Follow-ups in Political Discourse

Discourse Approaches to Politics, Society and Culture (DAPSAC)

ISSN 1569-9463

The editors invite contributions that investigate political, social and cultural processes from a linguistic/discourse-analytic point of view. The aim is to publish monographs and edited volumes which combine language-based approaches with disciplines concerned essentially with human interaction – disciplines such as political science, international relations, social psychology, social anthropology, sociology, economics, and gender studies.

For an overview of all books published in this series, please see
http://benjamins.com/catalog/dapsac

Volume 60

Follow-ups in Political Discourse
Explorations across contexts and discourse domains
Edited by Elda Weizman and Anita Fetzer

Follow-ups in Political Discourse

Explorations across contexts and discourse domains

Edited by

Elda Weizman
Bar-Ilan University

Anita Fetzer
University of Augsburg

John Benjamins Publishing Company
Amsterdam / Philadelphia

The paper used in this publication meets the minimum requirements of the American National Standard for Information Sciences – Permanence of Paper for Printed Library Materials, ANSI Z39.48-1984.

DOI 10.1075/dapsac.60
Cataloging-in-Publication Data available from Library of Congress:
LCCN 2015015826 (PRINT) / 2015019963 (E-BOOK)

ISBN 978 90 272 0651 0 (HB)
ISBN 978 90 272 6834 1 (E-BOOK)

John Benjamins Publishing Co. · P.O. Box 36224 · 1020 ME Amsterdam · The Netherlands
John Benjamins North America · P.O. Box 27519 · Philadelphia PA 19118-0519 · USA

In memoriam of Světla Čmejrková,
The Czech Language Institute of the Academy of Sciences,
a true linguist and friend

Table of contents

Following up across contexts and discourse domains

Introduction*

Anita Fetzer and Elda Weizman
University of Augsburg, Germany / University of Bar-Ilan, Israel[1]

1. Introductory comments

In our modern mediated and mediatized western societies, political discourse, viz. discourse by political agents and discourse about politics, has undergone dramatic changes, which are reflected not only in the domains of production, reception and mediation but also in its hybridization (cf., e.g. Berlin 2011; Fairclough 1995, 1998; Lauerbach 2004; Lauerbach and Fetzer 2007; Fetzer and Bull 2013), mixing genres, styles and communicative purposes, such as information and entertainment.

Political discourse can no longer be conceived of as a product only, i.e. as consisting of texts which have been produced by one political agent for some more or less specific set of addressees at some more or less specific local and temporal setting and thus as some kind of static notion. Analogously to more recent changes and developments in media discourse, political discourse has undergone a process of dynamization. Even a traditionally monologic genre or speech event such as political speech delivered to delegates at a party conference

* The chapters in this book are elaborate revisions of the contributions to the ESF Exploratory Workshop on "*Follow-ups Across Discourse Domains: A Cross-Cultural Exploration of Their Forms and Functions*", held at the University of Würzburg in *31 May – 2 June 2012*, (and see proceedings in Anita Fetzer, Elda Weizman and Elisabeth Reber, eds. *Proceedings of the ESF Strategic Workshop on Follow-ups Across Discourse Domains: A Cross-Cultural Exploration of Their Forms and Functions*. Würzburg: Universität Würzburg, 236–247. http://opus.bibliothek.uni-wuerzburg.de/volltexte/2012/7165/).

1. We are grateful to the contributors of this volume for their comments on the introduction, and to the reviewers for their valuable comments on the edited volume.

DOI 10.1075/dapsac.60.001int

gains its dynamic character not only through audience responses, but essentially through media coverage by public and commercial broadcasting services as well as live stream, by members of the audience using their personal gadgets and sharing their recordings, and by the numerous forms of citizenship talk, which involve interactions between ordinary, non-professional agents, as well as between them and activists and politicians. These forms of communication include various types of on-line interactive genres, such as web-based blogs and discussion forums, which may follow up on such discourse events as Prime Minister's Question Time in British Parliament (and its functional equivalents in other countries), panel interviews with audience participation and follow-up chat sessions with the politicians interviewed, mediatized party-political conferences with follow-up interviews and web-based discussion forums, live-reports of mediations concerning controversial decision-making processes, and rather spontaneously organized – and videoed – demonstrations, marches or sit-ins. In mediatized discourse, expectations for dynamic negotiations of information, stances and ideologies may thus become common ground, whereas the forms and functions of these negotiations vary according to the specifics of the web-communities and the participants' roles within them.

The process-orientation of political discourse has also become a constitutive part of political decision-making on both micro- and macro-levels of communication, regarding both professional politics and grassroots politics. E-mobility has thus not only changed the interpersonal domains of society, but has also transmitted public politics into the private domains of society, as is reflected in the participation of larger – and often also more heterogeneous – groups of society organising successful protests against macro-political decisions, such as youth unemployment in Spain, mass demonstrations in Egypt and other countries, or the planning and construction of extremely expensive public buildings in Germany. Moreover, e-mobility has supported the promotion of non-elite political discourse[2] and has provided citizens with necessary tools to engage in political decision-making processes and make their voices heard.

Political discourse can be transmitted through various types of media, and the formerly restricted access to semi-public, if not closed, political settings has provided members of society with the means of recycling selected excerpts of political events, if not the event as a whole, of commenting on them and inviting other members who have access to new media to comment on the recycled excerpts or on comments by the members. Political discourse has thus become a more and more dynamic endeavour, and because of its status as mediated discourse, it is

2. We would like to thank our reviewers for having pointed that out to us.

available to more and more participants and may thus be followed-up upon in different kinds of outlets. And what is more important is Clayman and Heritage's (2002, 241) observation that

> American citizens have a constitutionally protected right to remain silent in the face of police questioning, so that silence cannot be treated as incriminating in courts of law. But public figures have no such protection in the court of public opinion constituted by the news interview. In a nutshell, then, interviewees face a dilemma. There are various pressures – from interviewers, the audience, and subsequent media exposure – to "just answer".

Because of the less constrained production and reception formats in political discourse, which are primarily due to possession and access to the new media and their constitutive parts, it is not only interviewees but rather political agents in general who need to be prepared to be followed up on their performance. Political agents have been under more and more pressure to account for parts of their performances or on their entire performances, contextualizing and recontextualizing political claims they may have made in the past. In line with Watzlawick's cybernetic model (1967), communicators cannot *not* communicate, and follow-ups cannot *not* be followed up and thus generally tend to be taken up in political discourse.

This affluence of forms and functions of process-oriented political discourse is due to ongoing changes in modern and post-modern societies in general, and to our mediatized society and the so-called new media in particular. These modern technologies enable us to transmit information instantaneously to anybody who is a member of the web-anchored community, and contemporary perceptions accommodate interactivity, open-ended texts and constantly changing formats. Against this background, it is necessary to analyse not just political discourse as a product, to employ socio-pragmatic terminology, but rather as both process and product, accommodating the process of negotiating the validity of political claims.

To capture the dynamics of discourse in general and political discourse in particular, the communicative act of follow-up, which is a process-oriented concept par excellence, is expected to shed new light on the process-oriented nature of political discourse.

2. Follow-ups

Follow-ups are conceptualized in this volume as "communicative acts (or dialogue acts), in and through which a prior communicative act is accepted, challenged, or otherwise negotiated" (Fetzer, Weizman and Reber 2012) by ratified participants in the exchange or by third parties.They are furthermore perceived in the broad sense, not only as a sequential phenomenon defined by its particular status within a sequence but also as the carrier of pragmatic force, which is interdependent on the content of what is to be followed up, thus supporting an argument or rejecting it. As regards their sequential status, follow-ups express anaphoric reference by referring to the content or force of a prior communicative act. Unlike its original conception (Sinclair and Coulthard 1975), the communicative act of follow-up is not necessarily constrained by strict structural adjacency and thus by 3rd position. It may also span across longer sequences within the same discourse and be assigned the status of an object of talk, as is the case with follow-ups examined in the first part of this volume, *Follow-ups in the traditional media*, in the chapters by Bull, Hamo and Gruber, and it may span across discourses as is the case with the chapters by Ensink, Sauer and Schäffner in Part III, *Follow-ups across speech events*. To count as a follow-up across longer sequences and across discourses, the communicative acts and their constitutive parts to be follow-up need to be related semantically, pragmatically and / or discursively, and the nature of their connectedness needs to be assigned the status of an object of talk. Follow-ups may thus refer to one or more common discourse topics and assign them the status of an object of talk, or they may refer to a particular content and force and assign them the status of an object of talk. In all of these scenarios, the topic, content, force, their presuppositions and implication are considered relevant to the current stage of discourse. In the new media, follow-ups are afforded by technological developments and are thus accessible to all of the participants of the communicative event, as is discussed in the second part of the volume, *Follow-ups in the new media*, by Johansson and Sivenkova. Follow-ups have initially been defined as third-position elements located in the triad initiation-response-follow-up (Sinclair and Coulthard 1975). This triad is typically represented by the IRF (Initiation-Response-Follow-up) in classroom exchanges (ibid.). Follow-ups in their narrow definition are also produced in other contexts. For example, in political interviews the interviewer evaluates the interviewee's response (Fetzer 2007) or responds to the politician's equivocation (Bull 2012, this volume). In political discussion forums, speaker A posts a message which opens a discussion thread, the message is followed by reactions, and speaker A produces follow-up messages of confirmation or disagreement (Atifi and Marcoccia 2012), and in the diplomatic context, states submit reports on the implementation of international treaties to international organizations (IOs) and respond to comments by the IOs (Mikalayeva 2012, this volume).

Variants of prototypical third-position follow-ups include sequences where the follow-up is not performed by interlocutor A but rather by a third party, for example in comments on newspaper articles, where the article (= initiation) is commented upon by a reader B, and Reader C posts a comment on B (Weizman

2012). Interestingly, absence of follow-ups has also been described as a variant of the triadic follow-up, mainly when it carries an indirect meaning. For example, if in a TV interview an interviewer does not respond to an interviewee's answer (= response) to his or her previous question (= initiation), this absence of follow-up may be interpreted as an implicit consent, and be challenged (= a delayed follow-up) by a citizen (= a third party) in a discussion forum (Atifi and Marcoccia 2012). Another example of a follow-up absence is offered by diplomatic discourse on the implementation of treaties by state parties. For some treaties, state comments on the international organization's opinion are a highly conventional part of the exchange, and structurally occupy the third position in the triad state report (= initiation), international organization's opinion (= response), state comments (= follow-up). Their absence is meaningful and can constitute an object of talk (Mikalayeva 2012, this volume).

This volume accommodates a broader definition of follow-up, which views it as a non-initiative component of discursive negotiations, irrespective of its position in the sequence. On this view, a sufficient condition for the definition of a move as follow-up is its being initiated by a previous text. Its location as well as the cohesive relations with the initiation may vary (Fetzer 2000, 2012; Johansson 2006, 2012; Gruber 2012, this volume; Reber 2012; Weizman 2012, 2013). It may further be produced by an agent who was not supposed to take an active part in the exchange of ideas, such as an interpreter in an interpreter-mediated exchange (Schäffener 2012, this volume), and include multi-modality (Sauer 2012, this volume) and multi-directionality (Mikalayeva 2012, this volume). This broad definition has been shared by most of the views expressed in the 2012 workshop on follow-ups (Fetzer et al. 2012). For example, in a study of readers' comments on op-eds in Israeli national dailies, readers' comments are defined as follow-ups whether they are located at second position and respond to the initiative article, or at third position and respond to a previous comment (Weizman 2012). In this case, we are presented with a chain of follow-ups hierarchically organized in terms of position, such that the article is the initiation of 1st-order comment, whereas the 1st-order comment, and sometimes the article too, initiate the 2nd-order follow-up (ibid.). Thus, follow-ups necessarily have responsive properties, indicating how the preceding contributions are understood, and at the same time they may also have initiative features, introducing the next contributions (Linell 2009; Johansson 2012, this volume). The complexity embedded in chains of follow-ups is even accelerated in participatory multi-party interactions such as discussion forums, blogs and twitters. Whatever their position in the exchange is, follow-ups thus necessarily "involve recontextualization of an object of discourse (or parts of it) from another context, stance-taking, and the negotiation of new meaning" (Linell 1998, 154; Johansson 2006, 2012). And it is not only verbal performance, which may be followed up but also agents' non-verbal performance, including dress code (cf. Ensink 2012, this volume), facial expression or gesture, and the local and temporal setting as a whole (cf. Sauer 2012, this volume). The broad view suggested here further accommodates the large variation in the functions of follow-ups. Their uses have thus been accounted for in terms of positioning (cf. Hamo, this volume; Schäffner 2012, this volume), third-party involvement (cf. Schäffner 2012, this volume), evaluation and argumentation (Gruber, this volume), ratification, support, challenge and face wants (cf. Hamo 2012, this volume; Mikelayeva, this volume). The affiliative nature of meta-discursive follow-ups in interviews on Israeli TV may even challenge the basic view of follow-ups as necessarily dialogic (cf. Hamo, this volume). These variations are explored in this volume in range of cultural environments, such as the UK (Bull), The Netherlands (Sauer, Ensink), Israel (Hamo) and France (Johansson). Inter-cultural exchanges are studied through the analysis of diplomatic discourse (Mikalayeva) and interpreting (Schäffner), and cross-cultural comaprison (of the British, German and Russian contexts) is directly addressed by Sivenkova.

3. The contributions

The goal of the edited volume is to present up-to-date and original interdisciplinary research from the fields of linguistics, discourse analysis, socio-pragmatics, media communication, political science, and social psychology. The contributors have examined the heterogeneous field of political discourse and its manifestation in diverse discourse genres with respect to different degrees of directness in the presentation of politics and political information; different degrees of responsiveness, directness, indirectness and evasiveness in answering interviewer's questions; various manifestations of redundancy in mediated political discourse in general and in political statements in particular; professionalism and the de-construction of discourse identities in political discourse, to name but the most prominent research questions.

All of the chapters examine the forms and functions of follow-ups, that is, how a particular discourse, discourse topic or discourse contribution is taken up in discourse and negotiated between the communicators, and how it is commented on. Follow-ups are conceptualized as communicative acts (or dialogue acts), in and through which a prior communicative act is accepted, challenged, or otherwise negotiated. The discourses under investigation comprise political discourse across spoken and written dialogic genres considering (1) the discourse domains of political interview, editorial, op-eds and discussion forum, (2) their sequential organization as regards the status of initial (or 1st-order) follow-up, a follow-up of a prior follow-up (2nd-order follow-up), or nth-order follow-up, and (3) their discursive realization as regards degrees of indirectness and responsiveness which are conceptualized as a continuum along the lines of fully explicit and fully responsive not containing any attenuation devices.

Most of the chapters use compositional methodology. Within this common framework, perspectives vary representing (1) socio-pragmatics as regards context, sequentiality, participant format, communicative action, and implicature, (2) corpus linguistics as regards quantification of data in order to identify possible communicative patterns across discourse domains and cultures, (3) discourse analysis as regards the definition of genre, and (4) social psychology as regards face and face-work, and evasiveness.

The volume falls in three parts. The first part focuses on the analysis of follow-ups in the traditional media. Peter Bull's contribution *Follow-ups in broadcast political discourse: speeches, interviews, and parliamentary questions* analyses three distinct genres of political discourse: speeches, interviews, and parliamentary questions in the British television broadcasts. It gives particular attention to how the sequential triad is realized in equivocal and unequivocal responses by politicians to questions. At the conceptual level, it is argued that the notion of the follow-up can be usefully extended beyond the sequential triad to analyze not only sequential interactions over time, but also various forms of political action within and outside parliament. Helmut Gruber's contribution *Intertextual references in Austrian parliamentary debates: Between evaluation and argumentation* examines the debate contributions of Austrian MPs to the parliamentary debate following the inaugural speech of a new chancellor. In that particular context with a pre-established speaker order and fixed lengths of the contributions, the source of reference, the linguistic form of reference, and the rhetorical/ argumentative function of follow-ups are examined with political affiliation and time of statement delivery taken as independent variables. Michal Hamo's contribution *"I have nothing to do but agree": The reciprocal positioning of journalists and experts in broadcast television news discourse* explores the distinctions, hybridization and ambiguities of the reciprocal positioning of journalists and experts on Israeli television news items combining interviews with affiliated journalists and external experts. The analysis reveals a dominant pattern of a largely symmetrical positioning of senior journalists and experts as colleagues. A key positioning device contributing to this symmetry is the recurrent use of meta-discursive follow-ups with a preference for mutual alignment, support and agreement between journalists and experts.

The second part of the volume concentrates on follow-ups in the new media. Marjut Johansson's contribution *Bravo for this editorial! Users' comments in discussion forums* examines readers' follow-ups to editorials in comment sections in the online newspaper *Lemonde.fr*, focusing on the ways writers position themselves through the expression of their stances, mostly disagreeing explicitly or implicitly. Comments are conceptualised as follow-ups which carry not only responsive properties, but also initiative ones. Maria Sivenkova's contribution investigates *Metacommunicative follow-ups in British, German and Russian political webchats.* Adopting a cross-cultural perspective, the author tackles typical realisations of the new-media follow-ups in moderated and unmoderated discussions within online communities involving audiences, moderators and politicians. A typical pattern of online dialogue/polylogue organisation across cultural contexts is the insertion of evaluative follow-up moves in question-answer sequences and other sequences. Discussants in blogs may thus express support, reject or partially acknowledge criticisms, discipline other discussants, and improve their own previous contribution. Another typical pattern is the strategic use of non-evaluative follow-ups to account for some political action.

The third part of the volume adopts the perspective on follow-ups across speech events. Titus Ensink's contribution *Framing the Queen's head scarf: A case study of? follow-ups in Dutch politics* proposes a broad definition of follow-ups in political communication, conceived as any reaction to a politically relevant utterance, usually intended at influencing the electorate. Based on a case study (Queen Beatrix wearing a head scarf during a visit to a mosque), the analysis puts forward the importance of framing in influencing the public. It is argued that follow-ups in the political arena are mostly driven by attempts to gain media exposure rather than by interactional motivations. Christoph Sauer's contribution *Follow-ups in political talk shows and their visual framing* explores follow-ups in multi-modal political discourse. Based on the analysis of the Dutch talk show *Pauw & Witteman*, a distinction is made between *macro follow-ups*, which link different speech events (e.g. a talk show with previous news reports) and *micro follow-ups,* which link various modalities, mostly *visual framing* with verbal discourse, within the same speech event. The complexities and challenges presented by multimodal framing are discussed. Christina Schäffner's contribution *Follow-ups in interpreter-mediated interviews and press conferences* conceptualizes follow-ups in a broad sense, as thematic progression and speaker positioning towards prior talk. Analysing political interviews as well as press conferences and their transfer to news reports, she views the interpreter's renderings of the source text as follow-ups constituting moves in their own right. Drawing on political discourse analysis and translation studies, the analysis reveals that interpreters play a significant role in shaping the interaction, and take an active part in the role- construction of politicians. Liudmila Mikalayeva's contribution *Follow-ups in pre-structured communication: The case of treaty monitoring* investigates international treaty monitoring, which is viewed as a pre-structured, institutional communicative process, constituted by a series of multi-directed follow-ups that aim at building and sustaining the interlocutors' public images. Drawing on behaviourist and reflexive frameworks, the author discusses the negotiations of face wants in an inherently conflictual interaction, and sheds light on the construction of relations between states and international organizations while projecting a specific image into the public sphere.

References

Atifi, Hassan and Michel Marcoccia. 2012. "Follow-Ups in Online Political Discussions." In *Proceedings of the ESF Strategic Workshop on Follow-ups Across Discourse Domains: A Cross-Cultural Exploration of Their Forms and Functions, Würzburg (Germany), 31 May – 2 June 2012*, ed. by Anita Fetzer, Elda Weizman and Elisabeth Reber, 22–34. Würzburg: Universität Würzburg – [online]. URL: http://opus.bibliothek.uni-wuerzburg.de/volltexte/2012/7165/; URN: urn:nbn:de:bvb:20-opus-71656.

Berlin, Lawrence N. 2011. "Fighting Words: Hybrid Discourse and Discourse Processes." In *Context and Contexts*, ed. by Anita Fetzer and Etsuko Oishi, 41–65. Amsterdam: John Benjamins. DOI: 10.1075/pbns.209.04ber

Bull, Peter. 2012. "Follow-Ups in Broadcast Political Discourse: Speeches, Interviews, and Parliamentary Questions." In *Proceedings of the ESF Strategic Workshop on Follow-ups Across Discourse Domains: A Cross-Cultural Exploration of Their Forms and Functions, Würzburg (Germany), 31 May – 2 June 2012*, ed. by Anita Fetzer, Elda Weizman and Elisabeth Reber, 35–47. Würzburg: Universität Würzburg – [online]. URL: http://opus.bibliothek.uni-wuerzburg.de/volltexte/2012/7165/; URN: urn:nbn:de:bvb:20-opus-71656.

Clayman, Steven and John Heritage. 2002. *The News Interview*. Cambridge: Cambridge University Press. DOI: 10.1017/CBO9780511613623

Fairclough, Norman. 1995. *Critical Discourse Analysis: The Critical Study of Language*. London and New York: Longman.

Fairclough, Norman. 1998. "Political Discourse in the Media: An Analytic Framework." In *Approaches to Media Discourse*, ed. by Allen Bell and Peter Garret, 142–62. Oxford: Blackwell.

Ensink, Titus. 2012. "Framing as a Continual and Repetitive Process in Political Communication." In *Proceedings of the ESF Strategic Workshop on Follow-ups Across Discourse Domains: A Cross-Cultural Exploration of Their Forms and Functions, Würzburg (Germany), 31 May – 2 June 2012*, ed. by Anita Fetzer, Elda Weizman and Elisabeth Reber, 58–71. Würzburg: Universität Würzburg – [online]. URL: http://opus.bibliothek.uni-wuerzburg.de/volltexte/2012/7165/; URN: urn:nbn:de:bvb:20-opus-71656.

Fetzer, Anita. 2000. "Negotiating Validity Claims in Political Interviews." *Text* 20(4): 1–46.

Fetzer, Anita 2007. "Challenges in Political Interviews: An Intercultural Analysis." In *Political Discourse in the Media: Cross-Cultural Perspectives*, ed. by Anita Fetzer and Gerda Lauerbach, 163–196. Amsterdam: John Benjamins. DOI: 10.1075/pbns.160.10fet

Fetzer, Anita. 2012. "Quotations in Monologic and Dialogic Political Discourse." In *Proceedings of the ESF Strategic Workshop on Follow-ups Across Discourse Domains: A Cross-Cultural Exploration of Their Forms and Functions, Würzburg (Germany), 31 May – 2 June 2012*, ed. by Anita Fetzer, Elda Weizman and Elisabeth Reber, 72–86. Würzburg: Universität Würzburg – [online]. URL: http://opus.bibliothek.uni-wuerzburg.de/volltexte/2012/7165/; URN: urn:nbn:de:bvb:20-opus-71656.

Fetzer, Anita, Elda Weizman and Elisabeth Reber. 2012. "Introduction." In *Proceedings of the ESF Strategic Workshop on Follow-ups Across Discourse Domains: A Cross-Cultural Exploration of Their Forms and Functions, Würzburg (Germany), 31 May – 2 June 2012*, ed. by Anita Fetzer, Elda Weizman and Elisabeth Reber, 3–4. Würzburg: Universität Würzburg – [online]. URL: http://opus.bibliothek.uni-wuerzburg.de/volltexte/2012/7165/; URN: urn:nbn:de:bvb:20-opus-71656.

Fetzer, Anita, Elda Weizman and Elisabeth Reber (eds). 2012. *Proceedings of the ESF Strategic Workshop on Follow-ups Across Discourse Domains: A Cross-Cultural Exploration of Their Forms and Functions, Würzburg (Germany), 31 May – 2 June 2012*. Würzburg: Universität Würzburg, 2012. – [online]. URL: http://opus.bibliothek.uni-wuerzburg.de/volltexte/2012/7165/; URN: urn:nbn:de:bvb:20-opus-71656.

Fetzer, Anita and Peter Bull. 2013. "Political Interviews in Context." In *Analyzing Genres in Political Communication*, ed. by Piotr Cap and Okulska, Urzula, 73–99. Amsterdam: John Benjamins. DOI: 10.1075/dapsac.50.04fet

Gruber, Helmut. 2012. "Establishing Intertextual References in Austrian Parliamentary Debates. A Pilot Study." In *Proceedings of the ESF Strategic Workshop on Follow-ups Across Discourse Domains: A Cross-Cultural Exploration of Their Forms and Functions, Würzburg (Germany), 31 May – 2 June 2012*, ed. by Anita Fetzer, Elda Weizman and Elisabeth Reber, 87–106. Würzburg: Universität Würzburg – [online]. URL: http://opus.bibliothek.uni-wuerzburg.de/volltexte/2012/7165/; URN: urn:nbn:de:bvb:20-opus-71656.

Hamo, Michal. 2012. "*"I Have Nothing to Do But Agree"*: The Reciprocal Positioning of Journalists and Experts in Broadcast Television News Discourse." In *Proceedings of the ESF Strategic Workshop on Follow-ups Across Discourse Domains: A Cross-Cultural Exploration of Their Forms and Functions, Würzburg (Germany), 31 May – 2 June 2012*, ed. by Anita Fetzer, Elda Weizman and Elisabeth Reber, 107–120. Würzburg: Universität Würzburg – [online]. URL: http://opus.bibliothek.uni-wuerzburg.de/volltexte/2012/7165/; URN: urn:nbn:de:bvb:20-opus-71656.

Johansson, Marjut. 2006. "Constructing Objects of Discourse in the Political Broadcast Interview." *Journal of Pragmatics* 38(2): 216–229. DOI: 10.1016/j.pragma.2005.06.016

Johansson, Marjut. 2012. "Editorial and Its Comments: Follow-Ups in a Discussion Forum." In *Proceedings of the ESF Strategic Workshop on Follow-ups Across Discourse Domains: A Cross-Cultural Exploration of Their Forms and Functions, Würzburg (Germany), 31 May – 2 June 2012*, ed. by Anita Fetzer, Elda Weizman and Elisabeth Reber, 151–164. Würzburg: Universität Würzburg – [online]. URL: http://opus.bibliothek.uni-wuerzburg.de/volltexte/2012/7165/; URN: urn:nbn:de:bvb:20-opus-71656.

Lauerbach, Gerda. 2004. "Political Interviews as a Hybrid Genre." *Text* 24(3): 353–397.

Lauerbach, Gerda and Anita Fetzer. 2007. "Introduction". In Anita Fetzer and Gerda Lauerbach (eds), *Political Discourse in the Media*, 3–30. Amsterdam: John Benjamins. DOI: 10.1075/pbns.160.03lau

Linell, Per. 1998. *Approaching Dialogue. Talk, Interaction and Context in Dialogical Perspectives*. Amsterdam: John Benjamins. DOI: 10.1075/impact.3

Linell, Per. 2009. *Rethinking Language, Mind and World Dialogically: Interactional and Contextual Theories of Human Sense-Making*. Charlotte, NC: Information Age Publishing.

Mikalayeva, Liudmila. 2012. "Strategies of Response and Responsiveness in Diplomatic Communication." In *Proceedings of the ESF Strategic Workshop on Follow-ups Across Discourse Domains: A Cross-Cultural Exploration of Their Forms and Functions, Würzburg (Germany), 31 May – 2 June 2012*, ed. by Anita Fetzer, Elda Weizman and Elisabeth Reber, 178–191. Würzburg: Universität Würzburg – [online]. URL: http://opus.bibliothek.uni-wuerzburg.de/volltexte/2012/7165/; URN: urn:nbn:de:bvb:20-opus-71656.

Reber, Elisabeth. 2012. "Evidential Positioning in Follow-Ups in News Interviews." In *Proceedings of the ESF Strategic Workshop on Follow-ups Across Discourse Domains: A Cross-Cultural Exploration of Their Forms and Functions, Würzburg (Germany), 31 May – 2 June 2012*, ed. by Anita Fetzer, Elda Weizman and Elisabeth Reber, 205–220. Würzburg: Universität Würzburg – [online]. URL: http://opus.bibliothek.uni-wuerzburg.de/volltexte/2012/7165/; URN: urn:nbn:de:bvb:20-opus-71656.

Sauer, Christoph. 2012. "Framing in Talk Shows and Its Visualisation." In *Proceedings of the ESF Strategic Workshop on Follow-ups Across Discourse Domains: A Cross-Cultural Exploration of Their Forms and Functions, Würzburg (Germany), 31 May – 2 June 2012*, ed. by Anita Fetzer, Elda Weizman and Elisabeth Reber, 221–235. Würzburg: Universität Würzburg – [online]. URL: http://opus.bibliothek.uni-wuerzburg.de/volltexte/2012/7165/; URN: urn:nbn:de:bvb:20-opus-71656.

Schäffner, Christina. 2012. "Follow-Ups and Interpreter-Mediated Discourse." In *Proceedings of the ESF Strategic Workshop on Follow-ups Across Discourse Domains: A Cross-Cultural Exploration of Their Forms and Functions, Würzburg (Germany), 31 May – 2 June 2012*, ed. by Anita Fetzer, Elda Weizman and Elisabeth Reber, 236–247. Würzburg: Universität Würzburg – [online]. URL: http://opus.bibliothek.uni-wuerzburg.de/volltexte/2012/7165/; URN: urn:nbn:de:bvb:20-opus-71656.

Sinclair, John and Malcolm Coulthard. 1975. *Towards an Analysis of Discourse: The English Used by Teachers and Pupils*. Oxford: Oxford University Press.

Weizman, Elda. 2012. "Negotiating Irony through Follow-Ups: Readers' Comments on Op-Eds in the Daily Press." In *Proceedings of the ESF Strategic Workshop on Follow-ups Across Discourse Domains: A Cross-Cultural Exploration of Their Forms and Functions, Würzburg (Germany), 31 May – 2 June 2012*, ed. by Anita Fetzer, Elda Weizman and Elisabeth Reber, 263–276. Würzburg: Universität Würzburg – [online]. URL: http://opus.bibliothek.uni-wuerzburg.de/volltexte/2012/7165/; URN: urn:nbn:de:bvb:20-opus-71656.

Weizman, Elda. 2013. "Political irony: Constructing Reciprocal Positioning in the News Interview". In *The Pragmatics of Political Discourse: Explorations across Cultures*, ed.by Anita Fetzer, 167–190. Amsterdam: Benjamins, DOI: 10.1075/pbns.228.09wei

Watzlawick, Paul, Beavin, Janet H., and Jackson, Don D. 1967. *Pragmatics of Human Communication. A Study of Interactional Patterns, Pathologies and Paradoxes*. New York: W. W. Norton & Company.

PART I

Follow-ups in the traditional media

Follow-ups in broadcast political discourse

Speeches, interviews, and parliamentary questions

Peter Bull
University of York, York, United Kingdom

The concept of the follow-up as the third element of a sequential triad was originally formulated in the context of classroom discourse by Sinclair and Coulthard (1975). In this chapter, it is applied to the analysis of three distinct genres of political discourse: speeches, interviews, and parliamentary questions. Illustrative examples are drawn from television broadcasts with British politicians. It is proposed that the concepts of the follow-up and the sequential triad can be usefully applied to all three genres of political discourse. Their application also highlights significant gaps in the current research literature, most notably, how both interviewers and politicians follow up equivocal and unequivocal responses by politicians to questions. In addition, it is argued that the concept of the follow-up can be usefully extended beyond the sequential triad to analyze not only sequential interactions over time, but also various forms of political action within and outside parliament.

1. Introduction

"A person who asks a question has a right to talk again, after the other talks" (Sacks 1992, 49). In Sinclair and Coulthard's (1975) analysis of classroom discourse, teaching exchanges can be conceptualized in terms of a sequential triad: opening, answering, and follow-up moves. The follow-up move, which is typically produced by the teacher, takes place after the answering move as a reaction to the student's response. This move is considered vital in telling the students whether they have done what the teacher wanted them to do. Notably, if the follow-up is withheld, the students might think that they produced the wrong answer or that there is some kind of problem (McCarthy 1991, 16–17).

DOI 10.1075/dapsac.60.01bul

In this chapter, it will be argued that the concept of follow-ups is highly relevant to the analysis of political discourse.[1] Three distinct genres of political communication will be discussed: speeches, interviews, and parliamentary questions to the Prime Minister (PMQs). Illustrative examples are drawn from television broadcasts with British politicians, together with a case study, based on detailed textual analysis of follow-ups in two sessions of PMQs.

Each genre can be seen as representing a different form of political discourse: politicians addressing an audience (monologue), politicians questioned by professional interviewers, and politicians in debate with one another (PMQs) (Bull and Fetzer 2010). According to Thibault (2003, 44), "Genres are types. But they are types in a rather peculiar way. Genres do not specify the lexicogrammatical resources of word, phrase, clause, and so on. Instead, they specify the *typical* ways in which these are combined and deployed so as to enact the typical semiotic action formations of a given community". Finally, consideration will be given to the wider implications of the concept of follow-up in the analysis of political discourse.

2. Political speeches

Although a political speech is essentially monologic in form, it can also be understood as an interactive event. Notably, Atkinson (e.g., 1983, 1984a, 1984b) compared speaker-audience interaction to the way in which people take turns in conversation, although in the context of a political meeting, audience "turns" are essentially limited to gross displays of approval or disapproval (such as cheering or heckling). He pointed out that audience responses are not random, indeed, they are highly synchronized with speech: typically applause occurs either just before or immediately after a possible completion point by the speaker. This close synchronization suggests that audience members must in some way be able to project possible completion points in advance of their occurrence.

According to Atkinson (e.g., 1983, 1984a, 1984b), it is features in the construction of talk itself that indicate to the audience when to applaud. In particular, he identified two distinctive formulaic rhetorical devices: *three-part lists* and *contrasts*. In a three-part list (simply a list of three items), once the listener recognizes that a list is under way, it is possible to anticipate the completion point (the end of the speaker's utterance), thereby signalling an appropriate place to applaud. The contrast (or antithesis) involves the sequential juxtaposition of an item with

1. For a contrasting definition of follow-ups see, for example, Gruber, this volume.

its opposite. To be effective, the second part of the contrast should closely resemble the first in the details of its construction and duration, so that the audience can more easily anticipate the point of completion. According to Atkinson, contrasts and three-part lists are by far the most frequently used devices for inviting applause in political speeches.

In diplomatic speeches, different factors seem to come into play. An analysis of speeches delivered at the signing of the diplomatic accord between Israel and the Palestinian Liberation Organisation (September 1993) was conducted by Kurzon (1996). He noted the importance of certain keywords, such as "peace", "courage", and "gratitude", in evoking audience applause. He also noted that a change in tempo, usually a slowdown in speech rate, also evoked audience applause, whereas in contrast, Atkinson (1984b) observed that in political speeches there is often an increase in speech rate before the onset of applause.

If an audience fails to respond to applause invitations, speakers may actively pursue applause, termed a *pursuit* by Heritage and Greatbatch (1986). A common form of pursuit is to re-complete or simply repeat the previous point. Alternatively, speakers may re-summarize the gist of a previous point as a means of pursuing applause. A third form of pursuit involves a shift in what Goffman (1979) calls *footing*, for example, a speaker might shift from speaking on his/her own behalf to speaking on behalf of a collectivity (e.g., the government, or the political party s/he represents).

From the perspective outlined above, the pursuit may be regarded as the third part of a sequential triad, comparable to that identified by Sinclair and Coulthard (1975). At the same time, there are some notable differences. Firstly, the second element of this triad actually refers to the absence of a response, that is to say, a lack of applause from the audience, to which the speaker responds with a pursuit. Secondly, the absent response is not verbal, but nonverbal (i.e., applause). Thirdly, the pursuit itself may also be nonverbal as well as verbal, as illustrated below.

The following example comes from a speech delivered by Ed Miliband (former Leader of the British Labour Party, 2010–2015) to his party's annual conference (Liverpool, 27 September, 2011). Early on in the speech, Miliband said: "Ask me the three most important things I've done this year and I'll tell you; being at the birth of my second son, Sam". This extract can be understood in terms of two of the rhetorical devices identified by Heritage and Greatbatch's (1986) as types of applause invitation: the *puzzle-solution* and the *headline-punchline*. In the puzzle-solution device, the speaker begins by establishing some kind of puzzle or problem, and then, shortly afterwards, offers the solution – the important and applaudable part of the message. The headline-punchline device is structurally similar to the puzzle-solution format, although somewhat simpler. Here, the speaker proposes to make a declaration, pledge or announcement (headline) and then proceeds to make it (punchline). Thus, Miliband set a puzzle ("Ask me the three most important things I've done this year"), and then a headline ("I'll tell you"); this is followed by the solution/punchline ("being at the birth of my second son, Sam"), which should be the applaudable part of the message. But the audience did not applaud, there was a pause. Presumably, the audience was still waiting for items two and three, because Miliband said "Ask me the three most important things". Miliband then nodded his head during the pause, and the audience applauded. Arguably, the head nod might be understood as a nonverbal form of pursuit, indicating to the audience that Miliband was inviting applause at this point.

Hence, in this example, the sequential triad in the context of political speeches is extended to include nonverbal as well as verbal communication. As such, it may be seen as contribution to the growing research literature on the close interdependence between nonverbal communication and speech (e.g., Kendon 2004; McNeill 2005; Bull 2012a).

3. Broadcast political interviews

The concept of the sequential triad (Sinclair and Coulthard 1975) can also be applied to the analysis of broadcast political interviews. Such interviews characteristically take the form of question-response sequences; the interviewer is expected to ask questions, the politician is expected to reply (e.g., Greatbatch 1988; Clayman 1989; Heritage, Clayman and Zimmerman 1988). This is the principal means used by interviewers for creating and sustaining talk (Schegloff 1989), although they may also engage in non-questioning actions to open and close the interview (Heritage and Greatbatch 1991). Notably, however, as observed by Weizman (2008, 58) in her analyses of Israeli political interviews, deviations from these normative expectations may not necessarily be acknowledged, sanctioned or repaired.

A notable feature of broadcast political interviews is the extent to which politicians equivocate in response to interviewer questions. For example, Bull (1994) analyzed 33 broadcast interviews with British political leaders, broadcast between 1987 and 1992. Results showed a reply rate of only 46%, based on the analysis of 1,026 questions. (Reply rate was defined as the proportion of questions to which the politician gave a full reply). The results are notably similar to those of a completely independent study by Harris (1991), who found a reply rate of 39% with a different set of broadcast interviews, principally with Margaret Thatcher (Conservative Prime Minister, 1979–1990), and Neil Kinnock (Leader of the Labour Opposition, 1983–1992).

In comparison, it is interesting to consider reply rates in televised interviews with people who are not politicians. The late Diana, Princess of Wales, in her celebrated interview with Martin Bashir, replied to 78 per cent of questions (Bull 1997). Louise Woodward, the British au-pair who was convicted for the manslaughter of eight-month-old Matthew Eappen, in an interview with Martin Bashir replied to 70 per cent of questions (Bull 2000). Monica Lewinsky replied to 89 per cent of questions posed by Jon Snow in an interview concerning her affair with President Clinton (Bull 2000). The mean reply rate of 79 per cent across all three interviews is significantly higher than the mean reply rate of 46 per cent for the 33 political interviews reported above (Bull 2000).

How interviewers respond to equivocation by the politicians can be regarded as a form of follow-up. For example, one distinctive form of equivocation used by Neil Kinnock (former Leader of the British Labour Party, 1983–1992) was to make use of what were termed *negative answers*, in which he would state what would not happen instead of what would happen (Bull and Mayer 1993). Negative answers can be seen as a particularly ineffectual form of equivocation, because they simply invite the interviewer to follow up with a request for a positive answer (e.g., "That is why I'm asking what you would do", Sir Robin Day, interview with Neil Kinnock (1st June, 1987, BBC1 Panorama, general election campaign). In contrast, a distinctive form of equivocation used by Margaret Thatcher (former Conservative Prime Minister, 1979–1990) was to make personal attacks on the interviewer (Bull and Mayer 1993). Following such a personal attack, interviewers typically asked a new question in most instances (83 per cent) rather than following up the original question. Thus, whereas Margaret Thatcher's aggressive tactics had the effect of inhibiting the interviewers from pursuing follow-ups, the defensive tactics of Neil Kinnock simply invited further questioning on the same topic.

The above incidents are intended to demonstrate how particular follow-ups utilized by interviewers can be related to a politician's interview style. But these are only illustrative examples. Although the author has devised an equivocation typology which distinguishes between 35 different ways of not replying to questions (Bull and Mayer 1993; Bull 2003), there has been no comparable systematic analysis of interviewer follow-ups in response to equivocation by the politicians.

Arguably, an important aspect of an interviewer's communicative skills is how best to handle equivocation by the politicians (cf. Bull and Elliott 1998; Elliott and Bull 1996). Furthermore, this aspect of interviewer skill can be evaluated more effectively through the identification and analysis of different follow-up techniques used in response to political equivocation. In this respect, the application of the concept of follow-ups to broadcast political interviews is particularly useful, because it highlights a key feature of interviewing which hitherto has been largely neglected in the research literature.

4. Parliamentary questions

4.1 Prime Minister's Questions (PMQs)

PMQs are by far the most well-known form of parliamentary questions in the British House of Commons; these can also usefully be analyzed in terms of follow-ups. Like a broadcast political interview, PMQs take the form of question-response sequences. The principal difference is that the questions in PMQs are posed by politicians, not by professional political interviewers. Thus, whereas interviewers in broadcast interviews are expected to be impartial, there is no such requirement in PMQs. Indeed, Members of Parliament (MPs) can be as partial and as unashamedly partisan as they choose. Thus, opposition MPs can ask difficult and challenging questions, while government MPs can flatter the Prime Minister (PM) with toadying and obsequious questions.

PMQs take place while Parliament is sitting once a week every Wednesday, lasting for just 30 minutes. They always begin with the same tabled question to the PM, asking if s/he will list his/her official engagements for the day. All other questions are supplementary, hence they may have the important elements of unpredictability and surprise. MPs are protected by parliamentary privilege, which allows them to speak freely in the House of Commons without fear of legal action for slander. But they are also expected to observe certain traditions and conventions regarding what is termed "unparliamentary language". Specifically, they should not be abusive or insulting, call another member a liar, suggest another MP has false motives, or misrepresent another MP. The Speaker (who presides over House of Commons debates) may ask an MP to withdraw an objectionable utterance, or even *name* an MP, i.e., suspend the MP from the House for a specified period of time. Thus, in summary, MPs in PMQs must orient both to the expectation that dialogue should follow a question-answer pattern, and that they should refrain from unacceptable unparliamentary language.

The procedure of PMQs is as follows. Backbench MPs wishing to ask a question must enter their names on the Order Paper. (In the Westminster system, the Order Paper states the parliamentary business for the day. Backbench MPs are Members of Parliament who neither hold governmental office nor are spokespersons (frontbenchers) for the Opposition). The names of entrants are shuffled in a ballot to produce a random order in which they will be called by the Speaker. The Speaker then calls on MPs to put their questions, usually in an alternating fashion: one MP from the government benches is followed by one from the opposition benches. Notably, backbench MPs are limited to one question each. Thus, in terms of Sinclair and Coulthard's (1975) sequential triad, follow-ups from backbench MPs are not possible, because they are explicitly not permitted to pursue the PM's response with any further utterance (Harris 2001).

However, this is very much not the case for the Leader of the Opposition (LO), who may ask up to six questions, either as a whole block or in two separate groups of three. (The LO is conventionally the leader of the largest opposition party, currently the Labour Party). This means that the LO can pursue a specific topic through a series of questions. If the PM equivocates in response to a particular question, it is perfectly possible for the LO to follow up that particular issue in the next question. Conversely, if the PM replies to a particular question, it is of interest to analyze how this may be followed up by attacks on other aspects of government policy or performance.

PMQs are notorious for their adversarial discourse, and have been widely criticized on this account. Notably, when David Cameron (Prime Minister since May 2010) became Leader of the Conservative Party (6 December, 2005) he pledged to put an end to "the Punch and Judy politics of Westminster, the name calling, backbiting, point scoring, finger pointing" [Punch and Judy is a traditional popular British puppet show, which features domestic strife and violence between the two central characters, Mr. Punch and his wife Judy]. Subsequently, Cameron admitted that he had not kept this pledge, blaming the adversarial nature of PMQs (29 April, 2008). Similarly, according to John Bercow (2010), the current Speaker [the Speaker chairs the debates in the House of Commons], MPs "yell and heckle in a thoroughly unbecoming manner" providing "scrutiny by screech". Again, according to the late Simon Hoggart (2011), distinguished political columnist of *The Guardian* newspaper, "Prime Minister's Questions is increasingly like an unpleasant football match, in which the game played publicly is accompanied by all sorts of secret grudge matches, settlement of scores and covert fouls committed when the players hope the ref is not looking".

The authors of a recent major academic study of PMQs (Bates, Kerr, Byrne and Stanley 2012, 2) summarize as follows:

> .... there appears to be a general opinion among commentators, bloggers and viewers that PMQs has turned, from a relatively 'civilised' parliamentary session into something of a rowdy, mud-slinging spectacle catered more towards shallow political point scoring than serious scrutiny of prime ministerial activity.

At the same time, there are also commentators and critics who have spoken in praise of PMQs as a (potential) forum for serious, relevant debate and accountability (e.g., Sedgemore 1980; The Guardian 2010), and as a significant form of political opposition (Bull 2012b, 2013). Notably, there is nothing comparable to PMQs in the American political system. In the USA, the presidential press conference plays a much prominent role, where journalists have the opportunity to put questions to the president. But the president can "de-select" a journalist by not inviting him/her to future press conferences if s/he poses questions which are too awkward. In contrast, the PM has no right to de-select the LO, who may return to

PMQs week after week to persist in posing awkward questions. Despite its many detractors and deficiencies, PMQs offers a unique degree of political accountability, whereby the head of the UK government can be directly questioned, criticized and challenged by the political opposition.

Given the pre-eminence of PMQs, the relative dearth of serious academic research is surprising (Bates et al. 2012). However, there have been some studies of PMQs, both quantitative and qualitative, as reviewed below.

Quantitative studies can be summarized briefly as follows. Dunleavy and colleagues (Dunleavy, Jones and O'Leary 1990; Dunleavy, Jones, Burnham, Elgie and Fysh 1993) analyzed long-term trends in prime ministerial activity in the House of Commons. They found that answering questions has become more than four times as common as other modes of parliamentary intervention, which they claimed was principally due to the influence of PMQs. Giddings and Irwin (2005) found that the number of questions receiving an oral answer in PMQs in 2004 was less than half that in 1964; furthermore, whereas in 1964 there was a preponderance of backbench questions, by 2004 PMQs was dominated by the party leaders. Irwin, Kennon, Natzler and Rogers (1993) compared the number of questions tabled for PMQs in 1982 and 1989, and found a sharp increase in the number of oral questions tabled but a sharp decrease in the percentage of these which were substantive, rather than open questions. However, apart from the work of Irwin et al., these analyses tell us little about the content and structure of questions (e.g., the nature of the questions posed, and the nature of the answers given).

Qualitative studies of PMQs have been conducted by both Harris (2001), Bull and Wells (2012), and Bull (2013). In the context of Brown and Levinson's (1978, 1987) theory of politeness, Harris argued that much of the discourse of PMQs is composed of intentional and explicitly face-threatening acts (FTAs). She provided illustrative examples of a number of techniques whereby FTAs may be performed, such as asking disingenuous questions to which the questioner already knows the answer.

Bull and Wells (2012) conducted a more systematic investigation of different types of facework in PMQs, in which they identified six distinctive ways in which FTAs are performed in questions, and five in which the PM may counter FTAs in replies. They utilised the term *face aggravation* to refer to the aggressive use of facework, in which antagonists seek to score points at the other's expense (following Goffman 1967). Overall, they argued that face aggravation between the PM and LO is not just an acceptable form of parliamentary discourse, it is both sanctioned and rewarded, a means whereby the LO may enhance his/her own status. They further argued that PMQs should be regarded as another of the situations identified by Culpeper (1996), where impoliteness is not a marginal activity, but central to the interaction that takes place. The role of this adversarial discourse as a means of conducting political opposition was analysed by Bull (2013); this study is reported in much greater detail in Section 4 below.

Utilising both quantitative and qualitative techniques, the most substantive (and most recent) study of PMQs has been conducted by Bates et al. (2012). They compared the opening sessions of PMQs for the last five PMs from 1979–2010 (Thatcher, Major, Blair, Brown and Cameron). Their aim was to test a general perception that PMQs have developed into a focal point for shallow political point scoring rather than serious prime ministerial scrutiny. They found that the conduct of PMQs had become rowdier over the period sampled, with weekly sessions increasingly dominated by the leaders of the two main parties to the gradual exclusion of backbenchers.

The political effectiveness of this adversarial discourse was evaluated in a recent analysis of two sessions of PMQs in the context of the British phone-hacking scandal, with particular attention to the role of follow-ups (Bull 2013).

5. The British phone-hacking scandal: An illustrative example of follow-ups in PMQs

5.1 Contextual background

The British phone-hacking scandal has been an ongoing controversy involving the *News of the World* and other British tabloid newspapers published by *News International.* Employees of the newspaper were accused of engaging in phone hacking, police bribery, and exercising improper influence in the pursuit of publishing stories.

Of particular importance was the phone hacking of a 13-year-old English girl, Milly Dowler, who had been abducted on her way home from school (21 March 2002), and was subsequently found murdered (18 September, 2002). On 4 July 2011, The Guardian reported that journalists from the News of the World had hacked into her voicemail. It was further alleged that the reporters deleted messages when the mailbox was getting full, enabling them to listen to new messages, and thereby misleading the missing teenager's family into thinking that she was still alive. These allegations resulted not only in a huge public outcry but eventually in the closure of the News of the World, it being announced on 7 July 2011 that the paper would print its final edition on 10 July 2011. According to its final editorial: "Phones were hacked, and for that this newspaper is truly sorry… there is no justification for this appalling wrongdoing". However, although the newspaper admitted to phone-hacking, it did not admit to deleting messages from the teenager's voicemail. In fact, according to a subsequent statement from the Metropolitan

Police (9 May, 2012, http://www.bbc.co.uk/news/uk-18002180), some individual voicemails may have been deleted automatically, hence it was not possible to tell whether message deletions were automatic or intentional.

In context of this furore, Ed Miliband launched a wholesale attack on the PM and on News International in two sessions of PMQs (6 and 13 July 2011). There were four principal themes to Milband's attack: (1) a demand for a public inquiry into the culture and practices of British newspapers; (2) opposition to the News International takeover bid for BSkyB; (3) call for the resignation of Rebekah Brooks (chief executive of News International, and former editor of the News of the World); (4) criticism of Cameron for appointing another former editor of the News of the World (Andy Coulson) as his Director of Communications. Contextual information for each of these four issues is provided below.

5.2.1 *Demand for a public enquiry into the culture and practices of British newspapers*

A Tribunal of Inquiry in the UK is an official review of events or actions ordered by the government, typically into an issue of pressing public concern that must be investigated openly and fairly. Notably, a public inquiry does not necessarily mean that the evidence must all be heard in public, nor that the report will be made public (it may be given in private to the appropriate minister). However, interested members of the public and organizations may not only make (written) evidential submissions, but also listen to oral evidence given by other parties. The conclusions of the inquiry are delivered in the form of a written report, given first to the government, and soon after published in the public domain. The report will generally make recommendations to improve the future quality of government or management of public organizations. Notably, oppositional and pressure groups often demand public inquiries, but they are by no means always granted, not least because they may involve considerable expense, particularly in legal fees.

5.2.2 *News International bid for BSkyB*

News International is the main UK subsidiary of News Corporation, which was bidding to take over BSkyB. BSkyB is a British satellite broadcasting, broadband and telephony services company. News International is the second largest media group in the world in terms of revenue. If the bid had been successful, it would have created a media giant in the UK, whose revenues would dwarf all rivals, even the BBC. The takeover bid aroused huge opposition, both within and outside Parliament.

5.2.3 *Resignation of Rebekah Brooks*

Brooks was editor of two News International newspapers: the News of the World (2000–2003) and *The Sun* (2003–2009). Subsequently in 2009, she became chief executive of News International. Notably, the phone-hacking of Milly Dowler's voicemail took place during her editorship of the News of the World. According to *The New York Times* London reporter Sarah Lyall (2011), this meant "...... either that Ms. Brooks had no idea how the paper she edited was obtaining information about the Dowler family for its articles, or that she knew about the hacking and allowed it". In this context, Miliband called for her resignation as chief executive of News International.

5.2.4 *Appointment of Andy Coulson as Cameron's Director of Communications*

Coulson was a former editor of the News of the World (2003–2007), who was subsequently appointed as Cameron's Director of Communications in May 2010. Two of the paper's journalists (royal editor Clive Goodman and private detective Glenn Mulcaire) were jailed for phone hacking in January 2007, the offences having taken place when Coulson was editor. Although Coulson took ultimate responsibility and resigned his editorship, he claimed to know nothing of these offences at the time.

In addition, Coulson was criticized for his dealings with a private investigator called Jonathan Rees. Rees had worked for the News of the World for seven years, but was jailed for planting cocaine on a woman in order to discredit her during divorce proceedings. On release from prison, Rees was re-appointed by Coulson to the News of the World, where he continued to work until April 2008, when he was charged with conspiracy to murder his former business partner (a charge from which he was eventually acquitted for lack of evidence). According to The Guardian (11 March, 2011), Rees used a variety of illegal activities to obtain information while working for the News of the World, including buying information from corrupt police officers. Coulson denied knowledge of any of these activities.

Despite these denials, Coulson continued to be subject to repeated allegations that he was fully aware of phone hacking while editor of the News of the World, and eventually resigned his post as Cameron's Director of Communications (21 January 2011). In this context, Miliband attacked the PM for showing poor judgement in appointing Coulson to this post. Coulson has been arrested and charged with "intercepting communications without lawful authority" (i.e., phone-hacking) (24 July, 2012), for which he was subsequently convicted (24 June, 2014).

5.3 Analysis

The four issues discussed above provide the overall framework for the study conducted by Bull (2013), which presented a detailed analysis of question-response sequences and follow-ups between Miliband and Cameron in two sessions of PMQs (6 and 13 July, 2011).The extracts quoted below are taken directly from transcripts of these two sessions of PMQs.

5.3.1 *Setting up a public inquiry (Q1, Q2, 6 July; Q3, 13 July)*

In Q1 (6 July), EM asked for a full independent public inquiry: "Given the gravity of what has occurred, will the Prime Minister support the calls for a full, independent public inquiry to take place as soon as practical into the culture and practices of British newspapers?" Notably, Cameron conceded this straight away without demur (R1): "Let me be very clear. Yes, we do need to have an inquiry, possibly inquiries, as to what has happened".

In Q2 (6 July), Miliband followed up Cameron's response by upping his demands with more specific requests:

> He should immediately appoint a senior figure, potentially a judge, to lead this inquiry, make it clear that it will have the power to call witnesses under oath, and establish clear terms of reference covering a number of key issues: the culture and practices of the industry, the nature of regulation, which is absolutely crucial, and also the relationship between the police and the media.

In his response (R2), Cameron deferred on the specific details of the inquiry, but said he would consult with colleagues: "...... I don't want us to rush this decision. I want us to get it right, having discussed it with oth... with other party leaders, the Attorney-General and the Cabinet Secretary".

The following week (13 July), Miliband made a further demand, specifically that politicians (past and present) might be summoned to the inquiry to give evidence under oath (Q3): "Does he agree with me does he agree with me that if we expect editors and members of the press to give evidence under oath, so should current and p-past politicians?" Cameron also conceded this point (R3): "I–I agree with that".

Immediately following PMQs that day, Cameron made a statement to the House of Commons, announcing a two-part inquiry investigating the role of the press and police in the phone-hacking scandal. The inquiry was to be chaired by a senior judge, Lord Leveson. It would have the power to summon witnesses, including newspaper reporters, management, proprietors, policemen and politicians of all parties to give evidence under oath and in public. The Leveson Inquiry (as it became known) opened on 11 November, 2011. The formal evidence gathering phase of the inquiry finished on 24 July 2012, the report was published on 29 November 2012.

5.3.2 *News International bid for BSkyB*

In Q3 (6 July), Miliband asked: "Does the Prime Minister agree that the BSkyB bid should now be referred to the Competition Commission, to provide the breathing space that is required?" [The Competition Commission is a public body responsible for investigating mergers, markets and other enquiries related to regulated industries under competition law in the UK]. Cameron made no attempt directly to answer Miliband's question, claiming (R3) "On the issue of BSkyB, what we have done is follow, absolutely to the letter, the correct legal processes".

In his next question (Q4), Miliband reiterated the demand: "...... I–I know that this is difficult for him [i.e., the PM] but I strongly urge him to think again and send his decision to the proper authorities which is the Competition Commission. And as I say, this will provide breathing space for legitimacy and for the proper decisions to be made". In R4, Cameron simply reiterated his previous response: "I–I–I would say to him [i.e., Miliband] that the decision making has been through the proper processes, that it's right that the government acts legally in every way and that is what it that is what it has done".

In his next question (Q5), Miliband reiterated the point for a third time (Q5) "...... I hope that he will go off from this Question Time and think again, because it's in the interests of the media industry and the British public that this is properly referred to the Competition Commission in the way that all other bids are dealt with". Miliband then moved on to a different issue, that of the resignation of Rebekah Brooks (see Section 3 below). Cameron in his response (R5) to Q5 made no further reference to the BSkyB takeover bid.

Later that same day (6 July), Labour MPs tabled what is termed an Early Day Motion, calling on News Corporation to rescind its offer for BSkyB. [An Early Day Motion is one to be debated "on an early day", i.e., to be debated at an unspecified date in the future]. Over the next week, there was a huge public outcry against the News Corporation takeover bid, and the Early Day Motion was scheduled for debate the following Wednesday (13 July). At PMQs that day, Miliband put the following question to Cameron (Q2): "And does he further agree that if the House of Commons speaks with one voice today, and I hope he [i.e., the PM] will still come to the debate, that Rupert Murdoch should drop his bid for BSkyB, should recognise the world has changed, and he should listen to this House of Commons?" [N.B. "speaks with one voice" can be understood as referring to the debate on the Early Day Motion]. This time (R2), Cameron agreed with Miliband: "I agree with what the Honourable Gent Right Honourable Gentleman has said, and I think it's good that the House of Commons is going to speak with one voice". Later that same day, shortly before the Early Day Motion was due to be debated, News Corporation announced that it would be withdrawing its proposal to take complete ownership of BSkyB.

5.3.3 *Resignation of Rebekah Brooks*

In Q5 (6 July), Miliband shifted his attack from the BSkyB bid to a third issue, the resignation of Rebekah Brooks:

> Nobody is denying that Milly Dowler's phone was hacked and nobody is denying that it happened on the watch of the current chief executive of News International, who was editor of the newspaper at the time. Will the Prime Minister join me, if he believes in people taking responsibility, in saying that she should take responsibility and consider her position?

In response, Cameron (R5) equivocated by deferring responsibility to the police:

> .... everyone at News International is subject to one of the largest police investigations underway in this country. What I think is we should let the police do their work. They must follow the evidence wherever it leads and if they find people guilty of wrongdoing, they should have no hesitation but in making sure they're prosecuted.

Milband (Q6) followed up this response by explicitly drawing attention to Cameron's equivocation: "Mr. Speaker I don't know from that answer whether he [i.e., the PM] says that the chief executive of News International should stand down or not". Miliband then reiterated his point ("I am clear: she should take responsibility and stand down"), and moved on to another issue, the appointment of Coulson (see Section 4 below).

Two days later, in an emergency press conference, (8 July), Cameron stated that "....it's been reported that she [i.e., Brooks] had offered her resignation over this and in this situation I would have taken it" (transcribed from video, The Guardian, 8 July, 2011). At PMQs the following week (13 July), Miliband again reiterated his demand for Brooks' resignation (Q1): "Does the Prime Minister now agree with me that it is an insult to the [Dowler] family that Rebekah Brooks, who was editor of the News of the World at the time, is still in her post at News International?" This time, Cameron (R1) gave an unequivocal reply: "I've made very clear that she was right to resign, that resignation should have been accepted". The following day (14 July), the second largest shareholder of News Corporation, the Saudi Prince Al Waleed, called for Brooks' resignation in a BBC interview. On 15 July, Brooks resigned as chief executive of News International. The following year (15 May 2012), she was formally charged by the police with conspiracy to pervert the course of justice; however, she was subsequently acquitted on all charges (24 June, 2014).

5.3.4 *Appointment of Andy Coulson as Cameron's Director of Communications*

In Miliband's final question (Q6) on 6 July, he asked Cameron to acknowledge that he made a "catastrophic error of judgement by bringing Andy Coulson into the heart of his Downing Street machine". Cameron in his response (R6) made no specific reference to Coulson, but stated: "I take full responsibility for everyone I employ for everyone I appoint and I take responsibility for everything my government does". (Two days later (8 July), Coulson was arrested by the police, but was bailed and not charged).

At PMQs the following week (13 July), Miliband asked three further questions about Coulson. In Q4, he pointed out that while Coulson was editor of the News of the World, he had re-hired Jonathan Rees, who had been "jailed for seven years for a criminal conspiracy and who made payments to police on behalf of the News World". Miliband pointed out that this information had been passed on by The Guardian newspaper to Cameron's chief of staff. Miliband then asked "...... can the Prime Minister tell us what happened to that significant information that was given to his chief of staff?" Notably, as part of an extended reply (R4), Cameron stated explicitly that "... this information was not passed on to me...".

In the light of this response, Miliband pursued this issue in his next question (Q5), alleging that:

> .... this evidence [referring to the hiring of Jonathan Rees] casts serious doubt on Mr Coulson's assurances that the phone hacking over which he resigned was an isolated example of illegal activity. The Prime Minister says his chief of staff did not pass on this very serious information. Can he now tell us what information he proposes to take against his chief of staff?

Cameron in his response (R5) simply ignored Miliband's question: "...... do you know what, Mr Speaker, I think the public and the victims of this appalling scandal want us to rise above this and deal with the problems that this country faces".

In his final question (Q6), Miliband demanded that Cameron should "... publish the fullest account of all the information that was provided" and ".... apologise for the catastrophic error of judgment he made in hiring Andy Coulson". In an extended response, Cameron again made no specific reference to Coulson:

> ...... what the public want us to do is address this firestorm. They want us to sort out bad practices at the media. They want us to fix the corruption in the police. They want a proper public inquiry and they are entitled to ask, when these problems went on for so long, for so many years, what was it that happened in the last decade? What was it? When was the police investigation that didn't work? Where was the public inquiry over the last ten years? We've now got a full-on police investigation that will see proper prosecutions and, I hope, proper convictions, and we will have a public inquiry run by a judge to get to the bottom of this issue. That is the leadership I'm determined to provide.

However, at an emergency debate the following week (20 July), Cameron stated in relation to Coulson's appointment: "I regret, and I am sorry about, the furore it has caused" and that "If it turns out that he [i.e., Coulson] knew about the hacking, that will be a matter of huge regret and a matter for great apology" (as reported in Hansard). As noted above (5.2.4), Coulson was charged with phone-hacking (24 July, 2012), for which he was subsequently convicted (24 June, 2014).

5.4 Discussion

In evaluating the effectiveness of Miliband's questions, the concept of follow-up (Sinclair and Coulthard 1975) is extremely useful. Notably, it can be applied to both equivocal and unequivocal responses from the PM.

The following example is illustrative of how Miliband followed up an unequivocal reply by Cameron (Bull 2013). When Cameron (R1, 6 July 2011) conceded to Miliband's demand (Q1) that the PM set up a public inquiry into the culture and practices of British newspapers, Miliband in his next question (Q2) immediately upped his demands by asking for a judge to lead the inquiry with the power to call witnesses under oath. The following week (13 July, Q3), Miliband made a further demand that politicians (past and present) could be summoned to the inquiry to give evidence under oath. Although Cameron did not consent to these new demands immediately, he did concede them all in his statement to the House of Commons following PMQs on 13 July 2011.

The following examples are illustrative of how Miliband followed up equivocal responses by Cameron. When Miliband asked whether the PM would join him in calling for Brooks' resignation (Q5, 6 July 2011), Cameron in his response (R5) neither agreed nor disagreed with Miliband. Miliband in his follow-up question (Q6) explicitly drew attention to Cameron's equivocation ("Mr. Speaker I don't know from that answer whether he [i.e., the PM] says that the chief executive of News International should stand down or not"). At PMQs the next week, Miliband asked again (Q1) whether the PM agreed with him that Brooks should no longer be in her post. This time Cameron gave an explicit reply ("I've made very clear that she was right to resign, that resignation should have been accepted"). Miliband followed up Cameron's response with an explicit acknowledgment (Q2): "Mr. Speaker, I thank the Prime Minister for that answer and he's right to take the position that Rebekah Brooks should go".

However, it should be noted that Miliband's follow-ups to equivocal responses by Cameron were not always successful. Despite Miliband's repeated demands that Cameron apologise to the House of Commons for a "catastrophic error of judgement" in appointing Coulson as his Director of Communications, Cameron only eventually admitted that he regretted and was sorry about the furore it had caused (20 July, 2011).

The contrast between Miliband's follow-ups to these equivocal and unequivocal responses is striking. When Cameron conceded Miliband's demand for a public enquiry into the culture and practices of British newspapers, Miliband followed up with further demands. Conversely, when Cameron equivocated, Miliband followed up by repeating his questions – successfully with regard to Brooks' resignation, less so with regard to an apology for Coulson's appointment as Cameron's Director of Communications. Thus, the application of the concept of follow-ups to PMQ discourse can be seen to highlight the different strategies utilised by Miliband in response to equivocal and unequivocal responses.

The examples above also have implications for extending the concept of follow-up. The sequential triad, as originally identified by Sinclair and Coulthard (1975), comprised three elements (question/response/follow-up) occurring in strict temporal sequence. But in the case of Brooks' resignation, Miliband could be seen as "following up" his initial question (6 July, Q5) by putting the question again a week later (13 July, Q1). This is not a follow-up in the sense as strictly defined by Sinclair and Coulthard, but arguably represents a useful extension of the concept to the analysis of sequential interaction over time. From this perspective, given that the LO is entitled to ask up to six questions in each session, it is possible to see how topics are developed through all six question-response sequences. Thus, if the PM equivocates in response to a particular question, it is perfectly possible for the LO to follow up that specific issue throughout all the remaining questions. Conversely, if the PM answers the question, it is of interest to analyze how the answer may be followed up by attacks on other aspects of government policy or performance. Furthermore, given that the LO has the opportunity to ask a further six questions the following week, and in future sessions of PMQs, it is possible to investigate how a particular topic is followed up from one week to another, or over a period of weeks or months, or even years.

The concept of the follow-up can also be extended to the analysis of political action. In the case of the phone-hacking scandal, Miliband achieved substantive political gains with his questions at both sessions of PMQs. Thus, Cameron conceded a formal inquiry chaired by a senior judge, Lord Leveson, with the power to summon witnesses, including newspaper reporters, management, proprietors, policemen and politicians of all parties to give evidence under oath and in public. The bid by News International for BSkyB was withdrawn after a huge public outcry. Brooks resigned as the chief executive of News International. Finally, although Cameron never apologized for appointing Coulson as his Director of Communications, he distanced himself from Coulson in the emergency debate (20 July, 2011), acknowledging that he regretted and was sorry about the furore it had caused.

Of course, it is not possible to say in any of these instances that Miliband's questions at PMQs actually "caused" these events. But once Cameron had committed himself to setting up an inquiry into the culture and practices of British newspapers, it would have been extremely difficult for him to back down without serious loss of face, comparable to what has been referred to figuratively in a different context as "rhetorical entrapment" (Schimmelfennig 2001). Similarly, it is open to question whether Brooks would have actually taken the step of stepping down as chief executive of News International had not Miliband so publicly and explicitly called for her resignation.

6. Conclusions

In this chapter, it has been argued that the concept of follow-up as originally formulated in Sinclair and Coulthard's (1975) sequential triad is directly applicable to political discourse. Three distinctive genres have been considered: political speeches, broadcast interviews, and parliamentary questions.

In the context of political speeches, how politicians invite applause has been analyzed through the concept of rhetorical devices embedded in the structure of speech (e.g., Atkinson 1984a); if unsuccessful, applause invitations may be followed up through what have been termed pursuits (Heritage and Greatbatch 1986). These three elements (applause invitation, absence of response, and pursuit) were conceptualized in terms of Sinclair and Coulthard's (1975) sequential triad, but with several notable differences. Firstly, the second element of this triad refers not to a response but to its absence (i.e., the lack of applause). Secondly, the absent response is not verbal, but nonverbal. Thirdly, the pursuit itself may also be nonverbal, as well as verbal.

In the context of broadcast interviews, the concept of the sequential triad can be used to highlight substantial gaps in the research literature. Whereas question-response sequences have been analyzed in considerable depth, there has been little research on the third element of the triad, on how interviewers follow up the politicians' responses. Thus, whereas the author has devised an equivocation typology which systematically distinguishes between 35 different ways of not replying to questions (Bull and Mayer 1993; Bull 2003), there has been no comparable systematic analysis of how interviewers follow up equivocal responses. Furthermore, it would also be of interest to analyze how interviewers follow up responses where the politician does answer the question. Political interviewing can arguably be conceptualized as a form of communicative skill (cf. Bull 2011), and from this perspective, the concept of follow-ups highlights significant aspects of interviewer skill which have been largely neglected in the research literature.

In the context of parliamentary questions (PMQs), illustrative examples of notable difference between follow-ups to equivocal and non-equivocal responses by the PM were analyzed, and proposed as a topic for future research. From the analysis of PMQs, it was proposed that the concept of follow-ups could be extended well beyond a strict application of Sinclair and Coulthard's (1975) sequential triad to include other aspects of political discourse. Follow-ups can be analyzed over time, both within one particular interaction, and between two or more interactions, to investigate how particular political issues are taken up and pursued by the politicians. Another way of extending the concept of follow-ups is to consider whether the discourse so analyzed results in any significant form of political action, either within and/or outside Parliament. Although these possible extensions of the concept of follow-ups were considered in the context of PMQs, they are of course readily applicable to the genre of broadcast interviews and political speeches as discussed above, and arguably to other forms of political discourse as well.

To summarize, although the concept of follow-ups was originally identified in the context of classroom discourse (Sinclair and Coulthard 1975), the above analysis has shown how it can readily be applied to three distinct genres of political discourse, and extended to sequential interchanges over time, and various forms of political action. This analysis has also highlighted significant omissions in the current research literature, and pinpointed interesting topics for future research – in particular, how both interviewers and politicians respond to both the equivocal and unequivocal responses of politicians to questions.

From this perspective, it is perhaps not question-response sequences but the sequential triad that should be the primary unit of analysis in the context of broadcast political interviews and parliamentary questions.

References

Atkinson, Max. 1983. "Two devices for generating audience approval: a comparative study of public discourse and text." In *Connectedness in Sentence, Text and Discourse*, ed. by Konrad Ehlich and Henk van Riemsdijk, 199–236. Tilburg, Netherlands: Tilburg Papers in Linguistics.

Atkinson, Max. 1984a. *Our Masters' Voices*. London & New York: Methuen.

Atkinson, Max. 1984b. "Public Speaking and Audience Responses: Some Techniques for Inviting Applause." In *Structures of Social Action: Studies in Conversation Analysis*, ed. by Max Atkinson and John Heritage, 370–409. Cambridge & New York: Cambridge University Press.

Bates, Stephen R., Peter Kerr, Christopher Byrne, and Liam Stanley. 2012. "Questions to the Prime Minister: A Comparative Study of PMQs from Thatcher to Cameron?" *Parliamentary Affairs*: 1–28.

Bercow, John. 2010. "Speech to the Centre for Parliamentary Studies," 6 July. Retrieved 26 December, 2012, from the Rt Hon John Bercow MP web site: www.johnbercow.co.uk.

Brown, Penelope, and Stephen C. Levinson. 1978. "Universals in Language Usage: Politeness Phenomena?" In *Questions and Politeness*, ed. by Esther Goody, 56–310. Cambridge: Cambridge University Press.

Brown, Penelope, and Stephen C. Levinson. 1987. *Politeness: Some Universals in Language Use*. Cambridge: Cambridge University Press.

Bull, Peter. 1994. "On Identifying Questions, Replies and Non-Replies in Political Interviews." *Journal of Language and Social Psychology* 13: 115–131. DOI: 10.1177/0261927X94132002

Bull, Peter. 1997. "Queen of Hearts or Queen of the Arts of Implication? Implicit Criticisms and their Implications for Equivocation Theory in the Interview between Martin Bashir and Diana, Princess of Wales." *Social Psychological Review* 1: 27–36.

Bull, Peter. 2000. "Equivocation and the Rhetoric of Modernisation: An Analysis of Televised Interviews with Tony Blair in the 1997 British General Election." *Journal of Language and Social Psychology* 19: 222–247. DOI: 10.1177/0261927X00019002003

Bull, Peter. 2003. *The Microanalysis of Political Communication: Claptrap and Ambiguity*. London: Psychology Press.

Bull, Peter. 2011. "What Makes a Successful Politician? The Social Skills of Politics." In *The Psychology of Politicians*, ed. by Ashley Weinberg, 61–75. Cambridge: Cambridge University Press. DOI: 10.1017/CBO9781139026482.006

Bull, Peter. 2012a. "Gestures." In *Encyclopedia of Human Behavior*, ed. by Vilayanur S. Ramachandran (2nd edition), 248–254. Oxford: Elsevier. DOI: 10.1016/B978-0-12-375000-6.00180-4

Bull, Peter. 2012b. "Follow-Ups in Broadcast Political Discourse: Speeches, Interviews, and Parliamentary Questions." In *Proceedings of the ESF Strategic Workshop on Follow-ups Across Discourse Domains: A Cross-Cultural Exploration of Their Forms and Functions, Würzburg (Germany), 31 May – 2 June 2012*, ed. by Anita Fetzer, Elda Weizman and Elisabeth Reber, 35–47. Würzburg: Universität Würzburg – [online]. URL: http://opus.bibliothek.uni-wuerzburg.de/volltexte/2012/7165/; URN: urn:nbn:de:bvb:20-opus-71656.

Bull, Peter. 2013. "The Role of Adversarial Discourse in Political Opposition: Prime Minister's Questions and the British Phone-Hacking Scandal." *Language & Dialogue* 3(2): 254–272. DOI: 10.1075/ld.3.2.06bul

Bull, Peter and Elliott, Judy. 1998. "Level of Threat: Means of Assessing Interviewer Toughness and Neutrality." *Journal of Language and Social Psychology* 17: 220–244. DOI: 10.1177/0261927X980172005

Bull, Peter, and Fetzer, Anita. 2010. "Face, Facework and Political Discourse." *International Review of Social Psychology* 23: 155–185.

Bull, Peter and Mayer, Kate. 1993. "How not to Answer Questions in Political Interviews." *Political Psychology* 14: 651–666. DOI: 10.2307/3791379

Bull, Peter, and Wells, Pam. 2012. "Adversarial Discourse in Prime Minister's Questions." *Journal of Language and Social Psychology* 31: 30–48. DOI: 10.1177/0261927X11425034

Clayman, Steven E. 1989. "The Production of Punctuality: Social Interaction, Temporal Organization and Social Structure." *American Journal of Sociology* 95: 659–691. DOI: 10.1086/229329

Culpeper, Jonathan. 1996. "Towards an Anatomy of Impoliteness." *Journal of Pragmatics* 25(3): 349–367. DOI: 10.1016/0378-2166(95)00014-3

Dunleavy, Patrick, George W. Jones, and Brendon O'Leary. 1990. "Prime Ministers and the Commons: Patterns of Behaviour, 1868 to 1987." *Public Administration* 68: 123–140. DOI: 10.1111/j.1467-9299.1990.tb00750.x

Dunleavy, Patrick, George W. Jones, Jane Burnham, Robert Elgie, and Peter Fysh. 1993. "Leaders, Politics and Institutional Change: The Decline of Prime Ministerial Accountability to the House of Commons, 1868–1990." *British Journal of Political Science* 23: 267–298. DOI: 10.1017/S0007123400006621

Elliott, Judy, and Peter Bull. 1996. "A Question of Threat: Face Threats in Questions Posed during Televised Political Interviews." *Journal of Community & Applied Social Psychology* 6: 49–72. DOI: 10.1002/(SICI)1099-1298(199602)6:1<49::AID-CASP355>3.0.CO;2-H

Giddings, Philip and Helen Irwin. 2005. "Objects and Questions." In *The Future of Parliament*, ed. by Philip Giddings, 67–77. Basingstoke, Palgrave Macmillan.

Goffman, Erving. 1967. "Where the Action is." *Interaction Ritual: Essays on Face to Face Behaviour*, ed. by Erving Goffman, 149–270. Garden City, New York: Anchor.

Goffman, Erving. 1979. "Footing." *Semiotica* 25: 1–25. DOI: 10.1515/semi.1979.25.1-2.1

Greatbatch, David L. 1988. "A Turn-Taking System for British News Interviews." *Language in Society* 17: 401–430. DOI: 10.1017/S0047404500012963

Gruber, Helmut. Intertextual References in Austrian Parliamentary Debates: Between Evaluation and Argumentation. This volume.

Harris, Sandra. 1991. "Evasive Action: How Politicians Respond to Questions in Political Interviews." In *Broadcast Talk*, ed. by Paddy Scannell, 76–99. London: Sage.

Harris, Sandra. 2001. "Being Politically Impolite: Extending Politeness Theory to Adversarial Political Discourse." *Discourse & Society* 12: 451–472. DOI: 10.1177/0957926501012004003

Heritage, John, Steven E. Clayman and Don H. Zimmerman. 1988. "Discourse and Message Analysis: The Micro-Structure of Mass Media Messages." In *Advancing Communication Science: Merging Mass and Interpersonal Processes*, ed. by Robert Hawkins, Suzanne Pingree, and John Weimann, 77–109. Newbury Park: Sage.

Heritage, John and David L. Greatbatch. 1986. "Generating Applause: A Study of rhetoric and Response at Party Political Conferences." *American Journal of Sociology* 92: 110–157. DOI: 10.1086/228465

Heritage, John and David L. Greatbatch. 1991. "On the Institutional Character of Institutional Talk: The Case of News Interviews." In *Talk and Social Structure*, ed. by Deirdre Boden and Don H. Zimmerman, 93–137. Cambridge: Polity Press.

Hoggart, Simon. 2011. "Prime Minister's Questions – or an Unpleasant Football Match?" The Guardian, 14 December. Retrieved 26 December, 2012, from http://www.guardian.co.uk/politics/2011/dec/14/prime-ministers-questions-football-match

Irwin, Helen, Andrew Kennon, David Natzler, and Robert Rogers. 1993. "Evolving Rules." In *Parliamentary Questions*, ed. by Mark Franklin, and Philip Norton, 23–72. Oxford: Clarendon Press.

Kendon, Adam. 2004. *Gesture: Visible Action as Utterance*. Cambridge: Cambridge University Press. DOI: 10.1017/CBO9780511807572

Kurzon, Dennis. 1996. "The White House Speeches: Semantic and Paralinguistic Strategies for Eliciting Applause". *Text* 16(2): 199–224.

McCarthy, Michael. 1991. *Discourse Analysis for Language Teachers*. Cambridge: Cambridge University Press.

McNeill, David. 2005. *Gesture and Thought*. Chicago: University of Chicago Press. DOI: 10.7208/chicago/9780226514642.001.0001

Rawnsley, Andrew. 2012. "The Prime Minister has put his Judgment and Integrity on Trial." The Observer, 27 May. Retrieved 26 December 2012 from http://www.guardian.co.uk/commentisfree/2012/may/27/andrew-rawnsley-cameron-on-trial-at-leveson

Sacks, Harvey. 1992. *Lectures on Conversation*, Volume 1, ed. by Gail Jefferson. Oxford: Blackwell.

Schegloff, Emanuel A. 1989. "From Interview to Confrontation: Observations on the Bush/ Rather encounter." *Research on Language and Social Interaction* 22: 215–240. DOI: 10.1080/08351818809389304

Schimmelfennig, Frank. 2001. "The Community Trap: Liberal Norms, Rhetorical Action, and the Eastern Enlargement of the European Union." *International Organization* 55: 47–80. DOI: 10.1162/002081801551414

Sedgemore, Brian. 1980. *The Secret Constitution*. London: Hodder and Stoughton.

Sinclair, John and Malcolm Coulthard. 1975. *Towards an Analysis of Discourse: The English Used by Teachers and Pupils*. Oxford: Oxford University Press.

The Guardian, 2010.). "Editorial: In Praise of... Prime Minister's Questions," October 14. Retrieved 26 December, 2012, from http://www.guardian.co.uk/commentisfree/2010/ oct/14/in-praise-of-prime-ministers-questions.

The Guardian. 2011. "Murder Trial collapse Exposes News of the World Links to Police Corruption", 11 March Retrieved December 26, 2012, from http://www.guardian.co.uk/ media/2011/mar/11/news-of-the-world-police-corruption.

The Guardian, 2011. "I would have taken Rebekah Brooks Resignation, Says Cameron, 8 July., Retrieved 26 December, 2012, from http://www.guardian.co.uk/media/2011/jul/08/ rebekah-brooks-resignation-david-cameron.

Thibault, Paul J. 2003. "Contextualization and Social Meaning-Making Practices." In *Language and Interaction. Discussions with John J. Gumperz*, ed. by Susan L. Eerdmans, Carlo L. Prevignano, and Paul J. Thibault, 41–62. Amsterdam: John Benjamins. DOI: 10.1075/z.117.05thi

Weizman, Elda. 2008. *Positioning in Media Dialogue: Negotiating Roles in the News Interview*. Amsterdam: John Benjamins. DOI: 10.1075/ds.3

Intertextual references in Austrian parliamentary debates

Between evaluation and argumentation

Helmut Gruber
Vienna University, Austria

In this chapter, the contributions Austrian MPs deliver during the debate after the inaugural speech of a new federal chancellor are investigated under a discourse analytic and rhetorical-argumentative perspective. As the debate contributions refer only to a limited set of reference text, this specific communication situation provides a quasi-experimental setting in which "follow-up" moves in political discourse can be studied. MPs' follow-up moves during one inaugural speech debate (approx. 12 hours) are investigated on three dimensions: source of reference, linguistic form of reference, rhetorical/argumentative function of statement. Political affiliations of MPs and the time of statement delivery (during or after live TV broadcast) are taken as independent variables of the analysis. Results show that evaluation patterns change during time and that there are two "genres" of debate contributions: the "alternative policy focussed statement" and the "evaluation focussed statement" which display different linguistic and rhetorical/argumentative characteristics.

1. Uptake and follow-up: Towards a functional definition of reactive contributions in parliamentary debates

Apart from the strict procedural rules of interaction which are operative in all parliamentary systems, parliamentary debates follow also the interactive rules for casual conversation (Ilie 2010). Therefore, an analytic apparatus which accounts for discursive features of parliamentary follow-up utterances has to take into account the nature of follow-ups in everyday conversation as well as in institutional discourse.

Reactive utterances ("second pair parts", in conversation analytic terms) are often projected by their respective first pair parts. Much work on adjacency pairs, conditional relevance, and preference organisation in conversation analysis focus

DOI 10.1075/dapsac.60.02gru

on the initiating utterance of a sequence (for an overview see Hutchby and Wooffitt 1998) but also stress that each second pair part conveys recipient's understanding/interpretation of the respective first pair part (and thus provide the so-called "second-turn-proof-procedure", see Heritage 1984). This latter aspect of second pair parts is also of central relevance in Clark's (1996) conception of "uptake", i.e. the way an addressee takes up the conversational offer of a speaker proposing a joint project. Uptakes display addressee's construal of the illocution of the first part and thus may retrospectively (re)define the nature of the entire joint project as speakers learn through addressee's uptake how he/she defines the ongoing activity and may "let it go" even if the addressee's construal does not entirely correspond with speaker's "original" illocution. On the other hand, initial speakers may also evaluate and/or rebut an addressee's construal of speaker's illocution in a third position move if they do not accept addressee's displayed understanding of their initial move. For these reasons, Clark argues, addressee's uptake has in any case analytically and theoretically the same status as speaker's intention and both aspects have to be given equal relevance in a theory of communication as well as in the analysis of empirical data.

In public discourse with its complex audience design, interactants may exploit the structural opportunity of second speaker position for systematically misrepresenting/distorting the intended content of first speaker's contribution for an overhearing audience. Investigations of media and political communication have shown that addressees use reactive moves for redefining the content or re-framing the scope of the utterance they respond to (Drew 1992; Hutchby 1996) in order to influence or impress an overhearing audience. A comprehensive account of follow-up utterances thus should consider both aspects of paired utterances – the projecting force of first pair parts and the redefining force of second pair parts of conversational exchanges.

In media studies, the term "follow-up" is used for a specific kind of journalists' uptake of politicians' answers, especially journalists' question techniques in press conferences (for an overview see Eriksson 2011). In these studies, "follow-ups" are defined as journalists' second questions to a politician during a press conference. The use of a "second question" (by same journalist) signals (at the sequential and at the content level) that the journalist did not view the politician's answer to the first instalment of their question as sufficient. Journalists' "follow-ups" during press conferences thus signal an "adversarial stance" towards the previous answer or towards the respective politician (Eriksson 2011). In Clark's terms, these "follow-ups" are journalists' displays of their rejection of politicians' uptake of their original question and hence initiate extended acceptance phases.

The "display" of an adversarial stance is also related to the journalists' role as representatives of the general audience who can demand to get clear answers to their questions (Heritage 1985). The above definition of "follow-ups", however, is rather closely connected to the genre in which they are used, namely the political press conference or the political interview in a wider sense. In different genres, modified definitions of "follow-ups" may be appropriate or even needed.

The institutional setting of the inaugural speech debate which is under investigation here (cf. Section 3, Figure 1) provides MPs not only with the "power of summary" (Drew 1992) but also with the opportunity of evaluation and interpretation of the previous speech of the chancellor. MP's contributions display their (party-politically coloured) "uptake" of the new chancellor's inaugural speech and/or the government's program with the general proviso that both the inaugural speech and the government's program are monologically oriented statements (cf. Sections 3 and 4 below). Uptaking a primarily monological statement does not complete an action sequence but rather initiates one: it demonstrates the addressee's understanding of the monological statement and what he/she intends to do with it. In public political debate contexts, all these uptaking contributions are "stance-taking" (and "stance-displaying") utterances (cf. Klein 2000) and in this sense they are comparable to the "follow-ups" which have been investigated in press conferences, political interviews, and mass media settings. The stance displayed in MPs' contributions, however, is not necessarily critical but depends on their respective political affiliation: MPs of the government parties can be expected to praise the speech (or certain aspects of it) whereas opposition MPs are expected to criticise it. This display of stance is mainly directed towards the bystanding audiences (i.e. journalists and the general public) but also towards the primary audience (i.e. fellow politicians). Narrowing and specifying the definition provided in the introduction (Fetzer and Weizman this volume) and in Fetzer et al. (2012), a "follow-up" move in public political discourse may therefore be defined as follows:

> A "follow-up" move is any uptaking move which is noticeably related to the illocution or the content of a prior move and which (a) expresses a stance towards it and (b) initiates an action sequence that takes this prior move as its starting point.

This definition of "follow-up"[1] should hold for more political contexts than the parliamentary debates under investigation in this paper. The definition leads to a set of possible research questions as the relation between first move and follow-up move can be conceptualized and investigated on different levels:

1. Which is in contrast to Bull's definition in this volume: Whereas Bull investigates third position, ratifying utterances in adjacency pair sequences (e.g. question-answer sequences), the current definition of "follow-up" covers moves which are produced in response to first pair parts which do not project certain second pair parts.

- Follow-up as an aspect of context: which contextual variables influence the discursive characteristics of follow-ups which are produced in a certain situation?
- Follow-up as an aspect of illocutionary structure (activity structure): which types of follow-ups do certain first parts project? How "strong" is the projection force of a first part? – Does it allow for one, two, three, … n different follow-up illocutions/actions and which role does the context play for its projection force?
- Follow-up as an aspect of coherence structure: which kinds of coherence relations are established between first and second parts? – Are there strong and loose kinds of relations and by which (pragmatic) mechanisms are they inferred by participants (cognitive frames, conversational implicatures, search for relevance, etc.)?
- Follow-up as an aspect of discourse cohesion: which linguistic devices are used to signal the connection between the two (or more) parts of a follow-up sequence?

The parliamentary debate investigated here sets specific limits to the follow-up move characteristics listed above:

- A limited set of reference texts
- A strict time limit for each statement
- A pre-established sequence of speakers
- Clearly defined political affiliations and hence expectations of the general evaluative stance of statements
- A division of the event into a broadcast- and a non-broadcast phase

Combining these contextual characteristics with the general research questions above and the discourse characteristics of parliamentary debates which are discussed below (Section 2), the following research questions can be formulated:

1. To which reference statements do MP's uptaking utterances mainly refer – do MPs establish thematic connections to the previous inaugural speech (or the government program on which it is based) or do their follow-ups refer to previous debate contributions of other MPs (or to other reference texts)?
2. Which forms and mechanisms of uptake occur in a setting with strong institutional regulations for the debate sequence and in which mainly monological contributions are expected?
3. Which follow-up moves do MPs of different political affiliations (coalition vs. opposition parties) produce in response to the chancellor's inaugural speech?
4. Which specific setting characteristics account for the linguistic/discursive characteristics of MPs' contributions?

In the remainder of this paper, I will firstly characterise parliamentary debates as a typical instance of "front stage" political discourse that may be viewed under two complementary perspectives, a "deliberative" and a "symbolic". Then I provide more background information on the specific type of parliamentary debates I analyze in this paper. This is followed by an overview of the analytic categories which were used; then the results of the quantitative and qualitative analysis are presented. In closing, I discuss the relevance of the results for the questions which guided the analysis and will also present suggestions for further research.

2. Two kinds of and two perspectives on political discourse

Although political discourse may be seen as a typical instance of public communication which is aimed at and transmitted to multiple audiences by a variety of traditional and modern ("new") media, this view is only partly true. In fact two kinds of political discourse can be distinguished by employing Goffman's differentiation between "backstage" and "front stage" activities (Goffman 1959). Many instances of political discourse are not open to the general audience and the media (see Girnth 2002, 36, for a differentiation between different fields of "internal" and "external" political activity; Klein 2000 for a list of public and occluded political genres). In Goffman's terms these activities are performed "backstage" (Wodak 2011). Genres associated with these kinds of speech events include negotiations and deliberations between and within parties, drafting bills, but also hallway conversations etc. These "backstage genres" often provide the background for politicians' activities at the political "front stage".

"Front stage political activities" are performed for an audience comprising different groups with partly incompatible interests – fellow politicians of politician's own and of other parties, journalists who are interested in "good stories", interest groups, fractions of the general public who are directly affected by certain political activities, groups of the population with differing political views, etc. Typical genres which are realized in and associated with this kind of "front stage" political discourse are press-conferences, press releases, political interviews, political discussions in the media, public speeches, parliamentary debates, etc. These political genres are intricately related to different media genres (news stories, reports, commentaries, etc.) and communicative forms in traditional and new media (printed newspapers, internet newspapers, political broadcast programs, political websites and blogs, twitter messages, etc.) or they even take place in media settings (like many political discussions and interviews). The communicative purposes of these front stage genres are essentially two-fold: firstly they are directed towards their direct recipients and secondly they are directed towards an overhearing audience (cf. Clayman and Heritage 2002; Fetzer and Weizman 2006; Gruber 1993a; Heritage 1985; Kühn 1995; Nuolijärvi and Tiittula 2011). The resulting speech act characteristics of these genres of public political discourse have been referred to as "split illocutions" of political utterances which are attributed to the "staged" character of public political discourse (Hess-Lüttich 2007; Holly, Kühn and Püschel 1986; Strauss 1986).

The distinction between "front-stage" and "backstage" political discourse and their respective genres, however, are not sharp and categorical because (1) front stage genres do not have the sole function of proclaiming the results of backstage activities; rather, politicians will put their own (party-political) spin on the backstage issues they make public at front stage events; (2) front stage political interactions (e.g. public debates) may gain their own interactional dynamics and thus provide the public with genuine front stage political activities which are not rooted in previous backstage activities; (3) contents of backstage activities may "leak" into the general public through indiscretions performed on purpose by the involved actors or through investigative work of journalists who are always in search for exclusive stories. Nonetheless, Goffman's differentiation between these two kinds of activities (or "frames" as they are called in later phases of his theorizing) and their systematic interactional differences provide analysts of political discourse with an appropriate methodological framework for characterizing the different genres and especially for accounting for the different audience designs which are involved in the production and reception of these genres. Parliamentary debates are showcase examples of political front stage activities during which politicians exchange debate contributions that are often based on issues which had been subject of long and complicated backstage deliberations.

The political significance of parliamentary debates is judged differently by political scientists as well as by linguists investigating political discourse. Deliberative politics scholars assign a high value to (high-quality) deliberation which may be performed in hidden as well as in public political discussions (parliamentary committee meetings, parliamentary debates etc.). Their expectations of the deliberative quality of communication in public parliamentary debates are, however, inconsistent: there are arguments which support the expectation that backstage activities will show more argumentative quality (as they are not presented with a simultaneous appeal to the general public) as well as arguments to the contrary (in the sense that public discourse has a "civilising" effect which prevents speakers to use certain kinds of low-quality arguments). An empirical investigation of the deliberative quality in several parliamentary systems (Steiner, Bächtiger, Spörndli and Steenbergen 2004), however, showed a higher communicative quality for public parliamentary debates on most of the investigated indicators.

A view which is compatible with the deliberative politics approach is taken by linguistic scholars who are either influenced by Habermas' theory of communicative action (Habermas 1988) or who work within the pragma-dialectic framework (van Eemeren, Grootendorst and Kruiger 1987) and the pragma-rhetorical model of political discourse (Ilie 2010). They consider parliamentary discourse as serving two major functions, namely to solve problems and to construct identities of MPs. These two discursive aims may collide, but the (rational) solving of social and political problems is considered as the central communicative activity in parliamentary debates upon which identity construction strategies of individual MPs are piggybacked (cf. Ilie 2010; Plug 2010).

An almost opposed view of public political discourse is presented by Latour who argues against the common pleas for more "rationality" and "straightforward communication" in political communication (Latour 2003). Political discourse – in his view – has its primary function in creating and maintaining groups and group identities. The quality of political discourse thus may only be judged by considering the means through which these identities are created. A similar standpoint (with a more pessimistic undertone, however) towards public political discourse can be inferred from Crouch's considerations on the "postdemocratic" nature of most developed countries (Crouch 2008). Although he does not explicitly deal with the functions of parliaments in postdemocracy, his considerations suggest that – in his view – parliamentary discourse functions mainly as a symbolic facade which conceals that factual decisions are taken in "backstage" contexts by politicians who are influenced by industrial lobbies.

This second approach to public political debates is compatible with a group of linguistic scholars' view of parliamentary debates. According to them, parliamentary debate contributions do not aim at solving political problems but rather at persuading a secondary audience (Kühn 1995) and creating (and signalling) in-group vs. out-group memberships and often serve ceremonial functions in Goffman's sense (Goffman 1956) for the opening or closing of parliamentary procedures (cf. Klein 1991, 2000). Under this perspective, debate contributions are often characterised as monologues (Burkhardt 2004) with a high amount of intertextual references to other debate contributions (Bayley 2004) as their order of delivery is highly ritualised and follows the rules of the respective parliamentary system rather than the turn taking system of everyday conversations (see Bayley 2004). As a consequence of their highly institutionalized character, parliamentary debates are typical instances of "systems of genres" (Bazerman 1994) or "genre chains" (Swales 2004) comprising a variety of initiative and follow-up contributions/genres. In this view, the public parliamentary debate (and its respective contributions) serves mainly the purpose of (1) informing the followers of the own party in the general audience of the outcome of previous non-public deliberations and signalling a sense of coherence between members of the own party; (2) explicitly marking the differences between party standpoints; (3) and of opening up "rhetorical spaces" which can provide reference points for later (discursive and non-discursive) political actions.

In an attempt to integrate aspects of both of the above positions, parliamentary debate contributions can be investigated on two levels: (1) they can be viewed as moves in an argumentative discourse (in Habermas' sense) in which participants aim at a rational consensus that meets certain quality criteria – this content aspect covers the first of the above mentioned views; (2) under a symbolic perspective they can be investigated as elements of ritualised communicative events which are aimed at signalling messages far beyond their actual content – this ceremonial aspect takes into account the second of the above perspectives. These two perspectives do not correspond to the two levels of split illocutions of public political utterances mentioned above, i.e. both content and symbolic aspects of debate contributions may be aimed at either a primary or a secondary audience.

3. Political and institutional context of the investigated parliamentary debates

Before proceeding to the results of my study, I will shortly present some background information on the data I investigate in this paper. The parliamentary debates which follow the inaugural speeches of Austrian federal chancellors (for details of this genre see Gruber 2013) differ from usual Austrian parliamentary debates insofar as they contain (in principle) only one "initiative genre" – namely the chancellor's inaugural speech – and a vast number of follow-up contributions in which this speech is commented by the members of parliament (see below). This debate thus offers analysts of political discourse interested in content, forms and functions of follow-up contributions a quasi-experimental setting in which a very limited set of reference utterances/genres can only be followed by a very limited set of follow-up utterances/genres.

The chancellor's inaugural speech and the ensuing parliamentary debate take place a few days after the official formation of a new government in Austria. The party-deliberations which precede the government formation are typical examples of backstage political activities. They are conducted behind closed doors between the party which the president of the republic had entrusted with the formation of a new government (this is almost always the party which gained most votes in the preceding elections) on the one hand and (consecutively) all other parties which were elected in the Austrian parliament on the other hand. The formation of a new government is completed after the public presentation of the new members of government and the signing of the government program.

The inaugural speech of the new chancellor, however, is not a mere presentation of this program but its compilation and drafting is preceded by a diligent search for relevant data and facts from the single ministries. The institutional purpose of the speech is indirectly stipulated by the Austrian constitution which demands that each new government and its policy focuses have to be introduced to the national assembly, i.e. the first chamber of the Austrian parliament (Welan 1989). In fact, the actual political purpose of an inaugural speech consists also in signaling key aspects of the new government's policy to the bureaucracies of the different ministries, to different groups within the parties which form the government and – last but not least – to the media and the general public (Welan 1989).

These multiple purposes of the inaugural speech are reflected in its complex audience design and by the fact that it is part of two different systems of genres. Genre system I comprises the parliamentary debate after the inaugural speech during which every MP's debate contribution is expected to comment on the chancellor's speech (or on a very limited set of other utterances, see below). This first system of genres becomes the object of mass media coverage which establishes a second system of genres consisting of media reports and commentaries in different media. Figure 1 presents a diagrammatic representation of these two genre systems.

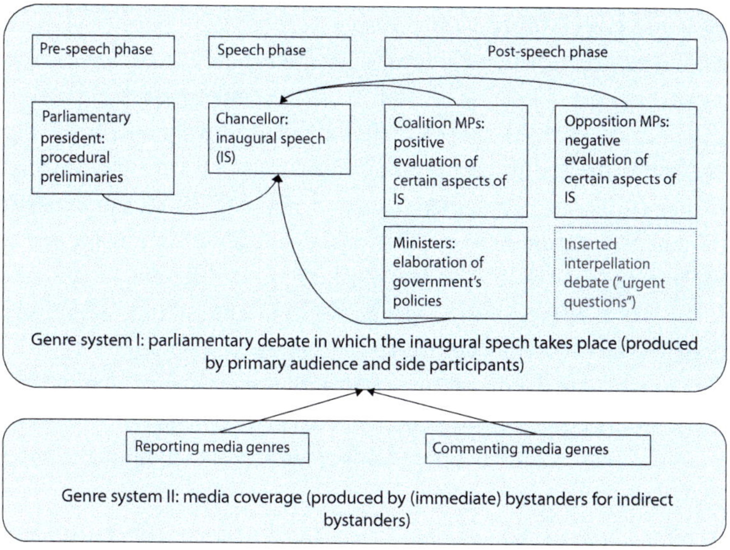

Figure 1. Genre systems in the inaugural speech debate

As Figure 1 shows, the parliamentary debate (as a front stage political activity) is characterized by a complex audience design in Goffman's sense[2] (Goffman 1981). The speech's "primary audience" ("ratified participants") are the MPs of the newly elected Austrian parliament with the members of the newly formed government as "side participants" ("unaddressed participants") and a group of direct "bystanders" who are watching the debate at the parliament's visiting gallery (journalists, members of the general public including the president of the Austrian republic). There is, however, also a large group of "indirect" bystanders who may either watch the live-broadcast of the debate or who will read the media reports and commentaries on the debate during the following days. During the debate after the speech, the audience structure of genre system I changes slightly: the ministers of the new government become primary audience members as they may be addressed directly during the MPs' statements and because they may also deliver statements which deal with the planned policies of their respective ministry.

The inaugural speech and the following parliamentary debate are the first front-stage political activities of the new government and the MPs of the newly elected parliamentary assembly. At the time of the debate, the government program has been already available for about one week in written form whereas the speech is delivered orally during the parliamentary session and (in most cases) no prior written version is available. Many MPs thus prepare their statements on the basis of the government program and comment mainly on this document rather than on the chancellor's speech (see below, Section 5.1).

Prior to the speech (during the pre-speech phase, cf. Figure 1), all parliamentary parties agree on a list and a pre-established sequence of speakers for each group, as well as on a "block" (i.e. total) speaking time for each party during the debate. The debate after the speech is then divided into time-slots during which speaking time is limited to certain intervals (i.e. a first time slot during which speakers may speak for 15 minutes, a second slot with 10-minute contributions, etc., until a debate period is reached in which speaking time is limited to three minutes). During these time slots, the speakers of the different parties take turns, i.e. each speaker is followed by a speaker of a different party. Additionally, the whole debate (starting with the pre-speech phase at 9.00 am) is broadcast live until 5.00 pm whereas the debate may last until the early morning of the following day. This complex arrangement of pre-established speaker order and speaking time limitations results in very limited opportunities for spontaneous interaction

2. Ilie (2010) and Zima and Feyaerts (2010) present similar adaptations of Goffman's conception of participant roles for parliamentary debates which is based on Clark's (1996) version of Goffman's original concepts. I use their terminology throughout this paper but during the introduction of the terms provide also Goffman's original terminology in brackets.

(except of the so-called "interruptive comments", Zima et al. 2010, which are not scrutinized in this study). As this study is based on the stenographic protocols of the Austrian parliament which are available online (http://www.parlament.gv.at/SERV/STAT/DOK/index.shtml) and which are edited before being published (cf. Zima et al. 2010) even less spontaneous interaction than in the original debates will be visible in the data. This lack of spontaneity does not influence the current analysis, which is not interested in sequential debate phenomena but rather in discursive properties of single contributions.

The parliamentary debate which is investigated here is part of a larger corpus of inaugural speech debates in the Austrian parliament (see Gruber 2013). For the current paper, the debate which followed SPÖ chancellor's Faymann inaugural speech was scrutinized. It took place on December, 3rd, 2008, between 09.04 am – 10.18 pm, the TV live broadcast lasted from 09.04 am to 5.00 pm. 127 debate speakers (from a total of 183 MPs) participated in the debate and contributed 136 debate contributions. 53 statements were delivered by government coalition party speakers of the SPÖ (Social democratic party) and ÖVP (Austrian people's party; Christian-conservative), 74 contributions came from the opposition parties FPÖ (Freedom party; right-wing nationalist- populist), BZÖ (Alliance for Austria's future; liberal-conservative spin-off from the FPÖ founded in 2002), and the Green party (left-liberal environmentalist).

4. Categories of analysis

The analytical categories for the present study were developed in an abductive way, i.e. neither a pre-established set of categories was applied nor was a bottom-up, grounded theory oriented approach taken. Rather, the categories were developed after reviewing the relevant literature and after a first exploratory reading of the data. The set of categories is intended to operationalize the following three basic dimensions of follow-up utterances which are relevant for investigating the research questions:

1. Source of uptake: to which previous utterance/event does the current statement refer?
2. Form of uptake: formal linguistic/discursive variants.
3. Rhetorical/argumentative function of debate contribution: critique/praise/presentation and support for own arguments/political standpoint with reference to a previous utterance.

These three dimensions will be elaborated in the following subsections.

4.1 Sources of follow-ups

As mentioned above, the choice of reference statements for the MPs' debate contributions seems to be limited to the inaugural speech and the government program; nonetheless a first reading of the debate showed that the MPs in fact refer to a greater variety of previous statements and/or events. Therefore the following set of categories was used to investigate the first of the above dimensions:

- The chancellor's inaugural speech: although it is the official reason for the parliamentary session, the chancellor's speech is only rarely referred to as it is delivered immediately before the debate.
- The government program: most contributions refer to (aspects of) the government program which is the most easily available text for MPs preparing their contribution.
- Previous debate contributions (of one of the new government's ministers, MPs of government parties, MPs of opposition parties): reactions to contributions which were delivered during the debate – they seem to constitute the most spontaneous type of contributions but this is not always the case (see below, Section 5.2).
- Previous political statement by:
  - Chancellor
  - Minister
  - Third persons

  Some MPs refer to prior political statements of the chancellor or of one of the current ministers (in the same or in a different political office). On very rare occasions references are also made to prior statements of non-politicians (e.g. experts). In most cases these references are used as starting points for criticism towards the current chancellor and/or government.
- Previous political event: Like previous statements, previous political events may serve as points of reference for MPs' contributions.

4.2 Forms of follow-ups – quoting and mentioning prior utterance

This second dimension was operationalized by relying on previous investigations of reported speech (Leech and Short 2007) in general and on types of reported speech in media discourse (Gruber 1993b; Weizman and Dascal 1991). In their widely used typology, Leech and Short distinguish between five categories of reported speech: direct quotation, indirect speech, free indirect speech, narrative report of a speech act, and narrative report of an action. These categories which describe different formal ways of discourse representation can also be ranked on a scale which comprises different degrees of current speaker's responsibility for the accurateness of the reported content. In direct quotations, current speaker's responsibility for representing the content of prior speaker's utterance content is highest whereas in narrative reports of actions it is lowest. Investigating different ways of quoting in news stories, Weizman and Dascal (1991) and Gruber (1993b) added the dimension of "author's alienation from quoted content". In their data (which stem from very different sources in newspaper discourse), they found that journalists use very short (often single word) direct quotes in their stories not only to give an accurate representation of previous speaker's utterance but also to express their dissociation from the respective speaker's utterance and hence implicitly (d)evaluate this speaker.

Combining and adapting these different types of reporting and taking into account the linguistic properties of the current material resulted in the following set of categories:

- Direct quotation as a starting point for a presentation of own policy suggestion.
- Short direct quotation as a means for implicit (d)evaluation of source text (and its producer).
- Topical mentioning of reference statement: using indirect speech and making reference to a single topic of a reference statement.
- Global mentioning of reference statement: using a narrative report of a speech act to make a general reference to a reference statement.
- Indirect mentioning of reference statement: in these cases, establishing a relation to a reference statement in the current utterance is only possible by relying on context knowledge.

4.3 Rhetorical and argumentative functions of follow-ups

The analysis of the third dimension needs a more differentiated set of categories than the two previous ones. Before going into details, it has to be mentioned that the analyses presented here were only based on those parts of MPs' debate contributions which refer notably to a reference statement or text. This means that (in the case of longer debate contributions which were delivered in the initial section of the session's debate phase) not always whole utterances but in some cases only parts of them were scrutinized. In these cases, the overall rhetorical structure and argumentation of the entire utterance was not analyzed but only the internal rhetorical and argumentation structure of the follow-up part(s) of these contributions. This is possible as all of these utterance parts are internally coherent discourse segments (which in fact constitute genres of their own, as will be argued in Section 6 below).

Secondly, it should be remembered that politicians' public debate contributions always combine argumentative, rhetorical means with evaluating devices (Klein 2000; Section 2 above). Therefore, the present categories for the third analytic dimension cover (1) evaluating aspects of the utterances and (2) the argumentative and rhetorical functions these evaluating devices serve.

Four aspects of the rhetorical and argumentative functions of the debate contributions were investigated by adapting and augmenting different aspects of appraisal theory (Martin and White 2007):

- The type of appraisal which is expressed towards a reference text/statement:
  - Affect: registering positive and negative feelings towards a stimulus
  - Judgement: attitudes towards others' behaviour (criticise, praise etc.): how should we/should we not behave
  - Appreciation: evaluation of natural and/or semiotic phenomena: what worth do phenomena have?
- The way of expressing appraisal: Martin and White (2007) distinguish between two general ways of expressing evaluations in texts. "Inscribed" appraisal expressions comprise all kinds of evaluative lexis which do not leave readers/addressees much freedom of interpretation. "Invoked" appraisal expressions, on the other hand, comprise instances of evaluative utterances which suggest a certain kind of evaluation towards a textual element but do not use explicitly evaluative lexis. The following short extracts provide examples from my data:
  - Inscribed evaluation: "Mr. Chancellor, what you impose on the Austrians is a bit strong" (Strache, FPÖ): expression of (negative) appraisal by using explicitly evaluating lexis: "you impose on the Austrians"; "[this] is a bit strong".
  - Invoked: "The planned measures of the new government are highly suitable for countering the upcoming economic crisis" (Haupt, ÖVP): inviting appraisal (positive evaluation) by pointing at positive consequences of government's planned actions.
- Intertextual orientation: this category is especially relevant in the case of utterances which refer to previous utterances. Depending on the linguistic form of uptake of the reference statement (cf. the second dimension of analysis) and to the content of the debate contributions, two poles of a cline of intertextuality were defined:
  - Explicitly heteroglossic utterances: these utterances establish an explicit relation to the utterance(s) of another speaker and express an explicit stance towards these reference-utterances (prototypical realization: "The chancellor/the government program says X but I say Y").

- Monoglossic utterances: these utterances do not display explicit relations towards prior utterance(s) and hence do not express a stance towards them (prototypical realization: "Policy X is wrong/right" which does not indicate to which source the actual utterance refers).

Different forms of discourse representation (see above) which are used in a follow-up utterance lead to different degrees of stance taking towards the respective utterance on the "heteroglossic – monoglossic" cline. The two categories, however, are not identical. As will be seen in Section 5, the use of "short direct quotations as a means for implicit evaluation of source text", a form of direct quotation, results in follow-up utterances which are positioned near the "monoglossic" pole (and far from the "explicit heteroglossic" end of the scale).

The operationalization of this subset of categories relies mainly on Bakhtin's original work on hetero- and monoglossia (Bakhtin 1986; Vice 1997) rather than on Martin and White's integration of Bakhtinian concepts into appraisal theory (Martin and White 2007).

- Dialogicity: Although "follow-ups" have been defined as utterances which take up a previous utterance, parliamentary debate contributions are characterized by a tension between monologue and dialogue (Burkhardt 2004)[3] which is caused by the general communicative function of parliamentary debates in modern societies (see Section 2). Debate contributions which are (by virtue of their name) parts of an exchange (the "parliamentary debate") thus can be expected to display dialogical and monological characteristics, albeit in different degrees. The category "dialogicity" places debate contributions on a cline between the two poles of (1) explicitly dialogical utterances (in which e.g. another speaker is explicitly addressed) and (2) utterances which do not overtly begin or continue a dialogue with another speaker. As a shorthand term, this second pole of the cline is labelled "monologic" although it has been argued elsewhere that purely monological utterances are not possible in political discourse (Gruber 2013; Reisigl 2007; Bull this volume).

The categories of the first two dimensions and a coding for "positive" vs. "negative" evaluation of the source utterance were performed by using the Atlas.ti coding tool for qualitative data analysis. All debate contributions were coded and a simple quantitative analysis was performed using the party affiliation of the speakers and

3. Burkhardt (2004) investigates German parliamentary debates which follow procedural rules that are different from the Austrian parliament. Nonetheless the two parliamentary systems are comparable.

the time of delivery of the contribution (during vs. after TV broadcast) as independent variables. The categories of the third dimension were additionally applied to a selected set of contributions and hence the results for these dimensions are qualitative and the generalizations drawn from them are preliminary.

5. Results

In this section, I will firstly present the results of the quantitative analysis (Section 5.1) and then proceed to the qualitative analysis of the rhetorical/argumentative functions of the contributions (Section 5.2).

5.1 Quantitative results

Table 1 shows that (on average) every coalition party MP produces 2 follow-up contributions and every opposition speaker uses more than 2 and less than 3 follow-ups in their debate contributions. The vast majority of the follow-up contributions (more than 50%) refer to the government program, but the second frequent kind of follow-ups consists of utterances which refer to a previous debate contribution (more than 20%). Only a rather small fraction of the follow-ups refers to the inaugural speech and to previous political events (less than 12%). References to previous political statements occur only very rarely.

Table 1. Frequency of references to source types in follow-ups

	Government coalition speakers (N=53)				Opposition speakers (N=74)				Total			
	Total / %		After TV/ %		Total / %		After TV/ %		Total / %		After TV/ %	
Inaugural speech	4	1.45	2	0.73	27	9.82	11	4	31	11.27	13	4.73
Government program	59	21.45	32	11.64	94	34.18	28	10.18	153	55.64	60	21.82
Previous debate contribution	35	12.73	16	5.82	23	8.36	8	2.91	58	21.09	24	8.73
Previous political statement	1	0.36	0	0.00	5	1.82	2	0.73	6	2.18	2	0.73
Previous political event	4	1.45	2	0.73	23	8.36	11	4	27	9.82	13	4.73
Total	103	37.45	52	18.91	172	62.55	60	21.82	275	100	112	40.73

That far more speakers refer to the government program than to the inaugural speech is not surprising as the text of the government program had been available at least a few days before the debate whereas the speech was delivered immediately before (see above, Section 3). The amount of references to previous debate contributions seems to indicate a rather high degree of dialogicity in the debate, a result which is to some extent contrary to Burkhardt's (2004) view who characterizes (German) parliamentary debates more or less as a succession of monologues that are only interrupted by dialogical interruptive comments. Furthermore, the results show that government coalition speakers do more often relate to previous debate contributions (and less often to both the inaugural speech and the government program) than opposition speakers do. This could indicate that government coalition MPs may have a higher debate orientation whereas opposition MPs might be more oriented towards commenting on the inaugural speech and/or the government program.

The way in which speakers refer to previous debate contributions, however, shows that the dialogical orientation in the follow-ups is rather superficial. Most references to previous statements belong to the category of global mentioning (and evaluation) of the reference statement without any detailed topical engagement. Results in Table 1 also show that about 50% of the follow-ups of government coalition speakers are produced after the broadcast phase of the debate whereas opposition speakers produce about 60% of their follow-ups during the broadcast phase (this result is further differentiated in Table 2).

References to the inaugural speech and to the government program cover the full range of formal referring devices and will be discussed in detail below. The cross tabulation in Table 2 shows the multi-dimensional distribution of the frequency counts for the categories "source of intertextual reference", "form of uptake", "global evaluation", "time of utterance", and "party affiliation of speakers", the most frequent categories are printed in bold italics (as the absolute counts in this complex table are rather low, no percentages were computed).

The results show that topical and global references are by far the most common ways of referring to a source text whereas direct quotations and indirect references are not used very frequently. Additionally, Table 2 shows that all negative evaluations of both the inaugural speech and the government program are produced by opposition party speakers whereas almost all positive evaluations come from government party speakers. This is not surprising, but at a closer look at the results at least one unexpected aspect surfaces: breaking down the results concerning positive vs. negative evaluations (irrespective of the form of reference) of either government program or inaugural speech according to the time of their delivery (i.e. during or after live TV broadcast) reveals that the majority of negative evaluations by opposition party speakers occurs during the live broadcast phase of the debate (82 negative evaluations during TV broadcast vs. 35 negative evaluations after TV broadcast) whereas the majority of the positive evaluations by coalition party speakers is produced after the live broadcast (27 positive evaluations during TV broadcast vs. 35 positive evaluations after TV broadcast).

Table 2. Counts for "appraisal of reference text" and "form of reference to source text" by party affiliation of debate speakers and debate phase

Form	Reference text	Appraisal	During/after broadcast	SPÖ	ÖVP	FPÖ	BZÖ	Green	Total
Direct	Inaugural speech	Negative	During			1		1	5
			after				1	2	
	Government program	Negative	During			4	3	2	12
			after			2	1		
Topical	Inaugural speech	Positive	During		2				4
			after	2					
		Negative	During			3	4		12
			after			2		3	
	Government program	***Positive***	***During***	***14***	***7***			***2***	***39***
			after	***14***	***8***	***2***		***2***	
		Negative	During			4	4	7	24
			after			5	2	2	
Global	Inaugural speech	Negative	During			2	1	4	10
			after			2	1		
	Government program	Positive	During	6	6				16
			after	3	1				
		Negative	During			***6***	***11***	***24***	***51***
			After			***5***	***2***	***3***	
Indirect	Government program	Positive	During	1	1				8
			after	4	2				
		Negative	During					1	3
			after					2	
Total				34	27	38	30	56	184

Considering the different audience designs of the debate during and after the TV broadcast phase (cf. above, Section 3) and the fact that the sequence of speakers is fixed in advance, these results indicate that the opposition parties (at least in this debate) were more successful in transmitting their various criticisms of both the government program and the inaugural speech to a general public than the coalition parties were in publicly praising the same texts for an overhearing audience.

5.2 Qualitative results

In a closer, qualitative analysis of the data, I try to integrate the results from investigating the first two analytical dimensions with the complex categories of the third dimension. Differentiating basically between positively vs. negatively evaluating contributions, the following analysis shows how different kinds of reference to a previous statement (i.e. their linguistic follow-up characteristics) place an utterance in various ways on the heteroglossic-monoglossic cline. Additionally, appraisal realizations, the different manifestations of dialogicity and their contributions to the rhetorical functions of the utterances are scrutinized.

5.2.1 *Positive evaluation and follow-up characteristics of debate contributions*

Firstly, I discuss the relationships between positively evaluating utterances, kinds of intertexuality and dialogicity, and sources of uptake found in the data (cf. Figure 2).

Figure 2. The heteroglossia – monoglossia cline: positive evaluation (mainly government parties) and follow-up characteristics

In positively evaluating utterances (which are mainly produced by government party speakers), three kinds of intertextual references are identifiable: "topical mentioning of reference statement", "global mentioning", and "indirect mentioning", whereas no forms of direct mentioning occur. The first two kinds of reference result in heteroglossic statements which allow a clear distinction between the reference statement and the MPs debate contribution, whereas the latter form of reference results in (almost) monoglossic utterances. Extract (1) presents an instance of the "topical mentioning of the government program" produced by SPÖ chief whip Josef Cap. It combines a topical reference to the government program ("20 billion € more budget assignment for cultural affairs") with a direct address to the minister ("congratulations, Madam Minister") whom Cap credits responsibility for this (alleged) success. The dialogical stance expressed through this direct address is, however, a mere rhetorical pose which Cap uses for publicly praising a newly appointed and (until then) publicly not very well known minister. The positive appraisal (a realization of the "judgement/social sanction/propriety" category) is inscribed into the utterance ("a handsome success").

Extract 1[4]

There are 20 billion € more budget assignment for cultural affairs in this government program. A handsome success – congratulations, Madam Minister! (MP Strache: [commenting interruption]) I think that this is important, also for signaling that we are a land of culture, a nation of culture. (Cap, SPÖ, 11:15)

Extract (1) is followed by a series of examples Cap presents in order to prove his positive evaluation presented in Extract (1). These examples (together with the stretch of text presented above as Extract (1)) combine to a discourse segment in which Extract (1) represents the nucleus and each example (i.e. each reference to the government program) serves as a satellite of an "evidence" relation (in terms of the coherence model of Rhetorical Structure Theory, Mann and Thompson 1987).

Extract (2) shows a representative example for a positively evaluative utterance with an indirect mentioning of the government program produced by ÖVP chief whip Karlheinz Kopf. The (indirect) reference to the government program in this segment is only inferable through the context of the statement (i.e. its production during the inaugural speech debate) and the mentioning of one specific initiative of the new government ("home care measures"). The utterance is thus (almost) monoglossic and monological (nobody from the primary audience is explicitly addressed). Similar to Extract (1), the appraisal (again a realization of the "judgement/social sanction/propriety" category) is inscribed ("the people's party thinks that it is absolutely right") and combined with a self-praise of the people's party whose activities during the coalition negotiations – in Kopf's view – represent the "volitional cause"-satellite (in terms of RST) for the measures which are positively evaluated.

Extract 2

This government puts a focus on home care with a whole bundle of measures, and – most of all – it sets this focus where it is necessary to put it: with the caring relatives! The people's party thinks that it is absolutely right – and we have cared for the fact that this issue can be found in the government's program – that this often neglected group of persons will get more support. (Karl Heinz Kopf, ÖVP, 11:45)

The qualitative analysis shows that in the group of positively evaluating utterances, dialogical statements occur only when the reference statement is topically referred to, and in these cases the dialogical orientation is a rhetorical pose of the speaker(as in Extract (1)). The argumentative/rhetorical function of these

4. The original German versions of Extracts (1)–(4) can be found in Appendix 1, all translations by the author (H. G.)

heteroglossic utterances consists mainly in highlighting and elaborating certain issues from the government program. The second utterance type in this group does not display an explicit dialogical orientation and their argumentative/rhetorical function consists in either highlighting/elaborating issues from the government program or in party-self praise.

Figure 3 shows how follow-up and evaluative characteristics interact in the schematic structures of these contributions. The two, partly different, schemata which are combined in Figure 3 illustrate their alternative rhetorical functions: in the topic-elaborating contributions (left branch of Figure 3), an "evidence" relation (in RST terms) is used at the top-level of the coherence structure to relate the evaluative part with the following content issues, on lower levels of the structure "elaboration" relations prevail. In the party self-praise statements (right branch of Figure 3), "volitional cause" relations prevail at the top level coherence graphs which indicate that the respective party cared for the praised policy issue in the coalition negotiations.

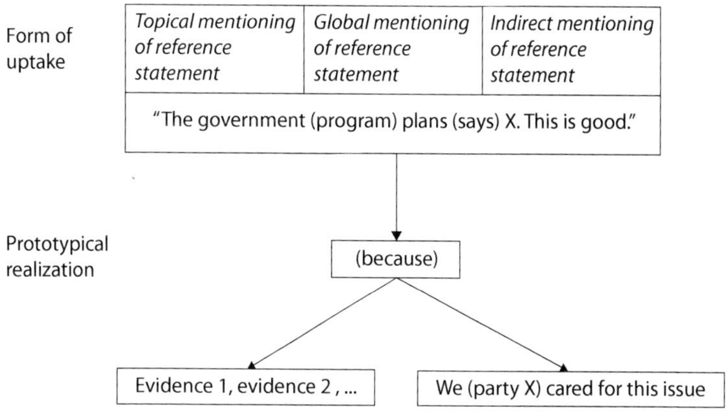

Figure 3. Positively evaluating statements: forms of intertextual reference and argumentative structure

In the positively evaluating statements, two kinds of appraisal are expressed (Martin and White 2007): judgement/social sanction/propriety and affect/satisfaction. No clear pattern of appraisal realization, however, emerges from the qualitative analysis: whereas in contributions which mention the reference statement only indirectly invoked appraisal realizations occur, in the two other kinds of reference, both appraisal realizations (inscribed and invoked) were found.

5.2.2 *Negative evaluation and follow-up characteristics of debate contributions*

The negatively evaluating statements show a greater formal variability of intertextual references and hence their stratification on the heteroglossic-monoglossic cline is more fine-grained (cf. Figure 4). Figure 4 shows that the two variants of direct quoting of a reference text/statement do not occupy neighboring nodes on the heteroglossic – monoglossic cline as they are used to perform markedly different argumentative/rhetorical functions. The heteroglossic, dialogic characteristic of the "direct quotation as a starting point for an alternative policy presentation" construes a sharp rhetorical contrast between government's and oppositions' policy plans expressed as moves in a (imagined) conversation. The weakly heteroglossic, monologic characteristic of the "direct quotation as a means for evaluating a source text/statement", on the other hand, invokes negative evaluation by ridiculing decontextualized phrases from a source text.

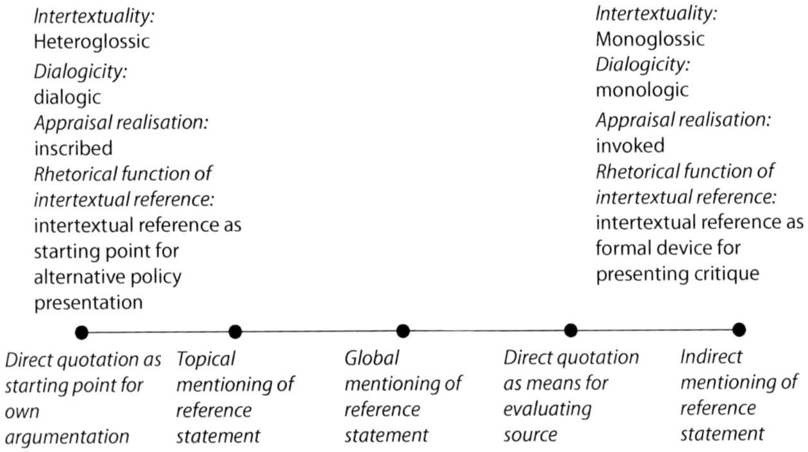

Figure 4. The heteroglossia – monoglossia cline: negative evaluation (opposition parties only) and follow-up characteristics

In the present study, the "direct quotation as a starting point for an alternative policy presentation" with its strong heteroglossic intertextuality is exclusively found in debate contributions from Green party MPs (cf. Extract (3)).

Extract 3

I tell you: this is exactly the point – which is listed under "aims" in the "health" chapter – that is wrongly defined, because it says: the focus of the government's health policy is on the patients' demands. Wrong! – The focus should be on the highest possible degree of health and ... (Karl Öllinger, Green Party, 16:45)

In Extract (3), Green party MP Karl Öllinger presents a direct quote from the government program ("the focus of the government's health policy is on patients' demands"), evaluates it (before and after the quote: "that is wrongly defined ... Wrong!") and then presents a series of health policy issues which he (or the Green party resp.) views as elements of an allegedly "right" health policy. The utterance is heteroglossic (use of direct quote) and dialogic (direct address of government: "I tell you") and expresses inscribed negative appraisal (of the "judgement/social sanction/propriety" category). The argumentative/rhetorical function of this statement is to construe an explicit rhetorical contrast between the government's policy plan (by using the direct quote as a starting point) and the (purportedly) better own (i.e. Green party's) policy alternatives. The dialogic orientation in this (and similar) statement(s) is at least more authentic than in the above cases of clear pseudo-dialogic "rhetorical posing" (cf. 5.2.1), although it cannot initiate an authentic dialogue because of the procedural debate rules. The argumentative scheme of contributions of this kind is illustrated in Figure 5.

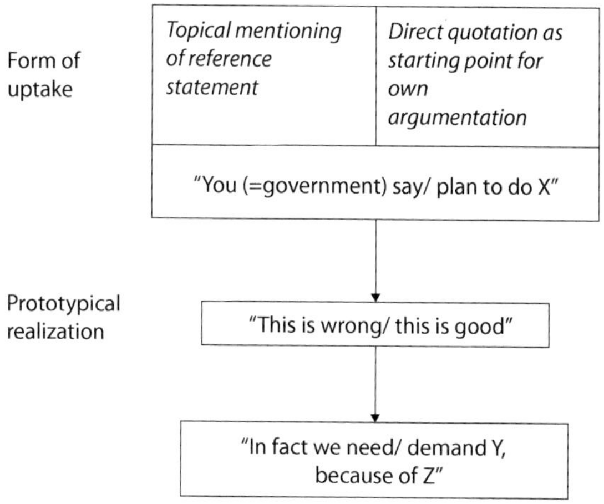

Figure 5. Negatively evaluating statements: forms of intertextual reference and argumentative structure; the Green party: Alternative policy focused statements (inscribed evaluation)

Figure 5 shows that the "alternative policy presentation" contributions use either (and mainly) direct quotations or instances of topical mentioning of a reference statement in order to realize a three-partite argumentation scheme which explicitly contrasts the (alleged) government position with an own political proposal. The central evaluative element is always realized as a token of the "judgement/social sanction/propriety" appraisal category (Martin and White 2007). Figure 5 also shows that the negative evaluation is sometimes realized as a (partly) positive evaluation of a policy planned by the new government. In these latter cases, speakers concede that the government is "on a good way", but that much more (and different) political efforts in the respective area would be needed – thus again a rhetorical contrast between planned government policy and own policy conceptions is construed.

The argumentative/rhetorical function of the direct quotations in these contributions differs fundamentally from the use of direct quotes in British MPs' parliamentary debate statements reported in Antaki and Leudar (2001). Whereas British MPs in Antaki and Leudar's study use direct quotes of their political opponents to support their own position, Austrian MPs in the current study use quotations in order to create an accentuated difference between a political opponent's standpoint and their own view of a certain topic. Both forms of uptake used in statements of this kind establish a strong heteroglossic, dialogic orientation whereas the use of the remaining three kinds of uptake (global mentioning, indirect mentioning, and direct quotations as a means for evaluating source) results in rather monoglossic, monological statements. As the uses of "indirect" or "global mentioning of a reference statement" (i.e. two ways of negatively evaluating the source text without presenting an own policy) result in an argumentative structure which is similar to the positively evaluating contributions no examples are presented here. The difference between these two kinds of statements lies only in the appraisal polarity. In the negatively evaluating statements, appraisal resources from "judgement/social sanction/propriety" category express a negative attitude whereas in the former kind of statements a positive attitude towards the reference statement is conveyed.

Direct quotations as a means for evaluating a source text realize almost monoglossic, monologic utterances in which the speakers use single terms or phrases from a reference statement in order to ridicule or negatively evaluate the source text. This rhetorical device was exclusively found in FPÖ and BZÖ speakers, Extract (4) provides an example from FPÖ MP Walter Rosenkranz.

Extract 4

There [in the government's program, HG] is permanently talked about "considering", "aiming at", "analyzing" and similar things. But there is no mentioning of implementing something, except it is something with "gender" – this popular term – namely gender budgeting. (Walter Rosenkranz, FPÖ, 21:11)

In his uptake of the government program, the speaker picks out some decontextualized words ("considering", "aiming at", "analyzing") and phrases which – allegedly – characterize the program as mainly oriented towards planning rather than towards implementing policies and contrasts this alleged hesitancy with gender policy issues which are (supposedly) announced in more concrete and determined terms in the program. The term "gender" (which is used as a foreign word in German) has an extremely negative connotation in right-wing political circles as it is associated with radical political feminism. The above statement thus combines a list of one-word (and one-phrase) quotes (taken out of their context) which are aimed at characterizing the government program as being either undecided or radical feminist. The statement shows no overt dialogic orientation, the speaker talks about the program rather than to its authors. This practice of ridiculing a reference statement rather than arguing against it provides the main resource for invoked appraisal expressions in the debate (NB that at least the above instance of this kind of follow-up occurs after the TV broadcast period, i.e. it is exclusively aimed at the speaker's primary audience).

The underlying argumentative scheme, combining forms of uptake with negative evaluation (without presentation of policy alternatives), is illustrated in Figure 6 (note that in the case of "direct quotations as means for evaluating source" only the "evidence" is linguistically realized as all other components of the prototypical realization remain implicit).

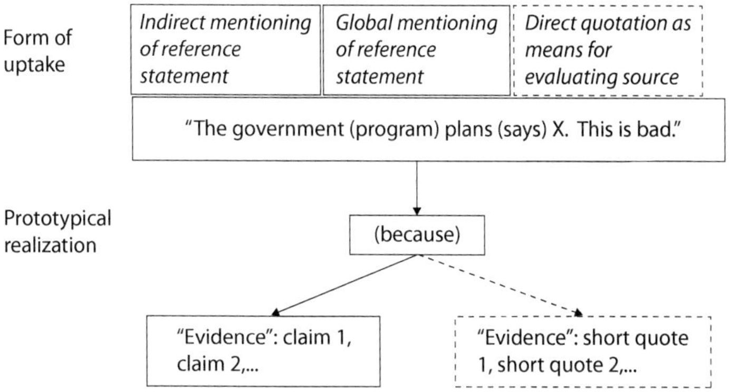

Figure 6. Negatively evaluating statements: forms of intertextual reference and argumentative structure; BZÖ, FPÖ, and Green party: Evaluation focused statements (inscribed or invoked evaluation)

The use of short direct quotations as a means for evaluating the source resembles quoting strategies which have been identified in mass media discourse (Weizman and Dascal 1991; Gruber 1993b) as a means for devaluing the source from which the quotes are taken. In this usage, the short quotes are employed as "evidence" for invoked negative appraisal, often realized from resources of the "appreciation/valuation" appraisal categories (Martin and White 2007).

The results presented here show that there is not only an expected and apparent difference between the debate contributions of government coalition and opposition MPs, but that the latter use two different rhetorical schemes for criticizing government policies in which different forms of uptake of a reference statement occur: one scheme explicitly refers to or quotes a source statement and provides argumentative and rhetorical space for elaborating an own alternative policy towards a certain topic whereas the other one merely mentions or alludes to a reference statement in order to criticize certain policies.

6. Conclusions and discussion

In this last section of the paper, I will apply a genre-perspective and argue that two general communicative purposes (and hence two genres) can be abstracted from the results – an "alternative policy focused genre" and an "evaluation focused genre". Furthermore, I intend to integrate the results from the empirical analysis with the broader considerations on the role of parliamentary debates in present day Western democratic societies already mentioned in Section 3 above.

Under a *genre-perspective* and foregrounding the *communicative purpose of the follow-up contributions* analyzed here, the analysis showed that two genres[5] of debate contributions seem to exist: the "alternative policy focused" genre and the "evaluation focused" genre. The *alternative policy focused statement* (Figure 5) is produced by Green party MPs and their audience are the other MPs and the general public (i.e. they are delivered during the TV-broadcast phase of the debate). The intertextual references which are used in these statements are "direct quotations" and "topical mentioning" of a reference statement, these serve as starting points for the presentation of an alternative policy towards a certain topic. The intertextual orientation in these statements is heteroglossic, and they display authentic dialogical elements (direct address of previous speaker, questions, etc.). The evaluations of the mentioned government policies is "negative", "inscribed", and realizes the "judgement/social sanction/propriety" category. The main purpose of this genre lies in criticising a planned government policy and presenting an own alternative.

5. There is some evidence that justifies speaking of "genres" when discussing these two kinds of contributions, yet it is not absolutely clear if they are really genres of their own: On the one hand, they have a clearly definable social purpose and many short contributions only contain one realization of the respective statement type whereas many longer contributions simply consist of a series of these statement types – this would justify using the term "genre" for these statement types. On the other hand, many of the longer debate contributions combine one or more instances of these statement types with other types (phases). A closer analysis of these complex long statements would be needed in order to determine whether these long debate contributions represent "macro-genres" (Martin and Rose 2008) in which these two respective genres are embedded.

The *evaluation focused statement* is used by speakers from all parties, the polarity of the expressed attitude, however, depends on whether a speaker is an opposition or government party MP (this genre thus combines the two argumentative schemata depicted in Figures 3 and 6). The intertextual references in these statements are "global mentioning of reference statement", "indirect mentioning of reference statement", and "direct quotation as means for evaluating source" (in the case of negative evaluations). The positive or negative evaluation of the reference text/statement is followed by evidence which is intended to support the respective evaluation or by the presentation of a reason why a certain (praised) policy was included into the government program. In the case of "direct quotations as means for evaluating a source", the quotations serve as evidence for the invoked negative evaluation of the source. The intertextual orientation of these statements is in most cases monoglossic (and only sometimes heteroglossic) and they are mainly monological. The evaluation of government policies is positive or negative, inscribed or invoked, and draws on all three appraisal resources: judgement/social sanction/propriety; appreciation/valuation; affect/satisfaction. The main purpose of this genre consists in either praising or criticising a planned government policy.

The rather frequent references to previous debate contributions and the various dialogical elements which could be found in some of the other forms of follow-up suggest at first glance a rather high dialogical debate orientation of many MPs and this result seems to contradict Burkhardt's characterization of parliamentary debates as a succession of monologues. But a closer look at the way MPs refer to previous debate contributions and at the realisation of the dialogical elements especially in the evaluation focused statements shows that the expressed dialogical stance in these statements is a mere rhetorical pose aimed at creating the impression of a dialogic orientation in front of an audience. Even the more authentic dialogical elements in the alternative policy focused statements do not (and cannot) initiate a dialogue in the given situation. One explanation for the occurrence of these quasi-dialogical contributions could be attempted by referring to the audience design of the speech event. MPs could be supposed to use the quasi-dialogical elements in their contributions in order to pretend conducting a real debate in front of an overhearing audience. This interpretation would be more in line with Burkhardt's view of parliamentary debates but it would additionally claim that (at least a rather high number of) MPs stage a debate for their audience while in fact another genre (political propaganda, in-group vs. out-group definition etc.) is realized. If we look, however, at the distribution of the quasi-dialogical statements on the time axis of the debate, we find them during as well as after the broadcast phase. The use of quasi-dialogical statements thus cannot only be attributed to speakers' orientation towards an overhearing (remote) audience.

What MPs do when they use dialogical elements in their contributions (and also if they do not use them) can be accounted for by referring to the deliberative politics approach mentioned above (Section 2) as well as by using Goffman's idea of ceremonies (Goffman 1956) and Klein's (2000) characterisation of parliamentary debates as symbolic events. In the deliberative politics approach, the use of dialogical elements during and after the TV broadcast phase of the debate can be taken as an indicator for politicians' aiming at an argumentative exchange with their fellow politicians from other political camps. The occurrence of two different genres with their differing ways of relating to previous statements and providing (or non-providing) own political alternatives can then be seen as instances of communicative actions of different quality. While the use of the "alternative policy focused" genre realizes communicative activities in which speakers visibly display an orientation towards the deliberation of different policy conceptions, the use of the "evaluation focused" genre indicates that speakers are not oriented towards deliberation but rather towards confrontation (or alignment) without presenting arguments. Under this perspective, the category system which was developed for analysing the data in this paper can also be used as a complementary tool for measuring discourse quality (in the sense of Steiner et al. 2004).

Viewing the debate as a ceremonial event (and political discourse primarily as a vehicle of group formation/maintenance, cf. Section 3), participants are primarily concerned with expressing an image of themselves and their relationship towards the other participants. By using (or not using) dialogical elements in their debate contributions and by using one of the two follow-up genres, MPs do not only act towards an overhearing audience but also towards their fellow MPs (of their own party and of the other parties). In the case of alternative policy focused statements, they project an image of themselves as topic-oriented, dialogue seeking politicians who offer alternative policy suggestions towards an issue. This stance is both oriented towards the own party (and its followers) and towards the political opponents. In the case of evaluation focused statements, the MPs project a self image of politicians who argue in line with their party affiliations. This stance is mainly oriented towards their own party (and its followers) and against the political opponents. In a political front-stage activity like a parliamentary debate, both aspects (i.e. the more content oriented deliberation focused view and the more image oriented symbolic view of parliamentary debates) interact in construing MPs' personae (Goffman 1959) or "public positive faces" (Gruber 1993a) both for an overhearing audience as well as for the fellow MPs (i.e. the primary audience).

The reversal of evaluation patterns during and after the live TV broadcast phase of the debate helps clarifying this point. *During the broadcast phase* (9.00 am – 5.00 pm) a predominance of negative evaluations from opposition party MPs was found and the majority of "direct quotations from government program" occurs. This implies that the rhetorical focus of the (opposition parties)MPs during this phase is on the "negative evaluation of government" and a "presentation of alternative policies" which can be interpreted as an orientation towards the overhearing audience in front of the TV screens.

After the broadcast phase (5.00 pm – end of debate) a predominance of positive evaluations of the government program and the inaugural speech by government party MPs was found. This implies a rhetorical focus on the "positive evaluation of government" by government MPs which is exclusively oriented towards the primary audience, i.e. the other MPs. These positive evaluations which are not oriented towards an overhearing audience obviously have an integrative function for the parliamentary groups.

For an integrative interpretation of the results reported in this paper, more research would be needed along the following lines: an analysis of more inaugural debates would be needed in order to identify patterns of opposition vs. government's, left vs. right wing parliamentary rhetoric (interviews with MPs could complement the results of the linguistic analyses). Furthermore, a comparison of "genres of follow-up moves" found in the present investigation with follow-ups in other political genres outside parliamentary debates (political media discussions, political interaction in the new media etc.) could show in which respects the results presented here are typical for parliamentary debates only and to which extent they are also relevant for other political contexts.

References

Antaki, Charles and Ivan Leudar. 2001. "Recruiting the Record: Using Opponents' Exact Words in Parliamentary Argumentation. *Text*, 21(4): 467–488.

Bakhtin, Mikhail. 1986. *Speech Genres and Other Late Essays. Edited by Caryl Emerson and Michael Holquist*. Austin/Texas: University of Texas Press.

Bayley, Paul. 2004. "Introduction: The Whys and Wherefores of Analyzing Parliamentary Discourse." In *Cross-Cultural Perspectives on Parliamentary Discourse*, ed. by Paul Bayley, 1–45. Amsterdam: John Benjamins. DOI: 10.1075/dapsac.10.01bay

Bazerman, Charles. 1994. "Systems of Genres and the Enactment of Social Intentions." In *Genre and the New Rhetoric*, ed. by Aviva Freedman & Peter Medway, 79–105. London: Taylor & Francis.

Burkhardt, Armin. 2004. *Zwischen Monolog und Dialog. Zur Theorie, Typologie und Geschichte des Zwischenrufes im deutschen Parlamentarismus*. Tübingen: Niemeyer Verlag. DOI: 10.1515/9783110910704

Clark, Herbert. 1996. *Using Language*. Cambridge: Cambridge University Press. DOI: 10.1017/CBO9780511620539

Clayman, Steven and John Heritage. 2002. *The News Interview : Journalists and Public Figures on the Air*. Cambridge: Cambridge University Press. DOI: 10.1017/CBO9780511613623

Crouch, Colin. 2008. *Postdemokratie*. Frankfurt am Main: Suhrkamp.
Drew, Paul. 1992. "Contested Evidence in Courtroom Cross-Examination: The Case of a Trial for Rape." In *Talk at Work*, ed. by Paul Drew and John Heritage, 470–521. Cambridge: Cambridge University Press.
Eriksson, Göran. 2011. "Follow-Up Questions in Political Press Conferences." *Journal of Pragmatics* 43: 3331–3344. DOI: 10.1016/j.pragma.2011.07.004
Fetzer, Anita and Elda Weizman. 2006. "Political Discourse as Mediated and Public Discourse." *Journal of Pragmatics* 38(2): 143–153. doi: 10.1016/j.pragma.2005.06.014
Fetzer, Anita, Elda Weizman, and Elisabeth Reber. 2012. "Introduction." In *Proceedings of the ESF Strategic Workshop on Follow-ups Across Discourse Domains: A Cross Cultural Exploration of Their Forms and Functions, Würzburg (Germany), 31 May – 2 June 2012*, ed. by Anita Fetzer, Elda Weizman and Elisabeth Reber, 3–4. Würzburg: Universität Würzburg – [online]. URL: http://opus.bibliothek.uniwuerzburg.de/volltexte/2012/7165/; URN: urn:nbn:de:bvb:20-opus-71656.
Fetzer, Anita and Elda Weizman. "Following Up Across Contexts and Discourse Domains: Introduction." This volume.
Girnth, Heiko. 2002. *Sprache und Sprachverwendung in der Politik*. Tübingen: Niemeyer. DOI: 10.1515/9783110946659
Goffman, Erving. 1956. "The Nature of Deference and Demeanor." *American Anthropologist* 58(3): 475–499. DOI: 10.1525/aa.1956.58.3.02a00070
Goffman, Erving. 1959. *The Presentation of Self in Everyday Life*. Garden City, NY: Doubleday, Anchor Books.
Goffman, Erving. 1981. *Forms of Talk*. Philadelphia: University of Pennsylvania Press.
Gruber, Helmut. 1993a. "Political Language and Textual Vagueness." *Pragmatics* 3(1): 1–29. DOI: 10.1075/prag.3.1.01gru
Gruber, Helmut. 1993b. "Evaluation Devices in Newspaper Reports." *Journal of Pragmatics* 19(5): 469–486. DOI: 10.1016/0378-2166(93)90006-B
Gruber, Helmut. 2013. "Genres in Political Discourse: The Case of the Parliamentary "Inaugural Speech" of Austrian Chancellors." In *Analyzing Genres in Political Communication: Theory and Practice*, ed. by Piotr Cap & Ursula Okulska (eds), 29–73. Amsterdam: Benjamins. DOI: 10.1075/dapsac.50.03gru
Habermas, Jürgen. 1988. *Theorie des kommunikativen Handelns* (3. Aufl., Bd. 1–2, Bd. 2). Frankfurt/Main: Suhrkamp.
Heritage, John. 1984. *Garfinkel and Ethnomethodology*. Oxford: Polity Press.
Heritage, John. 1985. "Analyzing News Interviews: Aspects of the Production of Talk for an Overhearing Audience." In *Handbook of Discourse analysis* (vol. 1,), ed. by Teun van Dijk, 95–117. London: Academic Press.
Hess-Lüttich, Ernest W. B. 2007. (Pseudo-)Argumentation in TV-debates. *Journal of Pragmatics* 39(8): 1360–1370. doi: 10.1016/j.pragma.2007.04.008
Holly, Werner, Peter Kühn, and Ulrich Püschel. 1986. *Politische Fernsehdiskussionen. Zur medienspezifischen Inszenierung von Propaganda als Diskussion*. Tübingen: Niemeyer.
Hutchby, Ian and Robin Wooffitt. 1998. *Conversation Analysis*. Cambridge: Polity Press.
Hutchby, Ian. 1996. *Confrontation Talk: Arguments, Asymmetries, and Power on Talk Radio*. Mahwah, NJ: Erlbaum.
Ilie, Cornelia. 2010. "Identity Co-Construction in Parliamentary Discourse Practices." In *European Parliaments under Scrutiny: Discourse Strategies and Interaction Practices*, ed. by Cornelia Ilie, 57–79. Amsterdam/Philadelphia: Benjamins. DOI: 10.1075/dapsac.38.04ili

Klein, Josef. 1991. "Politische Textsorten". *Aspekte der Textlinguistik* (Germanistische Linguistik 106/107): 245–278.
Klein, Josef. 2000. "Textsorten im Bereich politischer Institutionen." In *Handbuch der Text- und Gesprächsanalyse* (vol. 2), ed. by Gerd Antos, Karin Brinker and Sven F. Sager, 1589–1605. Berlin, New York: de Gruyter.
Kühn, Peter. 1995. *Mehrfachadressierung*. Tübingen: Niemeyer. DOI: 10.1515/9783110926835
Latour, Bruno. 2003. "What if we Talked Politics a Little?" *Contemporary Political Theory* (2): 143–164. doi: 10.1057/palgrave.cpt.9300092
Leech, Geoffrey N. and Michael Short. 2007. *Style in Fiction: A Linguistic Introduction to English Fictional Prose*. Harlow: Pearson Education.
Mann, William, and Sandra Thompson. 1987. *Rhetorical Structure Theory: A Theory of Text Organization*. Marina del Rey/California.
Martin, Jim R. and David Rose. 2008. *Genre Relations. Mapping Culture*. London: Equinox.
Martin, Jim R. and Peter White. 2007. *Language of Evaluation: Appraisal in English*. Houndsmills Basingstoke: Palgrave Macmillan. DOI: 10.1057/9780230511910
Nuolijärvi, Pirkko and Liisa Tiittula. 2011. "Irony in Political Television Debates." *Journal of Pragmatics* 43(2): 572–587. doi: 10.1016/j.pragma.2010.01.019
Plug, José. 2010. "Ad-Hominem Arguments in Dutch and the European Parliaments: Strategic Manoeuvring in an Institutional Context. In *European Parliaments under Scrutiny: Discourse Strategies and Interaction Practices*, ed. by Cornelia Ilie, 305–329. Amsterdam/Philadelphia: Benjamins. DOI: 10.1075/dapsac.38.15plu
Reisigl, Martin. 2007. *Nationale Rhetorik in Fest- und Gedenkreden. Eine diskursanalytische Studie zum „österreichischen Millennium" in den Jahren 1946 und 1996*. Tübingen: Stauffenburg.
Steiner, Jürg, André Bächtiger, Markus Spörndli, and Marco R. Steenbergen. 2004. *Deliberative Politics in Action. Analysing Parliamentary Discourse*. Cambridge: Cambridge University Press.
Strauss, Gerhard. 1986. *Der politische Wortschatz*. Tübingen: Narr.
Swales, John M. 2004. *Research Genres: Explorations and Applications*. Cambridge: Cambridge University Press. DOI: 10.1017/CBO9781139524827
Van Eemeren, Frans, Rob Grootendorst, and Tjark Kruiger. 1987. *Handbook of Argumentation Theory*. Dordrecht: Foris.
Vice, Sue. 1997. *Introducing Bakhtin*. Manchester University Press.
Weizman, Elda and Marcello Dascal. 1991. "On Clues and Cues: Strategies of Text-Understanding." *Journal of Literary Semantics* 20(1): 18–30. DOI: 10.1515/jlse.1991.20.1.18
Welan, Manfred. 1989. Regierungserklärungen in Recht und Politik. In *Was die Kanzler sagten: Regierungserklärungen der Zweiten Republik*, ed. by Maximilian Gottschlich, Oswald Panagl and Manfred Welan, 69–87. Wien: Böhlau.
Wodak, Ruth. 2011. *The Discourse of Politics in Action: Politics as Usual*. Basingstoke [u.a.]: Palgrave Macmillan. DOI: 10.1057/9780230316539
Zima, Elisabeth and Kurt Feyaerts. 2010. *Participant Roles and Layered Intersubjectivity in Austrian Parliamentary Debates*. Conference Presentation (*Vierte Konferenz der Deutschen Gesellschaft für Kognitive Linguistik*, Bremen).

Appendix 1

Original German texts of the extracts presented in this chapter:

Extract 1
Es sind in diesem Regierungsübereinkommen 20 Millionen € mehr für das Kulturbudget drinnen. Ein schöner Erfolg – Gratulation, Frau Minister! (Abg. Strache: [Zwischenruf]) Ich glaube, dass das wichtig ist, auch um zu signalisieren, wir sind ein Kulturland, eine Kulturnation.
(Cap, SPÖ, 11:15)

Extract 2
Im Bereich der Pflege setzt diese Regierung mit einem ganzen Bündel von Maßnahmen einen Schwerpunkt, und sie setzt ihn vor allem dort, wo es notwendig ist anzusetzen: bei den pflegenden Angehörigen! Die Volkspartei findet es absolut richtig – und wir haben auch dafür gesorgt, dass sich das in diesem Regierungsprogramm findet –, dass genau dieser oft unbedankten Personengruppe endlich mehr Unterstützung zuteil wird. (Karl Heinz Kopf, ÖVP, 11:45)

Extract 3
Ich sage Ihnen: Das ist genau der Punkt, der unter den Zielen, die im Kapitel Gesundheit angeführt werden, falsch definiert wird, denn da heißt es nämlich: Im Mittelpunkt der Gesundheitspolitik der Bundesregierung steht der Bedarf der PatientInnen. Falsch! Im Mittelpunkt müssten stehen die möglichst hohe Gesundheit und … (Karl Öllinger, Green party, 16:45)

Extract 4
Es wird hier [im Regierungsprogramm, HG] permanent nur von "ins Auge fassen", es "wird angestrebt", es "wird geprüft" und Ähnlichem gesprochen. Vom Umsetzen spricht man nicht, außer es handelt sich um etwas mit "Gender" – dieses beliebte Wort –, nämlich um das Gender Budgeting.
(Walter Rosenkranz, FPÖ, 21:11)

"I have nothing to do but agree"

Affiliative meta-discursive follow-ups as a resource for the reciprocal positioning of journalists, experts and politicians-as-experts in television news

Michal Hamo
Netanya Academic College, Israel

The present study explores the distinctions, hybridization and ambiguities of the reciprocal positioning of journalists and experts on the news, by examining a corpus of Israeli television news items combining interviews with affiliated journalists and external experts. The analysis reveals a dominant pattern of a largely symmetrical positioning of senior journalists and experts as colleagues. A key positioning device contributing to this symmetry is the recurrent use of meta-discursive follow-ups. These follow-ups exhibit a preference for mutual alignment, support and agreement between journalists and experts, and structure items as single co-authored arguments. The affordances of these patterns for politicians performing as expert interviewees and their possible detrimental implications for the social and democratic roles of the news are discussed.

1. Introduction

The frequency of interviews with affiliated journalists, members of the broadcasting institution, and with external experts (e.g., academics, political consultants, or retired public servants), has been and is continually rising in contemporary television news (Ekström and Kroon-Lundell 2011b; Kroon-Lundell and Eriksson 2010). This increasing salience has been discussed as the result of several larger scale changes in news discourse: it is part of a general trend of 'conversationalization'

* The present study is part of a research project on the discursive construction of authority and credibility in television news, supported by the Hamer research grant of The Israeli Second Authority for Television and Radio. My thanks to participants of the ESF exploratory workshop on follow-ups across discourse domains and to members of the Ross Priory group for research on broadcast talk for their helpful suggestions and comments on earlier versions of the article.

DOI 10.1075/dapsac.60.03ham

of the news through the spreading use of dialogical and interactional formats (Kroon-Lundell 2010; Montgomery 2007), and offers a relatively inexpensive and easy solution for the need to produce large and growing amounts of news content in a highly competitive and economically pressured environment. This need is intensified by the expansion and diversification of routine news editions throughout the day (Hjarvard 1994), and by the increasingly frequent rolling coverage of breaking news (Liebes 2003). Finally, it reflects the growing emphasis of the news on complementing information with analysis, interpretation and commentary (Albæk 2011; Ekström and Kroon-Lundell 2011b; Hopmann and Strömbäck 2010; Patrona 2012).

The present study explores journalistic and expert positioning on the news, by examining a corpus of Israeli television news items combining interviews with affiliated journalists and external experts. The analysis focuses on the recurrent use of meta-discursive follow-ups as a key discursive resource for reciprocal positioning. Follow-ups – defined here as meta-discursive comments which explicitly frame utterances as relating to any previous talk in the same item – allow interlocutors to negotiate and construct their respective roles, stances and alignment due to their dual nature. As follow-ups are both responsive and initiative, they indicate the interpretation of previous contributions of others, while at the same time framing and anticipating the status and function of the speaker's own contribution (Fetzer and Weizman this volume; Johansson this volume). As will be demonstrated below, such uses of follow-ups in news interviews encapsulate and reveal the ambiguities and hybridity of the genre and its sub-types.

2. Journalists and experts on the news

Interviews with journalists and with experts have been described as two distinct sub-types of the news interview, each characterized by different participant identities, goals and functions (Montgomery 2008).[1] Previous studies have documented systematic discursive differences between the various sub-types of the news interview, for example in the introduction of interviewees and the use of address terms, in question type, content and linguistic form, and in the interviewer's and projected audience's alignment with the interviewee (Montgomery 2008; Roth 2002; Weizman 2008). At the same time, in line with the growing hybridization of the news interview in general (e.g., Thornborrow and Montgomery 2010), the affiliated journalist and expert interviews exhibit high degrees of hybridity and ambiguity – both within each sub-type and between the two.

1. This distinction is part of a typology of four interview sub-types, which includes – in addition to affiliated and expert interviews – accountability interviews with politicians and public figures, and experiential interviews with 'ordinary' witnesses (Montgomery 2008).

2.1 The ambiguities of journalists' positioning

The growing interpretative emphasis of contemporary news leads to a rise in the salience of affiliated interviews offering analysis and commentary (Ekström and Kroon-Lundell 2011b). It also promotes shifts in the typical positioning of journalists on the news. Traditionally, journalistic authority has been constructed by highlighting professional practices and values – most prominently neutrality and objectivity – by emphasizing institutional affiliation and by downplaying personal authorship (Coupland 2001; Montgomery 2007). By contrast, the contemporary focus on interpretation gradually allows for a more personal positioning, which highlights individual journalists' recognizable personas, their superior knowledge in the fields they cover and their competence to successfully produce seemingly unchallengeable, extremely confident, sometimes opinionated personally-authored accounts and arguments (Ekström and Kroon-Lundell 2011b; Patrona 2012; Tolson 2011). This may be interpreted as part of a larger trend of personalization and celebritization of journalism, which is variously manifested across news genres – for example, in the rise of advocacy and partisanship in accountability interviews, or in the growing emphasis of news stories on journalists' performance as active agents in the field they cover (Higgins 2010; Hutchby 2011; Liebes and Kampf 2009; Marshall 2005).

The growing emphasis on the personal authority and expertise of individual journalists results in ambiguities in their positioning. First, as contemporary news discourse is informed by both traditional and emergent norms and practices (Montgomery 2007), it exhibits ongoing tensions between the professional and the personal positioning of journalists (Hamo 2010a), and an ambivalent positioning of senior journalists as both institutionally affiliated and autonomous (Ekström and Kroon-Lundell 2011b). Second, in parallel to the positioning of journalists in the socially privileged and powerful role of authoritative experts, contemporary news discourse also frequently presents them as representatives of public sentiments and common sense and aims at fostering an impression of similarity and solidarity between them and their audiences (Coupland 2001). Finally, while journalists, and in particular senior journalists, are commonly positioned in contemporary news discourse as highly knowledgeable experts, they are sometimes criticized as exhibiting quasi-expertise and possessing non-systematic and limited knowledge. Journalists have also been described as parasitic interactional experts, who rely heavily on expert sources whose knowledge they merely mediate to the public (Reich 2012; Tolson 2011).

2.2 The ambiguities of experts' positioning

While acknowledged by both practitioners and scholars as a distinct interview sub-type (Ekström and Kroon-Lundell 2011a; Montgomery 2008), the expert interview shares many functional and thematic characteristics with the affiliated journalist interview, as both are focused on information, explanation, background and analysis. The similarity between the two interview sub-types may have grew over time, as experts are increasingly featured on the news as commentators on current events, rather than as researchers presenting their own work (Albæk 2011). Like the affiliated interview, the expert interview may serve a dual function, and complement its explicit emphasis on providing information with room for expressing opinion (Montgomery 2007; Steele 1995). Both interview sub-types are supportive and position the interviewee as highly knowledgeable, competent and authoritative (Ekström and Kroon-Lundell 2011b; Montgomery 2008; Patrona 2012).

As the expert interview has received little scholarly attention in comparison to other sub-types of the news interview, the front-stage performance of experts on the news has yet to be thoroughly examined. By contrast, their backstage role in news processes has been the focus of research on news production and journalistic practices. These studies explored the relationships of journalists with expert sources and the contribution of the latter to the creation of news stories and frames, and reveal the complexity, ambivalence and variety of the expert-journalist relationship.

Journalists are increasingly dependent on expert sources both for background information and interpretative frameworks, and for securing the credibility and legitimacy of the news text. At the same time, journalists control and structure experts' media access, as they typically initiate contact with expert sources, and select expert interviewees according to their own media-oriented criteria (Albæk 2011; Steele 1995). In line with this mutual dependency, Albæk (2011) found two alternative scenarios, each accounting for about half of the journalist-expert backstage interactions in his study: in one, expert sources and voices are used by journalists to grant legitimacy to their own previously established frames and storylines; in the other, journalists and expert sources form a 'sparring partnership' and jointly develop and establish news frames.

Similar ambivalence and variety are evident in the front-stage positioning of experts in news discourse. Expert interviewees are typically presented as unaffiliated with the broadcasting institution, and accordingly, as offering an independent point of view, grounded in their superior knowledge and social legitimacy and prestige (Montgomery 2007). However, to successfully perform on the news, experts are required to adapt to the popular logic and discursive style of the media

(Lefstein 2008), and their backstage relationship with the news organization may be that of ongoing cooperation (Albæk 2011). Consequently, there may be discrepancies between the public discursive autonomous positioning of experts and their actual alignment and integration into news discourse.

Another source of ambiguity in experts' positioning is their affiliation with the social and professional arenas they analyze. Experts are typically presented on the news as neutral commentators, who explain and evaluate events from an unbiased perspective. However, they may in fact be involved to certain degrees in the events and institutions they discuss, as evident for example in the widespread reliance on retired public officials as expert commentators on the establishment they were once part of (Montgomery 2007; Steele 1995).

This ambiguity is evident in the fuzzy boundaries of the category of expert interviewees. The public definition of an expert and the profiles and backgrounds of interviewees and sources invited by news organizations to perform as experts have changed and widened over time (Albæk 2011). Accordingly, previous studies have adopted diverse definitions of expertise: from opposing experts to lay people while subsuming researchers, politicians and journalists all under the same label (Patrona 2006), or similarly discussing the performance of academics, journalists and political consultants as political experts, distinguished only from active politicians (Horsbøl 2010), to narrower definitions which separate experts from journalists (Kroon-Lundell and Eriksson 2010) or restrict the expert category to academics alone (Albæk 2011).

The tension between neutrality and involvement is particularly striking in the case of politicians performing as expert interviewees. Prototypically, politicians are interviewed on the news in the format of the accountability interview, which is characterized by high and increasing degrees of challenge, adversariality and hostility (Eriksson 2011; Montgomery 2008; Weizman 2008). These stand in sharp contrast to the respectful and supportive atmosphere of the expert interview (Montgomery 2008). Given the significant differences between the two interview sub-types, it is interesting to note that politicians may sometimes be positioned on the news as expert interviewees, who offer analysis and commentary on political processes and governmental actions.[2]

2. The appearance of politicians in expert interviews has been very common in the past (for instance, in the UK in 1980's), but has declined over the years (Montgomery 2007; Tolson 2011). This decline is part of a more general decrease in the relative salience of politicians in news discourse and its various interview sub-types, which stems from growing distrust of politicians among the public and the journalistic community (Ekström and Kroon-Lundell 2011b; Kroon-Lundell and Eriksson 2010; but see below for somewhat contrasting findings in the present corpus and for further discussion).

3. The present study

The present study aims at further exploring the distinctions and similarities between the affiliated journalist and expert interviews. It examines the ambiguities and hybridization of such interviews by focusing on the tensions between personal and professional authority and between independence and affiliation in the positioning of interviewees. Adopting a view of positioning as the contextualized dynamic reciprocal negotiation of identities, roles, stances and relationships (Weizman 2008), the present study aims at examining the ways these tensions are jointly worked out by journalists and experts through their use of meta-discursive follow-ups when appearing on the news together. To this end, it focuses on items combining both affiliated and expert interviews. Affiliated interviews were defined in the present analysis as interviews with journalists who are members of the broadcasting institution, and expert interviews – as interviews with unaffiliated non-lay participants (including academics, retired public officials and politicians) which exhibit the thematic, functional and discursive characteristics of the expert interview described above.

Such items were located in a database of Israeli television news, comprised of one composite week of weekdays (Sunday–Thursday), randomly sampled in January–April 2008. The database included all news shows broadcasted on prime-time and pre-prime-time (5 pm–10 pm) on Israel's three broadcast channels (the public Channel 1, the dominant commercial Channel 2, and its smaller commercial competitor, Channel 10).Within this database, a total of 20 items featuring interviews with both journalists and experts were located, transcribed and analyzed. These items appeared on a variety of news shows, including the main news editions of all three channels, highbrow news magazines (e.g., *Today on the news [Ha-yom ba-hadashot]*, Channel 1; *London and Kirshenbaum [London et Kirshenbaum]*, Channel 10) and afternoon tabloid news shows (e.g., *Six o'clock with Oded Ben-Ami [Shesh im Oded Ben-Ami]*, Channel 2; *Five o'clock with Rafi Reshef [Hamesh im Rafi Reshef]*, Channel 10). The items were reserved mainly for the extended coverage of highly newsworthy, at times breaking, news. Specifically, the corpus is dominated by the coverage of two very different events – the assassination of Hezbollah's Imad Mughniyah and the surprise annulment of a plea bargain in the sexual harassment trial of former Israeli president Moshe Katzav – which represent the diversity of hard news, including military, diplomatic, political and legal aspects of both foreign and domestic news.

The salience of extended breaking news coverage in the corpus supports the view of the affiliated and expert interviews as effective means for expanding and lengthening news discourse. It also results in textual hybridity, as some items in the corpus merge structural and discursive features of both routine news editions embedded in the schedules of broadcast channels, and rolling news typical of dedicated 24-hours news channels. While each item is contained within the line-up of a specific show, and adheres to its format, atmosphere and regular participants, some items also resemble rolling news discourse, as they are more extended, fluid, open-ended and multi-voiced than routine broadcast news items (Montgomery 2007).

In a previous study, the corpus was analyzed with a focus on participation frameworks and on the contents, functions and styles of the contributions of journalists and experts (Hamo 2012). The analysis revealed great diversity of reciprocal positionings, ranging from a clear role distribution, by which journalists report and experts analyze and comment, to a conflation of the two roles, by which both journalist and expert provide a mixture of facts, background, analysis and opinion. However, the dominant pattern that emerged was a largely symmetrical positioning of senior journalists and experts as colleagues, with only relatively delicate local distinctions between the two roles. This symmetry is discursively constructed through several devices. First, journalists and experts are positioned in parallel interactional roles of interviewees who answer questions, usually with no direct interaction between them. As interviewees, both journalists and experts are clearly distinguished from hosts-interviewers, and the differences in their professional and institutional affiliations are undercut. Secondly, experts and journalists are often symmetrically positioned by hosts, who ask both participants similar, sometimes identical questions. Thirdly, both interviewees produce functionally and thematically similar contributions, which combine facts, background and analysis and exhibit high degrees of confidence and authoritativeness (see examples below).

As indicated above, one discursive resource observed in this preliminary analysis as contributing to the symmetrical positioning of journalists and experts was the recurrent use of follow-ups. Accordingly, the present study set out to further explore their functions and implications for reciprocal positioning. As items in the corpus were typically structured as a sequence of separate interviews – usually an affiliated interview followed by an expert interview – to a certain extent the entire expert interview may be interpreted as following-up on the journalist's talk. However, the actual relationships between specific contributions in the two interviews are often implicit or equivocal. To ensure the valid identification of follow-ups, the present study adhered to participants' overt orientations to the relationships between their respective contributions: as specified above, follow-ups were narrowly defined as meta-discursive comments which explicitly frame utterances as relating to any previous talk in the same item, regardless of their sequential positioning or of the actual thematic or functional connections between them.

This relatively restrictive definition of follow-ups is also grounded in the recognition of meta-discourse as a highly significant positioning device both generally and in contemporary news discourse (Hamo 2010a). Meta-discursive talk often defines the interaction's participation framework, either explicitly or implicitly, for example through pronoun use. In addition, as it often explicitly labels the speech act or discursive function currently underway, it may entail the social role and stance of the speaker. For instance, when asked to discuss the possibility of retribution acts following the assassination of Imad Mughniyah (in a segment directly preceding Example (1) below), military commentator Yoav Limor opens by saying "A cautionary note, everything is based on our estimates, on our experience and so on" ("he'arat azhara, ha-kol mevusas al ha'arachotenu, al nisyonenu ve-chuley"). This meta-discursive comment functions as a disclaimer which pre-frames and hedges the analysis to follow. At the same time, it contributes to Limor's positioning in several ways: through the use of the first-person plural, it aligns him with an under-specified collective – either the journalistic interpretative community (Hamo 2010a), or, perhaps more likely, the Israeli intelligence community (see below for a discussion of the complicity of Israeli news media with the military establishment); it reflects and reinforces Limor's specific role as a commentator responsible for providing "estimates"; and finally, it underscores his "experience", and therefore his seniority and personal authority.

4. Follow-ups as a reciprocal positioning device

Meta-discursive follow-ups recur in the corpus. Given the typical structure of items mentioned above, they are frequently produced by experts, and more rarely by journalists. Meta-discursive follow-ups are multi-functional: by nature, they serve the textual function of maintaining and emphasizing inter-speaker continuity, coherence and cohesion, but often, they also contribute to the reciprocal positioning of participants. Example (1) includes three rather typical follow-ups produced by an expert, and illustrates how they construct the expert's and journalist's respective roles and their mutual alignment. Part of a lengthy item, the example begins as the host concludes an affiliated interview with the channel's military commentator, and introduces the external expert. Interestingly, she explicitly marks the expert interview as a resource for expanding and deepening news coverage ("let's really develop" ["bo'u be'ement nefate'ach"], turn 1).

(1) *Today on the news (Ha-yom ba-hadashot)*, pre-primetime highbrow news magazine, Channel 1, February 13 2008. As part of the breaking news coverage of the assassination of Hezbollah's Imad Mughniyah, the host, Keren Noibach (f),

interviews the channel's Arab affairs commentator Oded Granot, the channel's military commentator Yoav Limor, and Dr. Boaz Ganor, an expert on terror.[3]

1. Noibach: [>Okay, so let's really develop this issue and add to the conversation Doctor Boaz Ganor, an expert on terror from the Interdisciplinary Center in Herzliya.< Hello to you.
2. Ganor: Hello Keren.
3. Noibach: So Yoav actually here delineates the::: what would have happened, (.) if we'd been before the second, e Lebanon, war and what would have been then, how would look Hezbollah's reaction, to the hit on Mughniyah. Your estimate?
4. Ganor: *First, I have nothing ((to do)) but agree. h with Yoav,* e one should understand that Hezbollah, is perhaps one of the only organizations in the world, that not only wasn't deterred by a state for years, but succeeded in deterring a state, and I mean the state of Israel. It create:d two insights in the state of Israel, that i:f Israel hits, one of the leaders of the organization, then the reaction- or hits it >with another harsh blow, then the reaction will surely follow,< most likely against an Israeli or Jewish interest overseas, *and indeed was mentioned* Buenos Aires in- in its double move, and there were more examples throughout, e throughout history. It also accustomed us that if during an Israeli militar:y operation or an air strike civilians are hurt immediately it reacts with Katyusha ((missiles)), and these insights were learned in the state of Israel, and I think that the ((2006)) Lebanon war, this is at least what the prime minister declares, was meant to actually change these rules of the game, the bad ((rules))=

3. Examples are translated from the original Hebrew by the author. Full original transcripts and transliterations are available upon request. Transcription conventions: [words] – overlapping talk; = – overlatch; (.) – pauses, untimed; (…) – incomprehensible words; (words) – transcription doubt; .h – in breath; . – a falling intonation at the end of an utterance; , – a continuing rising intonation; ? – a rising intonation at the end of an utterance; WORD – high volume; °word° – low volume; word – emphasis; wo::rd – sound stretch; wor- – cut off; >words< – fast rhythm; <words> – slow rhythm; ((comment)) – transcriber's comments; *words* – meta-discursive follow-up. As the vast majority of participants in the corpus are men, gender is indicated only in the cases of women, with an (f). For reasons of space, transcripts do not include detailed visual data. The materials exhibit a shared visual pattern of a cyclic transition between medium shots of speakers; long shots of the entire studio; topically relevant, mostly archive, video footage, with the interaction in voice over; a split screen with two separate medium shots of speakers, side by side; and a split screen with a small medium shot of the speaker and a larger window presenting video footage. In addition, there is extensive use of subtitles identifying speakers and summarizing main points, and of a rolling news-bar at the bottom of the screen.

5. Noibach: =mm=
6. Ganor: =for Israel, that were established. There's no doubt, from my point of view at least, that- *I agree with that too, e with what Yoav said,* it doesn't matter by the way if Israel is responsible or not, and if it turns out tomorrow that in fact it was a Lebanese intelligence servi:ce, or or a Syrian, the- already now they're preparing in Hezbollah, for an operation (.) against Israel, for- a retribution operation, ((Turn continues))

In turn 3, the host summarizes the military commentator's previous contribution as an analysis proposing a hypothetical scenario, and then asks the external expert's for "your estimate" ("Ha'arachatcha"). This elliptical request allows for two possible interpretations: as inviting the expert to offer his own estimate of "what would have happened if we'd been before the second Lebanon war" ("ma haya kore ilu hayinu nimca'im lifney milhemet Levanon ha-shniya"), or as asking for his estimate of the scenario "Yoav actually here delineates" ("Yoav be'ement po mesartet"). Thus, while the host's opening move works to establish continuity between the two interviews, it leaves the specific relation between them ambivalent: the expert may be understood as invited to present his own analysis after the journalist has already given his, or as requested to evaluate the plausibility and quality of the military commentator's analysis. While the first interpretation highlights symmetry between the two interviewees, the second implicitly sanctions the expert's superior knowledge and authority, and positions him as providing independent corroboration for news discourse.

The expert opens his response with a meta-discursive follow-up ("I have nothing to do but agree with Yoav" ["Ein li ela lehaskim im Yoav"], turn 4). By framing his contribution as agreement, he affiliates with the journalist and supports his analysis. Moreover, the expert positions himself as redundant, unable to make any unique contribution to the discussion other than reiterate the journalist's analysis, thus highlighting their similarity. During the extended commentary that follows, the expert produces two additional follow-ups: the first ("and indeed was mentioned" ["ve-huzkar be'emet"], turn 4) merely serves the textual function of maintaining inter-speaker cohesion and coherence, by citing a previously mentioned fact. The second ("I agree with that too, with what Yoav said" ["ani maskim gam im ze, im ma she-Yoav amar"], turn 6) is again an affiliative follow-up. Here, the expert's ostensible superior status is not invoked, and the agreement conveyed may be interpreted as simply that between colleagues.[4]

4. The supportive frame is invoked again later, as the journalist draws on the expert's agreement as a form of independent authoritative corroboration strengthening his argument. Thus,

Overall, these meta-discursive follow-ups frame the item as a co-authored analysis. This analysis exhibits some of the key shared thematic, functional and stylistic characteristics of journalist and expert discourse in the present corpus: it is structured as a commentary which weaves opinion, speculation and factual background information into a single seamless argument. This argument is presented as personally authored and self-confident, through the combination of self-attribution ("I think" ["ani savur"], turn 4; "I agree" ["ani maskim"] turn 6) and markers of high deontic and epistemic modality ("one should understand" ["tzarich lehavin"], turn 4; "there's no doubt, from my point of view at least" ["ein safek, be-einay lefachot"], turn 6) (for these patterns in journalistic discourse, see Ekström and Kroon-Lundell 2011b; Patrona 2012; Tolson 2011; for further discussion, see Hamo 2012).

4.1 The construction of mutual alignment through the use of follow-ups

As Example (1) demonstrates, meta-discursive follow-ups are frequently used by experts to highlight agreement and alignment with previous statements by journalists. This recurrent use of affiliative follow-ups has dual effects on the positioning of both journalists and experts. As the expert is sanctioning the journalist's knowledge and analytic competence, he supports the journalist's authoritative persona as an expert in the field he covers. On the other hand, the journalist's knowledge and analysis are implicitly presented as requiring verification by a 'real' authority, highlighting the limits of his expertise. In a parallel manner, the expert is positioned as providing independent corroboration for news discourse, but at the same time, by aligning with the journalist, affiliates with news discourse.

These complex dual effects underscore the ambiguities of the journalist-expert relationship discussed above. However, alignment, co-authorship and symmetry seem to be the generally dominant effects, and are further supported by two additional patterns of use of follow-ups. First, the possible power hierarchy between expert and journalist is downplayed and symmetry is supported by the fact that journalists produce parallel meta-discursive follow-ups conveying agreement with experts – though more rarely, given the typical sequence of interviews, which gives them fewer opportunities to do so. Secondly, the preference for alignment and co-authorship is evident in the use of follow-ups to mitigate disagreement on the rare occasions it occurs. This is demonstrated by Example (2).

---

the supportive frame is extended and jointly developed over time. This is facilitated by the length of the item and by its unique structure, which interweaves three interviews together.

(2) *First Edition (Mahadura rishona)*, an afternoon news show, Channel 2, April 8 2008. As part of the coverage of the surprise annulment of a plea bargain in the sexual harassment trial of former Israeli president Moshe Katzav, the host, Oren Weigenfeld, talks to three participants, in two rounds of consecutive separate interviews: Guy Peleg, the channel's legal reporter, Amit Segal, the channel's political reporter, who spent the day covering the protests and reactions outside the courthouse, and law Professor Suzie Navot (f).

1. Weigenfeld: >In this story we are accompanied by, our reporters,< Guy Peleg and Amit Segal, and by the legal commentator, Suzi Navot, Hello to you all. We'll start with you Guy, ((any)) headline of the:: last minutes?
2. Peleg: ((Beginning of turn omitted: Peleg describes the anticipation of a statement by the attorney general)) we received just several minutes ago=
3. Weigenfeld: =Yes=
4. Peleg: =a press release, I will read its bottom line and with- and will add a word. eh- ((They)) write in the department of justice. In any case, it may be assumed that the implications of this move, are clear to Moshe Katzav, as was relayed at the time as part of the state's answer to the Supreme Court, before the plea arrangement, the clear tendency was that an indictment would be served, even for the gravest offences of which he was suspect, despite the difficulties involved. Now that the plea arrangement was annulled, the decision required under these circumstances will soon be made, and if we sum up, back at the time said ((attorney general)) Meni Mazuz, if there hadn't been a plea bargain we would have filed against Moshe Katzav, a severe indictment, including, a series of rapes, it seems to me that it can be estimated today after this announcement and the clear things, written by the ministry of justice, that the inclination (.) prior to the consultations, the inclination >of the attorney general,< is to create a new indictment, much more severe against Moshe Katzav that will include, the- the gravest sexual charge in the law books, the charge of rape.

((3 turns omitted: Weigenfeld and Peleg describe Katzav's surprising announcement of the plea bargain annulment; Weigenfeld introduces an insert – a statement by one of Katzav's attorneys.))

8. Weigenfeld: °Ok.° .h eh Professor eh Navot, the:: situation of annulling a plea bargain is, a quite rare situation, also the standing of Mazuz was a bit eh undermined, to say the least i:n this affair,

especially after ((Supreme Court Chief Justice)) Beinish then attacked the deal in court?=

9. Navot: =°Right,° the truth is that the whole affair, .h is a problematic affair, and to- today certainly was a very dramatic day maybe *in continuation to the things e .h that Guy said*, >it's true that we're going back< to the initial situation, and even if a very severe mm indictment would be filed, that is including rape charges, ((one)) must remember .h that against the- that indictment there are today dozens of pages, of an id::i- a do:cument submitted actually by Mazuz to the court when he tried to justify that amended indictment, .h who:le page:s where he actually details the problems he has, with the evidence, the problems that exist with the credibility of the complaining ((witnesses)), and these are the same complaining ((witnesses)) that today need, to stand, by his si:de, and need to support a new indictment. It wouldn't be possible to ignore .h th- that we're not going back, [it's] not a situation of zero, (but) we're going back >in a very problematic situation for the prosecutors.<

10. Weigenfeld: [°Yes°]

11. Weigenfeld: >Everything is ahead.< Amit Segal, you were there outside ((the courthouse)) with the demonstrators, of all sides, pro and con, describe for u:s a bi:t about what happened there?

((2 turns omitted: Segal and Weigenfeld describe the scene outside the courthouse; Segal introduces an insert – protestors' reactions to Katzav's arrival to the courthouse.))

14. Segal: =Yes, the really interesting thi::ng, is, how ((it)) was received, outside the message that came from inside of the annulment of the plea bargain, (then) the women's organizations were very happy, >you- will be able to see that also later on,< rea::l cries of joy, whistles and so on, this joy was premature. Because that this (.) annulment of the plea bargain that ((they)) fought so much eh for, including in the Supreme Court, comes for them, critically late, after Meni Mazuz (.) has already explained to the court, to- to the supreme court, (.) that there is no possibility, of convicting Katzav of the more serious charges, of rape, and e the indecent acts detailed >in the indictment draft,< n:o real possibility to see Katzav, e Katzav charged with (these) things by Mazuz >after the same Mazuz explained why this can't be done< ((Turn continues))

((7 turns omitted: Weigenfeld, Segal and Peleg describe reactions to the annulment in the political and legal arenas. Peleg introduces an insert – a statement by the attorney of one of the complaining witnesses.))

22. Peleg: ((Beginning of turn omitted)) and it seems to me:, *I will address here the comm[ents said] by my colleagues,*

23. Weigenfeld: [aha]

24. Peleg: em (.) regarding e the- clear things said by Meni Mazuz regarding the credibility of the complaining ((witnesses)), one mustn't forget that the m- head of the country's justice system, the Supreme Court Chief Justice, she said, so what if you have doubts, so what if there're disputes [(……)]

25. Weigenfeld: [Let the judges] decide=

26. Peleg: =exactly, let the judges decide, and from this moment ((on)) >I think that Meni Mazuz can feel< e at peace, and secure, with this kind of backwind from the Supreme Court Chief Justice, ((Turn continues))

Before turning to the analysis of the follow-ups in Example (2), note that the item's participation framework and its thematic and functional foci illustrate the ambivalence of journalists' and experts' reciprocal positioning and the tendency to conflate their roles in favor of a relatively symmetrical positioning. While the host's opening statement (turn 1) introduces the two reporters and the external expert separately, it does not distinguish between the unique roles each of them is expected to fulfill, but rather vaguely groups them together as "accompanying" ("melavim") the coverage. This conflation is furthered by the use of a journalistic role title ("commentator" ["parshanit"]) as a label for the external expert, law professor Suzie Navot.

Later, in his initial questions to each of the three interviewees (turns 1, 8 and 11), the host attempts to preserve functional differentiation: he asks the legal reporter to provide the latest update on the legal arena, the external expert to evaluate the current situation and its ramifications, and the political and field reporter to describe reactions in the public sphere. However, the reporters do not adhere to this distinction. Both begin their responses with factual reports which incorporate inserts from the earlier live coverage, but gradually shift to the more interpretative task of evaluating the plausibility of a severe new indictment, including rape charges, against former Israeli president Moshe Katzav, while drawing on background information on the Katzav affair in support of their assessments (turns 4 and 14). Thus, they re-position themselves in a role similar to the expert's. This symmetrical positioning is later reinforced by the legal reporter's reference to both the fellow reporter and the law professor as "my colleagues" ("amitay", turn 22), and by his insistence to maintain and defend his initial evaluation that a severe indictment is plausible after the expert has presented an opposing assessment, not yielding to her superior knowledge but rather positioning himself as her equal (turns 9 and 24).

The symmetry between expert and journalist is further supported by the use of follow-ups in the item. As mentioned, in turns 9 and 22–26, Law professor Suzie Navot and legal reporter Guy Peleg present contradictory evaluations. Both use affiliative follow-ups to frame their contradictory contributions in neutral, non-adversarial terms ("in continuation to the things that Guy said" ["be-hemshech la-dvarim she-amar Guy"] turn 9; "I will address here the comments said by my colleagues" ["ani etyahes po la-he'arot she-amru amitay"], turn 22), thus mitigating their disagreement and maintaining an orientation to inter-speaker coherence, continuity and alignment. Disagreement is further mitigated by both participants' use of impersonal forms to present counter-arguments ("It wouldn't be possible to ignore" ["i-efhsar yihiye lehit'alem"], turn 9; "one mustn't forget" ["asur lish-koach"], turn 24), and by the fact that Navot opens her contribution by conceding to some of Peleg's comments ("It's true" ["ze nachon"], turn 9). This use of follow-ups to mitigate disagreement stands in contrast to the use of follow-ups to highlight disagreement, challenge and criticism in others arenas of public discourse, such as online political discussions (Johansson, this volume; Sivenkova, this volume). Furthermore, such mitigation is particularly noteworthy in the context of Israeli mediated political discourse, which, due to the influence of the highly adversarial traditional Jewish-Israeli discursive style, typically exhibits a preference for intensified disagreement (Blum-Kulka, Blondheim and Hacohen 2002). Accordingly, the mitigation of disagreement in the present analysis provides strong evidence of the preference for agreement, mutual alignment and co-authorship between journalists and experts on television news (see below for discussion).

4.2 The expert interview's affordances for politicians

In contrast to evidence of a decline in the salience of politicians as news interviewees, both generally and more specifically as experts and commentators (see note 2 above; Ekström and Kroon-Lundell 2011b; Kroon-Lundell and Eriksson 2010; Montgomery 2007; Tolson 2011), the present corpus does include several appearances of politicians as expert interviewees who comment on current events. This somewhat surprising finding may be accounted for from several complementing perspectives. First, the corpus is dominated by the extended coverage of breaking news. It is plausible that under such unique circumstances, the pressing need to quickly find enough readily available and media competent interviewees leads news organizations to relax their usual distrust of politicians, who easily meet both these demands. Second, the use of politicians as expert interviewees in the corpus is reserved solely to the coverage of military, diplomatic and foreign news. It may be argued that news organizations clearly distinguish between the status of politicians in the domestic sphere and in the international arena: in the former, politicians are considered highly biased and manipulative interested parties whose media appearances should be both restricted and balanced through adversariality (Montgomery 2008; Weizman 2008). By contrast, in the latter they may be viewed as legitimate and respectable representatives of the interests and perspective of the nation state, who thus may perform as credible authoritative experts. Finally, the politicians appearing as expert interviewees in the present corpus are retired military officials. As the military establishment in Israel is highly valued and respected, these politicians' past records lend them authority and trustworthiness. Furthermore, reliance on the perspective of the military establishment, including the use of past and present military officials as expert sources, is commonplace in Israeli journalism. Thus, the present corpus may be somewhat culturally specific, reflecting the dominance of the military in the Israeli public sphere, and the complicity of both the journalistic community and the political arena with it (for reviews see Limor and Nossek 2006; Peri 2006).

While they may be uncommon and restricted to specific circumstances, opportunities for politicians to perform as expert interviewees provide them with unique and valuable affordances, as will be discussed below. Such occasions are extreme manifestations of the tension between neutrality and involvement inherent in the expert interview. Accordingly, their analysis may shed light on the sub-genre as a whole, as well as on some of its more frequent realizations, such as the regular use of retired officials or of active financial actors as experts on the news. Thus, the performance of politicians as expert interviewees merits close analytic attention.

As illustrated by Example (3) below, politicians may use the distinct conditions of the expert interview – including its respectful and supportive atmosphere and the preference described above for alignment with journalists – to foster a positive, authoritative and trustworthy public image. Example (3) features Dani Yatom, who is introduced at the beginning of the item as "a Knesset Member of the labor party who was a retired ((army)) general and also the head of the Mossad ((The Israeli Institute for Intelligence and Special Operations))" ("haver ha-Kneset mi-mifleget ha-avoda she-haya aluf be-milu'im ve-gam rosh ha-mosad"). Yatom illustrates the ambiguities of the positioning of expert interviewees in general, and of politicians as expert interviewees in particular. Like many expert interviewees, he is a retired official, who is accordingly somewhat complicit with the institutions he may be asked to analyze and evaluate (Mongtomery 2007). This ambiguity is exacerbated by the fact that at the time of the interview, Yatom's party was a member of the governing coalition, and accordingly, he may have been held accountable for representing Israel's official positions.

(3a) *London and Kirshenbaum (London et Kirshenbaum)*, highbrow pre-primetime news magazine, Channel 10, February 13 2008. As part of the coverage of the assassination of Hezbollah's Imad Mughniyah, and following two affiliated interviews, with senior Arab affairs correspondent Zvi Yehezkeli, and with military commentator Alon Ben-David, the host, Yaron London, turns to a third interviewee – the politician Dani Yatom.

1. London: =Dani Yatom, when, when e it's decided, em when Israel decides, to settle the score with someone, em how, what is the process of- by which we-=
2. Yatom: =I don't know, I don't know if Israel is behind this=
3. London: =No, behind this, no way,=
4. Yatom: And I don't know, I don't know who's doing this, or who did this, I know only that Imad Mughniyah was destined to die for many many years, and he's o:n the top part of the wanted list, of many many countries, including countries much bigger much stronger, and with much greater capabilities than, than our capabilities, for example the United States of America. An:::d he: e was responsible for many years, for all the secret activity of Hezbollah, that which even after its execution was not made public, (.) Hezbollah did not claim responsibility for it. He was not only, the master of hiding, *as was said here by Alon*, but he had a creative devilish mind. I think that this is the major loss for Hezbollah, in them losing one of the more creative planners, one of the more meticulous executors, because even after he executed ((terror)) attacks, it was very hard, to retrace his steps, for instance the investigatio::n regarding the two attacks i:n Buenos Aires, in Argentina, has taken many many years not just because of the fact, that the: authorities who investigated the attacks, on the Amia building, the Jewish community building, a::nd the Israeli embassy, e acted in a shoddy manner, but also because of the fact that Imad Mughniyah used to, leave, very few traces if any, and mo:st of the activities he did overseas, were a full cooperation with the Iranian intelligence. And there is in thi:s a great loss for Hezbollah, a remarkable e:: intelligence penetration, exceptional, and a >very very< great operational ability.=
5. London: =What were his assumed identities whi:le, in his stays overseas?

Yatom's hybrid status as an interviewee is reflected in the host's initial question, which asks him to provide privileged information on decision making processes in the Israeli government and security establishment (turn 1) – a question which calls for both demonstrating expertise and for being held accountable. The question is highly problematic for Yatom, as it presupposes that it is at the very least reasonable to assume that Israel is responsible for Mughniyah's assassination – a possibility which as a rule, Israeli officials blatantly refrain from addressing. Accordingly, Yatom refuses to answer the question, even hypothetically (turns 2–4).[5] He justifies this refusal by rejecting the hybrid positioning embedded in the question and re-positioning himself as strictly an expert ("I don't know… I know only" ["ani lo yode'a… ani yode'a rak"], turn 4). He refrains from talking about Israel and devotes an extended turn to detailed background information on its outgroup – Hezbollah and Mughniyah (turn 4). While doing so, he echoes and repeats some of the information provided earlier in the affiliated interviews, and uses a meta-discursive follow-up to emphasize continuity and alignment with them ("as was said here by Alon" ["kmo she-ne'emar kan al-yedey Alon"], turn 4). In the context of a political accountability interview, such a blatant topic shift and role re-negotiation would have been considered extremely evasive (Weizman 2008). Here, given the hybrid positioning of the politician-as-expert and the generally supportive setting of an expert interview, the same move goes unchallenged: the politician is allowed to continue his lengthy turn uninterrupted, and in turn 5, the host adopts and extends the new topical agenda and discursive role set by the interviewee.

This affiliative and supportive atmosphere is maintained throughout the rest of the item. It allows Yatom to continually re-negotiate his positioning and exploit its hybridity by carefully balancing different roles and subtly moving between them. For instance, in Example (3b) below, which closes the item, he takes the initiative by non-verbally requesting permission to speak (as evidenced by the host's reaction in turn 7). Again, the politician's initiative is supported and accepted by the host (turn 9). Once he gains the floor, Yatom provides an answer to the question on the advisability of assassinating terrorists (turn 10), originally addressed at the military commentator (turn 1). This emphasizes a symmetrical positioning of politician and journalist as fellow authoritative experts, who share the same entitlement to provide evaluations and judgments and produce parallel contributions.

(3b) *London and Kirshenbaum (London et Kirshenbaum)*, highbrow pre-primetime news magazine, Channel 10, February 13 2008. As part of the coverage of the assassination of Hezbollah's Imad Mughniyah, after concluding the interview with Dani Yatom, the host turns back to military commentator Alon Ben-David, with questions regarding possible retribution for Mughniyah's assassination. Following Ben-David's answer and a few questions and clarifications, the following interaction ensues.

---

5. It seems that the host acknowledges the sensitivity of the issue and anticipates Yatom's refusal to comment on it, as reflected by his many hesitations and false-starts in turn 1.

1. London: [Is it advisable- is it advisable- I rai:: think a theoretical question, is it advisable to eliminate such a person?
2. Ben-David: That's a very difficult question. Very difficult. Some will say to you, e there are people who should die, whatever the cost may be. As we have learned in the flesh-
3. London: Justice? Jus[ice?
4. Ben-David: [or-
5. London: A matter of justice?
6. Ben-David: A matter of stopping their activity. Bu[t, as we have learned after the attacks in Argentina,]
7. London: [Yes. (.) You want (after him?) Yes.]
8. Ben-David: The elimination of Abbass Mussawi both brought about a hundred and twenty casualties and raised Hezbollah, to a level of an organization much more dominant than [it was before. ((Theme music that signals a commercial break starts))
9. London: [Would you settle for a short sentence?=
10. Yatom: =In a short sentence, I think tha::t in the war on terror, which is a very very long and at times Sisyphean war, one should try and locate all the points of weakness and points of strength and hit them. And one of the major stre- strength points of any terror organization is the leadership, and one should carry out attacks there too.
11. London: Thanks very much.

Within the general symmetrical positioning in Example (3b), some differences are maintained. The military commentator's contribution is structured as a neutral expert analysis: it includes considerations both for (turns 2, 6) and against assassinations (turn 8). As some of these arguments are vaguely attributed to others ("some will say to you" ["yesh she-yagidu leach"], turn 2), and others are implied from a factual description of the past rather than explicitly stated (turns 6–8), the journalist's personal authorship is mitigated. This careful neutrality is atypical of journalistic expert discourse on the news, which tends to be highly opinionated, self-assured and personally owned (Ekström and Kroon-Lundell 2011b; Hamo 2012; Patrona 2012; Tolson 2011), and may stem from the complexity and moral sensitivity of the issue.

By contrast, the politician presents a confident unequivocal pro-assassination stand, uses high deontic modality ("one should try" ["tzarich lenasot"], "one should carry out" ["tzarich le-vatze'a"], turn 10) and underscores his personal commitment ("I think" ["ani hoshev"], turn 10). The status of his contribution is highly ambivalent: it may be interpreted as a typical instance of the confident and opinionated expert discourse in the corpus (Hamo 2012; see analysis of Example (1) above), but may also be understood as an expression of Yatom's personal political convictions, or even as the articulation of the official policy of the Israeli government by one of its legitimate representatives. This ambivalence is not taken up or clarified by the host or by the military commentator, who refrain from assuming a challenging 'watchdog' capacity. They do not develop the potential conflict between Yatom's and the military commentator's somewhat opposing views, criticize Yatom's pro-assassination policy or hold him accountable for its possible dire consequences. This may be partly explained by time constraints, as a commercial break is scheduled to start, but also results from the general supportive atmosphere of the expert interview and the preference for agreement discussed above.

Thus, Yatom uses key features of the expert interview and its combination with an affiliated interview in a single item – the supportive and respectful setting, the preference for alignment among participants and the possibility to dynamically re-negotiate their reciprocal positioning – to foster an authoritative persona, to construct an affiliative, rather than an antagonistic, relationship with the journalistic community, and to deflect accountability.

5. Conclusions

The present study reveals meta-discursive follow-ups to be a key reciprocal positioning device. Follow-ups are a specific local interactional phenomenon which echoes and encapsulates some large-scale trends of political discourse, such as its growing dynamization (Fetzer and Weizman, this volume). Accordingly, the micro-level analysis of the functions of follow-ups in positioning processes may provide the basis for some macro-level reflections on the (re)negotiated nature of social role, authority and expertise in contemporary news discourse and public sphere, to which we now turn.

Follow-ups were found to contribute to the construction of symmetry between journalists and experts on the news, which reinforces the ambiguities of journalists' and experts' positioning discussed above: such symmetry validates the status of senior journalists as experts in the fields they cover, thus underscoring their unique individual personas rather than their professional and institutional affiliations; and it reflects the alignment, cooperation and integration of external experts with news organizations and discourse. These findings provide further evidence of the ongoing and widespread hybridization of the news interview (Thornborrow and Montgomery 2010).

The recurrent use of affiliative follow-ups in items combining affiliated journalist and expert interviews reflects a preference for mutual support and agreement. It structures these items as offering a single co-authored analysis, while obscuring, rather than exploring, diverging perspectives and arguments. This co-authorship may be seen as the end result of more complicated backstage processes and relationships, as affiliated and expert interviews are based on extensive pre-planning. While structured as live spontaneous conversations, affiliated interviews are often collaboratively pre-scripted and rehearsed by interviewers and interviewees (Ekström and Kroon-Lundell 2011a). Expert interviews are grounded in background conversations between journalists and expert sources, including pre-interviewing and coordination of the interview's foci. Such practices allow journalists to obtain background information from experts and jointly negotiate the framing and perspective of the news story with them (Albæk 2011), and provide both parties with the opportunity to discuss and resolve any disagreements and conflicts in advance. Thus, the on-air reciprocal symmetrical and supportive positioning of journalists and experts as co-authors does not fully reflect the actual unique role played by experts in preparation of the news discourse. It may also obscure the full complexity of the expert-journalist relationships, which may involve various power asymmetries and conflicting individual interests and agendas. Accordingly, the present analysis demonstrates the importance of examining the news interview from an integrative approach, combining the attention of various traditions of media discourse analysis to front-stage performance with the focus of studies of journalistic practices on backstage processes (e.g., Ekström and Kroon-Lundell 2011a).

The symmetrical positioning of journalists and experts documented in the present study corroborates previous research on the Israeli news interview, which found a preference for symmetry, reciprocity and flexible re-negotiation of role distribution (Weizman 2008). As this preference echoes the traditional Israeli cultural ethos of mechanical solidarity, equality and informality (Hamo 2010b; Katriel 1991, 2004), it may be somewhat culturally specific. However, the preference for agreement found in the present study contrasts with the general preference for disagreement of both traditional Jewish-Israeli ways of speaking, and the highly adversarial and challenging Israeli mediated political discourse (Blum-Kulka et al. 2002; Weizman 2008). This discrepancy may be interpreted from two complementing perspectives. First, coupled with findings of previous studies, it may be understood as evidence of changes in Israeli ways of speaking, as both globalizing pressures and inner social trends lead to a growing orientation to harmony (Hamo 2010b; Katriel 2004). Alternatively, as previous studies on adversariality in Israeli media discourse examined political talk shows and political interviews (Blum-Kulka et al. 2002; Weizman 2008), it may be argued that the preference for agreement found in the present corpus is grounded in the specific institutional and generic conditions of news coverage. Accordingly, the present findings call for further research on the context-sensitivity of the reciprocal positioning of journalists and experts and of the patterns of use and functions of meta-discursive follow-ups, by examining them across cultural contexts and media genres.

Regardless of its origins and explanations, the preference for supportive co-authorship found in the present study may have detrimental implications for the social and democratic functions of news discourse. It demonstrates that television news often incorporate dialogical formats without realizing their affordances for promoting public discussion and representing divergent voices and perspectives. Rather, these formats may maintain and naturalize the hegemonic status of elite voices and perspectives (Fairclough 1995). This may be exacerbated in the case of expert interviews, which typically draw on a small homogenous elite group of potential interviewees (Steele 1995).

The adherence to a single hegemonic voice is especially troublesome in the particular format analyzed here, as items combining affiliated and expert interviews into a single co-authored analysis exhibit high degrees of coordination and complicity between several powerful social institutions. Thus, rather than complement, criticize and balance each other, the news media, various governmental branches, academia and socio-cultural elite are presented as sharing the same perspective and stance. In the present analysis, this complicity and its problematic ramifications are especially evident in the case of politicians performing as expert interviewees while deflecting accountability – a pattern which may extend beyond politics, for example to the frequent performance of investment bankers and analysts as seemingly neutral, authoritative and unchallengeable experts in the coverage of the economy (see Schejter and Davidson 2008 for a discussion of related tensions in financial news). Coupled with the typical discursive realization of expertise, in both affiliated and expert interviews, as highly self-confident, authoritative and seemingly unchallengeable (see Hamo 2012 for further discussion), the preference documented in the present study for symmetry, alignment and support may significantly restrict the potential of affiliated and expert interviews to promote audience involvement in the news, critical thinking and public discussion.

References

Albæk, Eric. 2011. "The Interaction between Experts and Journalists in News Journalism." *Journalism* 12(3): 335–348. DOI: 10.1177/1464884910392851

Blum-Kulka, Shoshana, Menahem Blondheim and Gonen Hacohen. 2002. "Traditions of Dispute: From Negotiations of Talmudic Texts to the Arena of Political Discourse in the Media." *Journal of Pragmatics* 34: 1569–1594. DOI: 10.1016/S0378-2166(02)00076-0

Coupland, Nikolas. 2001. "Stylization, Authenticity and TV News Review." *Discourse Studies* 3: 413–442. DOI: 10.1177/1461445601003004006

Ekström, Mats and Åsa Kroon-Lundell. 2011a. "Beyond the Broadcast Interview: Specialized Forms of Interviewing in the Making of Television News." *Journalism Studies* 12: 172–187. DOI: 10.1080/1461670X.2010.493328
Ekström, Mats and Åsa Kroon-Lundell. 2011b. "The Joint Construction of Journalistic Expert Identity in Studio Interactions between Journalists on TV News." *Text & Talk* 31: 661–681. DOI: 10.1515/text.2011.032
Eriksson, Göran. 2011. "Adversarial Moments: A study of Short-Form Interviews in the News." *Journalism* 12: 51–69. DOI: 10.1177/1464884910367588
Fairclough, Norman. 1995. *Media Discourse*. London: Edward Arnold.
Fetzer, Anita and Elda Weizman. "Following Up across Contexts and Discourse Domains: Introduction." This volume.
Hamo, Michal. 2010a. "'I haven't Dreamed that the Day will Come that we Talk about The Simpsons on Air': Self-Reflection in Broadcast Television News Discourse." Paper presented at the *annual Broadcast Talk Seminar*, University of Bologna, Italy, July 2010.
Hamo, Michal. 2010b. "'The Nation's Living Room': Negotiating Solidarity on an Israeli Talk Show in the 1990s." *Journal of Israeli History* 29(2): 175–190. DOI: 10.1080/13531042.2010.508945
Hamo, Michal. 2012. "The Reciprocal Positioning of Journalists and Experts in Broadcast Television News Discourse." Paper presented at the *annual Broadcast Talk Seminar*, Ross Priory, UK, July 2012.
Higgins, Michael. 2010. "The 'Public Inquisitor' as Media Celebrity." *Cultural Politics* 6(1): 93–110. DOI: 10.2752/175174310X12549254318863
Hjarvard, Stig. 1994. "TV News: From Discrete Items to Continuous Narrative? The Social Meaning of Changing Temporal Structures." *Cultural Studies* 8: 306–320. DOI: 10.1080/09502389400490471
Hopmann, David N. and Jesper Strömbäck. 2010. "The Rise of the Media Punditocracy?: Journalists and Media Pundits in Danish Election News 1994–2007." *Media, Culture & Society* 32: 943–960. DOI: 10.1177/0163443710379666
Horsbøl, Andres. 2010. "Experts in Political Communication: The Construal of Communication Expertise in Prime Time Television News." *Journal of Language and Politics* 9: 29–49. DOI: 10.1075/jlp.9.1.02hor
Hutchby, Ian. 2011. "Doing Non-Neutral: Belligerent Interaction in the Hybrid Political Interviews." In *Talking Politics in Broadcast Media: Cross-Cultural Perspectives on Political Interviewing, Journalism and Accountability*, ed. by Mats Ekström and Marianna Patrona, 115–134. Amsterdam: John Benjamins. DOI: 10.1075/dapsac.42.11hut
Johansson, Marjut. "'*Bravo for this Editorial!' Users' Comments in Discussion Forums*." This volume.
Katriel, Tamar. 1991. *Communal Webs: Communication and Culture in Contemporary Israel*. Albany, NY: SUNY Press.
Katriel, Tamar. 2004. *Dialogic Moments: From Soul Talks to Talk Radio in Israeli Culture*. Detroit, MI: Wayne State University Press.
Kroon-Lundell, Åsa. 2010. "Dialogues between Journalists on the News: The Intraprofessional 'Interview' as a Communicative Genre." *Media, Culture & Society* 32: 429–450. DOI: 10.1177/0163443709361171
Kroon-Lundell, Åsa and Göran Eriksson. 2010. "Interviews as Communicative Resources in News and Current Affairs Broadcasts." *Journalism Studies* 11: 20–35. DOI: 10.1080/14616700903119826
Lefstein, Adam. 2008. "Literacy Makeover: Educational Research and the Public Interest on Prime Time." *Teachers College Record* 110: 1115–1146.

Liebes, Tamar. 2003. "'Disaster Marathons': The Danger of Action News." In *American Dreams, Hebrew Subtitles: Globalization from the Receiving End*, 63–83. Cresskill, NJ: Hampton.
Liebes, Tamar and Zohar Kampf. 2009. "Performance Journalism: The Case of Media's Coverage on War and Terror." *The Communication Review* 12: 239–249. DOI: 10.1080/10714420903124135
Limor, Yehiel and Hillel Nossek. 2006. "The Military and the Media in the Twenty-First Century: Towards a New Model of Relations." *Israel affairs* 12: 484–510. DOI: 10.1080/13537120600745054
Marshall, P. David. 2005. "Intimately Intertwined in the most Public Way: Celebrity and Journalism." In *Journalism: Critical Issues*, ed. by Stuart Allan, 19–29. Berkshire, England: The Open University Press.
Montgomery, Martin. 2007. *The Discourse of Broadcast News: A Linguistic Approach*. London: Routledge.
Montgomery, Martin. 2008. "The Discourse of the Broadcast News Interview." *Journalism Studies* 9: 260–277. DOI: 10.1080/14616700701848303
Patrona, Marianna. 2006. "Constructing the Expert as a Public Speaker: Face Considerations on Floor-Claiming in Greek Television Discussion Programs." *Journal of Pragmatics* 38: 2124–2143. DOI: 10.1016/j.pragma.2006.04.006
Patrona, Marianna. 2012. "Journalists on the News: The Structured Panel Discussion as a Form of Broadcast Talk." *Discourse & Society* 23: 145–162. DOI: 10.1177/0957926511431505
Peri, Yoram. 2006. *Generals in the Cabinet Room: How the Military Shapes Israeli Policy*. Washington, DC: The United States Institute for Peace.
Reich, Zvi. 2012. "Journalism as Bipolar Interactional Expertise." *Communication Theory* 22: 339–358. DOI: 10.1111/j.1468-2885.2012.01411.x
Roth, Andrew L. 2002. "Social Epistemology in Broadcast News Interviews." *Language in Society* 31: 355–381.
Schejter, Amit M. and Roei Davidson. 2008. "'...And Money is Answer for all Things': The News Corp-Dow Jones Merger and the Separation of Editorial and Business Practices." *International Journal of Communication* 2: 515–542.
Sivenkova, Maria. *"Metacommunicative follow-ups in British, German and Russian Political Webchats."* This volume.
Steele, Janet E. 1995. "Experts and the Operational Bias of Television News: The Case of the Persian Gulf War." *Journalism & Mass Communication Quarterly* 72: 799–812. DOI: 10.1177/107769909507200404
Thornborrow, Joanna and Martin Montgomery (eds). 2010. "Special Issue on Personalization in the Broadcast News Interview." *Discourse & Communication* 4(2).
Tolson, Andrew. 2011. "Political Discourse in TV News: Politics and Change in UK Public Service Broadcasting." In *Talking Politics in Broadcast Media: Cross-Cultural Perspectives on Political Interviewing, Journalism and Accountability*, ed. by Mats Ekström and Marianna Patrona, 57–74. Amsterdam: John Benjamins. DOI: 10.1075/dapsac.42
Weizman, Elda. 2008. *Positioning in Media Dialogue: Negotiating Roles in the News Interview*. Amsterdam: John Benjamins. DOI: 10.1075/ds.3

PART II

Follow-ups in the new media

Bravo for this editorial!

Users' comments in discussion forums

Marjut Johansson
University of Turku, Finland

In this paper, I study how comments function as follow-ups in the discussion forums of online newspapers. Follow-ups recontextualize an object of discourse from its prior context to an ongoing context. A follow-up involves stance-taking, positioning, and negotiation of meaning. The data were obtained from one major French online newspaper called *lemonde.fr*. They consist of ten editorials with political and social topics, along with their subsequent comments. The first objective was to find out how, and by which linguistic means, writers express their stance and evaluate the editorials. It was found that they do it through axiological adjectives, explicit positioning, and various communicative acts, as well as by affective, epistemic, and ironic expressions. The second aim was to examine how the discussion forum posts target the prior discourse, and open up a negotiation, i.e., what types of responsive and initiative properties are used to negotiate the meaning. Findings indicate that the comments target either the content or the stance expressed in the editorial. By using them, users imply that they know more about the issue or they share the same view.

1. Introduction

Media convergence between "old media" and digital media has changed news-making practices and the reception of news on the Internet in many ways (Jenkins 2006, 3; Deuze 2008). Broadcast and print media are constantly being updated on the webpages of online newspapers and news sites. These types of news sites are digital communicative settings that combine different news genres. The contemporary news discourse is multisemiotic: traditional journalistic genres, such as news articles and editorials, and broadcast genres, such as news interviews, now in video format, are presented side by side, or in their own sections on news sites (Bednarek and Caple 2012, 2; Johansson 2014). They represent the institutional media in the sense that they are usually produced by media professionals. However, the more

DOI 10.1075/dapsac.60.04joh

significant change is that they are published along with user-generated genres that have become popular through social media, such as blogs and discussion forums.

In this paper, I focus on the discussion forum – or comment section – that follows editorials in online newspapers. The genre of discussion forum originates from social media, but in an online newspaper it forms a genre pair with traditional news genres, such as articles and editorials. In printed newspapers, letters to the editor are the traditional interaction between the institutional media's view of events and that of the readers. In online newspapers, comments can be considered as instantaneous user reactions to views about news items. Although these two media formats share this common feature, there are differences that separate them. First, online comment sections are far more numerous, but as they are usually placed at the end of news articles to allow rapid reactions, they are scattered throughout every section of the webpage of an online newspaper. Second, a reader might be required to log in before commenting on online newspapers. The messages can be moderated before publication, but they are not edited like traditional letters to the editor. The comment sections studied here are those of *lemonde.fr*, a major French newspaper that also has a print edition. It requires a login for its writers, but not for its readers. The comments to be studied are written in response to editorials, whose topics are socio-political, i.e., they discuss political or societal issues.

My main objective is to consider comments as follow-ups to the editorials. Follow-ups are communicative acts in which social actors express their opinions toward what has been said or written before, resulting in the negotiation of a meaning in the ongoing context. Follow-ups involve stancetaking and positioning. This shows an agreement or a disagreement by the users. I will specifically study those comments with a referential target of the editorial or the journal itself. In their posts, the users mention words such as *l'editorial* (the editorial) or *le journal* (the newspaper) that constitute an object of stance for them (cf. Section 4). My research questions are the following: (1) How do the writers express their stance, and position themselves in regard to the editorials? I will pay particular attention to how they evaluate a topic when agreeing or disagreeing. (2) How do follow-ups open up a negotiation of a meaning expressed in the editorials? How do they target the editorials? This will be done within the framework of a dialogic and socio-pragmatic approach on the one hand, and digital discourse analysis on the other.

In Section 2, I discuss the communicative genres involved – editorials and discussion forums which in this specific setting can be called comment sections. In Section 3, I specifically address follow-ups. I present my data and methods in Section 4. The analysis is divided into two sections: first, in Section 5, I analyze the stance, positioning, and the linguistic marking of agreement and disagreement, while in Section 6, I examine the posts as follow-ups, that is how the meaning of the editorials is negotiated.

2. Opinion genres: Editorial and comment section

Editorials and comment sections are both opinion genres that are organized in different manners. According to Charaudeau (1997, 138–143), news genres are determined by their relationship to the news event with which they are dealing. The news events differ, as do the ways of writing or speaking about them. *Reporting* and *commenting* are the two basic, monologic discourse activities, in which journalists express their positions in varying degrees of objectivity or subjectivity (Charaudeau 1997, 138–143). For example, generally, hard news is a reporting genre with objective positioning, while editorials are based on commenting with subjective positioning. Moirand (2007, 12) distinguishes genres based on the type of enunciative positioning containing subjective or objective features ("subjectivisée" or "objectivisée").[1] This distinction is, of course, not always clear-cut. The editorials and comment sections are both responsive to prior events and discourses. Their communicative activities, goals, and participants are different and will be discussed below.

2.1 Editorial

The *editorial* is a traditional journalistic genre written by editors to the readers. It comments on news events, and other issues, allowing editors to express their opinions in a conventional manner. Editorials can be signed or presented anonymously, but, through them, the newspaper can position itself as an institutional actor (Le 2010, 19). An editorial has recognizable characteristics. It is monologic, and its basic communicative activity is argumentative commenting. It is a responsive genre as its writers comment on news events and other issues. These can be any type of event, from accidents to political situations, but they can also be larger noteworthy societal issues from the recent past (Charaudeau 1997, 223; Moirand 2007, 143). In this genre, the writers strive to evaluate a topic and to argue for a particular point of view. According to Moirand (2007, 142), this "subjectivizing" genre is highly standardized, but the editors are not necessarily experts on the matters on which they express their views. Based on an extensive analysis of editorials in *Le Monde* as genre, Le (2010) considers editorials in a discursive communication identity framework. According to her, editorials are argumentative texts containing "constatives, i.e. speech acts stating how something is, most often

1. In the framework of French linguistics, enunciation is considered as the expression of utterances and how speaking subjects leave traces in their speech while expressing (cf. Benveniste 1966, 1974).

containing a negative evaluation in reference to socio-cultural code of values, and are followed by a directive" (Le 2010, 166). The negativity tends to become more pronounced in cases where the issue is extensively covered by the newspaper (Le 2010, 166). If the topic is further away from France, it is not as directive but still negative (Le 2010, 166). Despite the evaluation and argumentation, the subjectivity of the writer remains implicit, i.e., the genre does not (usually) contain personal pronouns or other linguistic markings that index the writer. Because the editorial is also a rather short text, its references to events have to be concise, based on event words or even stereotypes recognizable by the larger public (Moirand 2007, 9).

2.2 Comment sections as participatory journalism

A *comment section* – or discussion forum – in an online newspaper is a sub-genre as its sequential placement follows a news article or an editorial. Even though newspapers consider comment sections to be a form of participatory journalism, journalists themselves rarely take part in the online discussion with the users (Reich 2011).[2] The comment sections can be considered a communicative genre whose participants are mainly users (cf. Ensink 2012). They are generally the most widespread form of user-generated content in online newspapers compared to blogs, polls, citizen reporting, and crowdsourcing (Ruiz et al. 2011, 464). According to Reich (2011), newspapers can have either an interventionist moderation policy or a looser one in which comments are moderated either before or after publication. However, they are not free from irony, insults, and derogatory language, which make them controversial in newsrooms (cf. Weizman 2012; Ruiz et al. 2011, 465).

In studies on comment sections, media researchers have concentrated on finding out persons behind the comments, ethical issues, evolution of comments, how journalists evaluate them, or their rhetorical aspects (Reich 2011). In a study on German newspapers, Weber (2013, 9) found out that on average, approximately 20 users commented on a news item, while 10 percent of news articles received no comments. In addition, interaction between users remained rather low in most articles' comment sections (Weber 2013, 9). What is more interesting is that his study suggests that certain factors affect commenting. When the news topic can be considered proximal, i.e., it affects a social group of readers, such as the nation, it receives more comments and readers become more involved with each other (Weber 2013, 10). Ruiz et al. (2011, 476) found out that politics was the most commented topic in a study that considered several European online newspapers, but that most users (82.5 percent) do not comment more than once.

2. I thank Elda Weizman for bringing this information and publication to my attention.

One of the main questions in the research about online discussions is its nature as a democratic debate and its importance to the community, or rather the lack of it (Singer 2009; Weber 2013; Ruiz et al. 2011). However, the question about the nature of the discussion is rarely tackled. Ruiz et al. (2011, 476–480) make some interesting observations, i.e., some comments contain sources to back-up opinions, users mostly stay on topic, users quote other users if they have a counter-argument, and users acknowledge a good point made by an opponent. They found that there are cultural differences between the comment sections. In *NYTimes.com* and *Guardian.co.uk*, the diversity of points of view, argumentation, and the dialogue between users are more common than in *lemonde.fr*, *ElPaís.com*, and *Repubblica.it* (Ruiz et al. 2011, 483). The reason for this is that these latter newspapers have more homogenous readership communities than the previous ones, because their readers adhere to the ideological orientation of the newspaper (Ruiz et al. 2011, 483). The same kind of result was found by Richardson and Stanyer (2011, 1001). According to them, in British broadsheets, readers comment and interact, often attacking each other (Richardson and Stanyer 2011, 1001). However, on issues related to multiculturalism, arguments contained little evidence and had unexpressed premises, and symptomatic arguments were used fallaciously (Richardson and Stanyer 2011, 1001).

2.3 Discussion forums as written interaction

As Atifi and Marcoccia (2012) show, online discussions vary according to the situation and its participants: they distinguish between different types of discussions, such as comment sections in an online newspaper and discussions following a tweet of a politician. In general, online discussions are everyday discussions on a variety of topics in the social media. Their distinctive characteristic is the rather individual expression of opinions and experiences of private-sphere individuals whose real-life identities are not necessarily revealed. This anonymity also extends to their backgrounds and reasons for participation in the discussion.

The research on written asynchronous interaction on various online platforms has focused on several interrelated questions. Within the framework of computer-mediated communication, some basic questions about the interactional characteristics of online discussions have been studied. Such notions as the participation framework (Marcoccia 2004) and the coherence of discussion threads (Lambiase 2010) have been analyzed. Another perspective has been adopted by a group of studies that consider expressions of disagreement and emotions, as well as management of interpersonal relationships (Kleinke 2010; Langlotz and Locher 2012; Johansson 2012).

A general feature of online discussions is that users react at different times and do not necessarily read other posts in the discussion in which they are engaged. Posts may display connectedness with each other, or they may not. In the particular communicative genre of comment sections, organization of the posts is random and based on technological affordances, e.g., in the reverse order displaying the most recent post first. In this study, I propose that the online discussion to be studied is a written interaction that includes mostly monological posts that comment on a topic from various sources, and some dialogical posts in which participants engage in commenting to each other. Those comments that target the editorial, that is the text of the preceding genre, will be studied.

3. Follow-ups

3.1 Definition of follow-ups

The notion of follow-ups has been conceptualized in various ways from early studies of discourse structure (cf. Fetzer and Weizman; Gruber; Sivenkova, this volume; Sinclair and Coulthard 1975). In conversation analysis, preference organization or repair are examples of coming to terms with sequentiality (Schegloff, Jefferson and Sacks 1977). In media studies, there are several notions, such as remediation and intertextuality, that try to map the links of various media products and texts (Bolter and Grusin 1999; Fairclough 1992). All these approaches attest an investigation of interconnectedness of communication at various contextual levels. Here this is studied as follow-ups that are produced in context by social actors in a communicative activity (cf. Fetzer 2004).

Fetzer and Weizman (Introduction, this volume; Fetzer et al. 2012) define follow-ups as communicative acts (or dialogue acts) "in and through which a prior communicative act is accepted, challenged, or otherwise negotiated by ratified participants in the exchange or by third parties." Follow-ups are non-initiative components in dialogues (Fetzer and Weizman, Introduction, this volume). This view is a broad one: follow-up is a sequential phenomenon, but also a "carrier of pragmatic force" (Fetzer and Weizman, Introduction). This is a starting point for the definition presented below.

In this paper, a follow-up is understood as a communicative act of recontextualization, in which a social actor embeds something in the ongoing context (Linell 1998, 154; Johansson 2006, 2012). It involves an object of discourse or parts of it from a prior context (Johansson 2006). It also contains stancetaking, positioning, and a negotiation of new meaning (Linell 1998, 154; Johansson 2006, 2012).

The responsive features of follow-ups anchor them in the ongoing context (cf. Johansson 2012). They can be explicit or implicit. Explicit linguistic anchoring can be various types of meta-discursive devices, e.g. quotations are a typical example. The responsiveness can be based on a sequential position within a dialogue, for example, two adjacent turns in a discussion, textual devices that establish coherence. Or it can be within a genre system (cf. Gruber, this volume). I focus on this latter case, that is, comments that take the text of a preceding genre as their object of stance.

Follow-ups involve a negotiation of new meaning (cf. Linell 1998, 154; Johansson 2006). They do not contain only responsive properties, but they have a double function, as they also serve as initiative properties (cf. Johansson 2012). According to Linell (2009, 179–180), responses display understanding of prior discourses, while "initiatives introduce new material into the discourse" anticipating and projecting next contributions. They are not separate from each other but are *aspects* of every communicative act: "they are simultaneously present in any contribution or utterance" (Linell 2009, 179–180). This attests to the reflexivity of language use (Lucy 1993; cf. DuBois 2007).

3.2 Commenting, stancetaking and positioning in follow-ups

When commenting, social actors engage in a responsive communicative activity that considers events and issues that have taken place or have been told before. Commenting can target any part of an activity, its participation roles, content, manner, or the style in which this activity is constructed. When commenting, social actors express a stance, while the target of evaluation is an object of stance (DuBois 2007, 143). In stancetaking, social actors *evaluate* something, *position* themselves, and *align* or *disalign* – agree or disagree – with others (DuBois 2007, 163).

In this analysis, I will use *evaluation* to refer to linguistic activity with regard to a topic, while *positioning* will refer to how the social actors express their subjectivity in the production of utterances that allow others to determine their position (cf. DuBois 2007, 163; Moirand 2007). These are very closely related concepts. In regard to positioning, this view is similar to Weizman's (2008, 14) who considers positioning to be a way in which participants discursively inscribe themselves in situations. The positioning is simultaneously relational, determining how the participants establish relationships with each other (Weizman 2008, 14). These activities are constrained by the type of generic activity in which they take place. In the act of producing utterances, speakers leave traces of their subjectivity in their speech in a speaking situation (Benveniste 1966, 259, 1974, 80). However, there is no such thing as either an absolutely objective or subjective stance, but rather a gradual continuum between them (Kerbrat-Orecchioni 2006, 81).

Thompson and Hunston (2000, 5–6) define evaluation as the expression of stance or attitude consisting of opinion and reflecting values of the society in which a text has been produced as well as organizing the discourse and constructing relations between speaker and hearer. In a linguistic context, an evaluation can be positive or negative. Through evaluation, actors can express agreement or disagreement with previous actors depending on the genre, thus aligning or disaligning with them.

In ordinary conversation, one of the basic premises is the preference organization for the next activity (Schegloff et al., 1977). When a speaker claims knowledge about something and invites a co-speaker to share this, agreement is the preferred act, while disagreement is the marked one (Pomerantz 1984). However, this does not hold for conflict talk, or for other genres and contexts. In phases of disagreement, preference organization seems to change (Gruber 2001, 1823). Angouri and Locher (2012, 1551) propose that "disagreement is not an *a priori* negatively marked act," as the context determines what is acceptable in a given interaction. Several studies of spoken interaction show that disagreement is an ordinary phenomenon in professional contexts, decision making, problem solving, and political interviews and debates (Gruber 2001; Weizman 2008; Keisanen 2008; Angouri and Locher 2012). Similarly, in online forum discussions, as well as some other types of digital discussions, disagreement also seems to be an ordinary phenomenon (Kleinke 2010; Johansson 2012). Disagreement often involves the use of metadiscursive devices, such as quotations (Baym 1998).

In the research literature, a disagreement is a linguistic activity that can be referred to as a dispute, debate, quarrel, or conflict, among others (Grimshaw 1990, 11). The communicative acts of apology, gossip, insult, and so on could be part of a disagreement (Grimshaw 1990, 11). In an analysis of disagreement in a discussion forum, Kleinke (2010, 206) proposes that disagreement denotes "any non-supportive turn in which speakers express dissent with what has been said in a previous turn within the immediate talk exchange." In this type of online discussion, I will interpret disagreement as denoting a negative evaluation of some type which is accompanied by a negative positioning towards an object of stance. In sum, it shows a disalignment of a social actor to previous communicative action and/or discourse in the immediate or distant context. In spoken interactions, conflict is a way to manage a situation in which consensus has broken down (Vuchinich 1990, 119). In an online discussion, a consensus is not necessarily the goal of the participants in the first place, as will be demonstrated in the analysis.

Gruber (2001, 1823) distinguishes different types of disagreement in spoken interaction: overt disagreement with unmitigated expressions and a pragmatic one with a loose thematic link with a previous speaker. They are both directed backwards, and their projective features are weak (Gruber 2001, 1823). Unlike these, opposing questions also have projective properties, but they take up only one aspect of the previous speakers' turn (Gruber 2001, 1823–1824). Gruber (2001, 1826) distinguishes several types of questions that occur during conflict sequences. Explicit questions are marked with a meta-pragmatic utterance announcing a question that expresses disagreement (id., 1830–831). Rhetorical questions are very often the kind that speakers answer or at least imply the answer themselves (id., 1834–1835).

When disagreeing, the speakers or the writers can challenge something from a previous context. Challenging is a communicative activity that can be part of a disagreement. In spoken interaction, Keisanen (2008, 253) posits that:

> [...] challenges are constructed by displaying doubt toward a claim or a stance embedded in the prior turn, thereby suggesting that this stance or claim is problematic, and holding the recipient accountable for it. (Keisanen 2008, 253)

In challenging, social actors note that something is problematic while undermining the authority of those who have made the claim. In a broad manner, Fetzer (2007, 169) considers challenges to deny a communicative contribution's "truth and/or rejecting its appropriateness and its sincerity." According to Weizman (2008, 36), challenging includes pointing out one's own authority. In her view, challenge "embeds a conflict varying in degree of aggravation and explicitness" that targets the interactional or social roles of the participants (id., 36–37).

4. Data and method

The data came from a multilingual corpora of online discussions collected in 2008. In this paper, I use ten editorials and their comment sections from the online edition of the major French news site *lemonde.fr*. The topics of these editorials include global issues, such as the financial crisis of 2008 and the presidential election in the U.S., as well as French politics. In sum, the editorials are part of the public discourse about political and social issues. The editorials are listed in Appendix 1.

The editorials are nearly uniform in length, with each containing approximately 360 words. The comments are posted on the site in reverse order, the most recent being the first one users see. The number of comments per editorial varies from 19 up to 47 comments, with 339 posts in total. The total number of words is 22,344, while the average length of a comment is approximately 66 words. The online discussions are used without any modifications, except for the technical indications of the comment section.

The methodological approach consists of analyzing the posts as discourses in their context. The comments examined are those that comment explicitly on the editorials or the journal, i.e., they contain a direct reference to them. This constitutes their object of stance (cf. Dubois 2007, 163). First, these comments are retrieved by searching for the words *editorial, édito* or words that refer to the *journal* or *Le Monde*. They are indexical as they indicate a direct reference to the preceding communicative situation. In the data, there are 67 such posts, which is approximately 20 percent of all comments. These comments were written by 64 different writers, three of which posted twice (marked in bold in Table 1). Each editorial is numbered (E1–E10), and each writer is numbered (W1–W64) to protect their anonymity in order of the appearance of their posts (see Table 1).

Table 1. Posts and their writers from different discussions selected for analysis

	Number of posts	Writers
E1	8	W1–W6, **W5 + W6** twice
E2	1	W7
E3	12	W8–W19
E4	14	W20–W33
E5	5	W34–W38
E6	4	W39–W42
E7	6	W43–W48
E8	8	W49–W56
E9	8	W57–W63, **W18**
E10	1	W64
	67	

Second, the utterances are examined for the stancetaking and positioning in the linguistic context of utterances, and for how they construct agreement with or disagreement to the editorials (Section 5). In this part of the analysis, the stances are examined in terms of the lexico-grammatical elements that the writers use to evaluate, the types of communicative acts they express, and how they index their subjectivity. In addition, I pay attention how they use affective, epistemic, or ironic expressions (For the French, I use Kerbrat-Orecchioni 2006; DuBois 2007). Third, the posts are studied from the perspective of how they negotiate meaning and how the object of stance is evaluated (Section 6).

5. Taking a stance and positioning

5.1 Evaluations and positioning in agreeing and disagreeing

Most of the utterances containing a direct reference to the editorial are metapragmatic ones that comment on it. Most of the posts are negative; only seven posts contain positive evaluation. In this section, I distinguish between occurrences where the evaluations are similar, but are used either to agree or disagree.

The first two evaluations are explicit:

(1) Très, très *bon* éditorial [...] (E5, 7)
A very, very *good* editorial [...]

(2) Il est *tordant* cet édito! [...] (E1, 10)
This editorial is *extremely funny*! [...]

Both of these evaluations contain axiological adjectives, i.e., expressing value judgments (Kerbrat-Orecchioni 2006, 102–106). They both open a post, and Example (2) also opens a discussion thread. According to Gruber (1993, 476), these types of direct evaluations are found in text-initial positions in newspaper reports where they function as pre-sequences for argumentation in a news story. In Example (1), the adjective *bon/good* qualifies the whole editorial, while in Example (2), the choice of adjective (*tordant/extremely funny*) turns the evaluation into a negative and ironic one. In these utterances, the writers do not index themselves with any personal pronouns.

In the following Example (3), the positive evaluation is implicit, based on a comparison:

(3) *Cet éditorial* renvoie à la tradition anglo-saxonne de soutien affiché à l'un ou l'autre des candidats à la présidence américaine ("endorsment") [...] *Les éditos d'endorsment du NYT ou du Washington Post* montrent que l'on peu concilier *haute tenue* éditorial et engagement. (E3, 8)
This editorial refers to the Anglo-Saxon tradition of explicit support for one candidate or the other in American presidential elections ("endorsement") [...] *The endorsements in the NYT or in the Washington Post* show that it is possible to combine *high-quality* editorial and engagement.

This evaluation is situated at the beginning of a post. It is not the content, but the type of positioning expressed in the editorial, that is the target of the evaluation. This writer agrees with this, as she/he compares it with those in the U.S.

In the following example, the comparison is the same, but the evaluation is negative. In Example (3), the writer does not index her/himself, but in the next Example (4), the evaluation is expressed from an explicitly subjective standpoint:

(4) *J'adore* quand Le Monde veut se la jouer NY Times [...] Vivant aux Etats-Unis, *je rigole* quand *je lis* les editos des journaux francais "pompes" sur les editos anglo-saxons [...] (E3, 17)
I adore it when Le Monde wants to play the NY Times [...] Living in the U.S., *I laugh* when *I read* editorials in the major French newspapers about Anglo-Saxon editorials.

In Example (4), the writer uses first person personal pronoun several times, which foregrounds the writer's subjective stance and positioning (*j'adore, je rigole, je lis / I adore, I laugh, I read*). Here the explicit evaluation emerges from the fact that the two first verbs of adoration and amusement are used to convey a negative and ironic stance, as this writer considers that the French editorial does not match those in the Anglo-American newspapers that she/he claims to know due to her/his place of living (*Vivant aux Etats-Unis / Living in the U.S.*).

The writers can explicitly express their agreement or disagreement. In Examples (5) and (6), these writers omit the use of personal pronouns while the positioning is explicitly theirs:

(5) Tout à fait *d'accord* avec cet édito! [...] (E1, 8)
[I] *Agree* completely with this editorial!

(6) [...] *Pas d'accord* du tout avec cet édito *révélateur* [...] (E4, 14)
[...] *[I do] not agree* at all with this *revealing* editorial.

In Example (5), the writer uses an exclamation point to boost her/his judgment in an opening of a post, while in Example (6), the writer uses an axiological adjective to characterize the editorial at the end of the post (*révélateur/revealing*). They both boost their standpoints with intensifying adverbs (*tout à fait, pas du tout/ completely, not at all*).

In Examples (7) and (8), the evaluations are similar at the surface level, but convey different meanings. Here the writers position themselves in an intersubjective relationship in regard to the editorial. The positionings are based on a communicative act of congratulation:

(7) *Bravo* pour cet editorial! Pourquoi faudrait-il prendre un recul de principe, les lèvres pincées, devant cet élan d'espoir qui accompagnerait l'élection de B Obama à la présidence des Etats-Unis? [...] (E3, 30)
Bravo for this editorial! Why should [we] pull back in principle when we see this hope that accompanies the election of B.O. to the presidency to the U.S.? [...]

(8) *Bravo* Le Monde, cet édito signe "la vraie nature" du journal de ces dernières années [...] C'est un édito indigne de l'histoire du Monde! (E4, 13)
Bravo Le Monde, this editorial shows the "true nature" of the newspaper of these last years [...] It is an ignoble editorial in regard to the history of Le Monde!

In Example (7), the acclaim opens a post in which the writer agrees completely with the type of argumentation in the editorial. In Example (8), the first part of the acclaim – *bravo* – is ironic, as the evaluation is understood to reveal the nature of the journal as social actor. This writer also uses a negative adjective (*indigne/ignoble*) that qualifies the positioning of the editorial according to this writer.

5.2 Disagreement through affective, ironic, and epistemic stances

The expression of evaluations is also achieved through emotional language, thus disagreement is performed through an affective stance. In Example (9), anger is the emotion the writer says she/he feels when reading the editorial:

(9) *Je bondis d'indignation* en lisant cet editorial! [...] et voila que le journal en rajoute un couche en me sommant de ne pas manifester contre la calotte c'est le comble! [...] (E4, 1)
I get really angry reading this editorial! [...] and here the newspaper adding another layer telling me not to protest against the man of the cloth is the height of impertinence!

This emotional outburst opens a discussion thread after an editorial that discusses the pope's visit to France. In this post, the writer positions her/himself as a reader who has been given advice not to protest against the visit. The writer expresses disagreement through the description of her/his emotional state and affective noun *indignation/anger* (Kerbrat-Orecchioni 2006, 79).

A writer can perform a communicative act of thanking, but do it ironically. In this case, the writer denies the truthfulness of the claims made in the editorial:

(10) [...] *Merci* au journal Le Monde pour ses leçons d'idéologie pro euro mais rien dans cet édito n'est étayé [...] (E1, 43)
[...] *Thanks* to the newspaper Le Monde for its ideological lessons in favor of the euro but nothing in this editorial is guaranteed [...]

In the second part of this utterance, which begins by a connective *mais/but* this writer shows that she/he has more information about the issue. There are, however, other types of disagreement with the editorials. The writers could address the editors to ask for the source of their information:

(11) [...] *Je me demande* parfois qui renseigne "Le Monde"? [...] (E9, 31)
[...] *I sometimes ask* [myself] who informs "Le Monde"? [...]

This writer uses a reflexive, cognitive verb (*se demander / ask oneself*) that denotes asking in a rhetorical question (cf. Gruber 2001, 1834–1835). This writer wants to cast doubt on the information given in the editorial, and thus challenges its authority.

In a couple of utterances, the word *editorial* is used to refer to a quotation from the editorial that serves as a starting point for an argument that takes a negative stance towards the editorial:

(12) *dans l'*éditorial à la question faut-il quitter l'Afghanistan, on donne la réponse suivante: "Certainement pas car un départ marquerait la première défaite militaire de l'OTAN." *Vraiment*? [...] (E6, 2)
in the editorial to the question do the [troops] have to leave Afghanistan, there is the following answer: "Of course not because leaving would mark the first military defeat of NATO." *Really*? [...]

In Example (12), disagreement is expressed by the epistemic adverb (*vraiment/ really*) that follows the quotation. This adverb signals the astonishment of this writer and the fact that the writer knows more. It conveys an epistemic stance. It is a rhetorical question that opposes the preceding quotation challenging it (cf. Gruber 2001, 1834–1835). The same type of reaction can be seen in the use of discourse particles at the beginning of an utterance or in the use of exclamation.

(13) *Tiens*, Le Monde se prononce en faveur de M. Obama [...] (E3, 18)
Well, well, Le Monde pronounces in favor of Mr. Obama [...]

(14) Le Monde *adore faire la morale*! [...] (E5, 21)
Le Monde *adores moralizing*! [...]

Example (13) begins with a discourse particle (*tiens / well, well*) that, in this initial position, signals a reaction (cf. Dostie 2004, 150–151 for an analysis of *tiens*). It marks both the writer's understanding of the editorial and that it does not match his/her expectations. Therefore, it is ironic and comparable with the stance in Example (14). This writer identifies the type of communicative act and the argument that the editorial has put forward. Here the irony targets the moralizing discourse this writer has interpreted in the editorial.

In sum, in most cases, writers primarily express a negative stance for the purpose of disagreeing, but, in some cases, they agree. The stance is constructed in three principal ways. First, the writers evaluate the quality of the editorial by the use of especially axiological adjectives (Examples (1)–(2)) or compare the editorial with those of foreign newspapers (Examples (3)–(4)). Second, they position by expressing their agreement or disagreement directly (Examples (5)–(6)), and by performing communicative acts, such as congratulating or thanking, which can also be ironic or epistemic (Examples (7)–(8), (10)). Third, evaluations can be described by explicit expressions of negative emotional reactions, such as anger or sadness (Example (9)). They also use implicit means to convey their astonishment or discontent by the use of discourse particles or rhetorical questions at the beginning of their posts (Examples (11)–(13)). Finally, stance can be an ironic one revealing the opinion put forward in the editorial (Example (14)).

6. Posts as follow-ups

6.1 Disagreeing with the content of the editorial

In this section, I will study the posts as follow-ups, i.e., what type of negotiation of meaning is constructed. Their targets are the content and the positioning the newspaper takes in the editorial. Some of the comment sections begin with a post that contains total disagreement that targets the content of the editorial as empty:

(15) Un peu *creux* comme editorial, *non*? (E9, 1)
'A little *empty* [of content] as an editorial, *don't you think*?'

(16) Les éditos du Monde, depuis quelques temps, manquent singulièrement d'inspiration. Ou alors c'est le style de rédaction qui a changer. Toujours est-il qu'ils sonnent *creux. Et que c'est bien dommage.* (E3, 1)
For some time, the editorials in Le Monde have lacked inspiration. Or else it is the style that has changed. They always seem to be *empty. And that is a pity.*

These two opening posts come from different discussions, but they are strikingly similar (See Johansson 2012 for an analysis of Example (15)). They both give a negative evaluation of the content of the editorial using an axiological adjective (*creux/empty*) (Kerbrat-Orecchioni 2006, 102–106). They both contain elements that offer readers a possible point of negotiation: in Example (15), it is the evaluation of the content by modal elements (*un peu / a little*); in Example (16), it is the alternative that is offered as an explanation by connectives (*ou alors / or else)*. This negative stance serves as an invitation. Example (15) calls for other readers of the editorial to express similar views on the matter using the tag question (*non / don't you think*), while Example (16) expresses an emotional stance toward this type of editorial (*c'est bien dommage / what a pity*). It is also an implicit invitation to share this view.

The same type of positioning can also be found elsewhere in the discussions where the quality of the content is evaluated by comparison and disagreement is total:

(17) On attendait (*autrefois*) du Monde autre chose que ces *platitudes.* (E3, 10)
In the past, (one) could expect other things from Le Monde other than these *banalities.*

(18) Analyse *du cafe du coin* pour un edito!!! *Dommage.* (E9, 32)
This analysis is like that of *a local coffee shop*!!! *What a pity.*

In Example (17), the evaluation is based on a comparison with the content of past (*autrefois / in the past*) editorials. These posts invite other comment section participants to share this view of how the quality of the editorial and newspaper has changed. In Example (18), the editorial is compared to banal, everyday analysis (compared to that established in a *café du coin / local coffee shop*), and therefore unacceptable. This is regrettable according to this writer as the post ends with a concluding formula that expresses emotion about the situation (*Dommage / what a pity*).

There are also cases where total disagreement is based on the editorial being evaluated as wrong or lacking in facts. In these cases, the emotional component is present either as irony or an expression of sadness:

(19) *Tiens*, Le Monde se prononce en faveur de M. Obama. C'est donc nouveau, on peut voter pour le Président US! *Quelle démocratie*! (E3, 18)
Well, well, Le Monde pronounces in favor of Mr. Obama. This is new, we can vote for the President of the U.S.! *What a democracy*!

(20) *C'est tout? c'est tout* ce que le Monde a à dire sur la situation en Amerique dans son Editorial, *son papier-phare*?? *Quelle tristesse.* (E9, 19)
Is this all? Is this all that Le Monde has to say about the situation in America in its editorial, *its main text*?? *How sad.*

In Example (19), the post opens with a discourse particle (*tiens/well*) signaling the astonishment of this writer when her/his expectations are not met (see Example (13); Dostie 2004, 150–151). It recognizes the editorial as subjective by supporting Obama. This triggers an ironic exclamation about voting and a concluding formula that is also an exclamation about democracy. In Example (20), the post opens with a rhetorical question (*C'est tout / Is this all?*), which signals the same kind of reaction as the discourse particle in Example (19). This writer repeats this in the next utterance and evaluates the content as empty (as in Examples (17)–(18)) because there is a lack of agreement. According to her/him, the text does not measure up to the quality of an editorial (*son papier-phare / its main text*). Here the emotion is expressed in the concluding formula by an exclamation of sadness (*tristesse / sad*).

In some cases, the rejection is in the form of advice or a request for meaning that is not there:

(21) Il est utile de *rappeler* aux éditorialistes de LM que l'utilisation des signes de ponctuation dans les titres n'est pas interdite. *Un point d'interrogation après aurait fait une sacrée différence.* (E9, 30)
It is useful to *remind* the editors of LM that the use of punctuation marks is not forbidden in headlines. *A question mark after would have made a hell of a difference.*

(22) *Quel est l'intérêt* de cet éditorial? (E4, 43)
What is the point of this editorial?

In both of these examples, the meaning that the editorial conveys is being criticized. The editorial is about Barack Obama's possible election as the president of the U.S. in 2008. In Example (21), the stance expressed by the editorial is evaluated as too strong, as the writer suggests that the future is uncertain. The writer gives a piece of advice as she/he reminds (*rappeler*). The editors should have predicted the outcome of the election as the editorial is published before the election rather than presenting its outcome as certain. In Example (22), the writer poses a rhetorical question, challenging the whole meaning of the editorial (*Quel est l'intérêt / What is the meaning*).

6.2 Against the positioning of the editors and the newspaper

There are cases where the writers disagree with or challenge the type of positioning the editors have taken in the editorial. In Example (23), the writer disagrees with the editorial and its claim of supporting the wrong cause:

(23) Le Monde vole au secours de *l'idéologie monétariste* qui *nouc coûte* un point de croissance annuel depuis 25 ans (les chômeurs apprécieront), et qui protège surtout les rentiers [...] (E1, 14)
Le Monde comes to support *the monetary ideology* that *has cost us* one point of yearly growth for 25 years (the unemployed are thankful), and that especially protects renters [...]

In Example (23), this writer does not index her/himself – there are no explicit subjective personal markings in this example. This participant identifies the argument put forward by the newspaper (*l'idéologie monétariste / the monetary ideology*). She/he challenges it by providing additional information (the cost of the ideology, who is it for), thus undermining the editorial's argument.

In the following examples, the challenge put forward is a bit different:

(24) Le Monde *en fait des tonnes* sur la couleur de la peau en ce moment: *ne seriez-vous pas un peu en retard sur les mentalités?* (E3, 33)
Le Monde has *written a lot* about skin color at the moment: *aren't you a little bit behind on attitudes?* [...]

In Example (24), the writer challenges the editorial's positioning as incorrect. In the beginning, this writer refers to the amount of the writing (*a fait des tonnes / written a lot*). The post ends in a rhetorical question (cf. Gruber 2001, 1833). It is addressed to the editors directly by way of the second person plural pronoun (*vous/you*) and a negative interrogative. The writer suggests that she/he has more knowledge about this issue and has a position that is more up-to-date.

In Example (25), the writer considers the positioning expressed in the editorial to be untenable, and she/he takes an opposing position:

(25) L'éditorial évoque "les principes de liberté et de moralité qui fondent la communauté américaine et occidentale"; *cette "communauté occidentale" n'existe pas*, ou en tous cas *je démens en faire partie*: mes valeurs n'ont rien à voir avec celles de l'Américain moyen, *merci de le noter.* (E9, 17)
The editorial evokes "the principles of liberty and morality that are the foundation of the American and occidental community"; *this "occidental community" does not exist*, or at least *I refuse to be part of it*: my values have nothing to do with those of the average American, *please note this.*

In Example (25), the post opens with a quotation of the editorial. This serves as a starting point for an opposing stance expressed in the following utterances. The writer first denies the claim in the editorial (*cette "communauté occidentale" n'existe pas / this "occidental community" does not exist*). Then she/he excludes her/himself from it; here the writer uses a communicative act of refusing (*je démens en faire partie / I refuse to be part of it*). By doing this, the writer challenges the claim made by the editorial and detaches her/himself from this definition that is judged non-existent. The post ends with a concluding formula that includes an act of thanks addressed to the editorial (*merci de le noter / please note this*).

In the next examples, the writers consider the positioning of the editors to be incorrect and therefore attempt to correct it.

(26) *Comme je le précisais, et comme l'*éditorial tonitruant la *"victoire"* de l'€ *se garde bien de le signaler*, l'€ est en effondrement complet depuis septembre face au $, au F.S. et au Yen [...] (E1, 32)
As I stated, and as the editorial preaching about the "victory" of the euro does not mention at all, the euro has sunk completely since September in comparison with the dollar, the Swiss franc, and the yen [...]

(27) *Curieux édito, en forme de prêchi-prêcha*: ce que fait Sarko, c'est pas bien, *mais* les manifs des laïcs sectaires c'est pas bien non plus [...] (E4, 12)
Strange editorial, in the form of moralizing speech: what Sarkozy [the President of France] does is not good, *but* neither are the demonstrations of secular sectarians [...]

In Example (26), the post opens with two meta-pragmatic utterances that both report a quotation. The first reports what the writer has said, and the second signals that the editorial leaves something out in talking about the victory of the euro. This follow-up refers to a previous context, but the writer adds a fact that she/he considers accurate, thereby showing more authority. In Example (27), the post opens with an evaluation containing an axiological adjective (*curieux / strange*) and an identification of the type of communicative act in the editorial (*prêchi-prêcha / moralizing speech*). These serve the opinion of the writer who does not accept this, but it goes further by correcting a claim made in the editorial (*mais/but*).

In the last two examples, the writers address the editors directly:

(28) [...] Les éditorialistes du Monde voient décidément le monde *par le petit bout de la lorgnette*: on devrait leur conseiller la lecture du Monde Diplomatique! (E9, 18)

[...] The editors of Le Monde absolutely see the world *from a small corner of a monocle*: one should recommend to them that they read Le Monde Diplomatique!

(29) Depuis quand le monde se doit d'*influencer les lecteurs*? [...] (E3, 23)
Since when has Le Monde had to *influence its readers*? [...]

In Example (28), the writer challenges a position that she/he considers too narrow (reference to a monocle). It is yet another example of a writer who claims to have more knowledge than the editors. In Example (29), the evaluation indicates that the persuasion has gone too far. In other words, according to this writer, certain norms of editorial writing have broken down.

When disagreeing either with the content or the positioning of the editorial, the writers display their own interests in everyday political discourse, and how they do not share common ground with the editorial. On the contrary, these disagreements have several different goals that seem to emerge from different backgrounds.

6.3 Agreeing with the editorial

In some cases, the writers agree with the editorial by indicating where they find common ground with the content expressed in the editorial:

(30) *Tout à fait d'accord* avec cet édito! L'Euro a fait la preuve de son utilité [...] (E1, 8)

[I agree] completely with this editorial! The euro has proved useful [...]

In the beginning of the post, there is a meta-pragmatic utterance with a verbal construction denoting agreement (*d'accord/agree*). This serves as a starting point as the writer continues with the topic and underlines the main argument of the editorial.

(31) *Bravo* pour cet éditorial. *Pourquoi faudrait-il prendre un recul de principe, les lèvres pincées,* devant cet élan d'espoir qui accompagnerait l'élection de B Obama à la présidence des Etats-Unis? [...] (E3, 30)
Bravo for this editorial. *Why should one take a step back in principle, with clasped lips* in the face of this impulse of hope that would follow the election of B. Obama to the presidency of the United States? [...]

In Example (31), acceptance is demonstrated by a congratulation of the editor (*bravo*). The writer justifies this acceptance with a rhetorical question that is not a question that lacks information. Instead, the writer shows that the – engaged – positioning expressed in the editorial is correct and that there is no need for a different type of positioning (*Pourquoi faudrait-il prendre un recul / Why should one take a step back)*. This rhetorical question invites the reader to share this view – to reject criticism about the election. In Example (32), a positive evaluation opens the post:

(32) *Très, très bon éditorial*, qui place les banderilles là elles doivent être placées. Il fallait absolument être le premier, ou la première, à dénoncer l'antisémitisme […] (E5, 7)
A very, very good editorial that "places spears where they should be placed" [literal translation]. One absolutely had to *be the first* to denounce anti-Semitism […]

After the initial acknowledgement, this writer evaluates the critique of the editorial. In the second phrase, the writer recognizes that the newspaper has been the first one to take this position (*être le premier, ou la première / be the first*).

As result, it is possible to summarize the characteristics of the posts as follow-ups, i.e., how they respond to the editorial, and how they initiate a new negotiation of meaning. The writers mostly disagree with the content in the editorials (Examples (15) and (16)). They make negative remarks, give advice, and invite others to participate with them in the disagreement. In several cases, disagreement is accompanied by challenges, and by an affective stance of anger or sadness. The writers want to question the content of the editorials because they consider them empty, containing incorrect information, and lacking facts or analysis (Examples (18) and (20)). The editorials were also noted to be better in the past (Example (17)). The comments also target the positioning taken by the editors of the newspaper (Examples (23)–(29)). In these cases, the writers believe that the editors make assertions that are out of date, wrong, or too narrow. They do not agree with the way the newspaper, in their judgment, puts forward persuasive arguments to influence readers (Examples (21)–(22)). They use communicative acts of denial or refusal. The writers may signal their own positioning, and invite others to share the view with the use of rhetorical questions. When the writers express agreement, they demonstrate that they share common ground with the editorial (Examples (30)–(32)).

7. Conclusion

Contemporary online newspapers and news sites offer their readers the possibility of instantaneously commenting on news articles and editorials. When readers comment on editorials, they are responding to the opinion of the editorial about an event or a state of the world. The comment sections form an intersection where editorial views based on professional writing meet everyday opinions about the same topic. In this paper, the comment sections analyzed are those published on the major French national news site *lemonde.fr* about socio-political topics, i.e., they discuss political or societal issues. The comments whose object of stance was the editorial or the journal itself where chosen for the analysis.

The first research question was about the type of stance and positioning the users express in these posts, and how they evaluate or position when agreeing or disagreeing. In the analysis, the users mostly disagree with the editorial they are evaluating. They express either an evaluation with axiological adjectives that assign a certain value to the editorial (negative-positive). They position themselves by expressing their dis/alignment directly with the editorial, or perform communicative acts, such as thanking, congratulating, refusing, and denying in order to show their stance. The stance was also expressed with affective, epistemic, or ironic means.

The second question was about how these follow-ups negotiate the meaning and what do they target in the editorials. The target of critique was either the content or the stance and positioning expressed in the editorials. When considering the content, the users challenged the editorial for its lack of or inaccurate information. Thus, the users positioned themselves in the position as an authority on the news matters. In regards to the stance in the editorials, the same prevailed: the users attested to be more appropriate or up-to-date in their own views. In some cases, the users shared the same view as the editorials, accompanied with possible counter-arguments.

According to this analysis, follow-ups in discussion forums whose topics are socio-political are mostly based on disagreement with the editorial. Users also challenge the information put forward in them. The writers deny the validity of information or how it is expressed in the editorial. They strive to note that they have more information than the editorials express. However, justifications for having that knowledge or information can accompany the comments, but proof of their accuracy is rarely presented. Sometimes, the comments completely lack back-up for the claims being made. The affectivity and irony used by writers are those that most strikingly undermine their claims of lack of information.

In conclusion, comment sections are a user-generated sub-genre that forms a genre pair with the institutional news genre of editorials. Its contributions are polarized between agreement and disagreement with the editorial. The main goal of the participants is to question the information presented in the article and disagree with the institutional view expressed by journalists on sociopolitical issues. The contributions are not argumentative in the sense that they provide back-up or evidence to support their side of the argument, but mainly only imply that they have differing knowledge. The comments are affective and ironic. This indicates that the value of professional news writing is – if not undermined – at least questioned through this forum. They are not "participatory" in the sense understood in the ordinary rhetoric about social media – the users joining in the discussion to build knowledge together. Rather most of the writers align with each other in the act of disagreeing, thus participating in the creation of an entertaining moment of shared dissatisfaction.

References

Angouri, Jo and Miriam A. Locher. 2012. "Theorising Disagreement." *Journal of Pragmatics* 44 (12): 1549–53. DOI: 10.1016/j.pragma.2012.06.011

Atifi, Hassan and Michel Marcoccia. 2012. "Follow-ups in Online Political Discussions." In *Proceedings of the ESF Strategic Workshop on Follow-ups Across Discourse Domains: A Cross-Cultural Exploration of Their Forms and Functions, Würzburg (Germany), 31 May – 2 June 2012*, ed. by Anita Fetzer, Elda Weizman and Elisabeth Reber, 22–34. Würzburg: Universität Würzburg. [online]. URL: http://opus.bibliothek.uni-wuerzburg.de/volltexte/2012/7165/; URN: urn:nbn:de:bvb:20-opus-71656.

Baym, Nancy. 1998. "Agreements and Disagreements in a Computer-Mediated Discussion." *Research on Language and Social Interaction* 29 (4): 315–45. DOI: 10.1207/s15327973rlsi2904_2

Bednarek, Monika and Helen Caple. (eds.). 2012. *News Discourse*. London & New York: Continuum.

Bolter, Jay D. and Richard Grusin. 1999. *Remediation. Understanding New Media*. Cambridge, MA: MIT Press.

Benveniste, Emile. 1966, 1974. *Problèmes de linguistique générale*. [Problems in General Linguistics]. Tomes I–II. Paris: Gallimard.

Charaudeau, Patrick. 1997. *Le discours d'information médiatique. La construction du miroir social.* [Media Information Discourse. The Construction of the Social Mirror]. Paris: Nathan.

Deuze, Marc. 2008. "The Changing Context of News Work: Liquid Journalism and Monitorial Citizenship." *International Journal of Communication* 2, 848–65.

Dostie, Gaétane. 2004. *Pragmaticalisation et marquers discursifs. Analyse sémantique et traitement lexicographique*. [Pragmaticalization and Discourse Markers. Semantic and Lexicographic Analyses]. Bruxelles: De Boeck/Duculot. DOI: 10.3917/dbu.dosti.2004.01

DuBois, John. 2007. "The Stance Triangle." In: *Stancetaking in Discourse*, ed. by Robert Englebretson, 139–182. Amsterdam: John Benjamins. DOI: 10.1075/pbns.164.07du

Ensink, Titus. 2012. "Internet Newspaper Discussion Lists. A Virtual Political Arena?" In *Dialogue in Politics*, ed. by Lawrence N. Berlin and Anita Fetzer, 21–65. Amsterdam: John Benjamins. DOI: 10.1075/ds.18.05ens

Fairclough, Norman. 1992. *Discourse and Social Change*. London: Polity Press.

Fetzer, Anita. 2004. *Recontextualizing Context*. Amsterdam: John Benjamins. DOI: 10.1075/pbns.121

Fetzer, Anita. 2007. "Challenges in Political Interviews." In *Political Discourse in the Media. Cross-cultural Perspectives*, ed. by Anita Fetzer and Gerda E. Lauerbach, 161–195. Amsterdam: John Benjamins. DOI: 10.1177/095792650902000010704

Fetzer, Anita, Elda Weizman and Elisabeth Reber. 2012. "Introduction." In *Proceedings of the ESF Strategic Workshop on Follow-ups Across Discourse Domains: A Cross-Cultural Exploration of Their Forms and Functions, Würzburg (Germany), 31 May – 2 June 2012*, ed. by Anita Fetzer, Elda Weizman and Elisabeth Reber, 3–4. Würzburg: Universität Würzburg – [online]. URL: http://opus.bibliothek.uni-wuerzburg.de/volltexte/2012/7165/; URN: urn:nbn:de:bvb:20-opus-71656.

Fetzer, Anita and Elda Weizman. "Following Up Across Contexts and Discourse Domains: Introduction". This volume.

Grimshaw, Allen D. 1990. "Introduction." In *Conflict Talk. Sociolinguistic Investigations of Arguments in Conversations*, ed. by Allen D. Grimshaw, 1–20. Cambridge: Cambridge University Press.

Gruber, Helmut. 1993. "Evaluation Devices in Newspaper Reports." *Journal of Pragmatics* 19: 469–86. DOI: 10.1016/0378-2166(93)90006-B

Gruber, Helmut. 2001. "Questions and Strategic Orientation in Verbal Conflict Sequences." *Journal of Pragmatics* 33: 1815–1857. DOI: 10.1016/S0378-2166(00)00083-7

Gruber, Helmut. "Intertextual References in Austrian Parliamentary Debates: Between Evaluation and Argumentation." This volume.

Jenkins, Henry. 2006. *Convergence Culture: Where New and Old Media Collide*. New York: New York University Press.

Johansson, Marjut. 2006. "Constructing Objects of Discourse in the Broadcast Political Interview." In *Pragmatic Aspects of Political Discourse in the Media*, ed. by Anita Fetzer and Elda Weizman. *Journal of Pragmatics* 38 (2): 216–29.

Johansson, Marjut. 2012. "Editorial and its Comments. Follow-ups in a Discussion Forum." In *Proceedings of the ESF Strategic Workshop on Follow-ups Across Discourse Domains: A Cross-Cultural Exploration of Their Forms and Functions, Würzburg (Germany), 31 May – 2 June 2012*, ed. by Anita Fetzer, Elda Weizman and Elisabeth Reber, 151–164. Würzburg: Universität Würzburg – [online]. URL: http://opus.bibliothek.uni-wuerzburg.de/volltexte/2012/7165/; URN: urn:nbn:de:bvb:20-opus-71656.

Johansson, Marjut. 2014. "Reading Digital News: Participation Roles, Activities, and Positionings." *Journal of Pragmatics* 72: 31–45. DOI: 10.1016/j.pragma.2014.05.011

Keisanen, Tiina. 2008. "Stancetaking as an Interactional Activity. Challenging the Prior Speaker." In *Stancetaking in Discourse*, ed. by Robert Englebretson, 253–281. Amsterdam: John Benjamins. DOI: 10.1075/pbns.164.10kei

Kerbrat-Orecchioni, Catherine. 2006 [1980]. *L'énonciation. De la subjectivité dans le langage*. [Enunciation. About Subjectivity in the Language]. Paris: Armand Colin.

Kleinke, Sonia. 2010. "Interactive Aspects of Computer-Mediated Communication. Disagreement in an English and German Public News Group." In *Discourses in Interaction*, ed. by Sanna-Kaisa Tanskanen, Marja-Liisa Helasvuo, Marjut Johansson and Mia Raitaniemi, 195–222. Amsterdam: John Benjamins. DOI: 10.1075/pbns.203.15kle

Lambiase, Jacqueline J. 2010. "Hanging by a Thread: Topic Development and Death in an Online Discussion of Breaking News." *Language@Internet* 7.

Langlotz, Andreas and Miriam A. Locher. 2012. "Ways of Communicating Emotional Stance in Online Disagreements." *Journal of Pragmatics 44(12)*: 1591–606.

Le, Elisabeth. 2010. *Editorials and the Power of Media*. Amsterdam: John Benjamins. DOI: 10.1075/dapsac.35

Linell, Per. 1998. *Approaching Dialogue. Talk, Interaction and Contexts in Dialogical Perspective.* Amsterdam: John Benjamins. DOI: 10.1075/impact.3

Linell, Per. 2009. *Rethinking Language, Mind and World Dialogically. Interactional and Contextual Theories of Human Sense-Making.* Charlotte, NC: Information Age Publishing.

Lucy, John A. 1993. *Reflexive Language: Reported speech and Metapragmatics.* Cambridge: Cambridge University Press. DOI: 10.1017/CBO9780511621031

Marcoccia, Michel. 2004. "On-line Polylogues: Conversation Structure and Participation Framework in Internet Newsgroups." *Journal of Pragmatics* 36: 115–45. DOI: 10.1016/S0378-2166(03)00038-9

Moirand, Sophie. 2007. *Les discours de la presse quotidienne. Observer, analyser, comprendre.* [Discourse in the Press. Observations, Analyses, and Interpretations]. Paris: Presses Universitaires de France.

Pomerantz, Anita. 1984. "Agreeing and Disagreeing with Assessments: Some Features of Preferred/Dispreferred Turn Shapes." In *Structures of Social Action. Studies in Conversation Analysis*, ed. by Maxwell Atkinson J. and John Heritage, 56–101. Cambridge: Cambridge University Press.

Reich, Zvi. 2011. "User Comments: The Transformation of Participatory Space. Participatory Journalism." In *Guarding Open Gates at Online Newspapers*, ed. by Jane B. Singer, Alfred Hermida, David Domingo, Ari Heinonen, Steve Paulussen, Thorsten Quandt, Zvi Reich and Marina Vujnovic, 96–117. Malden, MA and Oxford: Wiley-Blackwell. DOI: 10.1002/9781444340747.ch6

Richardson, John E. and James Stanyer. 2011. "Reader Opinion in the Digital Age: Tabloid and Broadsheet Newspaper Websites and the Exercise of Political Voice." *Journalism: Theory, Practice and Criticism 12(8)*: 983–1003.

Ruiz, Carlos, David Domingo, Josep Lluís Micó, Javier Diaz-Noci, Koldo Meso, and Pere Masip. 2011. "Public Sphere 2.0? The Democratic Qualities of Citizen Debates in Online Newspapers." *The International Journal of Press/Politics* 16: 463–87.

Schegloff, Emanuel A., Gail Jefferson, and Harvey Sacks. 1977. "The Preference for Self-Correction in the Organization of Repair in Conversation." *Language* 54 (2): 361–82. DOI: 10.1353/lan.1977.0041

Sinclair, John and Malcolm Coulthard. 1975. *Towards an Analysis of Discourse.* London: Oxford University Press.

Singer, Jane B. 2009. "Separate Spaces: Discourse About the 2007 Scottish Elections on a National Newspaper Web Site." *The International Journal of Press/Politics* 14: 477–96. DOI: 10.1177/1940161209336659

Sivenkova, Maria. "Metacommunicative Follow-ups in British, German and Russian Political Webchats." This volume.

Thompson, Geoff and Susan Hunston. 2000. "Evaluation: An Introduction." In Geoff Thompson and Susan Hunston (eds.), *Evaluation in Text. Authorial Stance and the Construction of Discourse*, 1–27. Oxford: Oxford University Press.

Vuchinich, Samuel. 1990. "The Sequential Organization of Closing in Verbal Family Conflict." In *Conflict Talk. Sociolinguistic Investigations of Arguments in Conversations*, ed. by Allen D. Grimshaw, 118–138. Cambridge: Cambridge University Press.

Weber, Patrick. 2013. "Discussion in the Comments Section: Factors Influencing Participation and Interactivity in Online Newspapers' Reader Comments." *New Media & Society*, online, July 2013, 1–17.

Weizman, Elda. 2012. "Negotiating Irony through Follow-Ups: Readers' Comments on Op-Eds in the Daily Press." In *Proceedings of the ESF Strategic Workshop on Follow-ups Across Discourse Domains: A Cross-Cultural Exploration of Their Forms and Functions, Würzburg (Germany), 31 May – 2 June 2012*, ed. by Anita Fetzer, Elda Weizman and Elisabeth Reber, 263–276. Würzburg: Universität Würzburg – [online]. URL: http://opus.bibliothek.uni-wuerzburg.de/volltexte/2012/7165/; URN: urn:nbn:de:bvb:20-opus-71656.
Weizman, Elda. 2008. *Positioning in Media Dialogue*. Amsterdam: John Benjamins. DOI: 10.1075/ds.3

Appendix 1

Table 2. The data

	Title	Date	Words	Comments	Words
E1	L'euro protecteur	11/01/2008	363	47	3,511
E2	Réalisme made in USA	09/08/2008	354	22	1,299
E3	Pourquoi Obama	11/03/2008	381	53	3,452
E4	Un pape chez les laïques	09/11/2008	392	47	2,811
E5	Fait divers et politique	09/17/2008	349	22	1,425
E6	Un débat bienvenu	09/20/2008	359	33	2,464
E7	Retour au politique	10/09/2008	342	28	1,908
E8	L'Europe fait front	10/13/2008	373	19	1,179
E9	Dangereuse Amérique	10/14/2008	345	38	2,218
E10	Soigner la santé	10/21/2008	345	30	2,076
			3,603	339	22,344

Metacommunicative follow-ups in British, German and Russian political webchats

Maria Sivenkova
Minsk State Linguistic University, Belarus

The present study explores discursive functions and cross-cultural peculiarities of follow-ups containing metacommunicative utterances derived from political live webchats. It seeks to identify some typical patterns of online dialogue/polylogue organisation by filtering out discursive functions of metacommunicative follow-ups.

It is concluded that politicians and their audiences attempt to shape political interaction by inserting evaluative follow-up moves in question-answer or other types of sequences. Besides, non-evaluative follow-ups are also found to play a role in online political discussion. Both politicians and their audiences sometimes resort to metacommunicative justification, explanation and reasoning to defend their views, redress misunderstanding and otherwise ensure impression management.

As for cross-cultural similarities and differences, negative interdiscursive follow-ups that contain complaining sequences and requests to punish underperformance in other genres of political discourse occur most frequently in the British subset of webchat data. Russian politicians criticise the questioners approximately 2.5 times as often as their British counterparts and almost six times as often as German politicians. Neither German users nor German politicians complain about the complexities and challenges of political webchats, whereas both Russian and British users, as well as Russian politicians express doubts in the efficiency of this genre of political multi-party interaction.

1. Introduction

Similar to other types of participation, our political involvement often begins with a desire to provide a follow-up to a preceding contribution made by a political agent or by other participants in political discourse, for which the interactive nature of online media gives ample opportunity. The communicative act of follow-up broadly defined as a socially desirable but unobligatory type of conversational

DOI 10.1075/dapsac.60.05siv

input following a response (Stubbs 1983; McCarthy 1991; Coulthard and Brazil 1992; Francis and Hunston 1992; Döpke 1992; Cullen 2002) thus takes a central stage in the co-production of political meaning by elaborating on, clarifying or challenging a preceding discursive input and thus providing communicators with valuable feedback on how their previous contribution is viewed by the addressee.

Follow-ups are worth studying in online political discourse in general and in live webchat discussions in particular for several reasons. Firstly, the exchange structure of online discussion differs considerably from conversational structures found elsewhere. Yet it remains understudied despite the unique opportunity for investigating follow-up moves in online discussion.[1] In effect, in the genre of political webchat analysed in this paper, participants[2] – both politicians and audiences – are relatively free in satisfying their need to comment on previous strings of discussion, especially in comparison with many offline genres of political discourse possessing strict turn-taking rules.

It seems that the follow-ups politicians choose to generate in online discussions reflect the maximum communicative freedom they can publicly afford. As one commentator in the blog of Tom Watson, Member of Parliament, succinctly put it, "one of the nice things about Twitter et al. is that politicians <…> can be themselves on there, rather than hiding behind special advisers and media consultants. And if people are being themselves online, then every now and then they'll do something a bit daft online." (Mark Goodge in Tom Watson's blog, 01.26.12).

Secondly, although politicians retain significant discursive power in online political discussions,[3] online discussions of this type are usually less asymmetrical in terms of role distributions in comparison with other types of interactions in which follow-ups have mostly been investigated (e.g. teacher-student, parent-child, doctor-patient exchanges) (see a brief overview in Cullen 2002, 118). In effect, the discursive roles of guests and hosts in a political webchat session involve considerable challenge for both professional politicians and grassroot online activists, with the fragile balance of discursive power constantly shifting between multiple participants, and with the communicative act of follow-up taking a central role in the dynamic process of recontextualization of important objects of discourse and in the process of negotiation of new meaning.

1. Kneser, Pilkington, and Treasure-Jones (2001) and Ling (2006) applied Exchange Structure Analysis to investigate educational chat discourse, Hatter (2002) used Exchange Theory to uncover peculiarities of a recreational chat. As for online political discussions it seems that thay have not yet been approached from this perspective.

2. Webchat participants are sometimes referred to as "users" in this contribution, while politicians are called "guests" in webchats.

3. The author is grateful to the reviewer for pointing that out.

The present study focuses on metacommunicative follow-ups, that is, follow-ups containing metacommunicative utterances, and aims to address the following research questions: What are the discursive functions and some cross-cultural peculiarities of metacommunicative follow-ups in political live webchats? The chapter is structured as follows: after describing the data and defining follow-ups in online political discussion, the types of metacommunicative follow-ups in webchats are discussed and their discursive functions are analysed and summarised in the conclusion, together with several cross-cultural observations.

2. Data

The study is based on metacommunicative follow-ups, that is, follow-ups containing metacommunicative utterances obtained from ten British chats organized by Mumsnet, Netmums, Businesszone, Farmers Weekly, twenty Russian chats held by the *Novosibirsk press club, Zhivoj Angarsk, Russkij Obozrevatel, Starchat.ru, Online.newslab.ru, and* by LifeJournal user bb-mos, and twenty German webchats (*Blogsprechstunde, tagesschau-Chat, politik-digital, tacheles.*02-Chat, dol2day).

Interestingly, British Mumsnet webchats represent the only source of data explicitly taking a stance on the possibility of follow-ups as a communicative act. According to the Mumsnet rules of webchat participation available online, one question per member is allowed plus one follow-up for those members who have received a response. In all other webchats analysed for this study, follow-ups as communicative acts either remain unmentioned or are explicitly prohibited by moderators/rules of online conduct.

Excerpt (1) is as example of a typical three-partite sequence from a live Mumsnet webchat, in which user Roseformeplease asks the British Labour Party politician Alistair Darling, the chair of the Better Together campaign, a question about the possible consequences of the Scottish independence referendum, reads the politician's reply and provides a follow-up insisting on a more suitable answer. As we can see, each element of the three-partite sequence contains metacommunicative utterances, for example: 'These vital issues <...> have not really been addressed', 'I keep being asked this question', 'Please don't keep saying the same thing'.

Interestingly, rather than addressing the first responder (A. Darling), Roseformeplease uses her follow-up to address the other webchat guest, First Minister of Scotland A. Salmond, who is more vulnerable to the accusation of not spelling out his plans than A. Darling. The question is thus not simply repeated pragmatically speaking, but the follow-up is employed strategically to both signal Roseformeplease's dissatisfation with A. Darling's response and pass the floor to the other politician, whose answer probably interests Roseformeplease even more than that of A. Darling:

(1) **Question by Roseformeplease:** What will happen to my mortgage and the value of my property in the event of independence? These vital issues affecting ordinary voters have not really been addressed. And I am not a wealthy person, but an ordinary school teacher in a Scottish state school who has had enough to worry about this year with the massive pressure of Curriculum for Excellence.

Answer by Alistair Darling: I keep being asked this question, it's obviously a big worry for families. The short answer is that it all depends on the currency we use. And we still don't know, with eight days to go. <…>

Follow-up by Roseformeplease: Really worried about this. Mr Salmond, your response? Please don't keep saying the same thing, given that you have been told there will be no currency union. You must have thought through the consequences for those who are as concerned as I am.

(Mumsnet webchat with A. Darling, the chair of the Better Together campaign and A. Salmond, First Minster of Scotland, 10.09.2014)

It should be noted that webchats with politicians differ significantly in the three communicative cultures. British live webchats, especially Mumsnet, attract numerous audiences who actively contribute to the discussion before, during, and after the one-hour long interaction with the politician(s), with minimal intervention from the moderators. It is left to the guest's discretion whose questions and follow-up moves to react to or ignore and in which order. For this reason, webchat participants often compete for the politician's attention and monitor each other for proper behaviour online, which stimulates a great deal of metacommunication between politicians and users. Besides, politicians are expected to type their own answers.

In addition, the participants in the British webchats are significantly more critical of the guests, are accustomed to aggressively pressing for answers and explicitly express frustration if their contributions are not taken seriously, as the following comments from both sides of the same webchat demonstrate:

(2) Politician: I think people don't come on a site like this to cheerlead or simply say how great things are – they come on to express their worries and concerns. I'm slightly dismayed that Darren Henley and School Stars have been dismissed out of hand – I hope there will be a forum on the Henley Review. <…>
User: It's good that Ed came here but I too am dismayed at the facile nature of his responses given that there were several respondents here with sector knowledge and experience who were very willing to share their views with a member of the Government.

(Mumsnet chat with Ed Vaizey, Minister for Culture, Communications and Creative Industries, 31.01.2011)

By contrast, German live webchats with politicians, in my data, are heavily regulated discussions mostly mediated by a moderator (sometimes assisted by a co-moderator), who selects and sometimes analyses questions, supports participants' questions and repairs instances of communicative failure. Also, there are usually no pre- and post-interaction discussions, and politicians are sometimes assisted with typing. The differences in format explain to some extent why metacommunicative follow-ups are less frequent in German webchats, hence the higher number of German webchats included in the data.

As for the Russian webchats, they mostly resemble British chats in terms of the role of the moderator and in terms of user activity. Their audiences are usually larger than those in their German counterparts, but smaller than those participating in the British webchats analysed for the study. Besides, when dealing with top rank political guests online, participants of Russian political webchats often demonstrate greater communicative freedom and use a broader range of communicative strategies than their German or British counterparts do. As will be shown later, for many Russian users, the process of enquiring for political information seems to be frequently accompanied by a desire to be entertained and entertain others. In other words, political webchats are conceived more as an arena for 'politainment' than as an opportunity to hold serious political debate.

One may argue that the apparent differences in format make attempts at cross-cultural comparison of political webchats futile. However, it is this author's view that political webchats could and should be studied across cultures as a fascinating emerging genre of political discussion in the new media, with differences in characteristics of webchat sessions in German, Russian and English helping to illuminate various aspects of the communicative act of follow-up. It should be noted that this study deals with single instances of follow-ups as well as with excerpts of online discussions in which follow-ups receive conversational uptake. The latter are referred to as chains of follow-ups and defined as a combination of two or more follow-ups and responses from one or more users constituting one exchange:

Follow-up $_{n}$
Follow-up $_{n+1}$
Follow-up $_{n+2}$ etc.

In this study, chains of follow-ups allow examining some typical patterns of online dialogue/polylogue organisation. As will be shown later, for metacommunicative follow-ups, some of the most common patterns seem to be the expression of gratitude or apology for previous communicative acts, criticism of previous contributions, and endorsement of preceding discursive inputs.

3. Definition of follow-ups in political webchats

Follow-ups are defined in the study as "communicative acts (or dialogue acts), in and through which a prior communicative act is accepted, challenged, or otherwise negotiated" (Fetzer et al. 2012) "by ratified participants in the exchange or by third parties" (Fetzer, Weizman, this volume: p. 5). They follow responding or follow-up moves by the same/different participant(s) and may refer to communicative acts that happened elsewhere in offline and online genres of political and media discourse.

The origin of the definition and rationale for its several components will be briefly spelled out below. This definition is rooted in Exchange Theory with some modifications to embrace instances of follow-up questioning – one of the central communicative activities in political live webchats – and to account for some particular contextual constraints typical of live webchat interaction.

Based on the discourse analytic approach pioneered by Sinclair and Coulthard (1975) and developed in subsequent adaptations (see, for example, Stubbs 1983; McCarthy 1991; Coulthard and Brazil 1992; Francis and Hunston 1992; Döpke 1992; Cullen 2002), a follow-up is understood as an interactional move following a response to an opening move. In contrast to responses, follow-ups are conceived as a socially desirable but optional form of conversational input. In other words, unlike obligatory responses, "the interactional partner cannot be reprimanded for not supplying the follow-up" (Döpke 1992, 88). In live webchat interaction, however, the criterion of optionality is only partially applicable.

In webchats, the majority of initiations are questions to which politicians react with answers (responses), the follow-up moves containing an expression of gratitude for the answer and/or a follow-up question or evaluation ("Thanks for answering my private school q Diane. It's a good answer (politically)😁", Labour leadership contenders webchat, Sept. 6, 2010). In such three-part initiation-response-follow-up sequences, the third component may well be regarded as socially desirable but optional. At the same time, it is probably less desirable than in traditional offline three-partite sequences due to the contextual constrains of live webchats, with many users typically competing for the politician's attention and yearning to receive answers to their important questions within a limited time frame.

So it is often left to the discretion of webchat participants whether to provide follow-ups to the politician's responses to their questions. Some users prefer to save time and space so that fellow participants get an equal opportunity to see their questions answered, others might still be worried about producing a bad impression if they do not provide a follow-up, as the following comment demonstrates: "I have to leave in ten minutes to pick up the dc's from school. If I don't respond to the answer to my question – I'm not being rude. <<As you

were>>" (Mumsnet, Ed Miliband, Labour Leader and Leader of the Opposition, 01.12.2011). Additionally, many webchat participants use their follow-up moves as an opportunity to "smuggle" one or more supplementary questions and are reprimanded for this by fellow participants who are still waiting for answers to their initial questions, which is hardly conducive of social harmony ("Lots of people were in the queue before you").

In addition to conceptualising follow-ups as the third move in the three-part initiation-response-follow-up sequences studied by Exchange Theory, the present analysis also subsumes under follow-ups supplementary questions asked by interactants in some of the sub-genres of political discourse under specific circumstances (e.g. in parliamentary debates or live webchats).

From the point of view of Exchange Theory such follow-up questions are not defined as follow-ups, but are often viewed as initiation, response-initiation or re-initiation sequences. Yet in political linguistics follow-up questions may be regarded as a standard way to extend questioning sequences designed to evaluate, elaborate on, clarify or challenge the preceding answer. In other words, supplementary questions realise the functions typically ascribed to follow-up moves in Exchange Theory, although they do not always demonstrate the degree of unpredictability required from follow-up moves to be defined as such in existing definitions. Let us briefly review the components of the above definition of follow-ups.

The data analysed in the study show that politicians as well as other participants of online political discussions may comment not only on a prior communicative act, which constitutes the most frequent variety of follow-ups, but also on complete exchanges or transactions (hence the distinction between single and multiple follow-ups introduced in Section 4 below). These follow-ups are often evaluative, which is reflected in the component 'accepted, challenged' of the above definition.

Perhaps unsurprisingly, follow-ups in webchats are a vital resource in providing users' feedback on the politicians' impression management skills. If users like the guest they usually share positive feedback with the politician, as Example (3) shows, or praise him/her during the post-interaction discussion with other webchat participants. Similarly, if members of the online community form a negative impression of the guest they are likely to share it during the live session or after the politician leaves the webchat ("Sorry for the ramble but feeling totally hacked off and as if this whole webchat was nothing more than a publicity stunt", Netmums webchat with M. Miller, 23.03.11).

(3) northeastofeden 14:39:30: By the way thank you for coming to talk to us all. […]
swallowedAfly 14:40:37: yes i second northeastofeden – thank you and you are doing rather well. […]

northeastofeden 15:12:46: [...] I am off now, but thanks once again to Ed, I think you have come across really well.

(Mumsnet webchat with E. Miliband, Labour Leader and Leader of the Opposition, 1.12.2011)

Evaluative follow-ups of this type might allow to some extent measuring the effectiveness of politicians' communicative effort in online webchats, thus providing additional evidence for the interconnectedness of language and politics. Indeed, the feedback on politicians' performance online is often verbalised by audiences in the form of promises/refusals to vote for the candidate or his or her party ("OoooH! Ed Balls replied to me. I'll certainly have to vote for him now!", Mumsnet Labour leadership contenders webchat, 6.09.2010) or in the form of ironic comments about the politician's success online ("Goodness me, NF. You really are doing a sterling job of winning us over", Mumsnet chat with N. Farage, 24.02.11). At the same time, such responses may often be influenced by various political agendas of the webchat participants/organizers and as such they are not to be taken at face value.

Positive and negative evaluation, however, is not the only type of follow-up moves occurring in online political webchats. The component 'otherwise negotiated' covers non-evaluative types of follow-ups that contain metacommunicative justifications and/or explanations designed to ward off negative impressions audiences might develop on the basis of misconception or lack of information about politicians' true goals and motives.

The above-mentioned presence of multiple users is an important characteristic of online political discussion that needs to be reflected in the definition of follow-ups, hence the component 'They follow responding or follow-up moves by the same/different participant(s)'. Indeed, in addition to question-answer sequences that appear in politician-to-user and user-to-politician communication, follow-ups in live webchats are often found in user-to-user(s) interaction, expressing support and criticism of users/politicians and in moderator-to-user(s) interaction, disciplining the users and harmonising the communication flow.

Yet another consideration which should be taken into account when defining follow-ups in online political discussion is related to its intertextual and interdiscursive dimension. Indeed, in contrast to face-to-face or group conversational interaction, political follow-ups often refer to initiations and responses occurring elsewhere – in parliamentary debates or political interviews, during party conferences, political rallies or talk-shows, to name just a few, hence the final component of the definition of follow-ups, provided at the beginning of the section (follow-ups 'may refer to communicative acts that happened elsewhere in offline and online genres of political and media discourse'), and the distinction between intradiscursive and interdiscursive follow-ups that will be discussed in Section 4 below.

Related to the above idea, the component "by ratified participants in the exchange or by third parties" pays tribute to the openness of boundaries of contemporary political discourse accelerated by the new media.

4. Types of follow-ups in webchats

The present study explores discursive functions and cross-cultural peculiarities of metacommunicative follow-ups, that is, follow-ups containing metacommunicative utterances derived from political live chats. Such metacommunicative follow-ups refer to various aspects of politicians' communicative behavior online, such as the quality and quantity of provided information or the communicative strategies and communicative styles employed to do preceding and ongoing interaction tasks. In live webchats, such follow-ups are usually embedded in pre- or post-sequences to questions asked by members of an online community and to answers given by one or more politicians invited by webchat organisers to address the community. Example (4) demonstrates a user's evaluative follow-up critical of the politician's previous contributions to the live webchat:

(4) User: You're typing succinctly on MN today but sometimes your answers are very hard to decipher if I'm honest. Do you find it difficult to give a straight answer?
Politician: Thanks for your question. I'll help you with a clear answer – no!
(Labour leadership contenders webchat, 6.09.2010)

In contrast, follow-ups of the type "Thank you for helping families on low incomes" are not included in the study because they do not contain specific references to the politician's online or offline communicative behavior. Based on the number of communicative acts commented on, two types of follow-ups occur in my data: (1) single follow-ups referring to one particular preceding communicative act ("That's quite a facile reply if you don't mind me saying", Mumsnet Live Webchat with Ed Vaizey, Minister for Culture, Communications and Creative Industries, 31.01.11), (2) multiple follow-ups that comment on more than one communicative act or the whole transaction ("Many of your answers are the standard politician evasion because you think the public can still be fooled by that", Mumsnet Labour leadership contenders webchat, 6.09.2010). Moreover, based on their area of application, follow-ups may be (i) intradiscursive, i.e. referring to the same genre of political online discourse (webchat or blog discussion) and (ii) interdiscursive, i.e. relating to someone's communicative behaviour in a different genre of political or other discursive sphere. To illustrate the latter, a commentator might visit a blog to complain about the politician's communicative behaviour in a talk show or to expose the host's party colleague who had ignored questions from constituents. Such complaints occur mostly in the British subset of the webchat data, with references to other politicians' underperformance online or elsewhere serving as a strategy to boost the illocutionary force of interrogative sequences and convey a sense of urgency. Such sequences of complaints may be accompanied by requests to punish underperformance ("Can you give him a telling off please?", Mumsnet Live Webchat with David Cameron, Tory leader, 19.11.2009).

Interestingly, interdiscursive follow-up moves often refer to various online genres of political discourse: party websites, Twitter conversations, communication in social networks, as well as blogs and live webchats. Indeed, the politician's participation in the current webchat session or blog discussion is seen as a token of Internet affinity and a deep-rooted commitment to excellence in other forms of online communication. Underperformance in the field is therefore disapproved of and experts among the online audience provide metacommunicative advice, as Example (5) illustrates:

(5) Crumblemum: Hi Ed
Who does your twitter feed? It always seems a bit static and formal. I understand you can't do it all the time, but maybe you should go down the route of Obama (and the xfactor contestants) who does some himself but lets it be known when his staff are doing it – with (HQ) at end.
(Mumsnet webchat with Ed Miliband, 01.12.2011)

It should be noted that multiple interdiscursive follow-ups probably constitute threats to the politician's public face more than other types of follow-ups addressed in the study, with some users collecting multipoint 'dossiers' on politicians, exposing them for every imaginable communication error. Such follow-ups frequently receive conversational uptake from other discussants leading to a joint development of a long list of critical remarks produced online, to address which the politician often has no resources.

5. Discursive functions of follow-ups in online webchats with politicians

In webchats, politicians' primary interactional needs are to address as many questions as possible and to identify with the audience, because their success online is frequently judged by the number of questions they address during the live webchat interaction ('more answers = more competence'). Furthermore, such online webchat sessions are often held before elections and are increasingly regarded as an important way to win specific target audiences (e.g. about one million of UK mothers who are part of the Mumsnet online community in case of the Mumsnet webchats), which calls for the standard political skill of gaining votes by addressing specific needs of the target group ('more answers = better understanding of the voters' needs and/or more respect towards the online community').

Being confronted with multiple users pressing for answers, webchat guests usually have fewer possibilities than audiences to perform follow-ups. In this connection it can be hypothesised that actual performances of follow-ups highlight communicative situations in which important work-related attitudes are made explicit.

The Russian webchat data feature twenty-five metacommunicative follow-ups performed by politicians. In British and German data, there are twenty-two and twenty-one follow-ups respectively. These follow-ups serve a number of important functions listed in the table (see Table 1) and analysed below.

Table 1. Politicians' follow-ups in the three sets of webchat data

Function of follow-up	Sample, N		
	British	German	Russian
1. Criticism of questioner / audience	5	2	14
2. Denial of criticism	2	1	1
3. Apology, justification and explanation	4	2	1
4. Doing politics	2	2	1
5. Endorsement of questioner / audience	5	8	6
6. Acknowledgement, partial agreement with criticism	2	0	0
7. Improvement of response	1	4	1
8. Ambiguous	1	2	1

It should be noted that the categories of follow-ups presented in Table 1 partially overlap with those occurring in other genres of political discourse, for example, with a typology of equivocation in traditional media interviews developed by Bull and colleagues (Bull and Mayer 1993; Bull 2003, 114–122). The category 'attacking the question' lends itself particularly well to comparison, since it is obviously realised by way of meta-discursive remarks.

Category frequencies, however, differ significantly in political online discussion and traditional media. In particular, 'making political points' (type 4. 'Doing politics') is by far the most frequent strategy in televised interviews, but hardly occurs in the form of metacommunicative follow-ups in politicians' follow-ups and is more frequent in audience follow-ups in my data. The category 'attacking the question, in turn, is the second most frequent form of equivocation in traditional media interviews, whereas in my data, 'criticism of questioner / audience' is the most frequent type in the Russian webchats.

Apologies are extremely rare in televised interviews (Bull 2003, 122), but occur rather frequently in my data, together with justifications and explanations. However, apologies are difficult to compare: the apologies made by politicians in webchats usually concern some minor issues, whereas those made during televised interviews are usually very serious (cf. an apology for hitting the wrong button and an apology for an error of judgement that lead to serious consequences).

Let us analyse each of the eight types of functions of follow-ups in some detail. 'Criticism of questioner/audience', found in all the three sets of webchat data, refers to metacommunicative utterances that express disapproval of the addressee with a different degree of explicitness. They can occur as a response to criticism incorporated in the question or as a response to the preceding interaction in general and are designed to stop unwanted communicative behaviour or bring about changes in questioner/audience' communicative behaviour (*Druz'ja, ya prizyvaju byt' korrektnymi* – 'Friends, I call [you] to be tactful' as a reaction to an offensive remark about another local politician) or to provide the addressee with negative feedback (*Da, bojus', vy dejstvitel'no bol'ny* – 'Yes, I'm afraid you are really [mentally] ill' as a response to the questioner's baseless assumption about a fraud in the party).

As we can see from Table 1, Russian politicians criticise the questioners approximately 2,5 times as often as their British counterparts and almost six times as often as German politicians. In effect, 56% of Russian politician's metacommunicative follow-ups comprise criticisms of questioner/audience, whereas only 23% of British and 10% of German politicians' follow-ups are critical of audience's communicative behaviour. In the Russian data, the most frequent type of metacommunicative follow-up is criticism for having to repeat the same ideas (*Povtorjajus', odnako... Čitateli lentjai – ne xotjat čitat' čat sverxu* – 'I am repeating myself, however... The readers are lazy, they do not want to read this chat from the top'). In addition, Russian politicians expose webchat participants for not reaching their intended communicative goals, faulty logic, breaking the webchat rules, excessive directness, and even for spelling or lexical mistakes.

'Denial of criticism' covers cases when the politician denies the validity of the questioner's critical remarks by way of negating the criticism (user: *Ausgewichen!* – 'Evaded [the question]!', politician: *nicht ausgewichen* – 'I haven't evaded [the question]) or through the use of a lexeme alluding to the unjust nature of the accusation (*Vy nespravedlivy* – 'You are being unjust'). Such negations may also be extended with the politician's version of the communicative situation provided to support his/her credibility. Compare a response to criticism for inconsistency in (6):

(6) domesticslattern: Thanks EM and DM for answering my question. Your language is much stronger than I recall you using previously, but I suppose you modify it according to your audience.☺
DavidMiliband: Sorry but it is the same answer. eg "deadly and self defeating" is what I said in parliament.
(Mumsnet Labour leadership contenders webchat, 6.09.2010)

The third category – 'apology, justification and explanation' – deals with cases of impression management on the part of the politician. By explicating reasons behind particular communicative acts politicians try to ward off negative impressions audiences might develop on the basis of misconception or lack of information about politicians' true goals and motives. Such metacommunicative follow-ups may occur independently or in combination with criticism of questioner or denial of criticism, as the following response to criticism for slow typing demonstrates: "Older people type slower than younger people…please don't indulge in age discrimination! And i'm thinking about my replies which takes time. So give me a break sister!" (Mumsnet Live webchat with H. Harman, 25.11.2008).

In the webchat data, Russian politicians almost never apologise or provide self-justification/explanations related to their communicative activities to make themselves look better in the eyes of their audience, although they occasionally do it on a non-metacommunicative level (e.g. one politician had to provide justification for wearing an expensive watch). As for their British counterparts, one politician apologises for not getting back to the questioner on a different occasion, another politician has to explain why an advisor is typing his answers during the live webchat, yet another political agent explains an unfortunate choice of words that lead to a serious misunderstanding. The latter is a case of an allusion to classical mythology that was misinterpreted as a comment making light of rape, which brought about respective accusations in the live webchat and the politician`s justification: "I was referring to the rape of Europa – sometimes I know that using classical mythology can cause problems, and I certainly wasn't making a joke out of rape." (Mumsnet chat with N. Farage, Leader of the UK Independence Party, 24.02.11).

In one more follow-up of this type, the guest has to apologize and account for not posting for about 20 minutes due to a technical problem ("Sorry – laptop caught my campaign cold. I'm trying my best!"), although it was not his fault and despite the fact that the webchat organizers had already commented on the glitch and accepted responsibility for the delay in answering the community's questions, which highlights the relative aggressiveness of the genre of political discussion under study. Additionally, such follow-ups demonstrate that technology represents yet another important contextual constraint influencing the participants' chance of successful communication.

'Doing politics' is a category of follow-ups that refers to discursive manifestations of politicians' ingroup commitment, that is, communicative acts designed to promote one's own coalition and disparage the opponents (Bull, Fetzer and Johansson 2008). Compare the case of defending a party colleague (and a contestant for party leadership) against a reproach for not posting anything for a long time: "Andy is sitting next to me. I can confirm he is fine and typing away madly"

(Mumsnet Labour leadership contenders webchat, 6.09.2010). In the German webchat data, in one follow-up the politician's opponents are criticised for provoking too much media hype around their decisions; in the other instance the politician generates a multiple interdiscursive follow-up to disparage the opponents' argumentation flaws: *So argumentieren die Sozialdemokraten in Bayern immer. Das ist und bleibt ihr Problem* – 'The social democrats in Bavaria always argue this way. This is and remains their problem' (tacheles.02-Chat mit T. Goppel, CSU-Generalsekretär, 9.09.2003).

'Endorsement of questioner/audience' with the help of metacommunicative follow-ups is achieved primarily through the expressions of gratitude for constructive comments and agreement with opinions expressed by supporters. Interestingly, such comments' functions often go beyond phatic reaffirmation of positive attitude to the addressee. In effect, expressions of gratitude and agreement seem to be employed by politicians sparingly as a tool to highlight / encourage a high level of interactional achievement on the part of the user. For example, politicians praise members of online communities for suggesting clever policies, for providing a detailed analysis of a situation under discussion and for answering governmental questionnaires.

For instance, during the Netmums Coffee House Chat with Maria Miller, the then Work and Pensions Minister, the user named Jo A(227) has posted a detailed response to the green paper under discussion, which contained a number of interesting follow-up questions to the minister and a six-point "My conclusions" section. The minister responded with a gratitude and encouragement to submit further proposals, as exemplified in (7):

(7) Hi Jo, thank you so much for such a detailed and considered response and I look forward to reading your submission to the consultation. I can't answer all the issues that you have raised in the time I have available today but I'd like to pick up on your point regarding domestic violence as other people have asked this question too […]. (17.07.2008)

By contrast, responses received from other members of the Netmums Coffee House Chat are often only briefly acknowledged by the minister in her weaving comments of the type "Natalie S and Nicola B have raised the problem of parents who try to hide their real income levels", or are completely ignored by her.

The category 'acknowledgement, partial agreement with criticism' is found only in the British data. In one instance, the politician owns up to the fact that an advisor is typing his comments during the chat session although he already explained previously that he needed assistance as a slow typist. He has to reiterate explanation, after a post by one of his contenders attracts attention to this fact again ("Amazingly one of my rivals has an advisor (female) with him who is doing all his typing! I am too polite to say who"). Besides, the advisor in question also provides a metacommunicative follow-up to help the politician save face: "this is Ellie typing and I can confirm I am much better at it than Ed!" (Labour leadership contenders webchat, 6.09.2010). In the other instance, the politician reacts to an accusation of misrepresenting statistics with a concession: "Maybe I overstated 1 percent" in response to the question starting with "you regularly misrepresent statistics" (Mumsnet chat with N. Farage, Leader of the UK Independence Party, 24.02.11).

'Improvement of response' is a follow-up employed to enhance the politician's previous response or to improve a user's previous comment to help him/her save face, for instance by treating his/her previous comment as a joke. In the Russian data set, one politician employs this tactic to show that a user's previous inappropriate behaviour has been forgiven: *My vse ponjali,* čto *èto byla popytka* šutki. – 'We all understood it was an attempt at joke' by way of response to the user's self-critical follow-up: *Udalil svoj kament i prinošu izvinenjya* – 'Deleted my comment and proffer apologies' (bb-mos's webchat with V. Tor, 6.02.2011). Metacommunicative follow-ups of this type seem to demonstrate that interactional harmony and smooth interpersonal relationships play a role in online political discussion.

In all other instances, however, politicians employ metacommunicative follow-ups to improve their own comments, for instance, by providing a serious answer, as Excerpt (8) demonstrates. Arguably, the politician opts to provide a better answer to Chrisnelda's question to avoid handling the inconvenient question from koliba. Alternatively, the politician could have chosen to provide a serious answer as a follow-up to the humorous response for fear that his attempt at humor might not come across well.

(8) Moderator: Frage von Chrisnelda an Peter Friedrich: „Glauben Sie, dass die Zeit der „großen Volksparteien" vorbei ist?" […]
Peter_Friedrich: Zu Chrisnelda: Jein – tolle Antwort, gell? Typisch Volkspartei.
Moderator: Frage von koliba an Peter Friedrich: „Wenn Sie erlauben: Eine ganz grundsätzliche Frage zu Politikern: Diskutieren Politiker in diversen Ausschüssen genauso oberflächlich und unwissend wie in Talkrunden? Man hat oft das Gefühl, dass durch Rhetorik nicht vorhandenes Wissen überspielt wird. Liegt das vielleicht daran, dass Politiker zu schlecht bezahlt werden und die fähigen Leute in die Wirtschaft abwandern?"
Peter_Friedrich: **Nochmal zu Chrisnelda**: Ich glaube, dass die SPD wieder ein gesellschaftliches Lager bilden muss und kann, dass zum Kern den Vorrang der demokratischen Politik haben muss. Das kann auch wieder eine breite Bevölkerung ansprechen. (dol2day Chat mit P. Friedrich, Generalsekretär der SPD Baden-Württemberg, 14.05.2010)

(Moderator: Question from Chrisnelda to Peter Friedrich: "Do you think that the time of "large people's parties" is over?"
Peter_Friedrich: to Chrisnelda: Jein [both yes and no] – a great answer, isn't it? Typical of a people's party.
Moderator: Question from koliba to Peter Friedrich: "With your permission, a matter of principle for politicians: do politicians on various committees hold discussions as facile and ignorant as in rounds of talk? One often has a feeling that non-existent knowledge is covered up through rhetoric. Perhaps it's because politicians are too badly paid, and capable people leave for industry?"
Peter_Friedrich: **Once again to Chrisnelda:** I think that the SPD again must and can build a social camp having the advantage of democratic politics. That can also appeal to the population at large again.)

(dol2day Chat with P. Friedrich, secretary general of the SDP Baden-Württemberg and MP, 14.05.2010)

The other three examples of such follow-ups in German webchats reflect one important genre constraint. When having a discussion with multiple users, politicians often have to clarify that they wish to provide another comment referring to their preceding answer and indicate explicitly whose question they are now providing a follow-up to. For this, various metacommunicative utterances are employed: *Das bezog sich auf die vorherige Frage* – 'that was related to the preceding question', *Noch als Ergänzung* – 'as an addition to', *Nachtrag zur vorherigen Frage* – 'addition to the previous question'. Such metacommunication can be crucial to the overall success of the live webchat session.

Alternatively, the problem can be solved by indicating in the respective answer/follow-up the exact time at which the question was asked, as Excerpt (9) from a Russian chat demonstrates. Here, Sibirjačka is a webchat participant offering a piece of advice to the politician, and angarčanin is the moderator:

(9) 16:07:28 <Sibirjačka> angarčanin < 16:06:52> xotelos' by čtoby delali ssylku na tot vopros, na kotoryj otvečajut. Vremja ukazyvali
16:07:51 <angarčanin> 16:07:28 ok, podskažu
16:09:05 <angarčanin>: 16:07:28 16:07:51 podskazal. ždite

(16:07:28 <Sibiryachka> angarchanin < 16:06:52> It would be nice if references were made to the question being answered. By way of indicating the time.
16:07:51 <angarchanin> 16:07:28 ok, I'll tell him
16:09:05 < angarchanin >: 16:07:28 16:07:51 I have told him. Wait

(liveangarsk.ru, online chat with A. Kozlov, Mayor of Angarsk, 27.08.10)

What excerpts such as (9) seem to demonstrate is that Russian users may be more accustomed to online policial discussions than German counterparts and have developed efficient ways of dealing with technical issues online. By providing optimisation suggestions in the form of metacommunicative follow-ups Russian users help shape the negotiation of new meaning in the participatory multi-party interactions and contribute to the overall success of online political discussion.

Although many of the follow-ups discussed above may be defined to some extent as multifunctional, the category 'ambiguous' covers cases that defy categorisation by combining features of several categories. For example, statements like *Soweit ich das sehe, habe ich mich klar ausgedrückt* – 'As far as I can tell, I have expressed myself clearly' can be interpreted both as criticism of the questioner for making the politician reiterate the same point and as an attempt to justify the politician's refusal to answer the question again. Similarly, *Ich hoffe, damit ist die Frage halbwegs umfassend beantwortet* – lit. 'I hope with this is the question half comprehensively answered' seems to combine features of an apology for not providing an exhaustive answer and of an attempt to establish solidarity with the audience by demonstrating the respondent's good will and interactional achievement.

As we can see, different functions of follow-ups are relevant for different sets of webchat data. Politicians employ metacommunicative follow-ups to criticise or praise the addressee / audience and to deny criticism in all the three communicative cultures under study. Besides, some other culture/language-specific functions seem to play a role in politicians' online interactions. In particular, follow-ups are employed to partially accept criticism in the British data. In the German set of data, metacommunicative follow-ups are more frequently employed to improve the politician's previous contribution.

Moving on to audience's follow-ups, at least some members see live webchats with politicians as an opportunity to engage with politics by raising important issues ("KateMiddleton: <sigh> Our welfare state is at risk. Sensible questions people please. This is the leader of the opposition. Let's encourage him to oppose by asking the important stuff", Mumsnet with E. Miliband, Labour Leader and Leader of the Opposition, 01.12.2011). To this end, users press the politician for answers by repeatedly posing the same or similar question, criticise the politician if no satisfactory answer is provided, or resort to question substitutions ("I don't think he is going to answer my earlier question, so I am going to ask this…").

However, the tactics of pressing for answers and attracting attention to burning social issues at any cost seem to be culture-specific. For many Russian users, receiving information from politicians and making useful policy suggestions are not the only interactional tasks users have to fulfill while communicating with politicians online. Many Russian webchat participants are also interested in maintaining interactional harmony and good relationships with the politician, as metacommunicative comments such as *Ne xotite, ne otvečajte* – 'If you do not want to, do not answer' vividly demonstrate. Such comments seem to be indicative of awareness on the Russian users' part of some genre-specific constraints and of the complexities of the role as webchat guest. In effect, some questions may be too complex or too specific to be addressed online, whereas other issues may be regarded as inappropriate, inflamatory or face threatening. In combination with the ambiguous status of many webchat online discussions (e.g. public, semi-private or private), it seems only natural that some webchat participants express doubts about the appropriateness of their communicative contributions and are willing to allow the guest some interactional freedom in deciding which question to address and which to ignore.

Similar to raising important issues through incessant questioning, members regard debunking politicians' wrong beliefs as an important discursive task ("Yvette i feel compelled to tell you that your statement just there on Job Centre Plus is just not most people's experience", Mumsnet with Y. Cooper, secretary of state for work and pensions, 27.04.2010).

One interesting manifestation of channel-related user attitudes and perceptions in online political discussion becomes obvious when one considers the credibility-explicating follow-up moves alluding to the (relative) easiness of distributing lies online in contrast to offline genres of political discussion ("Aren't you glad you are typing that and not having to say it? 😁", Mumsnet with E. Vaizey, Minister for Culture, Communications and Creative Industries, 31.01.2011). Arguably, credibility-related problems in online political communication can have the same – if not more devastating – consequences, as many contemporary examples demonstrate.

Several British politicians received negative coverage in both mainstream and new media after their unconvincing appearance on Mumsnet. For instance, Mail Online had an article on D. Cameron, the then Leader of Opposition, who was repeatedly criticised for failing to answer questions about the Conservative policy on nappies for children with special needs, although his own disabled son, who had died earlier that year, was subject to this very same policy ("The mother of all ambushes: Cameron subjected to online inquisition from disgruntled middle-class parents during webchat on Mumsnet", http://www.dailymail.co.uk).

Seen from that perspective, follow-ups of the above type should probably be considered as a channel-specific credibility-related move synonymous with "You are lying" or "You are not telling us the truth" occurring elsewhere in offline political discourse. *One way of holding politicians accountable* in the data is to evaluate their performance by either approving their discursive input or by signaling discontent with their communicative behaviour ("I'm so angry! This man's flip answers didn't come close to addressing my concerns", Mumsnet with E. Vaizey, 31.01.2011).

In sum, discussing the politicians' or users' credibility seems to be one of the most important issues in online political webchats. Politicians get credibility boosts from supporters or challenges of their credibility from opponents (e.g. exposure for lying, expressing distrust, short narratives illustrating truth-related problems on the part of the politician). The latter can be accompanied by demands to provide evidence/arguments for one's credibility and advice on how to retain credibility.

When several members of the audience join forces in exposing the politician, long and particularly face-threatening chains of follow-ups are sometimes constructed. In such chains, the same metacommunicative utterance can simultaneously express solidarity with a previous commentator and criticism of the politician/coalition.

Moving on to positive evaluations, they are less frequent in the webchat data. Praise is sometimes incorporated in questions (see Example (10)) or is given in the post-interaction stage after the guest has left the online community.

(10) MsAnneThrope: Ed Miliband has been the only candidate to mention the importance of a better work-life balance for all – in his answers about Education and as one of his 5 key policies.What do the other candidates think about this subject, and do they propose any changes to our workplace culture, which is so un-family friendly for both men and women?
(Labour leadership contenders webchat, Sept. 6, 2010)

As for negative evaluations, they are, predictably, many and varied. Politicians are exposed for various communication flaws (e.g. evasion, picking up convenient questions, trotting out facile answers) and are pressured for more detailed/honest/serious answers and comments. These communication flaws can refer to mistakes made by the politician in the preceding stretch of current online discussion as well as to those made in other genres of offline and online political discourse (interviews, parliamentary debates, Twitter conversations).

Cross-cultural comparison of the Russian and British webchats under study reveals an asymmetry in requests and demands for a better communicative behaviour. In the Russian data, it is often the politician who demands a change of verbal behaviour on the part of the webchat participant(s), while in the British data the positions are reversed: webchat participants constantly challenge the guest and urge him/her to do better. For example, Mikhail Delyagin, leader of the Russian party "Motherland: common sense", repeatedly criticised other webchat participants for making spelling and lexical errors and for using net speak (e.g. *A teper' po-russki, esli ne složno* – 'And now in Russian, if it is not too much trouble'; *Na olbanskom pišite Medvedevu* – 'If you want to communicate in Olbansky[4] you should write to Medvedev', LiveJournal Chat with M. Delyagin, 17.05.2011). By contrast, Nigel Farage, leader of the UK Independence Party, is severely criticised

4. 'Olbansky' refers to a form of net speak popular in certain communities of Runet, the Russian-speaking segment of the Internet, characterised by deliberate misspelling as a form of creative activity. It is a Russian equivalent of LOLspeak.

by several Mumsnet webchat participants for inappropriate metaphors and unfortunate lexical choice. For example, by calling Italian politics 'sexy' the politician triggered a chain of metacommunicative follow-up moves in which users evaluated the appropriateness of the expression, as demonstrated in (11):

(11) Susiewho: [...] It's extremely offensive to judge Italian politics to be "Sexier" – why on earth would 'sexy' politics be a good thing anyway?? It's a very weird and creepy thing to say. Not well thought through at all. [...]
glasnost: [...] And to call Italian politics sexy, colourful etc is quite vomit inducing. It's actually debauched and corrupt. I was of an opinion that he was a misguided soul but now i know he's in utter bad faith. [...]
carminaburana: 'Sexy' doesn't have to have a sexual meaning – sexy can also mean 'interesting' – 'let's make this sexy' is a term often used in advertising etc. [...]
cakeywakey: Whatever the semantics Carmina, I'd expect an elected politician to choose his words more carefully – particularly in relation to Italian politics at the moment.
carminaburana: Sexy can mean 'flamboyant'. – Italian politics is certainly colourful – that's what I'm sure was meant here.
cakeywakey: Think we'll have to agree to disagree Carmina. Whatever the meaning, it was inappropriate.
(Mumsnet chat with N. Farage, Leader of the UK Independence Party, 24.02.11)

Apart from supplying metacommunicative follow-ups exposing politicians for previous communication glitches and urging them to perform better, members of the audience can resort to another way of showing displeasure with politicians' discursive input by way of offering halfhearted gratitude ("Thanks for kind of addressing the question"; "Thank you for at least trying to answer") and mitigated praise ("I like that answer, Ed, it seemed genuinely honest, albeit just the tip of the iceberg. Wish you'd take that kind of verve to the Lib Dems and show them that you believe you could do better with them...", Mumsnet with E. Miliband, Labour Leader and Leader of the Opposition, 01.12.2011).

One intriguing cross-cultural aspect of the above issue is related to politicians' and users' perceptions of the usefullness of political webchats as a genre of political participatory multi-party interaction. Interestingly, Russian users, Russian politicians and British users often express doubts as to the expediency of holding such multi-party interactions for fear of not getting serious answers due to genre constraints. As for British politicians, they reserve judgement and never offer any metacommunicative follow-ups on the issue, whereas German politicians occasionally highlight positive aspects of such interactions and never express doubts (*Man konzentriert sich auf das wesentliche* – 'One concentrates on the essential').

This finding seems to demonstrate that metacommunicative follow-ups can shed light on some important work-related attitudes that would remain implicit without a cross-cultural comparison. For British and German politicians, any interaction with potential voters – even in the framework of a largely experimental genre – unfolds in agreement with some general rules of politician-constituency interaction according to which expressing doubts about one's work can have detrimental consequences. For Russian politicians and audiences, policial webchats as a newly emerging genre of political deliberation are to be treated differently from well-established genres of political discussion. Applying the rules of offline discussion to the marginal online genre could come across as lack of flexibility and lack of understanding of norms of netiquette.

In addition to holding politicians accountable, metacommunicative follow-ups are employed by webchat members to discipline each other. The self-monitoring function of follow-up moves is realised when webchat rules are breached and the online discussion is disrupted or when politician's time is spent unproductively ("Can you not ask a more intelligent question than that?"). Besides, such follow-ups allow audiences to engage in impression management. Since many community members are concerned about their image as serious discussants to be reckoned with, instances of communicative behaviour that threaten that image are exposed and put an end to. Compare the two comments from a Mumsnet webchat with Ed Miliband, Labour Leader and Leader of the Opposition in (12), in which two webchat participants express concerns about their image:

(12) notsomumsie: FFS Asking (and answering) about bloody biscuits perpetuates the myth of stupid women. Get a grip. […]
lubeybaublely: Argh @ biscuit talk when I'm still awaiting many of the first page questions to be answered (including mine)
Do you know how many men on twitter think all we do is ask questions about biscuits? Ignoring all the decent, relevant questions we have asked. Doing nothing for ourselves here <rant over> (Mumsnet, 01.12.2011)

Another way of discipling each other in webchat discussions is related to the private/public divide. Interestingly, the status of online political discussions regarding the private/public dichotomy is perceived very differently by discussants, especially in the Russian data, as some of the metacommunicative follow-up moves demonstrate. Some users conceptualise online exchanges as either private or public discussions, while others rather think of them as semi-private conversations (*Učityvaja, čto èto ne intervju, a poluprivatnyj razgovor* – [Taking into account that this is not an interview but a semi-private conversation], liveangarsk.ru, online chat with A. Kozlov, Mayor of Angarsk, 27.08.10).

As for the British data set, webchat sessions are often perceived as private conversations having no impact on national policies: “Go on, be brave and answer… off the record, you understand (no one is listening in, honestly).” (Mumsnet Live Webchat with Ed Vaizey, Minister for Culture, Communications and Creative Industries, 31.01.11).

An idiosyncratic attitude towards the concept of publicity emerges from some of the Russian metacommunicative observations: the concept is occasionally used in negative contexts such as warnings, threats or refusals to go into detail (cf. the discussant's reaction to the politician's remark that the topic deserves a separate discussion: *Da, spasibo, čto drug druga ponimaem. No publično diskutirovat' ne stoit, osobenno zdes'. Takovy realii* – [Yes, I'm glad we understand each other. However, we should not discuss it publicly, especially here. This is reality], online chat with A. Kozlov, 27.08.10).

Besides, members' concerns with impression management become obvious though their post-interaction weaving comments in which they summarise their interactional gains – the number of questions answered by the guest and possible reasons of being ignored, as (13) shows:

(13) Madamimadam: […] But I think he simply thinks we're dyed-in-the-wool lefties (which I'm not). Or he wouldn't trot out such facile, supercilious answers. […] My confidence in the coalition has just rocketed after this…
(Mumsnet Live Webchat with Ed Vaizey, Minister for Culture, Communications and Creative Industries, 31.01.11)

As for moderators' follow-up moves, they are employed in live webchats to manage conversational flows, harmonise communication and make sure that rules are observed by all the participants. One specific task moderators of busy webchats have to handle on a regular basis is to curb users' frustration about not getting answers to their questions. Successful moderation in this case means preventing members from posting the same question many times and defending politicians from users' aggressive comments. Compare the moderator's justificatory and consolatory reactions (JustineMumsnet) to the chain of three follow-ups from the same user (Masserrato) in (14):

(14) Masserrato 14:29:29: Did you tell Ed that he will get a VERY bad name if he picks and chooses questions? […]
Masserrato 14:30:02: It looks as if he is seriously picking and choosing questions at the moment. […]
JustineMumsnet (MNHQ) 14:31:27: He has to pick by definition but he's just asked me what are the difficult ones, so again, please be patient! […]
Masserrato 14:31:36: Oh come on….you've jumped from the first question aeons ago and come to the last question. Sad. […]

> Masserrato 14:32:22: I would like to ask how Ed Milliband can stand in the House of Commons at question time and behave as if HIS party has nothing to do with the current crisis. I would like to see MPs agreeing on this issue and getting down to work together and at least pretending to support each other, instead of shouting at each other like hooligans. [...]
> JustineMumsnet (MNHQ) 14:34:24: Don't be sad, Masserrato, think Ed is answering your question right now 🙂.
> EdMiliband 14:35:36: Question Time is a terrible advert for politics. I take responsibility for some of the things we did wrong...
>
> (Mumsnet, Ed Miliband, Labour Leader and Leader of the Opposition, 01.12.2011)

One final note is due on the subject of humour and irony in metacommunicative follow-ups. Both users and politicians generally avoid humour/entertainment when doing the live question/answer sessions online. However, there seems to be considerable cross-cultural variation that becomes obvious through metacommunicative follow-ups.

In effect, not only Russian moderators but also Russian politicians and Russian users employ humour, irony and other techniques to express their stance and entertain. For instance, one Russian participant of a webchat changed his IP address *skuki radi* ('to get rid of boredom') in order to be able to ask his guest further questions. He made that strategy explicit in a metacommunicative follow-up, demonstrating, if not showing off, his digital competence; another Russian user imitated the guest's communicative style in a mock-serious follow-up comment in order to criticise the guest for having failed to address important issues; one Russian moderator employed a humorous formulation to ban a user from further webchat participation: '*vy otpravljaetes' v otpusk, do svidanija*' – 'You are going on holiday, goodbye.' The latter is hardly possible in the German or British data where moderators very seriously explain which transgressions cause the ban and remind the user about the importance of rules of online conduct.

As for British politicians and users, they also employ humour and irony in their metacommunicative follow-ups. For British politicians, the most frequently employed tactic seems to be using emoticons symbolising wink and offering follow-ups containing ironic gratitudes when responding to users' critical comments.

To sum up, being a guest of a live webchat is a challenging communicative activity involving many skills required to enact successfully in an oftentimes hostile communicative environment. Being confronted by multiple users pressing for answers within a limited timeframe, politicians participating in live webchats usually have fewer possibilities than audiences to perform follow-ups. Those instances when they do perform follow-ups reflect some important work-related tasks, such as stopping unwanted user behavior, defending themselves from unjust criticism, encouraging high-quality feedback from users.

6. Conclusion: Genre and cross-cultural peculiarities of follow-ups in online political discussions

In sum, the traditional definition of follow-up moves originating from the Exchange Theory needs to be modified to reflect some important contextual constraints of online political discussion in live webchats. In particular, it should reflect the presence of multiple participants eligible to generate follow-up moves, the possibility to comment on interactions occurring in other political and media online and offline genres, and the evaluative/non-evaluative dimension of conversational uptake.

As this study attemped to show, politicians' primary interactional needs are to address as many questions as possible and to identify with the audience, because their success online is frequently judged by the number of questions they address during the live webchat interaction ('more answers = more competence').

To this end, politicians attempt to shape political interaction by inserting evaluative follow-up moves in question-answer sequences or by providing evaluative follow-up moves after the question has been answered. Excellent performance is rewarded, underperformance is exposed and undesirable behaviour is stopped by way of evaluative metacommunicative follow-ups. As this study showed, endorsing comments seem to be employed by politicians sparingly as a tool to encourage a high level of interactional achievement on the part of the users.

However, evaluating others' communicative behaviour is not the only function of politicians' metacommunicative follow-ups in webchat political discussions. They can also be employed to manage impressions and ensure interactional harmony. For example, by explicating the reasons underlying particular communicative acts politicians try to ward off negative impressions audiences might develop on the basis of misconceptions or lack of information about politicians' true goals and motives. Such metacommunicative follow-ups may occur independently or in combination with criticism of questioner or denial of criticism, as was previously shown. In addition, metacommunicative follow-ups can be employed to improve the politician's or a user's comment, thus attending to face needs and contributing to interactional harmony. In addition, metacommunicative follow-ups serve to establish, boost and defend the politician's credibility.

On a lesser scale, metacommunicative follow-ups can serve to promote one's own coalition and to disparage the opponents.

As for audience's metacommunicative follow-ups, they are employed to hold politicians accountable, to manage impressions, and to discipline other users. The self-monitoring function of follow-ups is realised when webchat rules are violated and the online discussion is disrupted or when politician's time is spent inefficiently.

Moderators' follow-ups are employed in live webchats to manage conversational flows, harmonise communication and make sure that all the participants abide by the rules of online conducts. One specific task moderators of some aggressive webchats have to handle on a regular basis is to curb users' frustration about not getting answers to their questions.

It should also be noted that different follow-up moves have different chances of being addressed by the respondent. Asking follow-up questions in webchats often results in incomplete exchanges, because the politician is struggling with the influx of questions and comments from multiple participants and may overlook/ignore follow-up questions to address as many initial questions as possible.

In live webchats, cross-cultural differences become obvious if one pays attention to the differences in the format: British Mumsnet webchats are the liveliest – and the most aggressive – form of online discussion in comparison with more heavily controlled German webchats and with usually less densely populated but very active Russian synchronous discussions.

Cross-cultural differences along the lines presented here can be analysed on several levels, mostly: politicians' and users' perceptions of the usefullness of the genre and awareness of its constraints and the relevance of specific tactics to achieve one's communicative goals.

Metacommunicative follow-ups have been found to illuminate some important work-related attitudes that would remain implicit without a cross-cultural comparison of such follow-ups. For British and German politicians, webchat interactions develop in agreement with some general rules of politician-constituency interaction according to which no doubts about one's work are generally allowed. For Russian politicians and audiences, policial webchats as a marginal genre of political deliberation are to be treated differently from mainstream genres of political discourse. Applying the rules of offline discussion to the emerging online genre could be perceived as lack of flexibility and failure to understand the norms of netiquette.

My analysis of metacommunicative follow-ups in the three communicative cultures under study suggests that Russian webchat participants – both politicians and members of webchat audiences – are extremely aware of the limitations of this newly emerging genre of political communication and behave online accordingly. They joke, use irony, entertain themselves and others, make optimisation suggestions on how to deal with technical issues online, frequently criticise each other and express doubts in the sustainability of webchats as a genre of political discussion. Although some users believe they can do politics and influence decision-makers by way of challenging politicians during online political webchat sessions, both Russian politicians and Russian webchat audiences also try to build rapport, maintain good relationships online and attend to face wants (e.g. politicians help users save face, users grant politicians concessions as regards quality of forthcoming replies and follow-ups).

As for British webchat participants, they seem to focus primarily on ensuring that the politicians address their questions and that underperformance is exposed accordingly (e.g. complaints about party friends' performance in webchat sessions or elsewhere). At the same time, British webchat users represent the most sceptical group as regards estimations of efficiency of webchat sessions with politicians (e.g. abundant negative weaving comments). As for British politicians, in contrast to their Russian counterparts they never question the role of webchats as a form of online dialogue with citizens and seem to view them as yet another challenge to tackle as part of their communicative agendas.

Although German political webchats currently belong to marginal genres of political communication, German participants of webchat sessions demonstrate the most serious attitude towards this emerging genre. In effect, neither guests nor users complain about genre constraints.

In addition, several other peculiarities deserve mentioning. Negative interdiscursive follow-ups that contain sequences of complaints and requests to punish underperformance in other genres of political discourse occur the most frequently in the British subset of webchat data.

More manifestations of the arrogance of power were found in the Russian webchat data than in the German data (7 instances vs. 1): politicians sometimes dictated to other discussants how to behave verbally (although they were also being dictated to, as is more frequent in the British and German data).

Besides, an idiosyncratic attitude to the concept of publicity emerges from some of the Russian metacommunicative observations found both in blogs and webchats, with the concept being occasionally used in negative contexts such as warnings, threats, and refusals to go into detail.

In sum, follow-up moves are indispensable for high-quality online political discussions as an efficient way of conversational uptake.

References

Bull, Peter, Anita Fetzer and Marjut Johansson. 2008. "Prologue: Analyzing the Fine Details of Political Commitment." *Journal of Language and Social Psychology* 27 (4): 324–332. DOI: 10.1177/0261927X08322474

Bull, Peter and Kate Mayer. 1993. "How Not to Answer Questions in Political Interviews." *Political Psychology* 14: 651–666. DOI: 10.2307/3791379

Bull, Peter. 2003. *The Microanalysis of Political Communication. Claptrap and Ambiguity*. London: Routledge.

Coulthard, Malcolm and David Brazil. 1992. "Exchange structure." In *Advances in Spoken Discourse Analysis*, ed. by Malcolm Coulthard, 50–78. London, New York: Routledge.

Cullen, Richard. 2002. "Supportive Teacher Talk: The Importance of the F-Move." *ELT Journal*, 56 (2):117–127. DOI: 10.1093/elt/56.2.117

Döpke, Susanne. 1992. *One Parent, One Language: An Interactional Approach.* Amsterdam/ Philadelphia: John Benjamins. DOI: 10.1075/sibil.3

Fetzer, Anita, Elda Weizman and Elisabeth Reber (eds). 2012. *Proceedings of the ESF Strategic Workshop on Follow-ups Across Discourse Domains: A Cross-Cultural Exploration of Their Forms and Functions, Würzburg (Germany), 31 May - 2 June 2012.* Würzburg: Universität Würzburg, 2012. – [online]. URL: http://opus.bibliothek.uni-wuerzburg.de/volltexte/2012/7165/; URN: urn:nbn:de:bvb:20-opus-71656.

Fetzer, Anita and Elda Weizman. "Following Up across Contexts and Discourse Domains: Introduction." This volume.

Francis, Gill, and Susan Hunston. 1992. "Analysing Everyday Conversation." In *Advances in Spoken Discourse Analysis,* ed. by Malcolm Coulthard, 123–61. London, New York: Routledge.

Hatter, Jeffrey Mark. 2002. *The Application of Exchange Theory to Internet Relay Chat.* MA dissertation, supervisor: Dr. Susan Hunston. Birmingham: Centre for English Language Studies.

Kneser, C., R. Pilkington and T. Treasure-Jones. 2001. "The Tutor's Role: An Investigation of the Power of the Exchange Structure Analysis to Identify Different Roles in CMC Seminars." *International Journal of Artificial Intelligence in Education* 12: 63–84.

Ling, Lim Hwee. 2006. Constructing Learning Conversations: A Study of the Discourse and Learner Experiences of Online Synchronous Discussions. PhD thesis, Murdoch University.

McCarthy, Michael. 1991. *Discourse Analysis for Language Teachers.* Cambridge: Cambridge University Press.

Sinclair, John, and Malcolm Coulthard. 1975. *Towards an Analysis of Discourse.* Oxford: Oxford University Press.

Stubbs, Michael. 1983. *Discourse Analysis: The Sociolinguistic Analysis of Natural Language.* Oxford: Blackwell.

PART III

Follow-ups across speech events

Framing the Queen's head scarf

A case study on follow-ups in Dutch politics

Titus Ensink
University of Groningen, the Netherlands

In this chapter, follow-ups in political communication are conceived in a broad sense, as any more or less systematic consequence of or result from previous politically relevant communicative utterances and events, mostly implying an evaluation of the previous act. Since political communication by its very nature aims at influencing the electorate, follow-ups in general will pursue this goal. An important technique for influencing the public is *framing*. A frame embodies a particular view on a specific topic, and entails an evaluation. The success of a frame hinges on its continual repetition, so as to make them part of tacit background knowledge among the public. Politicians must use attention attracting devices in their communication to invoke and establish a certain frame, and to contest competing frames. In this contribution a specific case from Dutch politics will be analyzed, exemplifying this approach: Queen Beatrix wore a head scarf during a visit to a mosque. Dutch politicians and media reacted to her dress from within either of two competing frames: either giving in to an oppressive religion or ideology, or being polite by complying with the host's values. Politicians react almost exclusively to support their favorite frame.

1. Introduction

There is much more political communication than political history. Each day both politicians and citizens, speak and write in and through the media, about numerous political issues, without all these forms of communication having an immediately noticeable impact on the formation of policies, on decision-making or on creating legislation. Yet it is not likely that all these politically motivated utterances would be futile, or would have no consequences at all. It is fair to assume that these utterances serve primarily a function of political representation and image formation. The central question of this chapter is, how this function of political communication is realized. In Sections 2 and 3 I will argue that most political

DOI 10.1075/dapsac.60.06ens

statements which are made in response to each other (so as to create a series of follow-ups in a broad sense) have these image forming effects among the electorate as their main motive. The description of these effects may be based on the concept *framing*: political communication both invokes and reinforces a specific way of considering issues. The framework thus outlined will be demonstrated in an exemplary case study in Section 4.

2. Follow-ups in political communication

2.1 Follow-ups in a narrow and in a broad sense

Follow-ups in political communication may be conceived in a narrow and in a broad sense. In a narrow sense, follow-ups are conceived as the third turn in an interactional sequence *IRF*:

A: *I*nitiative,
B: *R*eaction,
A: *F*ollow-up on B's reaction.

The follow-up brings the sequence to a close, in general by evaluating B's reaction. This IRF-pattern has been identified in educational discourse where a teacher evaluates the pupil's answer (Mehan 1979, 52–53; Sinclair and Coulthard 1975, 48–49) and in interview discourse where the interviewer evaluates or acknowledges the interviewee's answer (Houtkoop-Steenstra 2000, 24–29). The IRF-sequence is alternatively sometimes referred to as *OAF*: Opening – Answering – Follow-up. In political communication, we might distinguish different types of sequences and concomitant follow-ups in different forms of political communication such as negotiations, parliamentary debates, or media interviews. Follow-ups in the narrow sense are restricted to forms of direct interaction between political actors.

In a broad sense, however, follow-ups of political communication may be seen as any more or less systematic consequence of or result from previous communicative utterances and events. Political communication occurs among many different actors who react to other actions whenever they deem a reaction appropriate. These reactions may occur in different situations, where actors in most cases are not co-present. These follow-ups thus do not belong to an interactional sequence in the strict sense, but they consist of any political communicative actions that are triggered by previous actions and that are seen as a reaction to them. These follow-ups should not be seen as an interactional reaction, but as a reaction made with a view to the general public, trying to influence public opinion. Follow-ups in a broad sense also imply an evaluation of the previous communicative act.

In this chapter, I will develop a framework for the description of follow-ups in this broad sense. This description should be linked to the different political actors and institutions, and their mutual relations. The political process encompasses the formation of power, exertion of power, policy making and decision making with respect to all relevant social issues, so as to resolve existing clashes of interest and warrant the continuation of the community. A wide variety of political actors is active in this process. Hence, follow-ups in political communication should be distinguished according to which participants are involved at the following levels:

1. The political leaders active in the central organizations and institutions of the state: the head of state, the government, members of parliament, leaders of political parties, et cetera. These have the power and authority to adopt policies and have them implemented.
2. The institutions that are politically active by virtue of their institutional mission: advisors and spin doctors, the civil service, lobby groups, leading economic players, (journalistic) media, et cetera. These institutions try to influence the processes at the first level on the one hand, and to make the political process known on the third level, on the other.
3. The civilian population, the electorate, the people, the public, or whatever term we want to use. In a principled democratic interpretation the electorate is the basis of sovereignty. In a cynical interpretation the electorate is what must be manipulated so as to secure political power and influence.

2.2 The network of political actors

The distinction of these three levels is necessary to describe follow-ups in political communication, because possible follow-ups show significant differences per level.

1. Follow-ups that occur on only the first level have the character of and can be described as more or less normal patterns of verbal interaction, where pragmatic rules as stated for speech acts and their associated perlocutionary effects remain valid. To a large extent, the Gricean cooperative principle may be assumed to be valid here. These remarks apply to e.g. discussions and negotiations between leading politicians, and to questions and answers between government and parliament, and so on. Political communication on the first level should be distinguished into two main categories, dependent on whether the communication is publicly visible. Many deliberations and negotiations among leading political actors are confidential and secret. On the other hand, many relevant forms of communication at this level are made directly visible to the general public. For instance, important parliamentary

debates can be followed directly on TV or via streaming video. The result is that – apart from face-to-face communication between representatives in the state's institutions – political communication patterns are strongly focused on the general public. When publicly speaking to a fellow politician, a politician performs a show for the public. And most politicians pay rather more attention to effects on the public than to effects on their fellow politicians.

2. On the second level, communication takes place again via normal interaction patterns: A spokesman at a press conference answers questions, a lobbyist tries to get into conversation with a politician. But communication on this level also aims at informing the public, at the same time creating and establishing certain images. Informing and creating images are different approaches with different goals, but in practice they are inextricably linked.
3. The civilian population is the most passive political actor on the one hand, on the other it is (at least in theory) the most important and powerful. Politics takes place both *on behalf of* and *under* the people. Politics is legitimized by elections, where 'the voter speaks'. But the voter 'speaks' only once every 4 years, and then that vote is a simple expression in favor of only one party or person. Many forms of political communication take place with a view to winning the vote for that one moment, in virtual or imagined elections. Yet the third level is not as passive as the official constitutional function of the electorate suggests. The electorate is permanently gauged through polls, and we are able to hear many expressions of the electorate in the media, such as citizen initiatives, blogs, internet initiatives, letters to media, approaches of lobby groups, et cetera. Individuals and institutions at levels 1 and 2 may show themselves to be susceptible for those expressions (see also Entman 2003, 419).

The levels outlined here with actors and their relationships can be summarized schematically as in Figure 1.

On the *national* level the Government (1) and Head of State (2) are the state's highest institutions. In most democratic states, these are controlled by a Lower House (3) and an Upper House (4). On the *international* level, political actions of and within states also influence, and are influenced by neighboring countries (5) and international organizations and associations (6).

The institutions of the state are advised by numerous economic, legal, environmental, statistical and other policy bodies and advisory organizations (8). These institutions are also approached by all kinds of interest groups and lobby groups (9), although on a less institutionalized and often unsolicited basis.

The media (7) take a special place in this scheme (visualized in the thick arrow in Figure 1). The media are the 'servants' of the public. Ideally, their mission is serious: to be informative and critical on behalf of the public. On the other hand, they

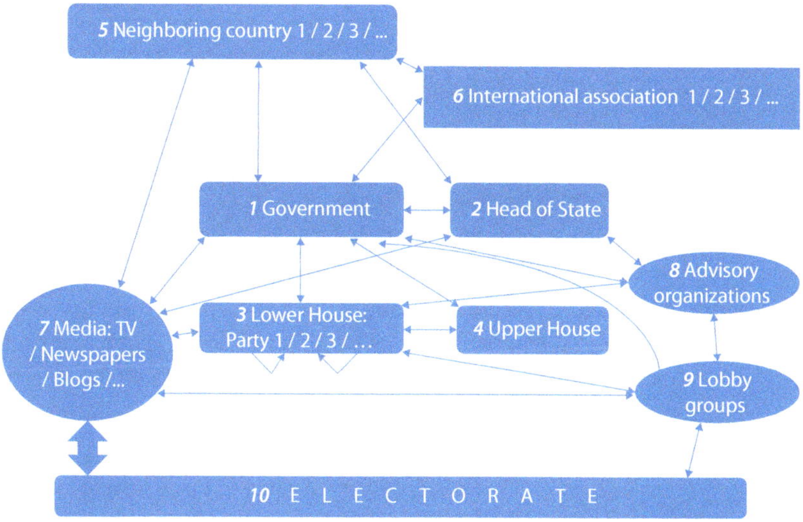

Figure 1. Network of political communicative relations

act as independent actors with their own agendas and missions, and in most cases media act as commercial organizations. As a result, media may act in cahoots with those in power if this fits their interests. Media developments of recent decades (especially the heavy emphasis on marketing and 'entertainmentisation') also led to a different mission: to score quickly, to find and make scoops, and to use politics as a means to generate media attention.

Finally, there is the electorate or the public (10). This is the most elusive and diffuse entity of the 10 actors/institutions contained in Figure 1. Nonetheless the electorate is the decisive actor, given the ultimate power of the people's vote. In comparison to the aforementioned actors (1–9), the electorate may be considered the most passive, but that is only partly true. The electorate is also able to express and organize themselves, in letters to newspapers, internet discussion lists, civil initiatives, pressure through lobby groups, and so on.

Between the institutions and actors there are a number of connecting lines through which various forms of communications take place: these connecting relations are expressed in Figure 1 by the many arrows. Note that in many cases there is 'two-way traffic' in the mutual relations. Obviously, not every form or act of communication may occur within any relationship. And therefore not any type of follow-up may take place within any type of relationship. But within each relationship symbolized by an arrow follow-ups are possible, and occur frequently.

Follow-ups in political communication must be characterized in terms of the relations of Figure 1. First, virtually everyone who is dealing with politics and political communication bears the scheme outlined in Figure 1 (or at least a similar one) in mind. Figure 1 makes it clear that 'politics' is not merely a matter of politicians or the political elite, but that this elite is in many ways connected to and both influences and is influenced by other people and institutions. On each arrow in this diagram communication takes place, which means that on each arrow in this diagram potentially relevant consequences ('follow-ups') can be found.

Second, from any political issue about which political communication takes place a timeline may be established showing which actors acted and reacted successively. It is important to identify the origin of the communication process: many forms of political communication are part of a semi-permanent process that has a barely identifiable starting point. In many cases of political communication most actors or institutions in the network (Figure 1) become active. Their actions and reactions should also be specified in discourse types. Among politicians, the dominant discourse types are debate, negotiation, and consultation. In the media, dominant discourse types are reporting, commenting, and evaluating, whereas we may find sometimes parody or satire. Between politicians and media representatives the dominant discourse type is the interview.

Third, whereas political communication aims at policy and decision making and the exertion of power, it is at the same time aimed at permanently influencing the public, because the legitimization of politics should be derived from and based on the public's consent. In this context, Erving Goffman's (1981) concept *footing* is relevant: although the electorate is seldom the direct addressee of political communication (Atkinson 1984), the public is nonetheless always a quasi-ratified bystander, as is often demonstrated in the analysis of political interviews (e.g. Clayman 1990). One of the consequences of the more or less explicit focus on the electorate is the sound-bite culture (Atkinson 1984, Chapter 5), particularly in the media representation of political communication. Quoting is a key technique in this representation (Waugh 1995). Political communication should also be seen in terms of the *front* and *back* (Goffman 1969, 32 ff) of communicative behavior.In Section 3, I discuss an important aspect of this permanent focus on influencing the public.

3. Framing

For the description of how intended images are created and established among the public, I propose to use two theoretical starting points (to be elaborated in 3.1 and 3.2), both of which relate to the core concept of *framing*. No person, object, event, or action is ever perceived in isolation. Any person (or object, or event) is perceived in context, within a network of meaningful relations specifying that person's (object's, event's) nature, role, goal, possibilities, and membership-relations. A *frame* is a mental structure specifying those meaningful relations. Consider the following simple but clear example.

If someone is asked: 'what do you see here?', then the most obvious answer would be:

Figure 2a. A running man (Bransford and McCarrell 1977, 378)

> 'In Figure 2a I see a man running, judging from his appearance probably an American football player who tries to catch the ball.' (Why is the man running? To catch the ball.)

Figure 2b. A running man (Bransford and McCarrell 1977, 378)

> 'In (b) I see a man chasing a woman, or else a woman who flees from the man.' (Why is the man running? To catch the woman.)

Figure 2c. A running man (Bransford and McCarrell 1977, 378)

> 'In (c) I see a man and a woman both fleeing from the lion.' (Why is the man running? To escape the lion.)

The point of this example lies in the fact that the drawing of the man in the three cases (a)–(c) is the same: the outer appearance of the man does not change. Only the relationship of the man with his environment changes, as a result of which the perception changes of the role the man plays: the running man performs different activities and pursues different purposes related to those activities in the three cases (a)–(c). Bransford and McCarrell (1977, 378) present figures (a)–(c) in order to illustrate '*object perception as a function or its role in events*'. Note that these perceptions are mutually exclusive: the running man is *either* involved in sports *or* chasing a woman *or* fleeing from a lion, but none of these at the same time. Note furthermore that this process works almost involuntarily: you choose from the available knowledge telling the world around you the most plausible form of knowledge to explain what you see, and from that moment on you see it that way. This is the essence of *framing*: to put an object into a preexisting cognitive structure: 'Frames are mental structures that shape the way we see the world' (Lakoff 2004, xv).

Frames are often conceived in a static and descriptive manner. That is, the concept is used for the description of all kinds of perception. Frames present a format for perceptions, even partial ones (Kuipers 1975; Ensink and Sauer 2003). The structure of the frame allows one to immediately recognize some object or event as what we think it is.

> One of the major results in the cognitive and brain sciences is that we think in terms of typically unconscious structures called 'frames' (sometimes 'schemas'). Frames include semantic roles, relations between roles, and relations to other frames. A hospital frame, for example, includes the roles: Doctor, Nurse, Patient, Visitor, Receptionist, Operating Room, Recovery Room, Scalpel, etc. Among the relations are specifications of what happens in a hospital, e.g., Doctors operate on Patients in Operating Rooms with Scalpels. These structures are physically realized in neural circuits in the brain. All of our knowledge makes use of frames, and every word is defined through the frames it neurally activates. All thinking and talking involves 'framing.' And since frames come in systems, a single word typically activates not only its defining frame, but also much of the system its defining frame is in. (Lakoff 2010, 71–72)

Between the perception of an event (an object, an acting person, and so on) and a cognitive frame there are two directions of influence. First, when confronted with an event one searches for a plausible frame in order to reach a plausible interpretation. But it is also possible, secondly, that a certain frame is already activated, forcing the perception of an event into that frame's pre-existing structure. Both directions play a role in political communication.

3.1 Frames as a structure, framing as a process

During the past few years, the concept framing has become increasingly popular in the analysis of political discourse and of media representations, mainly due to the (cognitive linguistically inspired) work of George Lakoff. The basic idea of 'frame' – there is a structure that makes even disparate observations meaningful – may be used *strategically* in political communication. Lakoff (2004, 2010) has pointed out the dynamic potential of framing. Although the premise is that frames act as unconsciously presupposed structures, you can also actively influence perception through such a structure. The audience doesn't see (political) facts, the audience sees specific presentations (i.e. *framings*) of facts. It makes no sense – if one does not condone the frame – to deny the frame because even the denial invokes the frame. (Compare e.g. the idea embodied in the title of Lakoff's book 'Don't think of an elephant': even the negation of a framing reinforces it, just as Nixon discovered when he said on television 'I am not a crook'. Or consider Marc Anthony's famous although fictitious political speech in Shakespeare's *Julius Caesar* describing Brutus as 'an honorable man', but *framing* him as the traitor who killed the really honorable Caesar: each time Brutus is mentioned as being honorable, the audience considers him as less honorable.) The intended structure is invoked, and repeated many times, both by the frame supporter and by anyone discussing with or reporting on the frame supporter. Frames thus derive their effectiveness from continual repetition: the success of a frame hinges on the repetition also by others:

> … one cannot avoid framing. The only question is, whose frames are being activated – and hence strengthened – in the brains of the public. (Lakoff 2010, 72)

Political propaganda is, considered from this point of view, in fact a matter of frame manipulation.

3.2 Media frames

The operation of frames in politics can be described by supplementing the role of frames in the media process. An overall diagram of frames in the media process is proposed by de Vreese 2003 and 2005 (Figure 3):

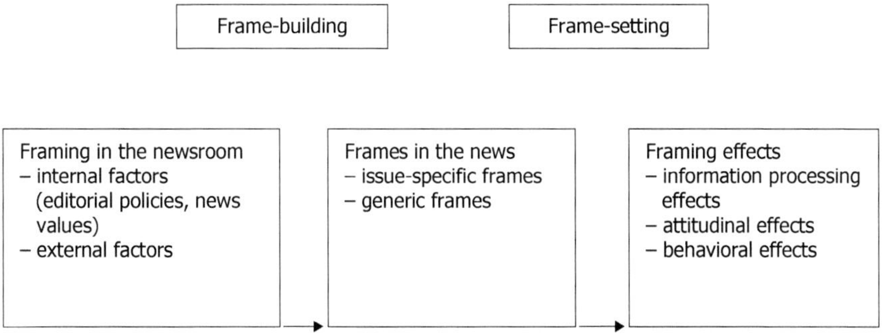

Figure 3. An integrated process model of framing (de Vreese 2003, 42 and 2005, 52)

A brief explanation of the key terms in this model, in the words of de Vreese (2005) himself:

> *Frame-building* refers to the factors that influence the structural qualities of news frames. Factors internal to journalism determine how journalists and news organizations frame issues (…). Equally important, however, are factors external to journalism. The frame-building process takes place in a continuous interaction between journalists and elites (…) and social movements (…). The outcomes of the frame building process are the frames manifest in the text. (2005, 52)
>
> *Frame-setting* refers to the interaction between media frames and individuals' prior knowledge and predispositions. Frames in the news may affect learning, interpretation, and evaluation of issues and events. This part of the framing process has been investigated most elaborately, often with the goal to explore the extent to which and under what circumstances audiences reflect and mirror frames made available to them in, for example, the news. The *consequences* of framing can be conceived on the individual and the societal level. An individual level consequence may be altered attitudes about an issue based on exposure to certain frames. On the societal level, frames may contribute to shaping social level processes such as political socialization, decision-making, and collective actions. (2005, 52) [all Italics in original]

Frame setting is described by Entman (2003, 418–423) in terms of *spreading activation* or *cascading activation*. Entman uses this concept derived from the literature on cognition as a metaphor for societal communicative processes: "The spreading activation of thoughts or 'nodes' within an individual's mind (…) has parallels in the way ideas travel along interpersonal networks and in the spread of framing words and images across the different media." (2003, 418) This idea is elaborated in a model of information 'cascading' down society, from the administration to other elites to the media, resulting in frames cascading down into the public. Entman points out, however, that there is also an opposite direction (cascading upward, so to speak), in the sense that ideas which appear in public opinion may influence, through media utterances, elites and ultimately the administration.

The ultimate goal of political communication is in the rightmost box of Figure 2: *framing effects* (cognitive, attitudinal and behavioral). It should be clear that the framing processes described in 3.1 should also be placed here. Politicians themselves (certainly the most successful ones) actively perform the first part of the process: *frame building*. The basic idea is that one should try to repeat a desired image (frame) as often as possible and possibly have it repeated also by others (in discussion, in quotation) to get it established in the process of *frame setting*. When this succeeds, a socially dominant image has been established. An image, once established, often becomes so to speak fact-free: people do not perceive facts but immediately use the pre-established image.

Entman (2003, 418) points out that frame building may lead to the dominance of one specific frame (often the one sponsored by the administration), but that the presence of the free press also may lead to frame parity, where the sponsored frame is contested by a counterframe "that puts together a completely alternative narrative, a tale of problem, cause, remedy, and moral judgment possessing as much magnitude and resonance (…)."

4. A case study: The Queen's hat-and-scarf

In Section 2 I offered a framework for the description of follow-ups (in a broad sense) in political communication, and in Section 3 I described the effects of framing. I will now combine both perspectives in the analysis of a single case which occurred in the context of Dutch politics. The case consists of a number of subsequent actions and reactions by a number of different actors, eighteen of which will be discussed here. In the chosen case there is not a specific policy decision under discussion. The case is rather determined by the fact that it starts with a communicative act that might have very well be ignored, without anyone reacting on it, in terms of its relevance for policy making. Yet the opposite happens: apparently the very first utterance contains something that makes it relevant for politically motivated communication. What is the relevance, and from where do subsequent follow-ups derive their relevance? That is the guiding question for the following analysis.

The method to be applied is as follows. In 4.1 a description of the subsequent communicative acts is provided, by showing how different relevant political actors react to the first incident and to one another. The description results in a chronological reconstruction, on the basis of which it is shown which actors from the network of political communication play a role. Subsequently, based on this description, in 4.2 the following questions are addressed: (1) which frames are dominant in the different reactions? (2) which political actors reinforce which frame in their reactions? (3) are there noticeable effects on the process of frame setting?

4.1 Description

#1.[1] In January 2012 the Dutch queen, Beatrix, brought a state visit to the United Arab Emirates. (Obviously this state visit itself was the result of prior agreements between governments or Heads of State of the Netherlands and the UAE, but what

1. Numbering in the form of #n represents the chronological order of events in the chain of subsequent communicative acts.

preceded the visit is irrelevant for the description of the case.) The program of the state visit also included a visit to the mosque of Abu Dhabi. During this visit, she was wearing a blue scarf on top of her hat (see Figure 4):

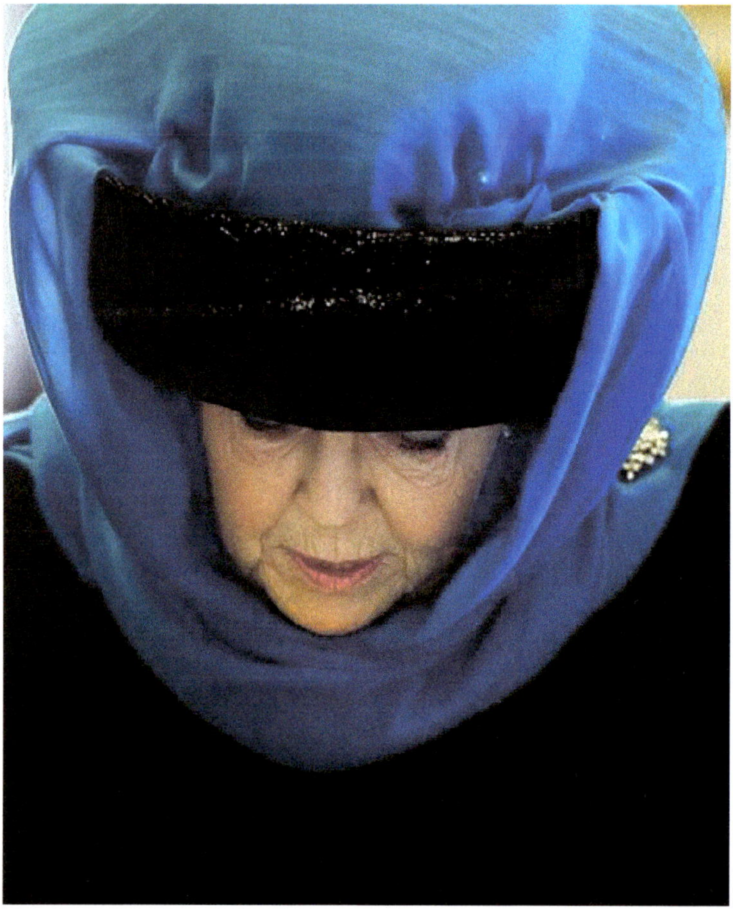

Figure 4. Dutch Queen Beatrix in Abu Dhabi, 8 January 2012

In general, the way a politician (or a person with an official function) is dressed is a matter of background perception. Although clothes do have a communicative function, this function most often is *ground* and only seldom *figure* (expressed in the well-known terminology of Gestalt Psychology).

How was the way she dressed perceived? Which follow-ups did take place as a reaction on her hat-and-scarf? How did the perceptions influence the nature of the series of subsequent reactions?

In other situations, these clothes might be perceived as some whim of fashion. Or, considering the fact that this fashion is worn by a royal person, it might be considered a variation or modernization of a crown. But the Dutch queen wore these clothes during her visit to a mosque, giving a specific meaning to her scarf: does this specific circumstance invoke a perception on the basis of a specific frame?

#2. Several Dutch media (newspapers, television stations) report about the Queen's visit to the mosque, in the first instance on their websites, on Sunday 12 January 2012, at about 9 a.m. An example of such a message is (1):

(1) **Beatrix draagt hoofddoek voor moskeebezoek Abu Dhabi**
zondag 8 januari 2012 10:16
Koningin Beatrix, kroonprins Willem-Alexander en prinses Máxima bezoeken zondag in het emiraat Abu Dhabi de Sjeik Zayed bin Sultan Al Nahayan-moskee. Voor het bezoek zijn Koningin Beatrix en prinses Máxima volgens moslimgebruik van top tot teen bedekt.
De Koningin droeg een abaya, een lang zwart alles verhullend gewaad en een blauwe hoofddoek. Prinses Máxima droeg een lange jurk met een hoofddoek.[2]

Beatrix wears headscarf for mosque visit Abu Dhabi
Sunday, 8 January 2012 10:16
Queen Beatrix, Prince Willem-Alexander and Princess Maxima visit the Sheikh Zayed bin Sultan Al Nahayan Mosque in the Emirate of Abu Dhabi on Sunday. For the visit Queen Beatrix and Princess Máxima were covered from head to toe according to Muslim usage.
The Queen wore an abaya, a long black robe veiling everything and a blue veil. Princess Máxima wore a long dress with a scarf.

Of course, her visit is reported on in later television news broadcasts, and in newspaper publications. Most of the (printed) newspaper publications, however, appeared one day later, on Monday 9 January, since Dutch newspapers do not have a Sunday edition.

#3. The dress chosen by the queen is clearly an adaptation to dress codes in the Islamic world, with respect to women, especially during a visit to a mosque. As such, the clothing of the queen has communicative value. How the hosts of the

2. http://www.elsevier.nl/web/Nieuws/Nederland/327143/Beatrix-draagt-hoofddoek-voor-moskeebezoek-Abu-Dhabi.htm.

- The word 'abaya' contained a link to the English Wikipedia entry about abayas.
- The name 'Princess Máxima' contained a link to a biographical note about Máxima on Elsevier's own website.

All URLs quoted in this paper have been accessed in October 2012.

queen, or the inhabitants of Abu Dhabi, perceived and evaluated her clothes would be a separate reaction (hence a follow-up), but that reaction is left out of consideration here.

#4. The leader of the Dutch left liberal party, *D66*, Alexander Pechtold, publishes the following message on *Twitter* (8 January 2012, 11.09):

(2) De Koningin naar een moskee? Heel NL zit trillend te wachten op reactie collega @geertwilderspvv ... Al wakker?
The Queen in a mosque? The Netherlands tremble and wait for Wilders's reaction ... Is he awake?

The interpretative background of this tweet is this. Given that, since the attacks on the Twin Towers on 11 September 2001, Islam is a permanent issue in Dutch politics, it is clear that the reported dress of the queen will be perceived and valued in that context. The Dutch politician who most clearly presents himself as anti-Islam is Geert Wilders (Ensink 2012a, 68). One of the most remarkable anti-Islam statements that Wilders has made is his proposal during a discussion in September 2009 in Dutch Parliament to introduce a *kopvoddentaks* 'head rag tax': a taxation on the wearing of head scarves by Islamic women (see Kuitenbrouwer 2010, 33–36 and 52; see also Ensink 2012a, 62). Wilders argued in favor of this proposal using the widely accepted argument in environmental policies that 'the polluter has to pay'. Pechtold is one of the toughest adversaries of Wilders in Dutch Parliament. Obviously, he is aware of the way the Queen's clothes may be seen from Wilders's perspective. In this tweet, Pechtold challenges Wilders, although not directly: Wilders is referred to in the third person, not directly addressed in the second person. Formulating the tweet this way makes clear that the challenge is meant to be noticed by the Dutch public in the first place.

#5. A popular Dutch weblog, *GeenStijl*,[3] puts a picture of Queen Beatrix, one of her hosts, her son, and her daughter-in-law (also wearing a long dress and a head scarf) on his website and asks the readers to post ironic or funny comments. Many internet users react to this call: the blog post contains 1075 reactions after a few days:

(3) Top die Kop!
Dinges, hare majesteit van GroenLinks, Wim-Lex & Máxima sightseeing in Abu Dhabi. Bedenk een kop en/of onderschrift. Of noem de mop waarom Wim-Lex moet lachen. Gaarne enige deftigheid betrachten. Dus niet zo vuil & vunzig als de heer @APechtold. Succes.

3. 'GeenStijl' means literally 'without style': tasteless, a bad way to behave. The dominant feature of the weblog is its anti-authoritarian, provocative and satirical approach of issues.

Update: Hopsakee. Daar zijn de **kamervragen** al.
Pritt Stift | 08-01-12 | 12:12 | Link | 1075 reacties |[4]

Fine that Headline!
Thingummy, her majesty of the GreenLeft, Wim-Lex & Máxima sightseeing in Abu Dhabi. Think up a headline and / or caption. Or tell the joke why Wim-Lex is laughing. Please exercise some dignity. Not so dirty and filthy as Mr @ APechtold. Success.
***Update**: Here we go. Here we have already the parliamentary questions.*

#6. Geert Wilders posts on 8 January 2012, 13.34, the following tweet:

(4) Wat heeft de Koningin te zoeken in moskee in Abu Dhabi? Met abaya en hoofddoek? Vragen met collegae vKlaveren/Elissen: bit.ly/x9PHG6
What's the Queen's business in a mosque in Abu Dhabi? With an abaya and a head scarf? Questions with colleagues vKlaveren/Elissen: bit.ly/x9PHG6

There is no sign in this tweet that Wilders reacts to Pechtold's challenge, as discussed in #4. Instead, Wilders refers to *vragen* 'questions', by offering a shortened URL (bitly). This link leads to the website of Wilders's party PVV, where some questions directed to the Dutch prime minister and to the Dutch minister of immigrations are formulated[5] (see #7).

#7. Dutch MPs have the right to ask (written) questions to Dutch government members, i.e. ministers and deputy ministers. These are obliged to answer within 3 weeks. The parliamentary questions and the answers by the government are part of the minutes of the Second Chamber. The three MPs of Wilders's PVV have formulated the following questions (5):

(5) Vragen van de leden Van Klaveren, Elissen en Wilders (allen PVV) aan de minister van Algemene Zaken en de minister van Immigratie, Integratie en Asiel over de islamitische hoofddoek van ons staatshoofd.

4. http://www.geenstijl.nl/mt/archieven/2012/01/top_die_kop_34.html
This blog post contained the following links:

- Abu Dhabi: link to an article about the Queen's visit on the website of Dutch national TV: http://nos.nl/koningshuis/artikel/328866-beatrix-naar-moskee-in-abu-dhabi.html;
- @APechtold: link to Pechtold's Twitter account, displaying the tweet discussed in #4: https://twitter.com/APechtold/status/155954148230184960;
- kamervragen: link to (x), showing the questions by three members of Wilders's PVV: http://www.geenstijl.nl/archives/images/kamervragenpvvbea.html

5. http://www.pvv.nl/index.php/component/content/article/71-joram-van-klaveren/5076-vragen-pvv-over-wanvertoning-in-abu-dhabi.html

1. Bent u bekend met het bericht 'Beatrix draagt hoofddoek voor moskeebezoek Abu Dhabi'(*Elsevier, 8 januari 2012)?
2. In hoeverre bent u het eens met de PVV dat de hoofddoek een symbool van islamisering, onderdrukking en discriminatie van de vrouw is?
3. En realiseert u zich dat ons staathoofd op deze wijze de onderdrukking van vrouwen legitimeert?
4. Had deze trieste wanvertoning niet voorkomen kunnen worden? Zo neen, waarom niet?

Questions by MPs Van Klaveren, Elissen and Wilders (all PVV) to the Minister of General Affairs and to the Minister of Immigration, Integration and Asylum on the Islamic headscarf of our head of state.

1. *Do you know the article (*Elsevier, 8 January 2012): 'Beatrix wears headscarf for mosque visit Abu Dhabi'?*
2. *Do you agree with PVV that the head scarf is a symbol of islamisation, suppression and discrimination of women?*
3. *Are you aware that our Head of State legitimizes the suppression of women in this way?*
4. *Could this sad failed performance not have been prevented? If not, why not?*

Of course, these questions have been sent to the ministers concerned through the appropriate channels, i.e. in written form and personally addressed. But at the same time these questions have been made public on the PVV's website, and Wilders drew the public's attention to them in his tweet.

The Prime Minister answers these 4 questions four days later, on 12 January, see #15.

#8. Later on during the day (8 January 2012), different media messages are published about the ongoing state visit and the reactions the state visit provokes. News sites update their messages or add new messages. Television news broadcasts report on the state visit, and show video footage of the queen during her visit.

As an example of media coverage the first newscast of Dutch national TV, *NOS*, at 12.00, is quoted here:

(6) Goeiemiddag. Koningin Beatrix is haar staatsbezoek aan de Verenigde Arabische Emiraten begonnen met een bezoek aan een moskee. De moskee in Abu Dhabi is een van de grootste ter wereld. De koningin, Prins Willem Alexander en Prinses Máxima kregen een rondleiding door onder meer het mausoleum en de bibliotheek van de moskee. De vrouwen in gepaste kleding, volgens de moslimtraditie van top tot teen bedekt.
Bij de moskee ligt Sheik Zayed begraven, de stichter van de Verenigde Emiraten. Het bezoek moet de relatie met de oliestaat verder verbeteren en vooral de Nederlandse handel een impuls geven. Morgen reist het gezelschap

> naar Dubai, en dinsdag naar Oman. Daar zou de koningin vorig jaar al langsgaan maar dat bezoek werd toen uitgesteld omdat het onrustig was in het land. Er werd gedemonstreerd tegen corruptie.
> Het bezoek aan de Emiraten is bijzonder, het is het 50e staatsbezoek van de koningin.[6]
>
> *Good afternoon. Queen Beatrix began her state visit to the United Arab Emirates with a visit to a mosque. The mosque in Abu Dhabi is one of the largest in the world. The queen, prince Willem Alexander and princess Máxima were given a tour including the mausoleum and the mosque's library. The women in appropriate clothing, according to Muslim tradition covered from head to toe.*
> *Near the mosque Sheik Zayed lies buried, the founder of the UAE. The visit is meant to improve the relationship with the oil state and to boost Dutch trade. Tomorrow the group travels to Dubai, and on Tuesday to Oman. The queen intended to visit Oman last year but that visit was then postponed because there was unrest in the country. There were demonstrations against corruption.*
> *The visit to the Emirates is special, it is the 50th state visit of the queen.*

The same item is repeated during the newscasts at 16.00 and 18.00,[7] with, however, one subtle difference. The sentence 'De vrouwen in gepaste kleding, volgens de moslimtraditie van top tot teen bedekt' *The women in appropriate clothing, according to Muslim tradition covered from head to toe* has been changed into 'De vrouwen in aangepaste kledij, volgens de moslimtraditie helemaal bedekt' *The women in adapted clothing, according to Muslim tradition completely covered.* At the end of this item in the newscast at 16.00 two additional pieces of information were added: Wilders's PVV considers the visit a failed performance because the head scarf is a symbol of suppression of women; for that reason, the political party has announced parliamentary questions. Furthermore, the RVD (the Dutch Information Service) has announced that the queen showed respect for the habits of the country she visits.

During the newscast of 20.00,[8] there has been a major change of wording. The broadcast opens with the short headline: 'Staatsbezoek koningin leidt tot kamervragen' *The queen's state visit leads to parliamentary questions.* The news item starts from a general point of view: the Dutch want to do business, but relations are sensitive. Only then the visit to the mosque is mentioned. After providing this information, the news anchor interviews a reporter on the spot. He

6. http://nos.nl/uitzending/55402-nos-journaal-1200-uur.html [00:04 – 00:59]

7. http://nos.nl/uitzending/55408-nos-journaal-1600-uur.html [00:05 – 01:28] and http://nos.nl/uitzending/55414-nos-journaal-1800-uur.html [01:08 – 02:27]

8. http://nos.nl/uitzending/55426-nos-journaal-2000-uur.html [00:28 – 04:30]

asks her whether the protests against the queen's clothing have been noticed in Abu Dhabi. The reporter answers that she also, as well as all tourists, wears these clothes. Subsequently, a short interview is inserted with the Minister of Foreign Affairs. He stresses the fact that the queen visited a place of religious worship: when visiting Jewish or Christian places of worship, she would adapt accordingly to prevailing prescriptions and rituals. The minister answers furthermore that the queen could have considered not to go to the mosque, but that, after the decision to go there, she could not consider anymore not to adapt her way of dressing. The reporter on the spot finally says that she has the impression that the reaction in the Netherlands has no influence on the atmosphere of the mission. The nature of the state visit as supporting business relations is finally once more stressed.

#9. On 8 and 9 January, many political actors, both MPs and government members, present their views on the issue. Most of the times, they are asked by media representatives. Several newspapers publish articles which consist of an enumeration of these reactions. A typical example is a two-page article in the Dutch newspaper *NRC Handelsblad*, published on Monday 9 January 2012. The headline of the article is: 'Links én rechts genieten van 'hoofddoekjesdag'' *Both left and right enjoy 'head scarf day'*. The newspaper article describes the development of the discussion in the Netherlands of the past one and a half days about the queen's head scarf. Next to this article, a photo is printed showing the queen in her controversial clothing, in the company of a number of sheiks and members of her entourage. Furthermore, the article discusses three themes in separate text boxes. First, the difficult relationship between the queen and PVV. Second, a comparison of clothing prescriptions in Islam, Christianity, and Judaism. Third, the comments by seven persons on this issue are presented: a Muslim entrepreneur, the editor-in-chief of a feminist magazine, a female Muslim politician from Amsterdam, a spokesman of the Netherlands Government Information Service, Alexander Pechtold's tweet (see #4), the editor-in-chief of a royalty magazine, and a rabbi.

#10. Most of the news sites reporting about the unfolding political discussion offer opportunities for internet users to react. Many readers use these opportunity. To give three examples:

- The news article on the website of the news magazine *Elsevier* quoted in (1)[9] shows 90 reactions, the great majority of them posted on 8 January 2012.
- The website of the Dutch newspaper *AD* ('Algemeen Dagblad' *General Daily Newspaper*) reports on 8 January 2012, 16.06, that PVV is going to ask parliamentary questions (quoted in (5)), and on the same day at 22.42 that the

9. See footnote 1.

> Dutch minister of foreign affairs, Rosenthal, defended the queen's clothing, saying the she acted out of respect for the habits, tradition and conventions of Islam.[10] Within two days, 185 reactions to the first report are posted, whereas the second report provokes 140 reactions.

Most of the posters of these reactions use an alias or nickname. As is most often the case in internet discussion lists (Ensink 2012b), these lists do not show any interactional coherence. Posters present their own opinions in their own right. The points of view that are expressed with some frequency in these lists are:

- Islam is degrading to women, hence it is a shame that the queen gave in.
- When Muslims come to the West they do not adapt to *our* customs whereas they expect us to do so when we visit Arab countries.
- It is time for the Netherlands to become a republic.
- It is all a matter of doing business.
- We also have to adapt to the demands of other religions.
- The queen was just right to show some respect.

#11. A popular Dutch television talk show, 'De wereld draait door' *The world keeps turning,*[11] has the habit of closing its daily programme with a short video clip, called 'Lucky TV', in which a parody or satire of some news item is presented. On 9 January, the clip starts by mentioning the fuss about the queen's head scarf, and its justification by the Government Information Service that it shows respect to the host's habits. To prove that this is the queen's normal routine, the Service 'shows' some pictures taken during the queen's recent visit to a Papua community in New Guinea. 'De majesteit draagt een traditionele tooi' *Her Majesty is dressed traditionally* the voice over comments, showing a nude woman among some equally nude Papuans; the queen's head is pasted on the nude woman's body. Subsequently, Prince Willem Alexander is shown, wearing a penis sheath. The one-minute clip closes with the statement: 'Minister van Buitenlandse Zaken Uri Rosenthal vindt het aanpassen aan lokale gewoonten "niet meer dan normaal".' *Foreign Minister Uri Rosenthal considers adapting to local habits "just normal".*[12] The short clip provokes many reactions from the public. Many people comment on Twitter and on internet

---

10. http://www.ad.nl/ad/nl/1012/Binnenland/article/detail/3110368/2012/01/08/Kamervragen-PVV-over-gewaad-Beatrix.dhtml and http://www.ad.nl/ad/nl/1012/Binnenland/article/detail/3110621/2012/01/08/Rosenthal-Koningin-toont-met-hoofddoek-respect.dhtml

11. See http://en.wikipedia.org/wiki/De_Wereld_Draait_Door. An idiomatic, non-literal, interpretation of 'De wereld draait door' is: the world goes mad.

12. http://www.luckymedia.nl/luckytv/2012/01/respect-voor-gewoontes/

discussion lists, either in a very positive (hilarious, brilliant satire) or a very negative way (tasteless, unworthy).[13]

#12. On 9 January 2012, the popular daily Dutch late-night talk show, Pauw & Witteman, spends some time on the issue of the queen's scarf. Normally, this daily show invites three to five guests who are involved in one of the themes to be discussed. The queen's scarf was not a planned theme on this evening.[14] One of the guests, however, was Hero Brinkman, a prominent member of Wilders's PVV, who was invited to discuss the authority of Dutch police officers. This circumstance gave the hosts the opportunity to discuss the queen's scarf, Wilders's tweet (#6), and the government's justification. (See also Sauer 2012 and Sauer, this volume). Brinkman offers a new interpretation of the queen's scarf. An expert on fashion has assured him that the queen's hat may be considered a modern symbol of the queen's crown. Hence, the fact that she wears a scarf on top of her hat and head means that she submits her monarchy to the demands of Islam.

#13. The Dutch newspaper *AD* reports on 11 January 2012 in a short article that the way Queen Beatrix was dressed is remarkably similar to the animation figure Merryweather in the animated cartoon *Sleeping Beauty* (Walt Disney 1959).[15] The article shows a portrait of the queen next to a screenshot of the cartoon, thus displaying the similarity.

#14. The Prime Minister provides his answers to the parliamentary questions (5) by three members of PVV on 12 January 2012. The answers are remarkably succinct: questions 2–4 (see (5)) are not answered separately, but collectively and indirectly. It is clear that the indirect answer to the three questions 2–4 is negative.

(7) 1. Ja.
2–4. Bij een bezoek van H. M. de Koningin aan een godshuis worden de daarbij behorende kledingvoorschriften gerespecteerd.[16]
1. Yes.

---

13. http://digitaleeditie.nrc.nl/digitaleeditie/NH/2012/0/20120110___/1_06/index.html#page6 and http://www.telegraaf.nl/binnenland/11271303/__Veel_reacties_montage_Beatrix__.html and http://www.telegraaf.nl/binnenland/11274682/__Geen__sorry__voor_naaktvideo__.html

14. http://pauwenwitteman.vara.nl/index.php?id=113&tx_ttnews[tt_news]=24724&calendartime=1326157200&cHash=933a63438945ab9b26f365b0cd461e83

15. http://www.ad.nl/ad/nl/1014/Bizar/article/detail/3115620/2012/01/11/Beatrix-lijkt-op-fee-Mooiweertje-van-Disney.dhtml

16. http://www.rijksoverheid.nl/documenten-en-publicaties/kamerstukken/2012/01/12/beantwoording-op-kamervragen-over-het-dragen-van-een-hoofddoek-door-hare-majesteit-de-koningin.html

2–4. Whenever Her Majesty the Queen visits a place of worship the corresponding dress code is respected.

Most Dutch media (newspapers, television stations and their websites) report the Prime Minister's answers. Neither Wilders nor other MPs of PVV react to these answers in a follow-up.

#15. On the final day of her state visit in Oman, on 12 January 2012, Queen Beatrix answered questions of Dutch newspaper journalists. In her opinion the commotion about the way she dressed was nonsensical, if only because women are not suppressed in the Arab Emirates. Covering her head during the visit to the mosque showed respect to the host's religion. The fuss did not surprise her, because she isn't easily surprised anymore. Her daughter-in-law, Princess Máxima, added that in the Arab Emirates two third of university students are women, and 70% of new entrepreneurs.[17]

#16. In several columns, op-eds and editorials different views on the issue are expressed. One commentator argues that equality rather than suppression is characteristic of the position of women in Oman, whereas a second commentator argues that state visits do not result in economic advantages.[18] The editorial of *NRC* argues that the queen should have kept her criticism (see #15) silent in view of her constitutional position, whereas the editor-in-chief of *Elsevier* argues: 'Het is onzin dat koningin Beatrix onzin geen 'onzin' mag noemen' *It is nonsense that queen Beatrix isn't allowed to call nonsense 'nonsense'*, because the foreign minister takes part in the state visit, thus warranting the government's backup of the queen's position.[19] On January 12, the newspaper *AD* asks a well known Dutch expert, author of several books on etiquette, to comment on the issue. According to her, one has to follow anywhere on the world prevailing rules when visiting a place of worship.[20]

#17. On 12 January 2012, an internet polling agency, *Peil.nl*, publishes the result of a very quick poll: the question 'Vindt u dat de Koningin bij het bezoek aan een

17. http://www.ad.nl/ad/nl/1012/Binnenland/article/detail/3117138/2012/01/12/Koningin-commotie-over-hoofddoek-echte-onzin.dhtml

18. http://digitaleeditie.nrc.nl/digitaleeditie/NH/2012/0/20120111___/1_14/index.html#page14 and http://digitaleeditie.nrc.nl/digitaleeditie/NH/2012/0/20120111___/1_14/NRC_20120111_1_008_article5.pdf

19. http://digitaleeditie.nrc.nl/digitaleeditie/NH/2012/0/20120112___/1_02/NRC_20120112_1_002_article6.pdf and http://www.elsevier.nl/web/Opinie/Commentaren/327614/Koningin-mag-onzin-gerust-onzin-noemen.htm?rss=true

20. http://www.ad.nl/ad/nl/1012/Binnenland/article/detail/3118640/2012/01/12/Deskundige-Rutte-heeft-gelijk-in-discussie-over-hoofddoek.dhtml

moskee in Oman geen sjaal over haar hoed had moeten dragen?' *Do you think that the Queen should not have worn a scarf over her hat when visiting a mosque in Oman?* is answered 'yes, she should not have worn a scarf' by 20% of the respondents, whereas 79% disagree.[21] These results are reported by most Dutch newspapers and their websites.[22] A few days later, on 15 January 2012, the same polling agency reports a new quick poll showing that Wilders's party PVV is going to lose 3 seats in parliament as compared to a poll one week earlier. This is ascribed to the fact that the earlier poll showed that many PVV-voters disagree with Wilders's position on the Queen's hat.[23]

#18. Wilders maintains repeatedly in media interviews his criticism of the Queen's clothing, and insists that he does not regret his criticism.[24] On 18 January he denies rumors that other MPs of PVV criticized his tweet (#6) and parliamentary questions (#7). He repeats his criticism that the queen legitimizes the suppression of women by wearing a scarf over her hat. In a television interview on 24 January he doubts the necessity of visiting mosques during a state visit, and he doubts the truth of the queen's argument that women are hardly suppressed in the Emirates (see #16), although he grants the queen her freedom of speech.

Follow-ups eventually do not occur anymore. The political issue disappears: it is not discussed anymore, there are no new developments.

4.2 Analysis

How may follow-ups be recognized and classified in this sequence of political communication? What is the role of the network of political actors? How can the concept framing shed light on this sequence? Are there noticeable effects on the

21. https://n6.noties.nl/peil.nl/
The website 'Peil.nl' has about 30.000 subscribers among whom quick surveys by email are executed. Between sending a collective email to a selection of about 1,000 or 2,000 of these subscribers and the publication of the results pass only a few hours. It should be noted that the question of the poll incorrectly refers to the Queen's visit to a mosque in Oman, whereas the whole issue started with a visit to a mosque in Abu Dhabi.

22. See e.g. http://www.elsevier.nl/web/Nieuws/Nederland/327573/Meeste-Nederlanders-vinden-hoofddoek-Koningin-prima.htm or http://www.telegraaf.nl/binnenland/11294325/__Nederlanders_geven_Beatrix_gelijk__.html

23. http://www.ad.nl/ad/nl/1012/Binnenland/article/detail/3122172/2012/01/15/PVV-blijft-zetels-inleveren-SP-even-groot-als-VVD.dhtml

24. http://www.ad.nl/ad/nl/1012/Binnenland/article/detail/3127620/2012/01/18/Wilders-blijft-achter-Beatrix-tweet-staan.dhtml and http://www.ad.nl/ad/nl/1012/Binnenland/article/detail/3135732/2012/01/24/Geert-Wilders-blijft-bij-opmerkingen-over-hoofddoek-Beatrix.dhtml

process of frame setting among the audience? I will answer these questions in the following nine analytical remarks.

1. In Section 1 I made a distinction between direct interactional follow-ups in a narrow sense, and follow-ups in general. Follow-ups in a narrow sense are almost nonexistent in the series of 18 utterances and reactions. There is a direct interaction between the parliamentary questions #7 and the response of the Government #14, but even here a follow-up in the sense of a third turn does not occur: after the response of the Prime Minister, the PVV offers no evaluation. In ##8, 9, 12, 15, 17 and 18 interaction occurs *within* the described events, but again direct follow-ups in the sense of third turns in interactional sequences are not visible. These interactions all aim to result in media messages (e.g. #9 and #15), or they occur as a form of direct media display, as in #12 where PVV MP Brinkman is asked by Pauw and Witteman about his reaction as part of a TV talk show. In #10 internet posters react on their own initiative to the blog's call for reactions, but the blog does not react to the posts, nor do posters react mutually, so interaction in a strict sense is also rather limited here.
2. After the news about the queen's dress became known (#2), the first reaction of a political actor in the Netherlands is Pechtold's tweet (#4). Noteworthy are two aspects to this tweet. First, the tweet is meant as a challenge to Wilders, but Wilders was not directly addressed (as he would have been in a personally addressed email or text message). A tweet is a public message for a general audience. Therefore, Pechtold's tweet is not a challenge to Wilders, but is meant to display to the public his willingness to challenge Wilders. Secondly, the tweet appeals to public common ground: knowledge about the current political situation is presupposed. The reason why '*The Netherlands tremble and wait for Wilders's reaction*' is not made explicit, but assumed to be known. Thus, although Pechtold challenges Wilders, he does so from Wilders' perceptual framework.
3. Analysis of the 18 subsequent reactions in terms of Figure 1 reveals the following. In Table 1 the reactions are coded for their place in the network. Four aspects stand out. First, some forms of communication that must have taken place are not perceptible to the audience, such as advising the queen or negotiating with the hosts, as is evident from the reaction of the Foreign Minister in the TV news (see #8). Second, most forms of communication between political actors occur with a view to the perception by the audience; this holds even for the parliamentary questions (#7). For that reason, many relations in the column 'Network relation' are doubly coded. Third, in several cases the audience is involved in the communication: in #5, a weblog invited readers' ironic comments, in #10 many internet users present their views on their own initiative, in

#17 a quasi-systematic survey of the electorate's opinion based on questioning a sample of the electorate is presented. Fourth, there is a distinction between reactions and utterances that are meant seriously and reactions that are non-serious in a frame analytic sense (Goffman 1974; Clark 1996, Chapter 12): ironic, satirical and parodic (#11, #13, and readers' reactions to #5).

Table 1. Overview of communicative events and location in the 'network'

Date	Event / Follow-up	Network relation
7–12 January 2012	#1. State visit by queen Beatrix to the United Arab Emirates; visit to a mosque in Abu Dhabi	2↔5
8 January 2012, 9 a.m.	#2. Reported by news media in the Netherlands	7→10
8 January 2012	#3. Reactions by host	5↔2
8 January 2012, 11.09 a.m.	#4. Tweet by Pechtold, leader of Left Liberals	3→3 3→10
8 January 2012, 12.12 a.m.	#5. Weblog *Geenstijl* calls for ironic or funny comments	7↔10 10↔10
8 January 2012 13.34	#6. Tweet by Wilders, leader of Freedom Party	3→10
8 January 2012	#7. Parliamentary questions by MPs of Freedom Party	3→1
8 January 2012	#8. Media messages about state visit and reactions	7→10 [embeds 7↔1]
8 January 2012	#9. Reactions from other politicians	7→10 [embeds 7↔1 and 7↔3]
8 January 2012	#10. Many posters on Internet reaction sites	10↔10 [through 7→10]
9 January 2012	#11. TV program airs parody	7→10
9 January 2012	#12. TV talk show	7→10 [embeds 7↔3]
11 January 2012	#13. Queen Beatrix noted as being similar to Disney animation figure Merryweather in *Sleeping Beauty*	7→10
12 January 2012	#14. Written answer (to #7) by Prime Minister	1→3
12 January 2012	#15. Queen Beatrix reacts to the press	7→10 [embeds 7↔2]
11–12 January 2012	#16. Columns, op-eds and editorials on relevant issues	7→10
12 and 15 January 2012	#17. Polling agency about reactions among the electorate	9↔7 9↔10
18 and 24 January 2012	#18. Wilders maintains in media interviews his criticism of the queen's clothing	3↔7 7→10

4. It should be noted that many forms of communication on the first level of political communication (see Section 1) are secret and not made public, such as talks between heads of state in preparation of and during a state visit, or talks between the prime minister and the head of state. In that sense, the description of this case in terms of (re)actions ##1–18 is necessarily incomplete. These forms of communication do not allow eavesdroppers or bystanders to be present (Goffman 1981).
5. Two frames appear to be dominant for the specific perception of the Queen's hat and scarf:
   a. The queen showed herself to be well-mannered toward her host, by adopting the host's values;
   b. The queen showed herself to give in to a tyrannical and misogynistic system.

   These two frames are derived from two deeper, more generic, frames pertaining to Islam:
   a″. Islam is a religion as any other major religion (as a consequence, one should respect that religion's rituals and habits);
   b″. Islam is a religion that has unique negative traits such as demanding complete submission from its believers, and fostering a culture of oppression of women (as a consequence, one should oppose and not respect those negative traits).

   These frames are more important than the concrete perception that is framed, and these frames existed already before the concrete perception took place. The queen's hat-and-scarf do not mean very much in themselves, they become meaningful when seen as fitting in either pattern a or b.

   Each frame is supported by actors (persons and institutions) who presuppose the frame, or who support and propagate the frame: the so-called frame sponsors (de Vreese 2003). These frames clearly are in a position of contestation (see Entman 2003, 418). The development of the contestation between these two frames may be seen in ##1–18, as follows: in #1 the 'fact to be framed' is presented (the queen and the scarf), in #2 this fact is connected to a visit to a mosque, thus making the mosque relevant for the interpretation of the fact, in #4 the expectation of a negative reaction based on frame b is thematized by a politician who does himself not support frame b, in #5 the public is invited to provide ironic reactions based on considerations that are obviously critical of Islam, in #6 the negative evaluation based on frame b is provided by its most active Dutch proponent, Wilders. On the other hand, the government and the head of state defend their viewpoint by explicitly stating frame a (in #8, #14 and #15). From that moment on, both frames are repeated in different utterances, by politically prominent actors, by commentators and by members of the public. Invoking these frames presupposes their relevance and their self-evident character. Frames are not explicitly formulated, but belong to the presupposed public common ground, i.e. knowledge about the current political situation. Even parodies presuppose these frames, for example, the parody described in #11 pushes the principle of frame a to the limit or even over the top.

Discussion between the frames is of course possible (and from a societal point of view desirable), but hardly ever occurs. This is shown in the fact that after the most explicit confrontation between both frames, i.e. the parliamentary questions #7 and their answer (#14), no follow-up takes place. No agreement is established, but there is also no continuation of the discussion. Both parties have made their point, the utterance of which is sufficient. Competition between frames thus appears to be rather a matter of frequent and clear utterance, rather than direct discursive confrontation. Between both frames there is, in fact, a situation of *frame parity* (see Entman 2003, 418).

6. In Section 2.2 de Vreese's process model for framing was presented. In the case described, frame building takes place only in a limited sense: the major frames for interpreting and evaluating matters concerning Islam existed already. The only question is: how should the queen's scarf be interpreted based on those frames? In terms of de Vreese's box for 'Frames in the news' this question may be formulated as: how is the issue-specific hat-and-scarf to be described in terms of the more generic frames pertaining to Islam? The more generic frames each have their own 'sponsors'. The fact that the queen appeared in a mosque wearing the scarf offered an opportunity for each of these sponsors to 'use' the queen's dress for promoting one's own point of view. Promoting frames occurs with a view to 'framing effects': reinforcing especially the public's attitudinal effects. Frame sponsors need the media in order to disperse their views. In that sense, media act as a 'service hatch' for political views, as in #2 and #8 in the described case. But media also play an active role, as in ##5, 11, 12, 13, and 16. The box 'framing in the newsroom' appears to be for the most part dependent on external factors.
7. In Section 2.2 Entman's idea of spreading activation of frames through society was discussed, resulting in his idea of a cascading model. Although the downward movement is dominant, there is also upward cascading, as exemplified in ##5, 10 and 17. In #5 (the call for ironic reactions) and #17 (the poll) upward cascading is invited, in #10 (internet posts) it is spontaneous. Whether invited or spontaneous, upward cascading is in these cases *reactive*. And upward cascading does not have the same impact as downward cascading.
8. Although the *issue* eventually disappears, the *frames* do not. The frames existed before the issue arose. The issue is, in fact, mainly used for reinforcing frames. That is, if the frames would not exist, the perception of the queen's clothes

would not have gained the meaning and relevance it actually did. Clothes are hardly ever politically relevant. They only became relevant after politicians noticed they could be framed in a specific useful way.

9. In the case described, there were hardly any directly interactional follow-ups in a strict sense. The nature of the follow-ups as described is apparently not interactionally driven, but driven by the desire to promote one's interests by gaining media exposure. The ideal of a frame sponsor is to have one's favorite frame invoked so as to let it become a part of tacit background knowledge. "Those frames that employ more culturally resonant terms have the greatest potential for influence", according to Entman (2003, 417). Ideally, frames are a presupposed basis on which to build policies.

5. Concluding remarks

The weak side of case studies is that they are not easily generalizable. Their strong side is the detailed picture they offer of the process under consideration. The case study presented in this chapter was chosen primarily for its at first sight non-political starting point, viz. the queen's clothing.

Subsequent reactions immediately made the seemingly non-political starting point highly political. In this light, one may assume that the characteristics of this case are not unique.

In the analysis of the follow-ups on queen Beatrix's clothing it is shown that political reactions are not driven by interactional motives: politicians do not wish to address Beatrix herself either for complimenting or for reproaching her. Rather, political reactions are driven by considerations of political opportunism, by the desire to be visible in the political arena. Reactions should generate media exposure, the general audience should notice the reaction. Reactions both presuppose and are aimed to reinforce a certain view of the world, in this case a certain framing. Follow-ups do not stop as a result of interactional behavior, they stop as soon as no more political value can be achieved, or as soon as all possibilities for publicity have been exhausted.

The approach of both political communication and media communication based on the central concept of framing has proved to be fruitful in this analysis. Different expressions of different actors could be brought down to a common denominator, thus allowing to see general tendencies in political discussions. Framing thus is not only relevant for communication studies but also for political studies.

References

Atkinson, John Maxwell. 1984. *Our Masters' Voices: The Language and Body Language of Politics* London: Methuen.

Bransford, John D. and Nancy S. McCarrell. 1977. "A Sketch of a Cognitive Approach to Comprehension: Some Thoughts about Understanding what it Means to Comprehend. Iin *Thinking: Readings in Cognitive Science* ed. by Philip N. Johnson-Laird and Peter C. Wason, 377–399. Cambridge: Cambridge University Press.

Clark, Herbert H. 1996. *Using Language*. Cambridge: Cambridge University Press. DOI: 10.1017/CBO9780511620539

Clayman, Steven E. 1990. "From Talk to Text: Newspaper Accounts of Reporter-source Interactions. *Media, culture and society* 12: 79–103. DOI: 10.1177/016344390012001005

de Vreese, Claes H. 2003. *Framing Europe. Television News and European Integration*. Amsterdam: Aksant Academic Publishers.

de Vreese, Claes H. 2005. "News framing: Theory and Typology." *Information Design Journal + Document Design* 13(1): 51–62. DOI: 10.1075/idjdd.13.1.06vre

Ensink, Titus. 2012a. "Framing as a Continual and Repetitive Process in Political Communication." In *Proceedings of the ESF Strategic Workshop on Follow-ups Across Discourse Domains: A Cross-Cultural Exploration of Their Forms and Functions, Würzburg (Germany), 31 May - 2 June 2012*, ed. by Anita Fetzer, Elda Weizman and Elisabeth Reber, 58–71. Würzburg: Universität Würzburg - [online]. URL: http://opus.bibliothek.uni-wuerzburg.de/volltexte/2012/7165/; URN: urn:nbn:de:bvb:20-opus-71656.

Ensink, Titus 2012b. "Internet Newspaper Discussion Lists: A Virtual Political Arena?" In *Dialogue in Politics* ed. by Lawrence N. Berlin and Anita Fetzer, 21–42. Amsterdam/ Philadelphia: John Benjamins. DOI: 10.1075/ds.18.05ens

Ensink, Titus, and Christoph Sauer. 2003. "Social-Functional and Cognitive approaches to Discourse Interpretation: The role of Frame and Perspective.", In *Framing and Perspectivising in Discourse*, ed. by Titus Ensink and Christoph Sauer, 3–12. Amsterdam: John Benjamins. DOI: 10.1075/pbns.111.02ens

Entman, Robert M. 2003. "Cascading activation: Contesting the White House's Frame after 9/11. *Political Communication* 20(4): 415–432. DOI: 10.1080/10584600390244176

Goffman, Erving. 1969. *The Presentation of Self in Everyday Life* Harmondsworth: Penguin.

Goffman, Erving. 1974. *Frame Analysis: An Essay on the Organization of Experience*. New York etc.: Harper & Row.

Goffman, Erving. 1981. *Forms of Talk* Oxford: Basil Blackwell.

Houtkoop-Steenstra, Hanneke. 2000. *Interaction in the Standardized Survey Interview: The Living Questionnaire*. Cambridge: Cambridge University Press. DOI: 10.1017/CBO9780511489457

Kuipers, Benjamin J. 1975. "A Frame for Frames: Representing Knowledge for Recognition." In *Representation and Understanding. Studies in Cognitive Science*, ed. by Daniel G. Bobrow and Allan Collins, 151–184. New York etc.: Academic Press. DOI: 10.1016/B978-0-12-108550-6.50011-2

Kuitenbrouwer, Jan. 2010. *De woorden van Wilders & hoe ze werken* [The words of Wilders and How they work] Amsterdam: Bezige Bij.

Lakoff, George. 2004. *Don't Think of an Elephant!: Know Your Values and Frame the Debate White River Junction*: Chelsea Green Publishing.

Lakoff, George. 2010. "Why it Matters how we frame the Environment." *Environmental Communication* 4(1): 70–81.
Mehan, Hugh. 1979. *Learning Lessons: Social Organization in the Classroom*. Cambridge, MA: Harvard University Press. DOI: 10.4159/harvard.9780674420106
Sauer, Christoph. 2012. "Framing in Talk Shows and its Visualisation." In *Proceedings of the ESF Strategic Workshop on Follow-ups Across Discourse Domains: A Cross-Cultural Exploration of Their Forms and Functions*, Würzburg (Germany), 31 May – 2 June 2012, ed. by Anita Fetzer, Elda Weizman and Elisabeth Reber, 221–235.
Sauer, Christoph. "*Follow-ups in Political Talk shows and their Visual Framing*", This volume.
Sinclair, John and Malcolm Coulthard. 1975. *Towards an Analysis of Discourse: The English Used by Teachers and Pupils*. Oxford: Oxford University Press.
Waugh, Linda. 1995. "Reported Speech in Journalistic Discourse: The Relation of Function and Text." *Text* 15: 129–173.

Follow-ups in political talk shows and their visual framing

Christoph Sauer
University of Groningen, the Netherlands

The chapter aims to provide corpus-analytical insights into the multimodality of political discourse in the Dutch talk show *Pauw & Witteman*.[1] The show combines conversations with video clips and other visuals. Thus, it realises a *macro follow-up* by linking talk items to (earlier) news reports that are shown before the talk starts: talk as a 'prolongation' of politics. Meanwhile, video clips or stills accompany the developing conversation: they may support, contradict, confirm or soften it. We consider this screening on the go a *micro follow-up* constellation. It works, among other things, as *visual framing* of the evolving verbal discourse: it triggers the exchanges and determines their lines. A corpus analysis of one week proves the show's multimodality that increases the meaning-making potential of socio-political media discourse and imposes visual authority on the speakers and participants. It turns out that classical interviews can remain as prominent accountability rituals ("set piece"), while additional forms of political conversation can diversify and become more fluid, such as in the way described here.

1. Introduction and research question

The Dutch public broadcast TV late-night talk show *Pauw & Witteman (P&W)* challenges guests, in particular politicians, with recent TV news reports, "YouTube" clips, Internet screen shots, projected "tweets" etc. and encourages them to react to the screenings (Huls and Varwijk 2011; Kee 2012; Ruigrok et al. 2012; Huls 2013). It is a live broadcast, which is highlighted by the applauding or laughing studio public. Political guests face a two-fold challenge. They are urged to acknowledge the screened news, and they must do so in the conversation, during which their

1. I would like to thank my reviewers both for valuable critical comments and appropriate advice. Faults that may rest are completely mine.

DOI 10.1075/dapsac.60.07sau

performance in maintaining their political role is checked in correspondence with visuals that are projected simultaneously onto the studio screens.

On the one hand, a talk topic is introduced first verbally by one host (sometimes already in combination with a visualisation), then a news report is projected onto the studio wall screens[2], and after the screening the talk starts prompted by the host's question, e.g.: "What do you think about this film?" Consequently, the topic of a news report initiates a talk topic and establishes the assumption that the emerging conversation reflects (yesterday's) news and operates as a 'variation' or 'continuation' of the news. We consider this constellation a *macro follow-up* and will try to find out how it works and which function it has in the show. Except for their *temporal* relationship – first screening, then discussion – there may be other functions. Since news reports, in general, are examples of *news framing* (de Vreese 2003) we shall take framing as one of the functions into account. A corpus analysis of one week *P&W* provides the appropriate data.

On the other hand, what follows after the screening of the clip is not a traditional interview, because already during the beginning exchanges other visuals appear on the studio screens. Politicians are expected to take the pictures into account explicitly. However, when politicians respond to the pictures and consider their meaning, other pictures can appear that ask anew for adjustment and comment. Thus, the visuals represent a 'claim' or an expectation by the editors who have prepared their projection in advance; this arrangement triggers verbal text and influences its wording.

We consider this constellation a *micro follow-up* that operates on two levels: *verbal text* and *visual framings*. Questions produce answers, answers comments, comments requests for clarification, and so on (as is shown, for example, by Bull (this volume), who regards the "sequential triad" by Sinclair and Coulthard 1975 as constitutive). So far, the third unit is a *micro follow-up* of the second one, the fourth of the third, and so on (Cullen 2002). In interviews without visual triggers, which depend completely on verbal text and body language, the interviewer's questions and reactions are the primary means to control the interaction (Clayman and Heritage 2002) resulting in verbal contributions that are micro follow-ups.

In the talk show *P&W*, however, visuals may take over many means of control. Their first appearance resembles an 'interjection' and produces an apt verbal follow-up. Thus, formulations depend on the projected visuals and sometimes visuals may replace verbal elements. How it works precisely is up to now not yet investigated. Therefore, we fall back upon research on *news discourse* (Montgomery 2007; Bednarek and Caple 2010), *multimodal communication* (Carter and Allan

2. TV viewers see the news reports on their home screens which are completely filled with them, which thus functions as a reminder of earlier news.

2009; Kress 2010; Sauer 2012), *speeches on television* (Sauer 2007, 2011), *media texts* (Meinhof 1994), *documentary films* (Nichols 2010; Sauer 2013; Nijdam-Akkerman and Sauer 2013) and *TV shows* (Graber 1989, 2012; Royce 2007; Montgomery 2007; Liu and O'Halloran 2009; Lauerbach 2010; Holly 2015; Richardson et al. 2012).

Especially, we want to establish *visual-verbal interrelations* in the talk show discourse, i.e. we are looking for moments when pictures and texts correspond with each other. We expect that these interrelations may also explain how TV viewers experience a talk show like *P&W*: not as verbal text, but as talk triggered by visualisations and accompanied by more screenings. Accordingly, the *micro follow-up* constellation shows that visuals prompt the discourse. Since this visual triggering of political discourse is not yet investigated, we propose to consider the screenings *visual framings* and to join research in *news framing* (Entman 1993; de Vreese 2003; Dahinden 2006). The conversations with screenings offer a *visual frame* to which the guests need to respond. A corpus analysis is aimed to find out how this operates. Still, we do not yet consider sound and music, due to missing expertise.

The talk show has an inner circle, hosts and guests who are surrounded by the studio public, and an outer circle, TV viewers who respond to their home screens. It is from the TV viewers' perspective that we investigate the follow-up constellations and their visual framings.

In Section 2 we describe some details of the talk show *P&W* in order to present what may be called its overwhelming visual appearance. Section 3 discusses the transition of political interviews from textual to multimodal realisation and their audience design. In Section 4, we work out the concept of follow-ups and our approach of the corpus analysis, in Section 5 we discuss the findings. Section 6 presents the discussion and conclusion.

2. The characteristics of the talk show "Pauw & Witteman"

The talk show is arranged so that TV viewers can (over)see and (over)hear the audio-visual and verbal events. They may, in particular, respond to the screenings of news films that are projected onto the studio screens and their home screens. This studio design and format concern the show's new discursive and visual style (see Pauw & Witteman 2010), which was initiated in September 2010 (for a general impression, see Figure 1, below).

The general disposition of the format is the screening of pictures that prompts the verbal discourse. It leads to an interview-like start of verbal exchanges between the hosts or just one of them and one guest or more. The guests are expected to enter the conversation by both reacting to the question as well as to the clips. Responses to the clips are explicitly welcomed: "How do you experience the film?" This goes beyond more conventional talk shows where the art of questioning depends on the hosts' skills and their entertaining or confrontational capacities (Vraga et al. 2012).

Figure 1. Impressions from the (new) studio in October 2010: studio walls are screens with the logo, photographs, and later films, cartoons, "tweets" etc. (source: Pauw & Witteman 2010)

The goal of the filmic inserts is a context-dependent confrontation. It is meant to provoke a reaction (an assessment or a comment) and to confine the next exchanges; hence, the discourse is *framed* by what the fragment represents and determined by the choice of language means by the hosts. Since no conversation starts without the screening of a video clip (from the news), this setting establishes a (temporal) *macro follow-up* constellation: what follows may be understood as a reaction to or prolongation of yesterday's news by the politician. The screening, at least, functions as a reminder: it reminds participants, studio public and TV viewers of what they already know about the news.

During the developing conversations, however, the screening of stills and other visual content continues. It is done mostly in correspondence with the sub-topics (prepared by the editors in advance) and functions as a filtering device: what is said is filtered by the screenings and what is screened frames the verbal discourse.[3] As a result, the talk show issue is a *macro follow-up* of a news topic and becomes

3. In German TV talk shows, video clips or film inserts – the so-called *Einspielfilme* – have a different function and style: they introduce the guests (often with heavily ironic voice-over commentary), they structure the sequence of items (by giving a short overview, discussing a content detail or provocatively illustrating a topic etc.), but hardly ever during the verbal exchanges themselves (Neufeld 2008; Maier 2009; Gäbler 2011; Klemm 2015). This occurs, e.g. in Belgium, too (De Smedt and Vandenbrande 2011). In the Netherlands, however, if there is an ironic tenor in a film clip at all, then it is caused by the original source or by the first questions by the hosts, but not by a voice-over text in the film itself. Therefore, footage in the talk show *P&W* is mainly used directly as discourse 'material', even during the talk itself when new inserts are projected. It is the general expectation that the talk realises a 'bridge' to the video clips.

condensed by visual framings, which operate as *micro follow-ups*: step by step (verbal discourse) and screening by screening (visual framings). We will come to this in a minute (see Section 4, below). In Figure 2 (below), the general sequential organisation of the show of ca. 60 minutes is illustrated.

Tune	2 min.	music and pictures
Introduction	5 min.	first by one host, then alternating by both hosts
Issue 1	12 min.	film clip, questions and answers, more visualisations, corresponding texts
Issue 2	12 min.	film clip, questions and answers, more visualisations, corresponding texts
Zap Service	up to 4 min.	screening of humorous filmic fragments of the day, mostly not related to talk show issues
Issue 3	12 min.	film clip, questions and answers, more visualisations, corresponding texts
Issue 4	12 min.	film clip, questions and answers, more visualisations, corresponding texts
Conclusion	3 min.	mostly by both hosts
Tune	1 min.	both hosts stand up and shake hands with all guests

Figure 2. Sequential organisation of the talk show P&W (during the corpus week, from Monday, 9 January, until Friday, 13 January 2012)

Apart from *confrontainment* sequences in the conversation (Klemm 2015), other screenings evidently are dedicated to *infotainment* purposes (Wonneberger et al. 2013), which are ratified by the participants' laughter (Timberg 1995).[4] Thus, the description by Vraga et al. (2012, 6) that political talk shows are "exchanges among pundits prompted by questions from a host" does not apply to the specific format here. Consequently, we see and hear more than talking heads alone, we see video clips before the conversations begin and screen projections during the exchanges. These screenings focus the TV viewers' attention perhaps more than the adjacent conversations. They also contribute to the complex dynamic multimodal design of the talk show.

4. Sometimes video clips are replaced by performances, like a rap with music, a classical musical performance, a political satirist, a band, a magician etc., and embedded in the verbal exchanges. Even candidates for the leadership of a political party were invited (in April and May 2012) and performed their debates in the show, which resulted in a completely different type of broadcast. Yet, it demonstrated the amount of variations that can be realised within this programme. It is open to discussion whether these other forms fit in with the talk show's potential, but the editors seem to look for innovations anyway. The show has run eight years and has stopped in the spring of 2014. The show *Pauw* that replaces *P&W* now is less visually structured and re-establishes more interview-like settings as such. Also only one host, namely *Pauw*, is present.

As concerns its dynamics, two factors prevail. The first one is the fact that four cameras are ceaselessly edited in short shots: a normal shot's length is six to ten seconds, but shorter shots are possible. The second factor is the fact that the screens on the studio walls (that TV viewers see as context of every shot or as home screen filling video fragment) often change, too. This may give the TV viewer the impression that the pictures reflect the moments when a specific verbal content is realised. A new picture seems to be linked to a new topic or sub-topic.

As concerns its multimodality, we experience the talk show's main characteristic as clip-related discourse and picture- (or camera-)dependent political performance (Meyer 2009). The refinement with which the visualisations are made and projected, chiefly in accordance with the expected verbal exchanges, is conducive to this characteristic. The show format applies pictures to stimulate verbal discourse: film clips are used to trigger formulations and, during the exchanges, to focus on sub-topics. Visualisations are mainly fragments from news reports, "tweets", photographs, cartoons from the press, parts of documentaries, etc. When they are projected to the screens then they provide a 'filter' of potential verbal contributions (see Figure 3, below).

Figure 3. Talk show of 9 January 2012 with, on the left, a "tweet" projection that elicits the discussion. Note that the guest's name and function is shown as text (for some moments only). On the right, of 13 January 2012, we see the studio screens that at this moment present a still photograph from earlier screened footage, about school situations

Pictures illustrate the topic and trigger the wordings, in particular when news reports predetermine the semantic domains, or when reactions to news reports result in "tweets" that can be projected to the wall screens.

3. Interviews in a talk show and their multimodal audience-related design

3.1 Visual-verbal discourse

Media talk is a growing field in discourse analysis and socio-pragmatics (see Scanell 2009 for an overview). However, what TV viewers *see* when they are listening to the talk mostly is *not* considered in the investigations (Greiffenhagen 2009). The predominant paradigm of conversation analysis, which determines the field of media interview investigations, tends to neglect or underestimate the visual part of TV (Clayman and Heritage 2002; Tolson 2006; Huls and Varwijk 2011; Hutchby 2011; Huls 2013). Also social scientists who investigate TV and other forms of media communication only touch slightly on the visual representations; so states Matthes (2009) in his overview that the lack of investigations of visual forms is a common practice. Nevertheless, it is always cameras that show the talking people's behaviour, including their body language and non-verbal communication (their "signalling", Clark 1996). Therefore, it is problematic to neglect visual impressions TV viewers are bombarded with. Accordingly, a minimal approach would be to regard the talk show *P&W* as *visual-verbal discourse.*

When the hosts' questions are preceded by film clips the first moves in the conversation are aimed at the clip content: a *(re)contextualisation* from audio-visual to verbal discourse.[5]

Undoubtedly, we sometimes find beginnings that resemble interviews, but a closer look reveals that the interview setting is abandoned quickly (Verhoef 2012).

The inevitable point of view of the multimodal discourse analysis is that of the TV viewers. It is for *them* that the discourse is realised and it is for *their* information processing that the arrangement of multimodal elements is built (Charaudeau 2002). What TV viewers see and hear is designed for their information purposes, and all preparations by the editors take the TV audience into account. Furthermore, the talk show has a double audience: the studio public that may response directly to the running discourse and to the video clips, and the TV viewers who overhear the conversations including the potential reactions of the studio public and "oversee" their non-verbal behaviour and the studio public's visible reactions as well as the projected footage. At the beginning moments of a sequence, the TV viewers process the information almost always from video fragments that fill their home screens completely (see also Figure 4, below).

5. The concept of "(re)contextualisation" in multimodal discourse is not as clear as it is in verbal discourse (but see Bolter and Grusin 1999: "remediation"). Due to limited space we restrict ourselves to the observation that conversations after the screening of a clip either offer (critical) evaluations of the pictures or consider only the words uttered by the reporter. It needs scrutiny to find more characteristic prolongation features.

3.2 Audience design

We assume that the position of viewers of TV and of documentary film match (Nichols 2010; Sauer 2009, 2012, 2013; Sauer and Akkerman-Nijdam 2013). Therefore, we apply *footing* (Goffman 1979, 1981) to approach their viewing role from the perspective of the "participation framework": TV and film viewers become "overhearers" who "overhear" and "oversee" the visual-verbal discourse (see also Gruber, this volume). This entails that the TV viewers' position depends on the *audience design* (Bell 1984, 2001): every information resource has to be arranged so that TV viewers find themselves supported in their information processing (van Leeuwen 2005; Carter and Allan 2009; Bednarek and Caple 2012). To put it in straightforward terms, the design of the talk show *P&W* is aimed at the TV viewers rather than the studio public. It is the TV viewer who is placed in the centre of the information processing. In other words, the multimodal discourse elements have to be *designed* as to support the TV audience's understanding. Hence, the TV viewers might be considered "overhearers" (Clark and Schaefer 1992; Clark 1996; Montgomery 2007; Bubel 2008) of the conversations inside the studio (including the studio public's "overhearing" of the discussions too). They must also be regarded as "overseers" (Sauer 2009, 2011) who "oversee" (Montgomery 2007, 146; Nichols 2010, 69 "overlook") the transmission peculiarities of the verbal exchanges, which are captured by cameras (Holly 2015). Because the cameras also show the synchronous visualisations in the speakers' background, the TV *audience design* is rather complex than straightforward. Consequently, the show is designed so as to encourage the viewers' expectation that their understanding will be supported. The basic line is that the TV viewers can see what hosts and guests are seeing too and that this seeing functions partly as a visible interruption and partly as triggering of the talk, which is indicated by the way the participants perceive the screen representations in the studio (Figure 4, below). This goes on and on, even if the talk only can be heard, but what one sees is not talk but talk in its context, at least. It takes on a more specific *visual* quality.

Like in the transmission of theatrical performances (Fischer-Lichte 2008), a conversation is going on in the inner circle, thus between hosts and guests. The conversation itself then needs to fulfil the requirements of *audience design*:

> Utterances are designed with overhearers in mind, on the basis of an estimate of the spectators' world knowledge and on the knowledge the participants have gleaned from interactions that the spectators have observed. This process is the screen-to-face equivalent of [...] "recipient design" in face-to-face conversation.
> (Bubel 2008, 66)

Figure 4. Left picture of 9 January 2012. Hosts and guests look at the screening of a news report while behind them a photograph represents the visual framing, here: the topic of the Queen's scarf. The news film itself fills the TV home screen completely. Right picture of 12 January 2012. A film trailer is shown as an introduction to a conversation with the film director (film about saving Jewish children during the Nazi occupation of the Netherlands)

The inner circle spectators (the inner overhearers) may response to the speakers' utterances, by means of applause, hissing, laughing, other ways of (dis-)approval etc. The TV viewers as outer spectators, however, necessarily must be provided with knowledge means that exceed the current inner circle (Sauer 2012), which dilates the inner speakers' *common ground* (Clark 1996). Therefore, it is the hosts' task to control the *audience design*, by requiring more adequate formulations: they ask disentangling questions, formulate specific requirements (Clayman 2007), or, concerning the accompanying visualisations, provide captures, descriptions or present more contextual information.

3.3 Complex functionality

In such talk show settings, it is not sufficient for a host acting as the person who provides the TV public during the conversation with necessary information resources ("speaking on behalf of the public", Clayman 2007). Moreover, when this *common ground* management becomes mundane in TV journalism then it also plays a role in managing the visual content in combination with the verbal one. Clayman's observation (2007, 243) fits with this specific context:

> Sometimes interviewers invoke the public simply to navigate from one phase of the interview to another, or more specifically to manage the transition across, and reconfiguration of, distinct participation frameworks.

The formulation "to invoke the public" opens a world of complex functionality. Hence, we see the shifting from one participation framework to another simply by the use of the full home TV screen for the presentation of a news film clip (alternating with shots from the studio and its public): It goes, in Goffman's terms, from "side participant" (studio public) to "bystanders" and "eavesdroppers" (summarized as "overhearers", TV viewers). Moreover, regularly we see also the realisation of a "reconfiguration", e.g. when a conversation phase becomes a small learning discourse in words and pictures (e.g. an expert demonstrating his expertise or an artist performing his art) or when it changes into an entertaining environment (e.g. with funny film pictures or humorous comments). Accordingly, the interview setting as such, thus without taking into account the peculiar TV features, is theoretically suboptimal to explain the forms and functions of the audiovisual discourse in this kind of talk show.

4. Conceptualisations of our approach

4.1 Follow-ups and visual framing: Macro and micro

In general, the talk show's character bridges a gap between (earlier) news and political reactions to this news by live conversations supplemented with pictures. Thus, it realises a *follow-up constellation* between earlier TV transmissions (mainly news reports) and verbal exchanges that aim at the presented focus. "Follow-ups are conceptualized as communicative acts (or dialogue acts), in and through which a prior communicative act is accepted, challenged, or otherwise negotiated" (Fetzer and Weizman 2012, this volume). This may function as an elaboration on the actual item, to put it neutrally, during the discussions (Sauer 2012). The constellation bears a predominant *temporal* quality: something must have been the issue of a public representation in the mass media in advance (a news show, an Internet web site, an article in the press), before it is able to become a talk show issue. We consider this a *macro* perspective, in that it combines news events from the (not long ago) past with actualisations now (the moment of the live conversation).

This macro perspective contributes to the shift from political discourse seen as a *product* (of an interview setting, e.g.) to political discourse seen as a *process* (in which politicians try to survive or to maintain their expected role). It is observable in talk shows of this format: they connect the reminder of yesterday news in the form of a video clip with actual interventions during the subsequent conversations. "Talk shows are the new political arena in our mediocracy. Here politicians must prove to the people how good they are" (Kleijwegt and van Weezel 2011, 34, transl. CS).

The follow-up comes into existence when the participants negotiate the clip's focus with each other. However, the verbal discourse is *framed* in a double way: by the visualisations prior to the talk and during the talk and by what is said to stimulate the talk (question or request). The first is the contribution of the talk show to the visual reality of politics, the latter is its realisation of some conventional ways of interviewing – as long as it takes, because after a short while a new visual will intervene in the ongoing discussion. This double framing process pushes the participants to 'place' their reactions within the frame and focusses the potential verbal meanings (Kress 2010, 152). In short, only what the pictures bring about might be a topic in the show, and verbal reactions are expected towards the screened pictures. This oscillation between the visual and the verbal characterises the *micro* perspective. It goes from pictures to words and back again. Thus, *P&W* combines macro with micro perspectives: (temporal) follow-ups of earlier news with visual frames that influence the verbal elaborations otherwise.

Furthermore, the temporal character of the macro follow-up constellation shows often in the fact that a talk show's result becomes a news item of its own the following day (see also Ruigrok et al. 2012). As such, it is usable for a new talk show issue. So we see a link between the past and the future. In the show, the reflection on previous behaviour (opinions, utterances) by politicians has the potential to increase and become a new news item. This common knowledge produces more provocative behaviour since politicians can be sure that conspicuous words or behaviour are picked up by other journalists, TV and blogs. In such a way, the talk show creates not only the talk of the day, but provides the TV public also with expectations of a 'chain' of political news. What was before, and what may come tomorrow is structured as the eternal follow-up that we already know from our landscape of the news in general (Landreville et al. 2010; Bednarek and Caple 2012). Figure 5 (below) presents a summary of these considerations.

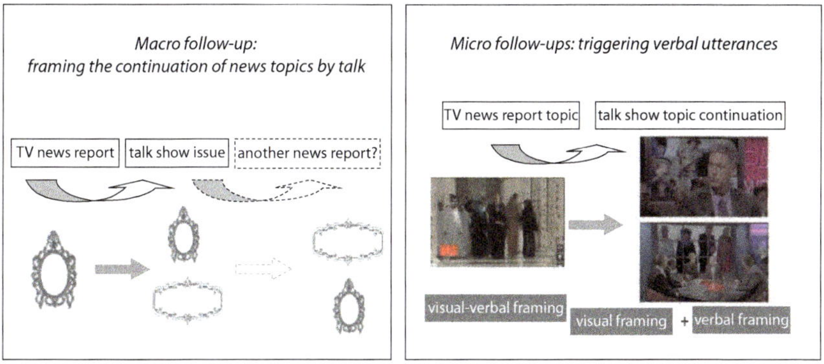

Figure 5. Macro follow-ups as continuation of the news and micro follow-ups that trigger discussion topics and sub-topics, apart from formulations, by visual framings

In contrast to general theories of *news framing* (de Vreese 2003; Matthes 2009), the visual framing of the discourse in *P&W* does not treat the TV viewers with a specific *P&W* worldview.[6] Instead, the TV public is focussed upon the topic continuation

6. However, in some investigations (Huls and Varwijk 2011; Huls 2013) as well as in the press (Ruigrok et al. 2012) the talk show *P&W* is seen as "biased" and more leftist than mainstream public television.

during the conversations, which functions obviously as visual support of the texts. Moreover, visualisations indicate for the TV viewers that the news from the video clips has something to do with the actual political conversations and thus demonstrates that political discourse and news discourse are intertwined with each other.

4.2 *Framing* and *news framing*

As it is said before (in Section 1, 2 and 4.1), we relate the peculiarities of the micro follow-ups to the *filtering-out* of topic elements that otherwise, i.e. *without* synchronous visualisations, would have had a chance to be elaborated on. But the topic elements that are shown on the screens are more prominent than not-shown elements and therefore may influence the ongoing conversation more than what remains invisible. These ways of filtering-out some potential elements and sticking to other ones are subject of research of *framing*, in particular *news framing*. Accordingly, news reports are always framed, i.e. they represent some aspects of the news and neglect other ones. Only what the news report tells counts as news, other aspects become irrelevant and are considered omitted. It is the ubiquity of *news framing* that allows us to regard it also as a source of more general framing devices. Thus, the filtering of a news issue that we experience as focus or accentuation can be described in terms of framing: so by Scheufele and Scheufele (2010) who ascribe this effect to the media system as such, or already by Entman (1993, 53) who says that frames "highlight some features of reality while omitting others", or by Lakoff (2004) who tries to counter framing realisations by reframing devices.

Therefore, we adopt work on *news framing* in order to investigate the filtering-out relations in *P&W*. De Vreese (2003) proposes "an integrated process model of news framing" that combines "frame-building" and "frame-setting". Frame-building bridges "framing in the newsroom" (by internal factors like editorial policies and news values, and by external factors like funding, political affiliation, competition in the news market, spin-doctors, lobbyists, interest groups) with "frames in the news" (like issue-specific frames and generic ones), such as *conflict* and *economic consequences*. Dahinden (2006) found three more generic frames: *progress, moral/ethics/law* and *personalisation*. Yet frame telling is unsatisfying since incomplete framing not often is recognised, although it seems to be realistic:

> In media texts, frames are often not fully worked out, in the sense that any given news story or television interview may be seen to frame some aspect of a given issue in a particular way, but may also contain some contradictory elements, which means that no coherent frame emerges. (Breeze 2013, 195)

So we may conclude that the visual framings in the talk show *P&W* in the first instance are not dedicated to make the discourse coherent.

Anyhow, news frames in general are not so much of interest here, since already framed news reports produce the 'material' that is used in *P&W* to stimulate the talk. What de Vreese (2003) calls "frame effects", however, that may generate effects in information processing, attitudes and behaviour, evolves in the micro perspective of the talk show as visual-verbal discourse. It forms a continuation of the news and not alone the news but also of the frames that were already used and realised in the news itself. We consider this constellation a kind of *quotation* device; it creates interview-like dispositions, since it leads to discussion and debate and can be stirred by confronting questions and pictures. And it urges the party, which is not represented in the frame, to act as to broaden the frame: to convert a non-quotation into a potential quotation.

4.3 Visual framing and visual-verbal interrelations

Research on visual framing in TV communication mostly is centred on speaking people, like presidential candidates in the U.S. (Coleman and Banning 2006) or news broadcasters' non-verbal behaviour (Coleman and Wu 2006). Coleman and Banning (2006, 324) expect "that television news images of candidates exhibiting positive or negative behaviours such as gestures and facial expressions convey impressions that might be flattering or unflattering", but this approach reduces the visual potentials TV viewers may response to (see also Haumer and Donsbach 2009). Furthermore, it is problematic to exclude other visual information that is provided by the *contexts* shown in which the candidates are exposed, or by other visuals that precede or may follow the candidates' pictures. Thus, the dynamic character of a news item has to be taken into consideration.

News anchors' role is another aspect. Their non-verbal behaviour is subject of study: they show either "emotions" or perform "neutrally" (Coleman and Wu 2006). There needs, however, to be more. This way of studying news shows lacks an approach of *multimodal* communication, at least of *visual-verbal discourse*. Consequently, visual framing needs a holistic approach and cannot be restricted to shots of hosts and politicians and their body language. *All events* that the cameras show, the loudspeakers produce and the editors put into the frame form the filtered information TV viewers have to deal with. Therefore, we need to look at "intersemiotic complementarity" (Royce 2007), "intersemiotic texture" (Liu and O'Halloran 2009), "Profilierungen" [visual-verbal contouring or modifications, CS] (Holly 2015) or combinations of "intersemiotic and intrasemiotic relations" (Bednarek and Caple 2012).

Even if one restricts oneself to talking people participating in conversations and strategically placed around a table (the traditional setting), the showing of the table and the showing of the speaking, responding and listening participants clearly link the visual impressions, which are caught by the different cameras and their continual editing, to the utterances by the participants (Holly 2015). A characteristic modern visual framing is the split-screen technique. It means that the TV home screen shows more than the natural environment of talk. It connects, e.g., two counterparts into one technical device so that TV viewers get a strong impression of *conflict*, which is a general framing strategy in talk shows; or it uncovers how a guest responds to the screening of a news film or shows a guest who comments on events screened (Figure 6, below).

Figure 6. Left picture, 9 January 2012: two politicians discussing the Queen wearing a scarf in a mosque in Abu Dhabi; they are captured even when their gazes are not directed towards each other but to the hosts (who lead the discussion). Middle picture, 10 January 2012: the guest is looking at the screening of a report on herself about high income (symbolised by the car) and bad leadership. Right picture, 13 January 2012: guest reacting to a clip

We may say that the split-screen technique supports the home viewer by framing the conflict between two guests, all the more when the speakers also use conflict language in their staged exchange, or by focussing visually upon the quarrel that is represented by the video clip. Thus, the split-screen technique used in *P&W* goes beyond traditional settings where talking heads form the main source of information. It frames visually what the TV viewer may respond to. The split-screen technique is one solution of the general problem of *visual-verbal interrelations*. Because a shot of a speaker cannot represent the total content of his words the speaker's picture has always a *partial* meaning (Sauer 2007, 2011). Only some components of the content can be represented in pictures, other ones not. By using the split-screen technique, one can easily add some pieces of the necessary content.

Research of visual-verbal interrelations relates components of the picture to components of the text and treats both resources as part of the holistic message. It studies "the interplay of the visual with the verbal" (Montgomery 2007, 94). What then are these components? As is already known from limitations of text-picture relationships in photojournalism (Stegu 2000; Sauer 2010), these components are "action components", as proposed by Meinhof (1994): *actors* (causes of actions/events, originators), *activities/events* themselves, *affected/effect/outcome* of the actions/events. However, texts and pictures are treated by many investigators as if they relate to these action components independently, as it were, although the meaning-inferring TV viewers experience holistic messages (Graber 1989). In a talk show with video clips these considerations are naturally more adequate and useful than in discussion-only programmes.

Meinhof (1994: 216–217) proposes three forms of verbal-visual interrelations in news that also may be applied to talk shows like *P&W*:

> *Overlap*: film footage and text share the same action component, e.g., film and text both refer to the same entity, such as a political leader or a flood, a police investigation, famine victims, etc.
>
> *Displacement*: film footage and text represent different action components of the same event, e.g., we see the effect of a disaster in pictures, with its cause reported in words, or the location of a strike, with its originators in the verbal report.
>
> *Dichotomy*: film footage and text represent action components of different events, e.g., we hear a text report on the crisis in Greece, whereas the pictures show the Acropolis in sunset.

Montgomery (2007) elaborates on Meinhof's categories, by focussing on "principles of intelligibility in TV news reports" and favouring a "closure between what we can see and what we can hear represented in televisual news discourse" by means of *co-reference*. The "principles" read as follows:

> Rule 1: For any referring expression in the verbal track, search for a relevant referent in the image track.
>
> Rule 2: Treat any element depicted in a shot in the visual track as a potential referent for a referring expression in the verbal track. (Montgomery 2007, 98)

Accordingly, at least one element in the visual track may serve as a potential referent for a referring expression in the verbal track; and complementary with it, referring expressions in the verbal track imply the search for a relevant referent in the image track. In general, these rules of co-reference take into account that no total or complete representation of the same content in the visual and verbal track is possible, thus only partial representations – which is philosophically grasped in the assumption that language means "underdetermine" communication, whereas pictures "over-determine" communication.[7]

7. We have not enough room to dwell on these philosophical questions here (but see Ranta 2011). That language "underdetermines" communication means that participants need to activate their language knowledge in order to infer the meaning; the lacking of a verbal element may have a great impact. That pictures "over-determine" communication means that participants quickly get an idea of the meaning, although the pictorial elements are always concrete and never general or abstract; so people need to subtract minor elements – which is also accentuated by the fact that missing elements or technical mistakes, e.g. in photographs, normally do not

Therefore, if we look for verbal-visual interrelations, we first start to find verbal co-references (that we underline in the protocols, see Figure 7 for an example, below). Then we try to establish the interrelations: not by assuming that the same content in pictures and texts is represented, but that a certain picture element has a referring expression in the text. We do so shot for shot (or in series of shots) and find several interrelations or "editing points" (van Leeuwen 2005, 184). But we also find many textual and visual elements that are not linked.

The Figure demonstrates the corpus description work. The shots are numbered, the text is transcribed (and translated), co-references are underlined, interrelations are interpreted: Displacement (1) since one sees "welcome", but not "today", Overlap (2) since a photograph of the scarf, the main topic, is shown, Overlap (3) since the trailer refers in music, pictures and text to the talk show *P&W*, D(isplacement)/O(verlap) (4) since welcoming words and gestures can be seen as well as the persons referred to, O/D/SP(EAKER CONTOURING) (5,6) since we see the greeting, the surgeon (as an object) and, later on, hear him talking (as a subject we can see and hear) with expertise about his work and using the head model that we see laying on the table (5).

Second, we track down the verbal-visual linking, but we restrict ourselves to the "editing points", the underlined verbal elements. Thus, we concentrate on the linked elements taking into account that no film picture might be a visual 'translation' of the text notwithstanding that TV viewers quickly build an overall meaning. Our main task here is to assess the relationships, whether they are *overlap*, *displacement*, *dichotomy* or other (Figure 7, above). The rest of a video clip, where no words are underlined and no co-references can be found, is regarded as open and needs some extra work of interpretation by the audience provided that this audience is willing to do so.

We require these practical solutions of the multimodality since the constellation of visual-verbal *overlap* is predominant in publications about text-image relations. In the first instance, however, it concerns talking heads, e.g. heads of state in a televised address (Bednarek and Caple 2012; Sauer 2007, 2011). But the *action component* we find in such shots is that of *actor* and the *action* is that of "talking" (cf. Jacobson's (1960) *phatic* function). Thus, TV viewers' meaning making depends on the words in total – and find nearly no support in the pictures themselves, at the most some contextual cues. Therefore, *overlap* can only be an exceptional case but more usual are *displacement* or even *dichotomy*.

---

cause interpretation problems. Don't try this, however, with words in a sentence! This principal distinction has as practical consequence, as far as a visually enriched talk show is concerned, that we concentrate on verbal and pictorial components that complement each other rather than expect a full content overlap when pictures are accompanied by texts.

Picture shots	Verbal Text (*translation CS in italics*) P = host Pauw, W = host Witteman VISUAL–VERBAL INTERRELATIONS	Music, sound (description)
 1	DISPLACEMENT P Het is vandaag maandag, maandag negen januari, de dag dat eh *P Today, it's Monday, Monday nine January, the day uh*	Beginning tune with logo, then
 2  3	OVERLAP de (.) hoofddoek van koningin Beatrix door veel kranten als belangrijk nieuws wordt gezien. *(.) Queen Beatrix's scarf by many newspapers is considered a major news item.* OVERLAP (music, pictures, text on screen)	picture from a news report with Beatrix wearing a scarf. Then tune alone with a series of standard pictures (a sort of trailer)
 4	DISPLACEMENT/OVERLAP P Welkom bij Pauw en Witteman *P Welcome to Pauw and Witteman* W Goedenavond *W Good evening*	Tune fades out, P speaking (public is applauding), then W speaking
 5  6	OVERLAP/DISPLACEMENT/ SPEAKER CONTOURING W Goedenavond dames en heren, bij ons aan tafel een Belgische chirurg, uit Gent om precies te zijn, Philippe Blondel. Die heeft als eerste Belgische chirurg, wat heet als eerste Benelux-chirurg, een geheel gezicht getransplanteerd. *W Good evening, ladies and gentlemen, here at our table a Belgian surgeon, from Gent to be precise, Philippe Blondel, who as the first Belgian surgeon, no as first Benelux surgeon, has transplanted an entire face.*	A model of a face or head lies on the table and is clearly visible (the seventh 'person' at the table?!)

Figure 7. Welcome by hosts P and W on January 9, 2012: first shots, co-references (underlined) and visual-verbal interrelations

In his investigation of camera editing in talk shows, Holly (2015) dismisses to the category of "talking heads" and proposes that of "Profilierung der Sprecher(selbst)darstellung" (*speaker contouring* or *modification*): a camera shot depicts the speaker's body language and his general appearance and the speaker's performance influences what one experiences as the meaning of the shot: anger, enthusiasm, commitment, but also expertise, skill, aptitude etc. Thus, these modifications may be useful when we try to explain how pictures showing talking people in visual-verbal TV representations contribute to the meaning making by TV viewers.

5. Findings

5.1 Macro follow-ups in the talk show and in the introduction

After one week of the talk show *P&W* – from Monday 9 January 2012 till Friday 13 January 2012 – we see that in all five broadcasts numerous macro follow-up constellations are realised, to be precise: *every* issue is a follow-up. However, not all issues are or can be visualised so that sometimes no film prompts the follow-up, e.g. when a medical operation for the first time has taken place (9 Jan. 2012), or when a political party's internal paper has been leaked to the press (12 Jan. 2012). In these cases, brackets [] are used. In Figure 8, below, we give a short overview of issues per talk show.

Day 1 Monday 9 Jan. 2012	1. Beatrix's visit to the UAE with scarf wearing 2. Young people who are aggressive towards police officers and ambulance staff and create problems for police officers Zap service 3. American primaries (clips from US media) 4. [Issue of face transplantation without news film]
Day 2 Tuesday 10 Jan. 2012	1. Court decision to re-install the head of the central institution asylum seekers 2. Countertenor Scholl's performance Zap service 3. Issue of violence in public transport after press reports
Day 3 Wednesday 11 Jan. 2012	1. [News about report Institute for Social Research: more money for primary education creates no better achievements] 2. News about shells in Syria that kill a journalist (breaking news) 3. [Haiti visit by Dutch-Haitian researcher] Zap service 4. Crime watch journalist Pieter R. de Vries about murderer Joran van der Sloot in Peru

Day 4 Thursday 12 Jan. 2012	1. Beatrix defends her scarf against her critics ("nonsense") 2. [Report Christian Democrats leaked to the press] Zap service 3. Film *Süskind* about saviour of Jewish children under German occupation (long issue, with many different conversations)
Day 5 Friday 13 Jan. 2012	Exceptional broadcast on "State of the Country", introduced by special trailer, with four guests who discuss the situation in the Netherlands on the basis of proposed items (by editors) and suggested film fragments (by guests themselves) used in the show: Ed Nijpels, MP VVD; Rick van der Ploeg, economist and prof.; Bert Brussen, journalist; Trudy Coenen, teacher VMBO (secondary vocational education, the most general secondary school) Zap service in between

Figure 8. Follow-up constellations that generate talk issues in P&W

Although nearly all issues in the talk show are follow-ups of news reports and therefore form a bridge between earlier news items and political topics that seem worth to be discussed more intensively, some topics are more focussed upon than other ones. This is clear from the introduction that prepares the TV viewers for the entire broadcast. In Figure 9, below, (with numbers from Figure 8, above, even if they differ from the sequence in the broadcast itself) we give an impression of the introductions of all five talk shows of our corpus. After the first issue, always the tune starts.

Four talk shows (day 1 till day 4) are unequivocally related to the news, thus form follow-ups to earlier news programmes in every conceivable way. And, by the way, their screening follows exactly the *news framing* of the original source, i.e., there is no obvious discrepancy. The relationship between earlier news and the actual talk show is always realised, even though some TV viewers may need some more time to remember exactly what the earlier news was about. But mainly, it is clarified by the hosts, as is the case on day 3, the visit to Haiti by a Dutch-Haitian female researcher, which was not a news item, but was broadcast by the Suriname news (former Dutch colony, with news also in Dutch); consequently, the editors projected it onto the screens. On day 4, an internal report by a political party was leaked to the press. It was treated as a news item of its own, although no film was available: the party logo and text were sufficient.[8]

8. On day 5, however, the show's format has been modified rather strongly. Because the four guests had been required to suggest their own topics as well as their own visualisations the show was a rather open mix of different visual means (photographs, films, news reports, documentaries etc.). This exceptional openness caused a structure that realised no follow-up constellation in the first instance, but a constellation that combined different filmic materials with verbal explanations and opinions by the guests themselves. The guests were, so to speak, able to create their own macro and micro follow-ups in text and pictures by discussing and commenting their own visually presented issues.

Day	Visual-verbal introduction	Verbal introduction only
1	 1 Beatrix's scarf in UAE	
	 2 General camera impressions	2 Announcement of discussion between two MPs about young people's violent against ambulances
	 3 American Republican Primaries	
2	 1 Recent Dutch Court decision	
	 2 Countertenor	
	 3 Violence in public transport	
3	 1 General camera impressions	1 Announcement of discussion about new report of Institute for Social Research
	 2 General camera impressions	2 Announcement of report from visit to Haiti one year after earthquake

	 3 Murder trial Peru	
	 4 Journalist killed in Syria	
4	 1 Beatrix's reaction to critics	
	 2 General camera impressions	2 Announcement of interview about internal report Christian Democrats
	 3 General camera impressions	3 Announcement of discussion about the new film *Süskind*
5	 Only news of the day – court decision in Peru – with visual intro	
	 A short trailer presenting the topic "State of the Country" (made especially for *P&W*	

Figure 9. The visual-verbal introductions in P&W with tune after the first issue and short references to the issues of the respective broadcasts

The *introductions* always start with a picture from the news of the day. Therefore, TV viewers can 'learn' from every introduction that the talk show *P&W* aspires after a follow-up of the (mainly) political news. It is realised verbally, visually or in visual-verbal form. Only on the occasion of day 5, the introduction shows another feature, namely after a short reference to the news of the day the court decision of a murder trial in Peru, which was an issue on day 3: it consists of the screening of a filmic summary in order to get the TV viewers in the right frame of mind. This can be considered an *Einspielfilm*[9] (a video clip or 'trailer' prepared by the editors that does not originate from the news). Yet, the follow-up constellation here is only postponed and not waived.

5.2 Micro follow-ups (visual framing): The case of Queen Beatrix's scarf

Our main example in this paragraph is the discussion about the Dutch head of state, Queen Beatrix, who paid a state visit to the United Arab Emirates (UAE) in the beginning of 2012 and, when visiting a mosque, was wearing a scarf draped around her hat (talk shows on day 1, day 4 and day 5)[10]. The discussion was *visually framed* by several photographs and film stills of her wearing a scarf – which was an appropriate visual motive for triggering verbal exchanges in the talk show and to control the discussion line.[11]

On day 1 (9 January 2012), the publication of the photograph in the newspapers, which was shown on the wall screens, caused a discussion between a MP of the *PVV* (literally 'Freedom Party', but in fact anti-Islam and populist right wing), a MP of the *PvdA* (Dutch Labour Party) and the editor in chief of the newspaper *De Volkskrant*. In this discussion, the discourse went from the visual (the scarf) to the verbal interpretation. It took two lines of argumentation, either "respectful behaviour in Islamic cultures" (thus pro) or "symbol of women repression" (thus con). The *macro follow-up* was realised by a video clip from yesterday's evening news (8 January 2012), the *visual framing* in the subsequent conversations by stills from this clip, by other photographs of different headgear of the Queen and by a "tweet"

9. See also footnote 3, above.

10. See also Ensink (2012, this volume).

11. Once a prepared editors' visual, a combination of photographs with a great amount of divers hats the Queen wore during the years, was used undoubtedly in the expectation that this specific topic would turn the TV viewers to her general habit of wearing remarkable hats (see also Figure 10, below, (c) and (d)). This line, however, was neither picked up by politicians nor by other guests so that the hosts (or the editors) then obviously skipped it already during the first minutes.

by the *PVV* leader Geert Wilders, which altogether urged the participants to react respectively. Thus, even if the discussion followed a certain line, a new *visual framing* caused an interruption or at least a modification in the course of the discussion.

On the second occasion (day 4, 12 January 2012), the *macro follow-up* was anew the screening of yesterday's news with one relevant item: that the Queen personally rejected the criticisms of her scarf wearing and underlined the diplomatic custom of adjustment to the culture of the visited country. It was told by the news correspondent who accompanied the Queen (a common form of *news framing*). Because the issue itself was elaborated on by a former female TV correspondent in the Middle East and a political reporter of the newspaper *NRC Handelsblad*, the discussion was more fundamental than the first time (on day 1). It went from "normal respect" via "freedom of choice to use or use not a headscarf" to "characteristic of a specific religious culture". It started with *visual framings* of broadcasts by the former correspondent who, in Teheran, always wore a headscarf in the news reports. The screening as such was an interruption of the developing discourse, as is often the case in *P&W* when a host says: "Shall we first see the film?" It triggered not so much the topic of Islamic culture as urged the correspondent to explain her then-behaviour.

All *visual framings* in this issue were presented as to *overlap* visually with the verbal discourse, even if the discourse itself developed in leaps and bounds.[12] Evidently, the editors had expected an elaboration on the government's policy, for they had prepared a short series screenings of confrontations between the *PVV* and the Queen. These *visual framings* once more provided for an interruption and produced eventually a loose form of discourse. Even the director of a film who was present took his chance and commented on the Queen's photograph: "... as a matter of fact I regard that headscarf as beautiful, very nice ..." As a result, the whole issue had a large degree of ritual communication and dutiful argumentation, maybe also due to the fact that there was no clear opponent at the table. Except for the interruptions, the visual-verbal interrelations were *overlap, displacement, speaker contouring*, but not *dichotomy*.[13]

12. Another important point in the conversations was the role of the Dutch government that, according to the political reporter, should have made, much earlier than it had done in fact, a clear acknowledgement of the head of state's right to respect the Muslim culture – and so should have protected her against political attacks. The latter point could not be illustrated by visuals, other than by repetitions of earlier photographs. So the *visual framing* of this part of the discussion was hardly supportive for the TV viewers.

13. *Dichotomy* was never found, due to the fact that visualisations that turned out not to trigger verbal exchanges very quickly disappeared from the wall screens.

On the third occasion on day 5 (13 January 2012), the talk show on the "State of the Country" used *visual framings* with the headscarf photograph of Beatrix, which we know already from day 1 and day 4, to confirm visually what the participants were saying on a certain moment. Because the exceptional format imposed upon every guest to suggest his own topic, the first one was "negativism in the Dutch political culture". One of the expectable sub-topics that the editors had prepared was the criticism of the Queen by the *PVV* that was framed by the meanwhile well-known photograph. The fourth topic was "provincialism" and it was framed too, only for a short moment, by a photograph of Crown Princess Máxima with headscarf. The conversation developed about how relaxed people in other countries, in contrast to Dutch people and politicians, experience the fact of adequate clothing by Muslims. Only one short *overlap* was produced that created a kind of 'interjection', which occurs when participants directly react to a new screening: "What a beautiful scarf, they say in UK", meaning not in Holland where some politicians regard it as ugly.

5.3 Visual-verbal interrelations

The analysis of talk show discourse that is visually framed by film clips and other visuals needs examinations of visual-verbal interrelations dependent on the state of affairs during the ongoing conversations. We deal with five problems:

1. verbal text that is linked to the news (the *macro follow-up*) and reacts to the hosts' questions who transform the clips' content into verbal utterances,
2. shots of speaking and reacting people (guests and hosts) edited by several cameras, which may include *speaker contouring modifications*,
3. shots of guests and hosts on the one hand, and studio public shots on the other hand, depicting the studio public's reactions to both the verbal and the visual discourse,
4. shots that capture visual framings in the speakers' visible background (the screen walls) so that beside the speaker also the screen representation can be perceived,
5. shots of the video clips that fill the TV home screen completely, whereas talk can be heard meanwhile (possibly, however, the original source's voice-over commentary first).

The *co-references* between the verbal track and the visual track are examined first. Not only screenings are examined, but also shots of guests pointing, looking or otherwise dealing with the pictures. Then we establish the *visual-verbal interrelations*, whether they are *overlap, displacement, dichotomy* or *speaker contouring*.

In Figure 10 (below), nearly all instances of visualisations are documented that serve for framing the verbal discourse in this sequence of the talk show. In all pictures selected by the editors and/or captured by the cameras we detect problem (4): an obtrusive-unobtrusive presence of the news in visual framings that urge the speakers time and again to turn to them. It contributes to the regular visual character of the talk show.

Problem (1) is the most general picture in the beginning of the show. In (a) (Figure 10), TV viewers see hosts and guests and on their background a photograph of Queen Beatrix; host Pauw is saying: "Today, it's Monday, Monday nine January, the day uh Queen Beatrix's scarf by many newspapers is considered a major item …" (underlined is the co-reference – what one sees when one listens to Pauw). The projection of the photograph focusses the viewers' attention instantly visually on the main subject and the words inform them verbally.

Figure 10. Visual framing in P&W on January 9, 2012 from the point of view of the TV viewers (during the first 5 minutes of the issue of Beatrix's scarf)

Problem (3), the representation of the inner circle surrounded by the studio public, is realised in (d), (e) and (i): we see the surrounding public that responses to the conversation by attentively looking, but is permanently visually co-framed by still photographs. TV viewers get the impression of a visual-verbal form of discussion that is experienced by visible studio public that acts on TV viewers' behalf. In pictures (b) and (g), name and affiliation in script are added, which is typical for the beginning of a sequence and informative for TV viewers. The pictures (a, b, c, d, g, h) represent problem (4): they give evidence to the fact that the discourse is visually related to and elaborates on the scarf (a), the headgear (c, d) and the discussion in the Dutch public opinion ("tweet" in b). A conflict determines the first sequence. One group (*PVV*, anti-Islam party, MP Hero Brinkman) pleas for not visiting a mosque in the host country, in accordance with his leader's "tweet" (b). The tweet shows what the group formulates. The other group (represented by the Dutch Labour Party MP Ahmed Marcouch, and the editor in chief of the newspaper *de Volkskrant*, Philippe Remarque) takes on the position that the scarf in a mosque symbolises respect and that the equation of scarf and repression is incorrect and based on an anti-Muslim ideology. The pictures (d, g, h) on the studio screens stimulate the discussion and keep on representing the topics.[14]

Problem (5), the home screen filling TV broadcast, shows in the beginning of this sequence: the screening of a news report. In (f) however, a still from this report fills the home screen completely, whereas the conversation is going on. It provides a visual framing that is a bit obsessive here, as if the editors claimed that TV viewers did not sufficiently become aware of the fact that the discussion is about a visit to a mosque.

Problem (2) is demonstrated in picture (h). Because the camera focusses explicitly on two guests talking with each other and puts all other context away, the TV viewers observe directly the conflicting situation that gives, together with the captured gazes, the speakers' appearances a clearer *contour*. The conflict comes to the fore explicitly, when the MP says (co-references are underlined): "And here I see a Muslim scarf draped around the crown [earlier he compared the Queen's hat with her crown, CS] of our Queen. And this symbol / there are millions / I think / I think the Dutch people agree with me that that this symbol never should have been used ..." The (medium) close-up shot excludes other visible elements and concentrates in full on facial expressions and body language, which thus functions as a *contouring* effect. Its result is that the MP is shown as angry and not fully rational at this moment.

14. From our point of view it is interesting that the visual framing mostly is realised by photographs and that these photographs *match* with descriptions and explanations in the participants' texts. In (c) and (d) several hats of Queen Beatrix are displayed, which operates as a *displacement*. But there are occasions on which the desired match cannot be produced (not even as *dichotomy*). One shot from the UAE where she had draped a scarf-like shawl around her hat (a), thus demonstratively not wearing a scarf (like other women in her entourage, see the news shot (f)), disappeared after a short while from the screens since it was not able to prompt the discussion. Even the prepared headgear photographs (d) vanished from the screens: no discussion evolved about them.

In general, there is a weak relationship between the words uttered and the shots. When the studio screens show corresponding visualisations then there is nearly no *overlap*, but mostly *displacement*. As far as the editing of cameras is concerned it is *speaker contouring*.

5.4 The visualisation of talk

Interviews are considered the main business of political communication on TV and in talk shows. But since we have nearly no real interview in our corpus, we study interview-like settings. What we might see, however, is not so much the setting itself as the way interview-like situations *change* during processing through the use of visual framings, through verbal reactions to screenings and, in general, through camera work. We may say they change from an interview-like beginning into a kind of debate, when other guests get involved, into an open-end and *zigzag* structure.

Since on day 5 another format has been applied, the normal talk show *P&W* presents in four days five issues that resemble interviews, at least in part. The majority of these appearances, however, develop into debates. So (see Figure 8, above) on day 1, there are two MPs discussing the wish of more respect for police officers (issue 2, day 1). The decision of a court to re-install the head of the central institution asylum seekers is reason to stage a sort of indictment discourse with many video clips that urge the guest to defend herself (issue 1, day 2). Later on a debate is initiated between a victim of violence in public transport and the director of the Dutch railways, department of travellers, about how people can react to acts of violence (issue 3, day 2). A report by the Institute for Social Research, which found that more money for primary education does not produce better achievements, is the reason for a debate between a MP and the highest representative of primary education (issue 1, day 3).

Only when an internal report of the Christian Democrats about the new course of the party leaked to the press, under the heading "Christian Democrats jerking to the left", an interview seems to start (issue 2, day 4). A former CD MP is invited to react to the questions. Later on a political reporter attending the show for other reasons is demanded to ask further questions: they change the setting into a debate. Since the director of a film (who belongs to issue 3 on this day 4) is present, he reacts to the current state of the debate too and broadens its impact. Thus, the conversation started as an interview opened by host questions and visually framed by the party logo (see Figure 11, below). Yet, quickly it changes into a debate between four persons. The debate was dominated by the former MP who, in her assertive role, was very often displayed in multiple pictures and combinations with other speakers, in a series of short shots. This sort of visual framing accentuated her predominant appearance and gave her a specific *contour* – which otherwise, e.g. in an interview, would be perceived as less predominant. Even though the tenor of the exchanges was considerably sharp, there was nonetheless enough room for laughing also by the studio public, which softened the focus and contributed to its zigzag configuration.

The quick move from an interview setting to a debate setting was clearly prepared by the editors. The hosts explicitly solicited for more arguments from other guests and showed expecting facial expressions. They stimulated the debate sphere, but after a while, after some debating, they steered the conversation towards a more specific question: about the future leadership of the party. They did so by presenting nine photographs of potential leaders (see Figure 11, below) and challenged the guests to comment on them. However, this visual framing did not succeed since the guests focussed only upon one figure. Therefore, and because of time reasons, the discussion faded out and the "zap service" was announced.

Figure 11. Interview-like setting between a politician, two hosts, a journalist and another guest (on day 4, 12 January 2012). First row: logo of the party and photographs of candidates for leadership. Second row: debate situation with journalist and other guest

We see that the *visual framings* (*contouring* by cameras and screening of logo and photographs of potential leaders, thus *overlap* and *displacement*) contribute to a more loose form of interview *and/or* debate. It is pointless relating the looseness of talk to the effects of the visual framings or to the habit of non-conventional acting by the hosts (Landreville et al. 2010; Vraga et al. 2012). Anyway, its connectedness can be inferred by the TV audiences. But we can observe that the *visualisation of interviews* in the talk show *P&W* urges politicians and other guests to execute a more visible or symbolic form of communicative behaviour.[15] What is adequate no

15. So did Henk Bleker (Kee 2012, 183–202). Former State Secretary for Economic Affairs Henk Bleker and boy asylum seeker Mauro Manuel met each other on the talk show of 28 October 2011. Mauro who had heard that he had to go back to Angola, although he lived more than eight

longer depends on the terms of content and rhetorical power, but on appearance, familiarity with media exposure as well as readiness to get involved in commenting on visualisations and films during conversations. Hence, verbal utterances and their content are less prominent in such TV settings.

6. Conclusion and discussion

The chapter regards the *follow-up* constellation as a general pattern of televised socio-political discourse. Also the creation of new news events by the talk show itself must be taken into consideration, for the never ending structure of the landscape of the news searches for new elements that resemble the well-known ones. Therefore, it is not news framing as such that occurs in the talk show; it is its re-use and its visualisation that matter.

Thus, our research shows that non-filmic issues are not favoured by the editors of the talk show *P&W*. Moreover, they do not seem to be interested in conventional talk any longer. Therefore, they apply not only the general *macro follow-up* setting by relating the talk show issues to the news of the day, but also a setting that allows for as much televisuality as possible. Hence, without news reports that precede the verbal exchanges no *TV talk* takes place. However, the format of *P&W* allows for numerous variations that are not yet fully investigated here, although our corpus shows a considerably broad spectrum of potential realisations. Amply, we elaborated on the show's specific multimodality by making use of the concept of *visual framings* in the *micro follow-ups* that are accompanying verbal utterances, triggering them or stimulating a short political performance. This occurred at many moments in the talk show and made it a really multimodal event.

It is the *micro follow-up* constellation that needs more scrutiny. It carries not only a wide range of variations, as our corpus has shown, but might also sometimes

years in the Netherlands, called vehemently for protest (in which he eventually succeeded, for he got a permanent residence permit on 3 April 2013). On this early occasion, however, Bleker defended his colleague CD Minister for Immigration, who was responsible for the announcement of permit ending, directly against Mauro. It was an exciting conversation that finished by Bleker writing a short note with an invitation to a football play and pushing it over to Mauro, fully captured by a camera. The "note to Mauro" became a symbol. It was mentioned in the discussion on 12 January 2012, although no pictures were shown. We think that the editors did not expect the mentioning of the Mauro case, and therefore did not prepare the pictures. Besides, for this double interview with Mauro and Bleker, Pauw and Witteman were awarded the *De Luis 2011 (the Louse 2011)*, the prize for the best Dutch language interview in this year. The awarding ceremony was on 29 March 2012 (http://pauwenwitteman.vara.nl/media/90644, accessed 15 November 2013).

show that verbal actions could be replaced by pictorial actions. This latter aspect is not yet worked out, also due to the absence of appropriate investigation methods.

Guests and hosts point to the pictures to underline a verbal confirmation. They look at the pictures to accentuate a certain verbal scope. They are encouraged to think about them and to pick up an element to elaborate on it. Very often, however, the screening of a video clip – and sometimes the showing of a photograph – is an *interruption* of the ongoing communication. On the one hand, it is caused by a technical necessity since the TV viewers get this clip on their home screens completely filled with the film, on the other hand, it cuts the lines of the argumentation and produces a topic shift. So visuals support the information processing, but at the same time disrupt the quality of the verbal exchanges and create an imbalanced or otherwise loose structure.

Looking at broadcasts of *P&W* and reflecting its political impact is a strange experience. For we see many politicians and hear theirs opinions, but we also see that our impression is influenced by the way they act and interact in the show. We consider the video clips and the flexible ways how politicians keep their balance, i.e., distinguish themselves from other politicians who are less balanced (Verhoef 2012). We participate in this process rather than perceive a result. Political communication presented in this way has an increasingly everyday character so that TV viewers may have the impression that they are part of the political play. Follow-ups suggest that political communication never ends, but they substantiate also that the TV viewer, just due to its everydayness, has less grip on them (Esser et al. 2012). This is already observed as a trend in the development of political communication on TV in a set of different European countries and as a tendency of the public service television in the Netherlands (Wonneberger et al. 2013).

To sum up, the social construction of reality – and of political reality – in the talk show *P&W* is its strict dedication to visual reality. You get what you *see*, but what you do not see you will not get. Only if a link with a visualisation can be established, the talk show may consume the issue. Its macro follow-up constellation, however, looks simple. There must be an occasion for the hosts to say "Let's first see the video" or "Before we continue, let's have a look".

References

Bednarek, Monika and Helen Caple. 2012. *News Discourse*. London: Continuum.

Bell, Allan. 1984. "Language Style as Audience Design." *Language in Society* 13 (2): 145–204. DOI: 10.1017/S004740450001037X

Bell, Allan. 2001. "Back in Style: Reworking Audience Design." In *Style and Sociolinguistic Variation*, ed. by Penelope Eckert and John R. Rickford, 139–196. Cambridge: Cambridge University Press.

Breeze, Ruth. 2013. "British Media Discourses on the Wearing of Religious Symbols." In *Verbal and Visual Rhetoric in a Media World*, ed. by Hilde van Belle, Paul Gillaerts, Baldwin van Gorp, Dorien van de Mieroop and Kris Rutten, 193–207. Amsterdam: Leiden University Press.

Bolter, Jay David and Richard Grusin. 1999. *Remediation: Understanding New Media*. Cambridge, Mass.: MIT Press.

Bubel, Claudia. 2008. "Film Audiences as Overhearers." *Journal of Pragmatics* 40 (1): 55–71. DOI: 10.1016/j.pragma.2007.10.001

Bull, Peter. 2015. "Follow-Ups in Broadcast Political Discourse: Speeches, Interviews and Parliamentary Questions". This volume.

Carter, Cynthia and Allan Stuart. 2009. "The Visual Culture of Television News." In *Using Visual Evidence*, ed. by Richard Howells and Robert W. Matson, 139–152. Maidenhead: Open University Press/McGraw-Hill.

Charaudeau, Patrick. 2002. "A Communicative Conception of Discourse." *Discourse Studies* 4 (3): 301–318. DOI: 10.1177/14614456020040030301

Clark, Herbert H. 1996. *Using Language*. Cambridge: Cambridge University Press. DOI: 10.1017/CBO9780511620539

Clayman, Steven and John Heritage. 2002. *The News Interview: Journalists and Public Figures on the Air*. Cambridge: Cambridge University Press. DOI: 10.1017/CBO9780511613623

Clayman, Steven. 2007. "Speaking on Behalf of the Public in Broadcast News Interviews." In *Reporting Talk. Reported Speech in Interaction*, ed. by Elizabeth Holt and Rebecca Clift, 221–243. Cambridge: Cambridge University Press.

Coleman, Renita and Stephen Banning. 2006. "Network TV News' Affective Framing of the Presidential Candidates: Evidence for a Second Level Agenda-Setting Effect through Visual Framing." *Journalism & Mass Communication Quarterly* 83 (2): 313–328. DOI: 10.1177/107769900608300206

Coleman, Renita and H. Denis Wu. 2006. "More than Words Alone: Incorporating Broadcasters' Nonverbal Communication into the Stages of Crisis Coverage Theory – Evidence from September 11." *Journal of Broadcasting & Electronic Media* 50 (1): 1–17. DOI: 10.1207/s15506878jobem5001_1

Cullen, Richard. 2002. "Supportive Teacher Talk: The Importance of the F-Move." *ELT Journal* 56 (2): 117–127. DOI: 10.1093/elt/56.2.117

Dahinden, Urs. 2006. *Framing. Eine integrative Theorie der Massenkommunikation* [Framing: An integrated theory of mass communication]. Konstanz: UVK.

De Smedt, Eva and Kristel Vandenbrande. 2011. "Political Television Formats as Strategic Resources in Achieving Journalists' Roles." In *Talking Politics in Broadcast Media: Cross-Cultural Perspectives on Political Interviewing, Journalism and Accountability*, ed. by Mats Ekström and Marianna Patrona, 75–92. Amsterdam/Philadelphia: Benjamins. DOI: 10.1075/dapsac.42.08sme

De Vreese, Claes H. 2003. *Framing Europe. Television News and European Integration*. Amsterdam: Aksant.

Ensink, Titus. 2012. "Framing as a Continual and Repetitive Process in Political Communication." In *Proceedings of the ESF Strategic Workshop on Follow-ups Across Discourse Domains: A Cross-Cultural Exploration of Their Forms and Functions, Würzburg (Germany), 31 May – 2 June 2012*, ed. by Anita Fetzer, Elda Weizman and Elisabeth Reber, 58–71. Würzburg: Universität Würzburg – [online]. URL: http://opus.bibliothek.uni-wuerzburg.de/volltexte/2012/7165/; URN: urn:nbn:de:bvb:20-opus-71656.

Ensink, Titus. 2015. "Framing the Queen's Headscarf: A Case Study on Follow-Ups in Dutch Politics." This volume.
Entman, Robert M. 1993. "Framing: Toward Clarification of a Fractured Paradigm." *Journal of Communication* 43 (4): 51–58. DOI: 10.1111/j.1460-2466.1993.tb01304.x
Esser, Frank, Claes H. de Vreese, Jesper Strömbäck, Peter van Aelst, Toril Aalberg, James Stanyer, Günther Lengauer, Rosa Berganza, Guido Legnante, Stylianos Papathanassopoulos, Susana Salgado, Tamir Sheafer and Carsten Reinemann. 2012. "Political Information Opportunities in Europe: A Longitudinal and Comparative Study of Thirteen Television Systems." *The International Journal of Press/Politics* 17 (2): 247–274. DOI: 10.1177/1940161212442956
Fetzer, Anita, Elda Weizman and Elisabeth Reber. 2012. "Introduction." In *Proceedings of the ESF Strategic Workshop on Follow-ups Across Discourse Domains: A Cross-Cultural Exploration of Their Forms and Functions, Würzburg (Germany), 31 May – 2 June 2012,* ed. by Anita Fetzer, Elda Weizman and Elizabeth Reber, 3–4. Würzburg: Universität Würzburg – [online]. URL: http://opus.bibliothek.uni-wuerzburg.de/volltexte/2012/7165/; URN: urn:nbn:de:bvb:20-opus-71656.
Fetzer, Anita and Elda Weizman. 2015. "Introduction". This volume.
Fetzer, Anita, Weizman, Elda and Elisabeth Reber (eds). 2012. *Proceedings of the ESF Strategic Workshop on Follow-ups Across Discourse Domains: A Cross-Cultural Exploration of Their Forms and Functions*, Würzburg (Germany), 31 May – 2 June 2012. Würzburg: Universität Würzburg – [online]. URL: http://opus.bibliothek.uni-wuerzburg.de/volltexte/2012/7165/; URN: urn:nbn:de:bvb:20-opus-71656.
Fischer-Lichte, Erika. 2008. *The Transformative Power of Performance: A New Aesthetics.* London: Routledge.
Gäbler, Bernd. 2001. "*... und unseren täglichen Talk gib uns heute!" Inszenierungsstrategien, redaktionelle Dramaturgien und Rolle der TV-Polit-Talkshows* ["... and give us today our daily talk!" Production strategies, editorial dramaturgies and the role of TV political talk shows]. Frankfurt am Main: Otto Brenner Stiftung.
Goffman, Ervin. 1979. "Footing." *Semiotica* 25 (1–2): 1–29. DOI: 10.1515/semi.1979.25.1-2.1
Goffman, Ervin. 1981. *Forms of Talk.* Philadelphia: University of Pennsylvania Press.
Graber, Doris. 1989. "Content and Meaning. What's it all about?" *American Behavioral Scientist* 33: 144–52. DOI: 10.1177/0002764289033002004
Graber, Doris. 2012. *On Media: Making Sense of Politics.* Oxford: Oxford University Press.
Greiffenhagen, Christian. 2009. "News Interviews: Clayman and Heritage's 'The News Interview'." In *Doing Social Science: Evidence and Methods in Empirical Research.* ed. by Fiona Devine and Sue Heath, 167–192. Basingstoke: Palgrave Macmillan.
Gruber, Helmut. 2015. "Intertextual References in Austrian Parliamentary Debates: Between Evaluation and Argumentation". This volume.
Haumer, Florian and Wolfgang Donsbach. 2009. "The Rivalry of Nonverbal Cues on the Perception of Politicians by Television Viewers." *Journal of Broadcasting & Electronic Media* 53 (2): 262–279. DOI: 10.1080/08838150902907918
Holly, Werner. 2015. "Bildinszenierung in Talkshows. Medienlinguistische Anmerkungen zu einer Form von 'Bild-Sprach-Transkription.'" [Visual production of talk shows. Media-linguistic remarks on a type of 'picture language transcription']. In *Polit-Talkshows. Interdisziplinäre Perspektiven auf ein multimodales Format* [Political talk shows. Interdisciplinary perspectives on a multimodal format], ed. by Heiko Girnth and Sascha Michel, 123–144. Stuttgart: ibidem-Verlag.

Huls, Erica. 2013. "Politieke Partijdigheid in Talkshow-Gesprekken." [Political Bias in Talk Show Conversations]. In *Studies in Taalbeheersing 4*. ed. by Ronny Boogaart and Henrike Jansen, 157–169. Assen: Van Gorcum.

Huls, Erica and Jasper Varwijk. 2011. "Political Bias in TV Interviews." *Discourse & Society* 22 (1): 48–65. DOI: 10.1177/0957926510382836

Hutchby, Ian. 2011. "Non-Neutrality and Argument in the Hybrid Political Interview." *Discourse Studies* 13 (3): 349–365. DOI: 10.1177/1461445611400665

Jakobson, Roman. 1960. "Closing Statement: Linguistics and Poetics." In *Style in Language*, ed. by Thomas Sebeok, 350–377. Cambridge, Mass.: MIT Press.

Kee, Peter. 2012. *Het Briefje van Bleker. Over Intriges op het Binnenhof, Politici, Spindoctors en Pauw en Witteman* [Bleker's Note. Parliamentary Intrigues, Politicians, Spin Doctors and Pauw and Witteman]. Amsterdam: Atlas Contact.

Kleijwegt, Margalith and Max van Weezel. 2011. "Op tv, of roemloos ten onder." [On TV, or perish ingloriously]. *Vrij Nederland*: 17 Dec. 2011.

Klemm, Michael. 2015. "Wenn Politik auf Einspielfilme trifft. Zur multimodalen Argumentation in der politischen Fernsehdiskussion *hart aber fair*"." [When politics meet video clips. On multimodal argumentation in the TV discussion *hart aber fair*]. In *Polit-Talkshows. Interdisziplinäre Perspektiven auf ein multimodales Format* [Political talk shows. Interdisciplinary perspectives on a multimodal format], ed. by Heiko Girnth and Sascha Michel, 97–122. Stuttgart: ibidem-Verlag.

Kress, Gunther. 2010. *Multimodality. A Social Semiotic Approach to Contemporary Communication*. London: Routledge.

Lakoff, George. 2004. *Don't Think of an Elephant! Know your Values and Frame the Debate*. White River Junction (VT): Chelsea Green.

Landreville, Kristen D., R. Lance Holbert and Heather L. LaMarre. 2010. "The Influence of Late-Night TV Comedy Viewing on Political Talk: A Moderated-Mediation Model." *International Journal of Press/Politics* 15 (4): 482–498. DOI: 10.1177/1940161210371506

Lauerbach, Gerda. 2010. "Manoeuvring between the Political, the Personal and the Private: Talk, Image and Rhythm in TV Dialogue." *Discourse & Communication* 4 (2): 125–159. DOI: 10.1177/1750481310363980

Liu, Yu and Kay L. O'Halloran. 2009. "Intersemiotic Texture: Analyzing Cohesive Devices between Language and Images." *Social Semiotics* 19 (4): 367–388. DOI: 10.1080/10350330903361059

Matthes, Jörg. 2009. "What's in a Frame? A Content Analysis of Media Framing Studies in the World's Leading Communication Journals, 1990–2005." *Journalism & Mass Communication Quarterly* 86 (2): 349–367. DOI: 10.1177/107769900908600206

Meinhof, Ulrike. 1994. "Double Talk in News Broadcasts." In *Media Texts: Authors and Readers* ed. by David Graddol and Oliver Boyd-Barrett, 212–223. Clevedon: Multilingual Matters.

Meyer, Thomas. 2009. "Visuelle Kommunikation und politische Öffentlichkeit". [Visual Communication and the Political Public Sphere]. In *Strategien der Visualisierung. Verbildlichung als Mittel Politischer Kommunikation* [Visualisation strategies. Pictoriaism as a mean in political communication], ed. by Herfried Münkler and Jens Hacke, 53–69. Frankfurt am Main: Campus.

Montgomery, Martin. 2007. *The Discourse of Broadcast News. A Linguistic Approach*. London: Routledge.

Neufeld, Johannes. 2008. *Interaktion in politischen Talkshows. Eine Inhaltsanalyse der Formate ANNE WILL, hartaberfair und Maybrit ILLNER* [Interaction in Political Talk Shows. A Content Analysis of Two Different Formats]. Frankfurt am Main: Grin. (Master Thesis, University of Mainz).

Nichols, Bill. 2010. *Introduction to Documentary*. Bloomington: Indiana University Press. Second Edition.

Pauw, Jeroen and Paul Witteman. 2010. *4 okt. 2010 – Nieuwe lokatie Pauw & Witteman* New location P & W]. http://pauwenwitteman.vara.nl/media/8716 (accessed 11 November 2013).

Ranta, Michael. 2011. "Stories in Pictures (and Non-Pictorial Objects): A Narratological and Cognitive Psychological Approach." *Contemporary Aesthetics* 9. http://www.contempaesthetics.org/newvolume/pages/article.php?articleID=619 (accessed 11 November 2013).

Richardson, Kay, Katy Parry and John Corner. 2012. *Political Culture and Media Genre: Beyond the News*. London: Palgrave Macmillan. DOI: 10.1057/9781137291271

Royce, Terry D. 2007. "Intersemiotic Complementarity: A Framework for Multimodal Discourse Analysis." In *New Directions in the Analysis of Multimodal Discourse*, ed. by Terry D. Royce and Wendy L. Bowcher, 63–109. New Jersey: Erlbaum.

Ruigrok, Nel, Joep Schaper, Kasper Welbers, Carina Jacobi, Pauline van der Beek and Sandra Wagemakers. 2012. *Impact van Pauw en Witteman*. Amsterdam: Nederlandse Nieuwsmonitor. www.nieuwsmonitor.net/d/190/Pauw_en_Witteman_pdf (accessed 12 November 2013).

Sauer, Christoph. 2007. "Christmas Messages by Heads of State: Multimodality and Media Adaptations." In *Political Discourse in the Media*, ed. by Anita Fetzer and Gerda Lauerbach, 227–273. Amsterdam/Philadelphia: Benjamins. DOI: 10.1075/pbns.160.13sau

Sauer, Christoph. 2009. "Geschwätzigkeit und Stille. Eine Problemskizze zum Filmdialog." [Loquacity and silence. A problem sketch of filmic dialogue]. *Fenster – Zeitschrift für Zeichen und Wirkung* 1 (3–4): 117–141.

Sauer, Christoph. 2010. "Hingucker und/oder Wegleser. Niederländische Pressebilder (fast) ohne Text." [Looking and/or reading away: Dutch press photographs with (nearly) no text]. In *Kontexte und Texte. Konstellationen literalen Handelns*, ed. by Peter Klotz, Paul R. Portmann-Tselikas and Georg Weidacher, 301–325. Tübingen: Narr.

Sauer, Christoph. 2011. "On Multimodal Communication: Televised Christmas Messages by Heads of State." In *Conjunctions and Disruptions. Communication, Information and Media Studies in Europe*, ed. by María J. Pando Canteli, 193–219. Bilbao: University of Deusto Press.

Sauer, Christoph. 2012. "Multimodality and Performance. Britain's first Holocaust Memorial Day (BBC on January 27, 2001)." In *Dialogue in Politics*, ed. by Lawrence N. Berlin and Anita Fetzer, 241–307. Amsterdam/ Philadelphia: Benjamins. DOI: 10.1075/ds.18.16sau

Sauer, Christoph. 2013. "Memoria in Documentary Film: How Spectators Remember Sequences and Actualize Public Memory." In *Verbal and Visual Rhetoric in a Media World*, ed. by Hilde van Belle, Paul Gillaerts, Baldwin van Gorp, Dorien van de Mieroop and Kris Rutten, 389–413. Amsterdam: Leiden University Press.

Sauer, Christoph and Marrit Nijdam-Akkerman. 2013. "Hoe Gaan Woorden en Beelden Samen? Over de Verhouding van Tekstinformatie en Beeldinformatie in Documentaires." [How do Words and Images Interact? On the Relationships between Text and Image Information in Documentaries]. In *Studies in Taalbeheersing* 4, ed. by Ronny Boogaart and Henrike Jansen, 303–313. Assen: Van Gorcum.

Scanell, Paddy. 2009. "Review Essay: The Liveness of Broadcast Talk." *Journal of Communication*, 59, E1–E6. DOI: 10.1111/j.1460-2466.2009.01460.x

Scheufele, Bertram T. and Dietram A. Scheufele. 2010. "Of Spreading Activation, Applicability, and Schemas: Conceptual Distinctions and their Operational Implications for Measuring Frames and Framing Effects." In *Doing News Framing Analysis: Empirical and Theoretical Perspectives*, ed. by Paul d'Angelo and Jim A. Kuypers, 110–134. New York: Routledge.

Sinclair, John and Malcolm Coulthard. 1975. *Towards an Analysis of Discourse: The English Used by Teachers and Pupils*. Oxford: Oxford University Press.

Stegu, Martin. 2000: "Text oder Kontext: zur Rolle von Fotos in Tageszeitungen." [Text or Context: On the Role of Photographs in Newspapers]. In *Bild im Text – Text und Bild* [Picture in the text – text and picture], ed. by Ulla Fix and Hans Wellmann, 307–324. Heidelberg: C. Winter.

Timberg, Bernard M. 1995. *Talk Shows*. http://www.museum.tv/eotv/talkshows.htm (accessed November 7, 2013).

Tolson, Andrew 2006. *Media Talk: Spoken Discourse on TV and Radio*. Edinburgh: Edinburgh University Press.

Van Leeuwen, Theo. 2005. *Introducing Social Semiotics*. London: Routledge.

Verhoef, Jesper. 2012. *Talkshowinterviews met Politici. De Rol van Beeld en Beeldfragmenten voor Gespreksdeelnemers en TV-Kijkers* [Political Interviews in Talk Shows: The role of Pictures and Visual Inserts for Participants and TV Audiences]. Master Thesis. Communication and Information Sciences. Groningen: University.

Vraga, Emily K., Stephanie Edgerly, Leticia Bode, Jasun D. Carr, Mitchell Bard, Courtney N. Johnson, Kim Young Mie and Dhavan V. Shah. 2012. "The Correspondent, the Comic, and the Combatant: The Consequences of Host Style in Political Talk Shows." *Journalism & Mass Communication Quarterly* 89 (1): 5–22. DOI: 10.1177/1077699011428575

Wonneberger, Anke, Klaus Schoenbach and Lex van Meurs. 2013. "How Keeping up Diversifies: Watching Public Affairs TV in the Netherlands 1988 – 2010." *European Journal of Communication* 28 (6): 646–662. DOI: 10.1177/0267323113501150

Follow-ups in interpreter-mediated interviews and press conferences

Christina Schäffner
Aston University, Birmingham, UK

This chapter investigates the nature of follow-ups in interpreter-mediated interaction. The data come from international press conferences and interviews. The involvement of an interpreter as an active participant in the exchange between politicians and journalists has consequences for analysing question – response – follow-up patterns. Follow-ups are understood here in the wider sense of thematic progression and speaker positioning towards prior talk. The chapter illustrates effects of interpreter-mediated encounters on role construction and positioning of politicians. It also illustrates how different interpreting modes and institutional arrangements influence the flow of the interaction and subsequent recontextualisation processes such as the transfer of a press conference to news reports. It is argued that multiple and multilingual data can enrich the analysis and may lead to different interpretations, also in respect of follow-ups.

1. Introduction

In an increasingly globalised world, politics is increasingly international too. Political events in one country often have consequences for other countries as well, and more and more decisions are taken at supranational levels, such as the United Nations or the European Union institutions. Conducting politics requires communication, which leads to a variety of discursive events (e.g. meetings of heads of state, state visits, parliamentary debates) and institutional types of political discourse (e.g. treaties, speeches, press releases). For international politics, a significant amount of such texts and discourse is made available in several languages. This means that very frequently translation and interpreting play an important role in political settings. International institutions often have a dedicated translation and interpreting service to cater for these needs (for the EU institutions see Koskinen 2008; Wagner et al. 2012, for the United Nations see Cao and Zhao 2008; and Baigorri-Jalón 2004 with specific reference to interpreting).

DOI 10.1075/dapsac.60.08sch

Translation also plays a more or less important role at a national level. For officially multilingual countries, it is a quite widespread phenomenon that politically relevant texts (e.g. legislation, policy documents) are made available in the relevant languages, and often websites of governments are multilingual (e.g. French, Dutch, German for the Parliament of Belgium, http://www.belgium.be/fr/la_belgique/pouvoirs_publics/autorites_federales/parlement_federal/) or bilingual (e.g. Welsh and English for the Parliament of Wales, http://www.assemblywales.org/cy/index.htm). In predominantly monolingual countries (such as Germany, France, England), government websites are not normally multilingual, but they too may include texts in other languages. This applies, for example, to speeches which have been made available in translation. Sometimes an advance translation of a speech is handed out to journalists before a state visit. Similarly, when politicians travel abroad, or when they welcome foreign politicians to their own countries, the meetings are often mediated by an interpreter. Such meetings or state visits may conclude with a press conference, which, too, may be conducted with the help of interpreters. The discursive event of a press conference brings politicians and journalists together, i.e. representatives from the domain of politics interact with representatives from the domain of journalism. Another discursive event which is often conducted with the help of an interpreter is the political interview. The involvement of an interpreter means that these discursive events are not just forms of dialogic interaction but actually triadic exchanges (Mason 2001). Both press conferences and political interviews involve question and answer sequences and thus make them worthwhile to investigate for follow-ups. In this chapter, I will illustrate interpreter-mediated press conferences and political interviews and explore what the involvement of an interpreter means for investigating follow-ups. The main question this chapter tries to answer is therefore: What are the consequences of interpreter-mediated encounters for our understanding of follow-ups (who follows up on whom and what and how)? The analysis of examples of triadic exchanges in the context of political discourse will thus also contribute to reflecting on the question: what counts as a follow-up?

2. Conceptualising follow-ups in interpreter-mediated exchanges

In analysing dialogic interaction, follow-ups have often been described as the third part of the exchange, as initially proposed by Sinclair and Coulthard (1975). That is, a speaker A, who had initiated an exchange, reacts to the response of speaker B, thus positioning him- or herself towards prior talk. In this three-move sequence, the third move takes up the content and/or the force of either the initiating move or the response. When political interviews are mediated by an interpreter, the interaction, seen in structural terms, is more complex. The triadic exchange involves three participants, i.e. interviewer, interpreter, and interviewee, with the interaction, however, involving a doubling of each turn. For example, the exchange starts with a question initiated by the interviewer in language A, this question is rendered into language B by the interpreter, the interviewee responds in language B, and this response is then rendered again into language A by the interpreter. Strictly speaking, the interviewee responds to the interpreter's words, and any subsequent follow-up question the interviewer may wish to ask is motivated by the interviewee's response as rendered by the interpreter. Research in Interpreting Studies has shown that interpreting is not just an exercise in repeating exactly in another language what a speaker has said before. That is, an interpreter is not just an invisible mouthpiece but rather an active participant in the exchange. This active role of the interpreter as the third partner in an interview will also have to be taken into account for any reflection on what constitutes the third part of an exchange and what is an initiating or a reactive move.

Depending on the discursive event, the interpreting mode may be simultaneous or consecutive. Simultaneous interpreting (i.e. the interpreter renders a politician's words into another language in real time, while the speaker continuously speaks) is often used for the delivery of speeches in formal setups (such as speeches in the European Parliament). In that case, the interpreter is often placed in a booth wearing a pair of headphones and speaks into a microphone. The audience too listens to the interpreter's rendering via headphones. Simultaneous interpreting can also be used at meetings of a small group of people, and is then often performed as whispered interpreting (*chuchotage*) with the interpreter being close to the person(s) requiring interpreting. In consecutive interpreting, the interpreter renders what was said after the speaker has finished, with speakers breaking down their message into manageable turns. Consecutive interpreting normally involves note-taking, unless the turns are very short. Whereas simultaneous interpreters in their booths are usually invisible to the audience, an interpreter working in the consecutive mode is often positioned close to the speaker(s) and thus visible to the audience. If consecutive interpreting is used, the individual turns are more clear-cut, since only one speaker has the floor at each time, which makes identifying a potentially 'third' part in the exchange somewhat easier.

In the case of international press conferences, the discursive flow is not necessarily characterised by coherence and cohesion between adjacent moves, since questions can be asked by several journalists, and a question may well refer back to an earlier part of the exchange, or even to a previous discourse. In the analysis below, I will therefore use the concept of follow-ups in a wider sense, combining structural aspects and thematic progression of the exchange. That is, I will look at how a specific topic or a prior communicative act is taken up and developed through complex interchanges. This broader view of follow-ups as communicative acts which are initiated by a previous text is in line with the positions of the contributors to this volume. Fetzer's view of follow-ups as moves which "refer anaphorically to other discourses and import relevant content, force and/or context into an ongoing discourse" (Fetzer 2012, 74) seems to focus on intertextual relations, i.e. moves within a discourse which only refer to some prior discourse. In my analysis below, I also count as follow-ups references to prior moves within the ongoing discursive event of an interview or a press conference. Since political interviews and press conferences as discursive events involve journalists, it is quite normal that these journalists will report about the event subsequently in their respective mass media, thus recontextualising the initial discursive event. For example, a journalistic article published in a newspaper reports on a press conference held the day before and also includes some direct quotes made by politicians at this initial event. Such processes of recontextualisation go hand in hand with transformations, e.g. additions, deletions, substitutions, rearrangements, which, in turn, result in certain arguments and topoi gaining legitimacy and power (as illustrated for example by Blackledge 2005). I will therefore also use the concept of follow-ups by extension for exploring relationships between interviews and/or press conferences and subsequent news reports (for consequences of recontextualisation processes on the visibility of translation and interpreting see also Schäffner 2012b). My main concern in this chapter, however, is to investigate how (if at all) the fact that the exchange is mediated by an interpreter impacts on the thematic and interactional progression of the exchange.

3. Political Discourse Analysis and Translation and Interpreting Studies

Within the discipline of Translation Studies, the translational practices in the fields of politics and journalism are still largely under-researched, although news translation has recently seen more attention (e.g. Bielsa and Bassnett 2009; Kang 2007; Valdeon 2008; van Doorslaer 2009). Analyses of translated or interpreted political discourse have identified the significance of institutional contexts, ideological aims, and agency (e.g. Schäffner 2012a, 2012b; Schäffner and Bassnett 2010). Whether a political speech is translated or interpreted has consequences for the textual make-up since translation strategies differ from interpreting strategies. Such differences were illustrated by Stage (2002) and Munday (2012) who compared the interpreter's output with the written translations of speeches by US-Presidents Clinton and Obama, respectively. In his analysis of US-President Barack Obama's 2009 inaugural address, Munday noticed that a reduction of the force of the attitude occurs more often in interpreting compared to written translation (for example, the use of a more general noun such as *killing* instead of *slaughtering* in the interpreting). His comparison also revealed that interpreters use omission or reformulation, while translators tend to (over-)explicate in the case of context-dependent instances and culturally sensitive aspects. Pöchhacker (2012) analysed the output of several interpreters who rendered Obama's inaugural address into German. His main interest was in investigating to what extent the simultaneous interpreters who were working under different, and sometimes extremely difficult conditions managed "to retain, or re-create, the rhetorical effect of the original" (Pöchhacker 2012, 130) and which strategies they employed, illustrated with forms of address, metaphorical expressions, and parallelisms.

Among the few cases of analysis of interpreter-mediated interviews in the context of politics are the studies by Wadensjö (2000) and Baker (1997). Wadensjö (2000) explored the interpreter's performance in an interview with the former Russian president Boris Yeltsin, which was broadcast live on Swedish radio. She examined a variety of divergences between the original Russian and the interpreter's Swedish version, suggesting that the "interpreter's performance is affected first and foremost by the nature of the assignment and the communicative genre", i.e. by the "conventions of 'news interview talk'" (Wadensjö 2000, 233). Her study was based on an interactionistic approach to interpreter-mediated encounters. In her case study of a televised interview with Saddam Hussein, broadcast by the British channel ITN in 1990, Baker (1997) explored the effects of psychological and cultural constraints on interpreter strategies in political interviews. She illustrates possible "implications of the use of certain strategies in terms of reinforcing cultural stereotypes, constructing a convenient image of the enemy, and enabling or obstructing an understanding of the other's points of view and priorities" (Baker 1997, 112).

Both Wadensjö and Baker make use of concepts from Discourse Analysis, such as turn-taking mechanisms, face work, or shifts of footing. Discourse Analysis and Interactional Pragmatics have also often informed the analysis of interpreter-mediated interaction in courtroom, police, and healthcare settings, with scholars investigating, in addition to the aspects mentioned above, the dynamics of the triadic exchange, including question types, politeness strategies, positioning, the use of first or third person, as well as role perceptions (e.g. Roy 2000; Hale 2004, the contributions in Mason 2001). Follow-ups, however, have not yet been investigated in a systematic way from the perspective of Translation and Interpreting Studies. This chapter is thus also an attempt at closing this gap (see also Schaffner 2012c).

The chapter is based on an analysis of written transcripts of interpreter-mediated interviews with politicians and international press conferences, video recordings, and news reports. The data are multilingual, or more precisely: monolingual but available twice in the respective languages of the interactional partners involved. While watching video recordings (or live transmissions, if possible) a researcher can normally hear only one voice if simultaneous interpreting is provided, i.e. the voice of either the speaker or of the interpreter. Video recordings of press conferences are usually accessible only from the website of the host, whereas transcripts are often provided on the websites of both partners (governments, political parties). The inaudible voice of the other speaker can thus be 'discovered' in the written transcripts. This chapter will illustrate how the use of such multiple data can reveal otherwise hidden interaction strategies and constraints of institutional arrangements. I will focus in particular on potential consequences of interpreting modes and institutional settings for the flow of the interaction and follow-ups.

4. Interpreter-mediated political interview: Who has the power?

In her analysis of direct, monolingual media interviews, Weizman (2008) has shown that follow-up moves (although not conceptualised as 3rd-position elements) also contribute to the positioning of the participants. In the dialogic interaction of an interview, a "complex system of interactional and social roles and identities is established through negotiations" (Weizman 2008, 3), and "positioning involves assignment, shaping and negotiations of reciprocal relations between all parties involved in the interaction" (Weizman 2008, 16). In the interaction, participants can be positioned in respect of their social roles (i.e. their roles outside the interaction itself) and their interactional roles (i.e. roles and obligations in the specific interaction).[1] The positioning of politicians can also be affected to various degrees in interpreter-mediated encounters with consequences for the construction of their identities (as illustrated in Schäffner in press).

In media interviews, positioning is also a matter of power relationships. Fetzer and Bull (2013, 85) state that journalists can demonstrate their professional skills by asking precise questions and critical follow-up questions, and Weizman (2008) illustrates an asymmetry of power in media interviews as it can be seen in the length of turns, in interruptions, in topic initiation, in agenda management, etc. In political interviews, where we have one journalist interviewing one politician, follow-ups too can be a form of agenda management and thus reflect power. In my corpus of interpreter-mediated political interviews and press conferences, I have not encountered any example of a journalist's follow-up question (in the narrower sense of an immediate reactive move to a response by the interviewee)

1. Hamo (this volume) adopts a similar view of positioning in her discussion of its dynamic construction through the use of follow-ups.

being motivated by an interpreter's inaccurate rendering or possible misinterpretation. A likely reason for this is that interpreters who work at such high levels for heads of state or government are highly qualified and experienced. Another, and more relevant reason for the data I have gathered is that the interviews as they were made available to the public are hardly ever the live interviews. It is quite common that transcripts of interviews undergo revision (for content, politically-sensitive arguments) and amendments (for grammar and style) before they are made publicly available (on a website, in a newspaper, for a TV news report), as I illustrated previously with an interview with Vladimir Putin and subsequent media reports in several newspapers (Schäffner 2010). The example I want to use here goes beyond a more narrow linguistic analysis of written transcripts and also reflects on institutional arrangements.

The example is a TV interview which the well known CNN journalist Larry King conducted with the then Russian Prime Minister Vladimir Putin, and aired on 1 December 2010. The interview was conducted via satellite, with King situated in the CNN studio in Washington and Putin in a room in Moscow, in front of a TV set. Putin was answering King's questions in Russian, and simultaneous interpreting into English was provided, with the interpreter speaking with a heavy Russian accent and not very fluently. A video recording of this interview was initially available on YouTube shortly after the interview had been conducted, but it was removed later and is thus not accessible anymore. However, the interview can be accessed from the Russian prime minister's website (http://premier.gov.ru), where we find transcripts in both Russian and English (the English one on http://premier.gov.ru/eng/events/news/13147/), and a video in Russian only. In this video, we hear Putin's words in Russian and Russian interpreting of King's questions. In the video initially available on YouTube, the constellation was the opposite, i.e., we could hear King's questions in English and the interpreted English of Putins' responses. The website of the *Voice of Russia* (http://english.ruvr.ru/2010/12/02/36107249.html) provides a transcript of the interview in English, with an additional note saying "as provided by the Russian prime minister's website". From the website of this broadcasting service, it is possible to watch a news report in which a journalist based in the studio in Moscow is talking in English with another reporter based in Washington, and extracts from the interview are incorporated. Here again, simultaneous interpreting of Putin's words into English is provided. However, this time another interpreter is used, who is also speaking with a Russian accent, but much more fluently. This signals that this recording was redone at a later stage. After the initial transmission of the interview, some respondents in blogs on the CNN website criticised the simultaneous interpreter for a poor performance, which seems to have been another reason for re-recording the interpreted rendition of Putin's responses.

When we compare the transcripts of the interview on the CNN website (which is preceded by the sentence "This is a rush transcript. This copy may not be in its final form and may be updated" (http://transcripts.cnn.com/TRANSCRIPTS/1012/01/lkl.01.html) to those on the Russian websites mentioned above, we also note differences. Moreover, when we listen to the re-recorded interpreting from the *Voice of Russia* website and at the same time read the transcript provided there, we also notice discrepancies between the written and the spoken word. All these differences point to institutional practices, and they are particularly striking in respect of thematic progression, follow-ups and interaction management. The transcript on the CNN website is a record of the complete interaction, and includes the following:

(1) KING: We will be right back with the prime minister of Russia, Vladimir Putin. We'll ask about the situation on the Korean Peninsula right after this.
(COMMERCIAL BREAK)
KING: We're back with Vladimir Putin, the Prime Minister of Russia [...] What, Mr. Prime minister, is your assessment of the Korean Peninsula? [...]

King's turn after the commercial break can be treated as a content-based follow-up in that it returns to the theme announced in his prior turn. Later on in the interview, we encounter a similar situation (turn numbering added for ease of analysis):

(2)
1. KING: Will you – will – will you go to Zurich to make a personal appeal?
2. PUTIN: Well, I've been reflecting on that. [...] I've been enjoying –
3. KING: All right, we'll be right back...
4. PUTIN: – the sport through all my life. I love soccer.
5. KING: All right, let me get a break on time. We'll be right back with more of the prime minister following this.

(COMMERCIAL BREAK)

6. KING: Something, Mr. Prime Minister, I don't think you've ever been asked. We have quite a dispute about it in America. What is the Russian policy toward gays and lesbians in your military?
7. PUTIN: Well, I'd like to finalize my statement regarding whether I go to Zurich or not.
8. KING: OK.
9. PUTIN: I think it would be better for me not to be there prior to these elections – [...]
10. KING: I've got –
11. PUTIN: – so that it would not appear as an element of pressurizing their decision on my part.
12. KING: I gathered that.
13. PUTIN: Now, as regards to the attitude toward gays and lesbians, [...]

Contrary to Example (1) where the theme of the Korean Peninsula was introduced before the commercial break, there are no immediate cohesive devices linking King's turns 5 and 6 in Example (2). The *more of the prime minister* is rather vague and does not specify a theme. The *this* in turn 5 clearly refers to the break, and is thus a reference to something outside the communicative interaction. After the commercial break, King immediately introduces a totally different topic (in 6). Putin, however, returns to the prior topic, using a metacommunicative comment (*I'd like to finalize my statement*) to signal explicitly his speaking right and also the thematic coherence to the unfinished theme (King's initial words *go to Zurich* are taken up again, although we need to bear in mind that these are the words the interpreter had used). We can thus speak of a follow-up which is both content-based and force-based. It can be interpreted as a follow-up initiated by Putin in order to complete his comment on a specific topic (i.e. content) and also in order to re-establish the authority of his political position by not immediately accepting the new topic (he does eventually take it up in turn 13). Denying an immediate response is a strategy of positioning oneself towards the interlocutor, and in this case a form of challenging the preceding move (i.e. force). Putin obviously felt he had been denied his interactional role as an interviewee by being cut short, and indeed, interrupting a politician in the middle of his answer can be seen as face threatening. In terms of the social role, we can say that by reclaiming his right to speak, Putin asserted his superior position, which was accepted by King (*OK*). What is most interesting in this example, however, is that both speakers' power is subordinate to the power of the media institution. As said above, the interview was shown on CNN, one of the world's largest news organisations, which depends on income from companies and private sponsors. Ensuring that a commercial break is realised at the time and with a duration as previously agreed is more important than letting people finish a conversation. The economic policy of the news channel thus determined the timing of the interview, which neither the journalist nor the politician were allowed to ignore. Participant positioning is thus also largely determined by wider institutional practices and values. On Putin's official website, Extract (2) is presented as follows in the English version (the Russian one is identical in structure and content):

(3) 1. **Larry King**: Will you go to Zurich to make a personal appeal?
2. **Vladimir Putin**: You know, that's something I thought about, of course. But I think that now, when FIFA members are coming under such pointed attacks and attempts to disgrace them, they need the space to make an objective decision without any external pressure.
As you know, I've been keen on sport all my life, and I love football but I don't think I should appear there before the

	vote lest my presence be regarded as an attempt to exert some kind of pressure on the decision-making process.
3. **Larry King:**	Something, Mr Prime Minister, I don't think you've ever been asked. [...] What is the Russian policy towards gays and lesbians in your military?
4. **Vladimir Putin:**	I've tried to answer similar questions before. [...]

As we can see, Putin's answer is presented as one long and coherent turn, the language is more formal (e.g. *pointed attacks, disgrace, lest my presence, exert some kind of pressure*), and there is no reference to commercial breaks. In short: the follow-up has been deleted. The same editing processes were made to the video recording, which is one long smooth question-answer interaction. These editing processes too reflect the power of the institution, but in contrast to the economic and commercial values which are relevant to the media institution CNN, the values for the political institution of the Russian government are of an ideological nature. The re-recording of Putin's answers with another interpreter is embedded into these ideologically-determined aims and contributes to the presentation of Putin as a powerful politician who is the main agent in managing the interaction.

5. Follow-ups at press conferences: Constraints and opportunities

Whereas in political interviews, journalists can initiate a topic, and are even expected to do so, this is not normally the case at press conferences. What is more common at press conferences is that journalists take up a particular issue that had been mentioned in the politicians' statements and ask questions in order to explore it further. That is, agenda management is possible for journalists through selecting an issue and making a politician react to it. In this way, journalists can also exert power by giving prominence to a specific topic and/or sensitive political issue.

Bhatia characterizes press conferences as "mediatization of political action" (Bhatia 2006, 176), and Fetzer and Bull (2013, 85) state that politicians "perform political actions in the public, mediatized arena". International press conferences are structured and ritualistic discursive events, normally starting with statements by the politicians, at first by the host, then by the guest(s). After the statements, there is usually the opportunity for the journalists present to ask questions. The interaction is regulated in that the number of questions journalists are allowed to ask is often limited in advance. Moreover, attention is given to the fact that journalists are evenly selected, thus giving speaking rights to journalists representing media from the host and the visiting politician's country. With journalists not being allowed to take the floor for a second time, the opportunity to ask a follow-up question in the sense initially proposed by Sinclair and Coulthard is thus severely restricted at press conferences.

At the discursive event of a press conference, it is also very common that one politician takes up and elaborates further on a topic introduced by the other politician. Such instances too can be characterised as content-based follow-ups since they contribute to the thematic progression. They are often signalled explicitly by meta-communicative formulations, as illustrated in Extract (4) below from a joint press conference between the German Chancellor Angela Merkel and the British Prime Minister David Cameron, held on 21 May 2010 in Berlin.

(4) **Cameron:** Thank you very much, Chancellor, for inviting me here today and thank you for what you have said. [...]
As you said, we started with an interesting conversation about how you best operate a coalition, something you have great expertise in. [...]
(http://downingstreetsays.com/briefings/0110/04/22/8388)

What you have said and *as you said* are cohesive devices, establishing a coherent link to a topic introduced before by Merkel, and signalling Cameron's intention to add his position and opinion. Politicians also often explicitly state that they agree to a point made by the other politician before, or that they support an argument. This may happen as well in the response move. Journalists often address a specific question to both politicians, and it is normally in the response of the second politician that explicit reference is made to the first politician's arguments and that agreement and support is voiced. Thematic progression can thus be characterised as a series of follow-up moves in terms of both content and force. So far, I have not yet encountered examples where the second politician would challenge or disagree to the statement of the first politician. This may be due to the nature of a joint press conference at which politicians perform together rather than against each other.

Meta-communicative phrases such as *as you said* are also often used by journalists at the start of their questioning turn to indicate which topic they wish to pursue, or in other words: which they wish to follow up on. Example (5) below from a joint press conference of the French President Nicolas Sarkozy and the German Chancellor Angela Merkel, held on 6 February 2012 in Paris, illustrates this use of meta-communicative phrases (*comme vous le disiez, vous avez dit*) by a journalist:

(5) **QUESTION** – Monsieur le Président, Madame la Chancelière, comme vous le disiez, la crise grecque menace à nouveau. Monsieur le Président de la République, vous avez dit que [...]

(Literally:
Question: Mr President, Madam Chancellor, as you already said, the crisis in Greece is again getting dangerously acute. Mr President, you have said that [...])
(http://www.elysee.fr/president/les-actualites/conferences-de-presse/2012/conference-de-presse-conjointe-de-nicolas-sarkozy.12958.html)

In some cases, journalists actually use the very formulation *follow up* to indicate their communicative intention, as in Extract (6) below from a joint press conference by Angela Merkel and US-President Barack Obama, held on 19 June 2013 in Washington:

(6a) Q Mr. President, I wanted to follow up on your comments about the Taliban talks. When you announced those talks yesterday, you praised Afghan President Hamid Karzai as being courageous for being willing to take that step [...] And, Chancellor Merkel, you mentioned that PRISM came up in your discussions today with President Obama. [...]
(http://www.whitehouse.gov/the-press-office/2013/06/19/remarks-president-obama-and-german-chancellor-merkel-joint-press-confere)

The use of *follow up*, or *follow on*, by itself does not constitute a follow-up move. The follow-up move is more extensive, with the topic a journalist wants to explore mentioned and then elaborated on and leading to a question which reflects the journalist's positioning towards the topic, or more precisely: towards the politician's earlier comments on the topic. In Extract (6), the follow-ups refer to prior statements made by both Obama and Merkel in the discursive event of the press conference and also to statements they made in different prior discursive events (discursively realised as *when you announced those talks yesterday*, *in your discussions today*). These are examples of Fetzer's (2012) wider definition of follow-ups as references to other discourses, even if the relevant content has been imported as indirect speech and combined with an evaluation (*you praised Afghan President Hamid Karzai as being courageous*).

The use of *follow up* by the journalist signals the communicative intention, and this strategy has been reproduced by the interpreter, who rendered the journalist's words into German as "Ich möchte auf die Taliban-Gespräche zurückkommen" (Literally: I would like to come back to the Taliban talks.). Later on in this press conference, we encounter another case of a journalist asking a follow-up question which is explicitly signalled as such as a *Nachfrage*, the German equivalent noun to follow-up question. This time the question is asked in German with the journalist in the first part of her turn enquiring when Guantanamo will be closed down. She then continues as follows:

(6b) Frage: Herr Präsident, [...]
Ich habe eine Nachfrage zur NSA. Sie haben gerade auf Deutschland verwiesen. Ist der Grund dafür, dass Sie besonders Deutschland so ausspähen lassen, dass es auch hier ein besonderes Gefährdungspotenzial gibt?
Frau Bundeskanzlerin, wie bewerten Sie es, dass der Friedensnobelpreisträger Obama auch über Deutschland einen Drohnenkrieg führt? Darf er das nach deutschem Rechtsverständnis?
(http://www.bundesregierung.de/ContentArchiv/DE/Archiv17/Mitschrift/Pressekonferenzen/2013/06/2013-06-19-pk-merkel-obama.html)

A literal translation of the first part of her turn would be:

> I have a follow-up question on the NSA. You have just referred to Germany. Is the reason that you allow spying especially on Germany that the potential risk of danger is particularly high here?

The term *NSA* had been used by Obama before in his response to the first journalists's question concerning the PRISM programme. So the journalist's follow-up here is a thematic progression and she also repeats the word used by Obama. She then adds a question addressed to Chancellor Merkel. Her turn was rendered into English as follows:

(6c) Q Madam Chancellor, Mr. President. [...] And now, as regards Asia, are you singling out Germany because there's a big risk here?
And, Madam Chancellor, the Nobel Prize winner, Obama is waging a drone war also via Germany. And is he allowed to do that, according to German law?

The erroneous rendering of *NSA* as *Asia* could probably have been caused by the interpreter not being able to hear the speaker very clearly. When we watch the video which is accessible from the website of the German government, we notice that the journalist pronounced *NSA* the English way. It may also be due to the acoustics that the function of the follow-up had not been understood by the interpreter, who might have assumed that a new topic is to be introduced (*and now*). The break-down in the coherence let Obama ask for clarification:

(6d) THE PRESIDENT: Let me see if I understood your question properly. The first question was related to policies back home, related to Guantanamo or the death penalty. And then you wanted to talk about drones, or did you just want to focus on the drone question? I just want to make sure that I'm responsive to your question.

In their answers, both Obama and Merkel talk about the use of technologies, such as unmanned drones, as part of counterterrorism activities, but neither addresses the issue of the NSA spying in Germany. In consequence, since the journalist's follow-up question had not been rendered as such by the interpreter, it was not answered.

What we also notice at press conferences in respect of follow-up questions is that a journalist may take up a question asked by another journalist before and invite the politicians to comment. This strategy may be used if a journalist feels that the response given was not sufficient or convincing enough, or if they want to explore an issue from a different perspective. I will illustrate this in Examples (7) and (8) below. The first example comes from the same Merkel-Sarkozy press conference as Example (5) above. The table below shows the transcript on the website of the French government, where we normally find complete transcripts of the exchange, and the transcript of this exchange on the website of the German government (http://www.bundeskanzlerin.de/Content/DE/Mitschrift/Pressekonferenzen/2012/02/2012-02-06-merkel-sarkozy.html?nn=74446), together with my own literal renditions into English and turn numbers added.

(7)

Turn number	French transcript	Literal translation into English	German transcript	Literal translation into English
1	**Question:** Madame la Chancelière, pour suivre la question de ma consœur, vous avez laissé bercer votre intention de soutenir la candidature du président de la République. Pouvez-vous nous dire pourquoi?	**Question**: Madam Chancellor, to follow on from my colleague's question, you have expressed your intention to support the candidacy of the president. Can you tell us why?	**Frage:** Frau Bundeskanzlerin, ich schließe an das an, was meine Kollegen gefragt haben. Sie haben gesagt, dass Sie die Kandidatur des französischen Präsidenten unterstützen möchten. Können Sie uns sagen, warum Sie das tun?	**Question**: Madam Chancellor, I follow on from my colleagues' questions. You have said you would like to support the candidacy of the French president. Coud you tell us why you are doing this?
2	**Sarkozy:** C'est vous qui annoncez ma candidature ce matin.	**Sarkozy**: It is you who announced my candidacy this morning	**Sarkozy**: Sie haben jetzt meine Kandidatur angekündigt, wenn ich das richtig verstehe.	**Sarkozy**: You have now announced my candidacy, if I see this correctly.
3	**Question:** Non, pas du tout. Si vous vous présentiez, excusez-moi, j'ai oublié cette simple condition…	**Question**: No, not at all. If you were going to announce it, sorry, I forgot this condition …	**Zusatz:** Wenn Sie antreten würden.	**Addition:** If you were to stand as candidate.
4	**Sarkozy:** J'en étais très flatté, très heureux, je n'aurais pas osé vous le demander…	**Sarkozy**: I'm very flattered, very honoured, I wouldn't have dared to ask you…	**Sarkozy**: Das schmeichelt mir sehr. Ich hätte es nicht gewagt, Sie darum zu bitten, das zu tun. Aber so, wie die Frage gestellt wurde, konnte man denken, dass Sie meine Sprecherin sind.	**Sarkozy**: I'm very flattered. I wouldn't have dared to ask you to do this. But the question, as asked, could let one think you were my spokesperson.
5	**Question:** Pardon.	**Question**: Sorry.		
6	**Sarkozy:** Mais la question, présentée comme elle était, laissait à penser que vous étiez ma porte-parole.	**Sarkozy**: But the question, as asked, lets one think you were my spokesperson.		

7	**Question:** Non, pas du tout…	**Question:** No, not at all…		
8	**Sarkozy:** Mais là, vraiment, je ne voudrais pas vous imposer cela.	**Sarkozy:** I really wouldn't want to impose this on you.	**Zusatz:** Das würde ich Ihnen nun wirklich nicht antun. Aber vergessen wir das. Ich meinte: wenn Sie zufällig kandidieren würden. Sie machen heute ein gemeinsames Fernsehinterview. Das ist vielleicht auch ein Beweis für die Unterstützung der Bundeskanzlerin in Ihre Richtung. Frau Bundeskanzlerin, ich möchte Sie ebenfalls fragen, ob François Hollande Ihnen Angst macht, […]	**Addition:** I really wouldn't want to do this to you. But let's forget about this. I meant: if by coincidence you were to stand as a candidate. You are doing a joint TV programme tonight. This too may be proof of the Chancellor's support for you. Madam Chancellor, I would also like to ask you if you are afraid of Francois Hollande […]
9	**Question:** J'oubliais cette condition, si par hasard, vous étiez candidat…	**Question:** I forgot this condition, so if you by coincidence were to announce your candidacy…		
10	**Sarkozy:** Voilà.	**Sarkozy:** Quite.		
11	**Question:** C'est vrai que l'on a tous ressenti, ici, que cette émission de télévision que vous faîtes en commun ce soir est peut-être aussi une preuve du soutien que Madame la Chancelière vous apporte, peut-être que je me trompe? Je voulais savoir, Madame la Chancelière, si François HOLLANDE vous fait peur […]	**Question:** It is true that we have all felt you doing a joint TV programme tonight is probably also proof that Madam Chancellor supports you, if I'm not wrong. I would like to know Madam Chancellor if you are afraid of Francois Hollande […]		

The journalist starts by explicitly introducing her question as a follow-up to a question asked by another journalist (*pour suivre la question de ma consœur*). It is also interesting to see that each turn by the journalist is indicated as *Question* in the transcript, even if in terms of content and speech acts they have a different function, for example, as an apology (in (5)). This consistency in using *Question* is also an indication of the prototypical role assigned to journalists in press conferences. In the German transcript, *Zusatz* ('addition') is used for the subsequent turns of the journalist after the initial *Frage* ('question'), which equally indicates the continuation of the questioning role of the journalist.

We can see in turn (1) that a question was explicitly addressed to the German Chancellor (*Madame la Chancelière, […] vous avez […] Pouvez-vous nous dire pourquoi?*). Sarkozy's intervention is thus, strictly speaking, not in a coherent relationship to the preceding turn. In terms of interactional roles, he assumes speaking rights which are not motivated by the questioner's communicative intention. By doing so, he positions himself in his social role as an authority, as the only person authorised to declare his candidacy, even if the whole exchange seems to be underpinned by a rapier-like irony. This quick exchange between Sarkozy and the journalist, with partly overlapping speech (more noticeable when watching the video recording) obviously caused some problems for the simultaneous interpreter. When watching the video, which is accessible from the website of the French government, we only hear French, i.e. Sarkozy's original words, and the interpreting into French. Simultaneous interpreting into German was provided for Merkel (and journalists), noticeable from the headphones Merkel wears, but we cannot hear the German interpreter's voice. The transcript available on the website of the German government is much shorter, compared to the French transcript, with the exchange between Sarkozy and the journalist (11 turns and 220 words in total) condensed to 5 turns and 163 words in total.

What this German transcript also shows is that Sarkozy's statement (*Mais là, vraiment, je ne voudrais pas vous imposer cela.* – 'I really wouldn't want to impose this on you.') was assigned to the journalist, and the journalist's admission *J'oubliais cette condition, si par hasard, vous étiez candidat* ('I forgot this condition, so if you by coincidence were to announce your candidacy') was turned into a rather firm statement (or commissive speech act) *Aber vergessen wir das* ('Let's forget about this'). It is only this change of the speech act which could be characterised as an inaccurate rendering by the interpreter. The combination of turns 8 till 11 in the orginal exchange to just one turn in the German transcript, however, is not the interpreter's fault. It is impossible to tell if the audience present at the actual press conference who relied on the interpreting (Chancellor Merkel in the first instance, and also journalists) were able to identify what was said by whom, but since they could observe the exchange between Sarkozy and the journalist, several modes of input could be used for meaning construction. Users of the transcript which was put up on the website of the German government, however, do not have the added benefit of oral or visual input and will end up with a somewhat different interpretation of the nature of the exchange and the interpersonal relationship between Sarkozy and the journalist. The main causes for such a divergent interpretation need to be sought in the institutional practices and concern questions such as: Who writes up transcripts of an interpreter's output? Do they check the transcript against the actual discursive event before the text is put on the website? Are the interpreters themselves asked to check the transcript? Who takes the final decision? To find the answers to these questions, research will need to go beyond the analysis of discourse features and investigate institutional contexts, for example through ethnographic research methods.

Whereas in this case (Example (7)), the minor inaccuracies in the interpreter's rendition can be explained with reference to the speed of the exchange which imposed time constraints, the final example will illustrate how the planning for the provision of interpreting services combined with a journalist's political agenda resulted in a specific construction of a politician.

6. (De)Constructing a politician

This final example is a press conference which US President Obama held on 19 January 2011 in Washington with the then President of the People's Republic of China, President Hu. At this event, the interpreting provision is much more complex, and becomes obvious only when watching the video. Simultaneous interpreting was provided for the initial statements by the two politicians. Then the question-answer session starts, and in the transcript on the White House website (available at http://www.whitehouse.gov/the-press-office/2011/01/19/press-conference-president-obama-and-president-hu-peoples-republic-china) we see that the first question, asked by Ben Feller of Associated Press, is presented as a follow-up question.

(8a) Q Thank you very much. I'd like to address both leaders, if I may. President Obama, [...] I'd like to follow up specifically on your comments about human rights. Can you explain to the American people how the United States can be so allied with a country that is known for treating its people so poorly, for using censorship and force to repress its people? Do you have any confidence that as a result of this visit that will change? [...].
And, President Hu, I'd like to give you a chance to respond to this issue of human rights. How do you justify China's record, and do you think that's any of the business of the American people?

The journalist explicitly mentions *follow up* in his turn, and specifies the topic to which it is related (human rights). However, it is not only a case of a content-based follow-up, but the follow-up can also be seen as force-based and implicature-based (see Fetzer 2012), in particular in the questions addressed to President Hu. The journalist challenges Hu (*How do you justify China's record ...*), with *record* implying all the negative aspects listed before (*treating its people so poorly, censorship, repress its people*). The transcript then continues as follows:

(8b)
1. PRESIDENT OBAMA: First of all, [...] Let me address the other issue, and a very serious issue [...] But that doesn't prevent us from cooperating in these other critical areas. I apologize. I thought we had simultaneous translation there. So I would have broken up the answer into smaller bites.
2. Q (Speaking in Chinese.)
3. PRESIDENT OBAMA: I'm sorry, I'm getting it in Chinese.
4. Q I'm from China Central Television. [...] So, President Hu Jintao, I would like to ask you the question, [...] So I would like to ask President Obama [...]

5. PRESIDENT HU: (As translated.) I would like to take this question from the lady journalist. I think that the exchanges between our two peoples represent the basis and the driving force behind the growth of our relationship [...]

The transcript on its own seems somewhat incoherent: why would Obama finish a statement with an apology? Why is there a reference to Chinese? Why would Hu start his turn with accepting a question which had already been asked? When we watch the video, the sequence of the communicative acts appears somewhat different. Obama gives a relatively long answer (311 words in total) to the first question asked by the American journalist which ends with *these other critical areas*. At this stage, we hear somebody speaking in Chinese, and a few seconds later we hear a voice-over from another speaker informing us in English that *The question is translated*. In the video, we can see a man (one of the interpreters?) going to President Hu and whispering something in his ear, but only for a few seconds before he disappears again. At the end of the interpreter's utterances in Chinese, there is a short pause, and it is here that Obama says *I apologize. [...]*, acknowledging problems with the interpreting provision. Obviously the simultaneous interpreting had stopped after the statements, which also explains Obama's next comment *I'm getting it in Chinese*. The video shows him putting on the headphones again, but the question by the Chinese journalist was only subsequently interpreted into English in the consecutive mode. The sentence *I would like to take this question from the lady journalist* by President Hu was also uttered before she actually asked the question.

The whole press conference then continues with consecutive interpreting, both for the journalists' questions and the politicians' responses, which makes the whole event rather long. The next question asked by the journalist Hans Nichols from Bloomberg can again be analysed as a follow-up, both content-based and force-based. It refers back to the first question asked by Feller in terms of the topic (human rights), and challenges Hu in an even more forceful way by accusing him of having avoided answering the question when it was first asked (although he hedges his question by politeness formula: *I was wondering*):

(8c) 1. Q Thank you, Mr. President, President Hu. President Obama, with your respect and permission, because of the translation questions, could I direct one first to President Hu?

2. PRESIDENT OBAMA: Of course.

3. Q Thank you.
President Hu, first off, my colleague asked you a question about human rights, which you did not answer. I was wondering if we could get an answer to that question. [...]

4. PRESIDENT HU: (As translated.) First, I would like to clarify, because of the technical translation and interpretation problem, I did not hear the question about the human rights. What I know was that he was asking a question directed at President Obama. As you raise this question, and I heard the question properly, certainly I'm in a position to answer that question. [...]

In structural terms, the follow-up does not take the third position since another question had been asked before (the one by the Chinese journalist), and it is also not the same speaker who produces a follow-up but another one. We can say that instead of the traditional exchange structure Initiation – Response – Follow-up we have a sequence of Initiation (the initial question by Ben Feller, which in itself is phrased as a follow-up to a topic addressed in the prior statements) – Follow-up (by Hans Nichols, which, however, is preceded by Obama's response to Feller's questions, another question by the Chinese journalist, and responses to this question by Hu and Obama) – Response (the answer by President Hu). Moreover, Hu's response is preceded by speech acts of justification. We need to bear in mind, however, that Nichols' follow-up was interpreted consecutively into Chinese, that Hu's response was in Chinese, and that what we read in the transcript in English are the interpreter's words. The more complex interaction thus is: Feller's question in English – its consecutive interpreting into Chinese – Obama's response in English – its consecutive interpreting into Chinese – a question by the Chinese journalist in Chinese – its consecutive interpreting into English – the response to this question by Hu in Chinese – its consecutive interpreting into English – the response to this question by Obama in English – its consecutive interpreting into Chinese – Follow-up by Nichols in English – its consecutive interpreting into Chinese – the response to this question by Hu in Chinese – its consecutive interpreting into English.

Moreover, Extract (8c) is somewhat different to Examples (4) to (7) above, which were follow-up questions mainly in content rather than in force. In this case, the journalist (Nichols) produces a follow-up not in order to challenge or to evaluate a response by a politician, but in order to elicit a response which had been expected in this specific discursive event but had not been given. This second order follow-up is relatively short in its discursive realization, just repeating the topic (*human rights*) and reminding the audience of the initiating move (*my colleague asked you a question*) and of the missing response (*which you did not answer*). What we thus also see here is the teamwork of the journalists who collectively produce the follow-up.

Extract (8c) also shows that interpreting itself became the topic of the exchange, and it was used as a reason by Hu to reject the accusatory challenge of the journalist's (i.e. Nichols') follow-up. We can say that the positioning of President Hu is largely determined by the follow-up question by Nichols, which can also be characterised as a face-threatening act, and confirms the observation by Clayman and Heritage (2002) that journalists have become less deferential and more aggressive in questioning politicians. In his interactional role, President Hu is positioned as unresponsive and un-cooperative, and in his social role he is positioned as a less credible politician. This positioning of President Hu as unresponsive and lacking in credibility was enhanced further by the mass media. In media reports, journalists added evaluative comments concerning Hu's interactional strategies and thus his behaviour, including non-verbal behaviour (*laughed, held a palm up and smiled*). The following examples from a blog in *The Guardian* (9), a CNN news ticker (10) and an article in *The Washington Post* (11) illustrate this (underlining mine).

(9) […] Asked by a US reporter about human rights, Obama gave a lengthy reply but Hu embarrassingly refused to answer.
Later at the press conference, another US reporter asked Hu why he had not answered the human rights question. Hu laughed and blamed a problem in translation, saying he had not realised the question was aimed at him, but he would now answer it.
(http://www.guardian.co.uk/world/richard-adams-blog/2011/jan/19/hu-jintao-china-barack-obama-live)

(10) Then came the "lost in translation" moment that turned the press availability into what felt like one long Chinese-language lesson. It started when both presidents were asked about human rights in China. Mr. Obama answered but, in a confusing moment, Mr. Hu did not. Instead, the translator began translating Mr. Obama's answer. Then they went on to another question. So another U.S. reporter asked the human rights question again, hinting the Chinese president might have tried to avoid it. President Hu was not amused: "First, I would like to clarify, because of the technical translation and interpretation problem, I did not hear the question about the human rights," he said. […]
(http://politicalticker.blogs.cnn.com/2011/01/19/a-lost-in-translation-press-conference/)

(11) […] the Associated Press's Ben Feller rose and asked a gutsy, forceful question. […] Obama answered. The translator translated. All eyes turned to Hu – who said nothing. Instead, he looked to a woman from China Central Television […]
But the next questioner, Bloomberg's Hans Nichols, gave Hu a lesson in press freedoms. "First off, my colleague asked you a question about human rights which you did not answer," the lanky newsman advised the Chinese strongman. "I was wondering if we could get an answer to that question."

> [...] During the translation of Nichols's question, Hu held a palm up and smiled, as if he couldn't see what all the fuss was about. "Because of the technical translation and interpretation problem, I did not hear the question about the human rights," he explained – falsely, as it turns out.
> (http://www.washingtonpost.com/wp-dyn/content/article/2011/01/19/AR2011011905552.html)

The direct quotes by President Hu incorporated in English in these reports are actually the voice of the interpreter. In any case, by including extracts from press conferences as direct quotes and further elaborating on topics, these mass media reports too function as follow-ups in the wider sense (see also Johansson, this volume). They can be characterised as discursive events (communicative acts) which accept, or reject, or challenge (parts of) prior discursive events. In this way, recontextualisation of a prior event in a new setting can reinforce existing ideological opinions and values (see also Hodges 2008 on the politics of recontextualisation).

7. Conclusion

Political arguments cross linguistic, cultural, socio-political, and ideological boundaries as a result of translation and/or interpreting. In interpreter-mediated interaction, responses to questions are strictly speaking responses to the question as rendered by the interpreter, and in the same way, the response too is transmitted back by the interpreter. The interaction at an interpreter-mediated discursive event such as a political interview or a press conference is thus much more complex than at a similar monolingual event where we have a direct exchange between politician(s) and journalist(s). This complexity means in the first instance that follow-ups cannot be characterised as 3rd position moves in an exchange, since the interpreter's rendering of a preceding move actually constitutes a move in its own right. Interpreters (and by extension translators) are active agents who play a significant role in shaping the interaction. They are legitimate participants in the discursive event, and their performance and the output of their performance cannot be ignored or underestimated.

A question to ask then is how exactly the involvement of interpreters influences the thematic progression and the communicative force of the interaction, and here specifically of press conferences and interviews. Are there any noticeable differences in respect of follow-ups in interpreter-mediated encounters compared to the 'normal', monolingual ones? As said above, I use 'follow-ups' to refer to moves which take up a topic of a prior communicative act (either within the ongoing discursive event or in some prior discourse) and which express the speaker's stance towards this prior act or topic. Both political interviews and press conferences are discursive events which are characterised by question-response sequences, with a more direct relationship between these two moves in interviews (although research has also shown that politicians are often evasive in their answers, see e.g. Fetzer 2002). Both the journalist as the interviewer and the politician as the interviewee can follow up on a prior topic at any time in the interview, elaborate on it and/or challenge it, thus positioning themselves to the topic and to the interactional partner. At press conferences too, follow-ups can occur at any stage in the question-answer session and can also be follow-ups to prior questions. This is due to the nature of international press conferences where the number of questions which can be asked is limited and where journalists are normally only granted speaking rights once. Moreover, since more than two interactional partners are involved, follow-ups can also be initiated by a politician to refer to prior talk by the other politician, or by a journalist to refer to a prior question by another journalist, as illustrated in the examples above. Concerning the question asked at the beginning of this chapter ('who follows up on whom and what'), we can say that there is more variety and complexity at press conferences than in interviews.

Whether an interview or a press conference is mediated by an interpreter or not does not have effects on their overall structure and function. In fact, politicians seem to be quite used to working through interpreters (at least in the examples in my corpus), and they even may forget their turns are interpreted. This could be seen in Example (7) where Sarkozy's rapid exchange with the journalist made it extremely difficult for the interpreter to keep up. The mode of interpreting may also have an impact here: whereas in the simultaneous mode (most commonly used in my corpus of press conferences), both interpreters and politicians need to react immediately, the consecutive mode gives them more thinking time. That is, while a politician, or a journalist, is waiting for the message to be rendered by the interpreter, they have some time to reflect on their next move or whether they wish to follow up on a prior move. Such thinking time can also be provided by extra-discursive factors such as the commercial breaks in the Putin-King interview.

The interpreting mode may also account for differences in the discursive realization of follow-ups. As illustrated above, follow-up moves are often explicitly introduced by metacommunicative expressions (e.g. *as you said, I would like to follow up on*) which function as cohesive devices to signal the thematic progression. Interpreters do not always reproduce these metacommunicative expressions literally. More detailed research would be required to see whether such metacommunicative expressions are rendered more often and more closely in simultaneous interpreting than in consecutive interpreting. However, the question of how follow-ups are discursively realised in interpreter-mediated encounters cannot be reduced to analysing the rendering of metacommunicative expressions. As I have illustrated above (especially Examples (3) and (6)), follow-ups are also omitted, although this does not normally happen because of interpreters' incompetence, but rather as the result of institutional arrangements. These arrangements can concern the spatial position of the interpreter in relation to the speakers which may affect what interpreters can actually hear and see. In videos we can often see that microphones are given to journalists when they already started their question, and in transcripts we read *off-mic* or *akustisch unverständlich* ('not understood acoustically') in such cases. Transcripts of interviews and press conferences on websites of governments or media institutions have often undergone some revision before they are released to the public, either for political reasons (as in the re-recording of the Putin interview with Larry King) or for stylistic reasons, or for both. The revisions which may or may not happen (as in Example (7), where no checking of speakers occurred before the transcript was released) are also evidence of institutions' attitude to and awareness of interpreting (and translation). This holds true as well for mass media which regularly include direct speech of politicians in their reports without any indication that what is quoted are the words as rendered by interpreters (as illustrated in Examples (9) to (11)). By extension, reports about discursive events such as interviews and press conferences in mass media can also be characterised as follow-ups in that they are thematically related to a prior discourse and express a stance towards it.

As I have tried to illustrate, if researchers use a variety of sources (such as transcripts in various languages, video recordings, news reports) the analysis can be enriched and may lead to different interpretations. Investigating interpreter-mediated political interviews and press conferences from the perspective of Translation and Interpreting Studies can thus add new insights into the nature of follow-ups and into the institutional practices and constraints which impact these discursive events.

References

Baigorri Jalón, Jesús. 2004. *Interpreters at the United Nations. A history.* Salamanca: Universidad de Salamanca.

Baker, Mona. 1997. "Non-Cognitive Constraints and Interpreter Strategies in Political Interviews." In *Translating Sensitive Texts: Linguistic Aspects*, ed. by Karl Simms, 111–129. Amsterdam: Rodopi.

Bhatia, Aditi. 2006. "Critical discourse analysis of political press conferences". *Discourse & Society* 17(2): 173–203. DOI: 10.1177/0957926506058057

Bielsa, Esperança, and Susan Bassnett. 2009. *Translation in Global News.* London and New York: Routledge.

Blackledge, Adrian. 2005. *Discourse and Power in a Multilingual World.* Amsterdam and Philadelphia: John Benjamins [Discourse Approaches to Politics, Society and Culture 15]. DOI: 10.1075/dapsac.15

Cao, Deborah, and Xingmin Zhao. 2008. "Translation at the United Nations as Specialized Translation." *The Journal of Specialised Translation* 9: 39–54.

Clayman, Steven E., and John Heritage. 2002. "Questioning Presidents: Journalistic Deference and Adversarialness in the Press Conferences of Eisenhower and Reagan." *Journal of Communication* 52(4): 749-775. DOI: 10.1111/j.1460-2466.2002.tb02572.x

Fetzer, Anita. 2002. "'Put Bluntly, You Have Something of a Credibility Problem': Sincerity and Credibility in Political Interviews." In *Politics as Text and Talk: Analytic Approaches to Political Discourse*, ed. by Paul Chilton, and Christina Schäffner, 173–201. Amsterdam and Philadelphia: John Benjamins. DOI: 10.1075/dapsac.4.10fet

Fetzer, Anita. 2012. "Quotations in Monologic and Dialogic Political Discourse." In *Proceedings of the ESF Strategic Workshop on Follow-ups Across Discourse Domains: A Cross-Cultural Exploration of Their Forms and Functions, Würzburg (Germany), 31 May – 2 June 2012*, ed. by Anita Fetzer, Elda Weizman and Elisabeth Reber, 72–86. Würzburg: Universität Würzburg – [online]. URL: http://opus.bibliothek.uni-wuerzburg.de/volltexte/2012/7165/; URN: urn:nbn:de:bvb:20-opus-71656.

Fetzer, Anita, and Peter Bull. 2013. "Political Interviews in Context." In *Analyzing Genres in Political Communication*, ed. by Piotr Cap and Urszula Okulska, 73–99. Amsterdam and Philadelphia: John Benjamins [Discourse Approaches to Politics, Society and Culture 50]. DOI: 10.1075/dapsac.50.04fet

Hale, Sandra. 2004. *The Discourse of Court Interpreting: Discourse Practices of the Law, the Witness and the Interpreter*. Amsterdam and Philadelphia: John Benjamins. DOI: 10.1075/btl.52

Hamo, Michal. *"I have nothing to do but agree": Affiliative Meta-Discursive Follow-Ups as a Resource for the Reciprocal Positioning of Journalists, Experts and Politicians-as-experts in Television News*. This volume.

Hodges, Adam. 2008. "The Politics of Recontextualisation: Discursive Competition over Claims of Iranian Involvement in Iraq." *Discourse & Society* 19(4): 483–505. DOI: 10.1177/0957926508089940

Johansson, Marjut. *Bravo for this editorial! Users' comments in discussion forums*. This volume.

Kang, Ji-Hae. 2007. "Recontextualization of News Discourse: A Case Study of Translation of News Discourse on North Korea." *The Translator* 13(2): 219–242. DOI: 10.1080/13556509.2007.10799239

Koskinen, Kaisa. 2008. *Translating Institutions: An Ethnographic Study of EU Translation*. Manchester: St Jerome.

Mason, Ian (ed). 2001. *Triadic Exchanges. Studies in Dialogue Interpreting*. Manchester: St. Jerome.

Munday, Jeremy. 2012. *Evaluation in Translation. Critical Points of Translator Decision-making*. London and New York: Routledge.

Pöchhacker, Franz. 2012. "Obama's Rhetoric in German: A Case Study of Inaugural Address." In *Discourses of Translation*, ed. by Beverly Adab, Peter A. Schmitt and Gregory Shreve, 123–137. Frankfurt am Main: Peter Lang.

Roy, Cynthia. 2000. *Interpreting as a Discourse Process*. New York and Oxford: Oxford University Press.

Schäffner, Christina. 2010. "Politische Interviews im Blick der Translationswissenschaft." In *Translationskultur revisited. Festschrift für Erich Prunc*, ed. by Nadja Grbic, Gernot Hebenstreit, Gisella Vorderobermeier and Michaela Wolf, 319–339. Tübingen: Stauffenburg.

Schäffner, Christina. 2012a. "Unknown Agents in Translated Political Discourse." *Target* 24(1): 103–125. DOI: 10.1075/target.24.1.07sch

Schäffner, Christina. 2012b. "Press Conferences and Recontextualisation." In *Ensayos sobre traducción jurídica e institucional. Essays on legal and institutional translation*, ed. by Icíar Alonso Araguás, Jesús Baigorri Jalón, and Helen J. L. Campbell, 69–83. Granada: Editorial Comares [Interlingua 106].

Schäffner, Christina. 2012c. "Follow-Ups and Interpreter-Mediated Discourse." In *Proceedings of the ESF Strategic Workshop on Follow-ups Across Discourse Domains: A Cross-Cultural Exploration of Their Forms and Functions, Würzburg (Germany), 31 May – 2 June 2012*, ed. by Anita Fetzer, Elda Weizman and Elisabeth Reber, 263–276. Würzburg: Universität Würzburg – [online]. URL: http://opus.bibliothek.uni-wuerzburg.de/volltexte/2012/7165/; URN: urn:nbn:de:bvb:20-opus-71656.

Schäffner, Christina. in press. "Speaker Representation in Interpreter-Mediated Press Conferences." *Target*.

Schäffner, Christina, and Susan Bassnett (eds). 2010. *Political Discourse, Media and Translation*. Newcastle upon Tyne: Cambridge Scholars Publishing.

Sinclair, John, and Coulthard, Malcolm. 1975. *Towards an Analysis of Discourse*. Oxford: Oxford University Press.

Stage, Dorthe. 2002. "Comparing Types of Interlingual Transfer." *Perspectives* 10(2): 119–134. DOI: 10.1080/0907676X.2002.9961438

Valdeón, Roberto. 2008. "Anomalous News Translation. Selective Appropriation of Themes and Texts in the Internet." *Babel* 54(4): 299–326. DOI: 10.1075/babel.54.4.01val

van Doorslaer, Luc. 2009. "How Language and (Non)Translation Impact on Media Newsrooms. The Case of Newspapers in Belgium." *Perspectives* 17(2): 83–92. DOI: 10.1080/09076760903125051

Wadensjö, Cecila. 2000. "Co-Constructing Yeltsin – Explorations of an Interpreter- Mediated Political Interview." In *Intercultural Faultlines. Research Models in Translation Studies I: Textual and Cognitive Aspects*, ed. by Maeve Olohan, 233–252. Manchester: St. Jerome.

Wagner, Emma, Svend Bech, and Jesús M. Martínez. 2012. *Translating for the European Union Institutions*. Manchester: St. Jerome.

Weizman, Elda. 2008. *Positioning in Media Dialogue*. Amsterdam and Philadelphia: John Benjamins [Dialogue Studies, 3]. DOI: 10.1075/ds.3

Follow-ups in pre-structured communication

The case of treaty monitoring

Liudmila Mikalayeva
Albert-Ludwig University of Freiburg

This contribution outlines two theoretical frameworks – behaviorist and reflexive – for considering the discursive interaction between states and international organizations within treaty monitoring (a process of assessing states' compliance with international treaties). Monitoring is seen as a communicative process, aimed at building and sustaining the interlocutors' public images and constituted by a series of multi-directed follow-ups. This definition emphasizes the importance of anticipation and silence in pre-structured diplomatic communication. The two suggested frameworks lie across the ontological divide. The behaviorist framework relies on an actor/speaker-oriented view of social interaction, conceives of actors as rational, strategizing beings performing cost-benefit calculations to define their discursive choices, and conceptualizes the participants' concern with their public image in terms of face wants. The reflexive framework looks at how states and international organizations (IOs) use the monitoring exchange to (re)construct their relationship while projecting a specific image into the public sphere. Continuity of the interaction, intensity and regularity of the exchange within treaty monitoring provide IOs with sources of power and thus allow rebalancing the initially asymmetrical set-up. The frameworks are illustrated using the example of the monitoring mechanism of the Council of Europe's Framework Convention for the Protection of National Minorities.

1. Introduction

Report-based monitoring is a ubiquitous case of diplomatic communication; it is a typical implementation mechanism in many areas of international law. Thus, the United Nations' human rights regime is largely based on the regular submission of reports by state parties to international organizations (IOs), which provide the states with a detailed feedback on legislation and policies, and indicate ways to improve compliance with the treaty (Alston and Crawford 2000; Alfredsson et al. 2001; Alston 1995). All states are involved in multiparty communication on

DOI 10.1075/dapsac.60.09mik

international norms, although they engage in this communication with differing enthusiasm and openness. States are thus held accountable on an international level, their policies and discourse are subjected to scrutiny, and their compliance with international obligations is regularly tracked and evaluated (Henkin 1994).

In the last two decades, the issues of compliance with international norms and the role of IOs in maximizing it have attracted a lot of academic attention. Scholars have developed and applied a dozen various theories (Bradford 2004) to explain how and why states follow international rules and norms in the absence of a world government able to force them to do so. These theories rely on two kinds of ontology. Theories based on a *positivist* understanding of social reality (behaviorist approaches) make sense of monitoring exchanges by looking at the institutional characteristics of participants – power relationships, and stable geopolitical interests and identities. In contrast, theories based on a *constructivist* ontology (reflexive approaches) conceptualize the identities and the interests of participants as well as the relationships between them as endogenous to communication and dynamically constituted within it (see Wiener 2004). The discursive part of treaty monitoring can be meaningfully studied within either perspective. Such a study can provide international relations scholars with a better understanding of how international organizations function, what the choices states and IOs make in the monitoring are and how these choices affect the treaty monitoring's efficiency. On the other hand, a deeper insight into treaty monitoring as a type of political and diplomatic communication can give discourse scholars tools to account for the pre-structured character and contextual constraints of many discursive genres in this domain.

This contribution looks at treaty monitoring as a communicative exchange and a discursive interaction. I complete theories developed within international studies and political science with insights from pragmatics and discourse analysis. I extend the behaviorist and reflexive approaches with compatible explanations of how discourse functions and what exactly happens when states and IOs exchange written documents during treaty monitoring. The two frameworks focus on social images of the interlocutors as elucidated through communication. The first framework builds on a positivist take on social image in communication (face) and highlights the ways the treaty monitoring's conflict potential is mitigated by strategic communicative interaction. The second framework is grounded in a constructivist view of social images as endogenous to communicative exchanges – contested, negotiated, and constantly (re)interpreted – and privileges a dynamic account of relationship-building within treaty monitoring.

I start by acknowledging that treaty monitoring is a *process*, involving various actors,[1] and that it is *interactional* – constituted by the actors' reaction to the

1. In addition to states and IOs, other actors may be involved as well: local populations, civil society, NGOs, etc.

international norms the treaty contains, to each other and each other's utterances. Monitoring can be conceptualized as a series of utterances reacting to each other, and thus lends itself to analysis in terms of follow-ups. The interactions included in the monitoring are to a large extent formalized and pre-set: the list of participants, their roles and moves are prescribed by the treaty and the rules of procedure. As in the case of many other types of political communication, we are dealing here with scripted, pre-structured communication (see Gruber, Bull, Schäffner, this volume). To account for this important dimension of diplomatic, political and legal communication, I propose to define follow-ups in pre-structured communication as *a reaction (utterance or absence of utterance) to another utterance, produced or anticipated within the given communicative exchange*. This definition is compatible with both frameworks I propose.

In the remainder of the introduction, I briefly outline and compare the positivist and the reflexive frameworks. Section 2 then offers a step-by-step elaboration of a definition of follow-up suitable for pre-structured communication. Section 3 presents and illustrates the behaviorist framework, followed by Section 4 focusing on the reflexive framework. I conclude with a short summary and an outlook on possible future research.

The behaviorist framework: My first framework relies on the behaviorist understanding of compliance and a related legal-technical view of treaty monitoring. Within this approach, monitoring is an assessment of how well states comply with their treaty obligations. It is a process of comparing state practices with objective and stable international norms and deciding whether there is a fit (compliance) or a misfit (non-compliance) between the two: "compliance refers to all behavior by subjects or actors that conforms to the requirements of behavioral prescriptions" (Young 1979, 4). Although this process may be procedurally complicated and biased by political considerations, it is rather straightforwardly carried out in a step-by-step manner by a special body within the IO hosting the treaty. A big challenge in this process is the major structural asymmetry between the IO and the state. Hurd rightfully notes that "all of the politics, practice, and law of international organizations takes place in the puzzling shadow of state consent" (Hurd 2011, 9). What is puzzling is that states allow IOs to judge their policies and to limit their sovereign decision-making.

Whatever the solution to the puzzle, monitoring is a highly challenging task for the IOs; it has a high conflict potential and calls for a scrupulously measured approach to procedural and linguistic choices. A theory of discursive exchange, which appears to be particularly suited for the study of such exchanges, is politeness theory, as developed by Brown and Levinson (1987) based on Goffman's theory of face. It looks mostly at how interlocutors manage to mitigate threats to their social images by using specific communicative strategies and tactics. Monitoring – by definition full of face-threatening acts of criticism and advice – is a fertile terrain for the deployment of such strategies, ready to be studied. Discursive analysis of monitoring adopting this framework and using the concept of follow-up would zoom in on the discursive strategies and tactics of parties responding to face-threatening acts produced by their interlocutor.

The reflexive framework: While behaviorists see international norms as stable and focus on state behavior as a reaction to norms, reflexive theories of compliance "stress the role of discursive interventions as social practices" (Wiener 2004, 190) and underline the importance of norms' interpretation and negotiation. Norms are shared understandings, and their implementation cannot be based on a passive 'consumption' of ready-made postulates. Social, political and ideological processes of constitution and contestation of norms, values and identities take shape in the form of discourse and are reflected in official documents, political debates or policy documents (Wiener 2004, 201). The mediated character of social reality makes compliance elusive. If the meaning of norms is intersubjectively defined, compliance is to be found in the state's and its interlocutors' *understandings* of what constitutes a breach of obligations and what is to be acknowledged as compliant behavior (Bull 1977). Studying compliance from this perspective means addressing communicative processes leading to the establishment of intersubjective understandings of norms and behavior.

The scope of the monitoring exchange is then seen as much wider than checking article-by-article respect of the treaty. Its object and product is also the relationship between the state and the IO: it is within the monitoring exchange that this relationship is developed and defined. Thus, we cannot talk about social images of the state and the IO being "maintained" and "attended to" in the exchange. From the point of view of reflexivists, social images get actualized only within the exchange and are endogenous to it. Brown and Levinson's theory gives way to a relational theory of communication, a dialogical view on interactions and being (Baxter and Montgomery 1996; Bakhtin 2006). Within this framework, a multidirectional definition of follow-ups is called for, and the focus of discourse analysis shifts towards understanding how the relationship between the parties is built via follow-ups on other utterances and silences within the monitoring exchange.

Table 1 summarizes the two frameworks. The major difference concerns understandings of the *nature* of the monitoring process and of the main *object* of the interaction. Within the behaviorist framework, the gist of the theoretical extension I perform is to recognize that institutional actors, such as states and IOs, have face and face wants, which they attend to in the potentially highly conflictual monitoring exchange. These processes can be fruitfully studied with the help of politeness theory, revealing the complex facework the parties engage in by consecutively following up on each other's utterances. The central focus of the reflexivist extension is on the monitoring interaction as constitutive of the relationship between the state and the IO. It foregrounds discursive processes of identities' and interests' negotiation, identifies sustained communication as one of the major sources of IOs' power, and prioritizes a more complex, multidirectional definition of follow-ups (responsive, anticipatory, initiative).

Table 1. Summary of the two frameworks

	Behaviorist framework	**Reflexive framework**
Theory of treaty monitoring	Legal assessment of compliance with stable norms	Discursive negotiation and contestation of norms' meaning and of the relationship between the participants
Theory of discursive exchange	Face theory for the study of the conflictual interaction	Relational theory for the study of the constitutive exchange
Definition of follow-up	Consecutive *Metaphor*: a chain	Multidirectional *Metaphor*: a kaleidoscope
Question	How do the speakers mitigate the conflictual potential of the interaction?	How do the interlocutors build their relationship within the discursive exchange?
Example	Strategies mitigating the inevitable face threats	Struggle defining authority and legitimacy

2. The definition of follow-ups in pre-structured communication

In the introduction to this volume, Fetzer and Weizman initially define follow-ups as communicative acts through which a prior communicative act is reacted upon and negotiated (page xi). This section defends the need for a more nuanced definition of follow-ups in pre-structured communication, such as treaty monitoring.

2.1 Structure of treaty monitoring

Since the 1970s, when international report-based mechanisms were first developed to monitor states' compliance with the United Nations' human rights treaties, the basic procedure has not changed much. Typically, states are invited to submit *regular reports* describing measures they undertake to comply with the treaty. Then, a special body within the IO (monitoring body) considers the report, as well as other authorized evidence, and issues a *statement* on the degree of compliance. Sometimes, states are allowed to *comment* upon this statement, agreeing or disagreeing with the findings and conclusions of the monitoring body. The cycle concludes when the political body of the IO issues a final *official account* of the state's policies in light of the treaty. The sequence is repeated every four years or so, depending on the treaty.[2]

How treaty monitoring works in practice will be illustrated based on the Council of Europe's Framework Convention for the Protection of National Minorities (FCNM).[3] The main participants of this exchange are presented in Table 2. The task of monitoring is entrusted to the Committee of Ministers – the political body of the Council of Europe, which is "assisted" in this task by – that is, delegates the bulk of monitoring to – the Advisory Committee of the Framework Convention (AC; Article 26.1), composed of eighteen experts who act in their personal capacity. A dedicated Secretariat assumes day-to-day organizational tasks, and has a major influence on the content of the monitoring documents. On the side of the reporting states, a specialized department within the Ministry of Foreign Affairs, tasked with preparing and filing reports and comments, is the direct interlocutor of the AC.

Table 2. Main participants in the monitoring exchange of the FCNM

Reporting state	Council of Europe
Ministry of Foreign Affairs: – Specialized department or section (e.g., a Human Rights department) – coordinates information gathering; drafts Reports and Comments; provides other information as requested by the Advisory Committee – Political department – supervises	Advisory Committee: – Working group on the state – gathers information; drafts Opinions; may request additional information from the state – Expert from the state concerned (when available) – consultative participation – Whole Committee – discusses and adopts the Opinion
Other relevant ministries (Education, Culture) and organs (Ombudsman) – provide information to the Ministry of Foreign Affairs	Secretariat of the Framework Convention – supports information gathering and drafting; coordinates monitoring
(Depending on the state) Civil society and non-governmental organizations – provide information to the Ministry of Foreign Affairs; directly file "shadow reports"	Committee of Ministers – provides political supervision; adopts a final Resolution

When a monitoring cycle starts, states submit Reports, followed by AC's Opinions, to which states may react with Comments. Comments update the Council of Europe on developments in state policies and circumstances before the Resolution is adopted by the Committee of Ministers. Normally, state Reports are long

2. See a more complete graphical representation of the cycle in (OHCHR 2005, 20).

3. The treaty was adopted in 1995 on the wave of the shock at ethnic violence in Southern Europe. The roots of the treaty reach much deeper; it emerged after decades of discussions within the Council of Europe (de Boer-Buquicchio 2008, 1–2). It entered into force in 1998, and in 1999 states started submitting initial reports.

(10–200 pages), Opinions and Comments are shorter, but still quite extensive and detailed (10–30 pages), and Resolutions are short (1–2 pages). Documents are usually available in the official language(s) of reporting states and in English (French translations are not always commissioned, for financial reasons). Opinions are published only together with Comments, which reflects respectfulness of the state's legitimate interests and its right to react to, interpret and refute critique. The written part of the interaction is complemented by an oral part (formal and informal), where members of the AC and of the state's administration meet and discuss the Framework Convention and its implementation.

2.2 Simple consecutive follow-ups

To sum up, the written part of the exchange starts with a report, followed by a compliance statement, followed by state's comments, followed by a formal final account (Figure 1).

1st state report → *Compliance statement* → *State comments* → *Final account* → *2nd State report...*

Figure 1. Simple consecutive follow-ups

In terms of the initial definition suggested by Fetzer and Weizman (this volume), a compliance statement is a follow-up on the content and formulation of the prior state report, while states' comments follow up on a compliance statement.[4] This definition calls for a step-by-step analysis of the communicative interaction and makes a lot of sense within the behaviorist understanding of treaty monitoring. Section 3 demonstrates how a behaviorist theory of communication (face theory) operates with this definition: it is used to study the discursive strategies of coping with the conflictuality of the exchange. However, the image of communication as a chain of consecutive utterances does not do justice to the complexity of the exchange.

2.3 Complex consecutive follow-ups

The limitations of the chain metaphor become evident already at the third step of monitoring, when states' comments are issued. States' comments can be a follow-up on the report at the same time as a reaction to the compliance statement of the monitoring body. The final account by the political body of the international

4. In this analysis, utterances are very long; their boundaries are marked by changing turns within the exchange. It is also possible to consider lower-level follow-ups, responding to particular fragments of these large utterances, as illustrated in Section 3.

organization may be even more complex, reacting and relating to all three communicative acts taking place within the monitoring cycle before it (Figure 2). Every new cycle of monitoring complicates the landscape: the second state report potentially responds to all prior communicative acts of the first cycle. When we get to the fourth cycle (currently underway), we can only hope to keep track of all cross-references and inter-textual cues – and will almost surely fail. The initial definition by Fetzer and Weizman does not preclude this complexity, as long as follow-ups respond to chronologically prior communicative acts. They recognize that follow-ups "may also span across longer sequences within the same discourse" (Fetzer and Weizman, this volume, xi). Still, this definition does not tell the whole story.

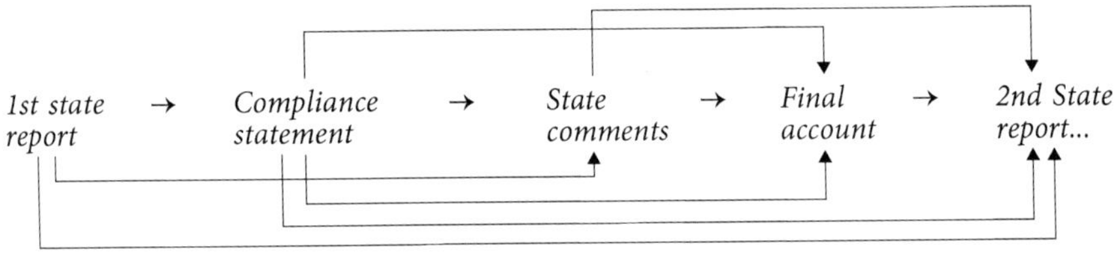

Figure 2. Complex consecutive follow-ups

2.4 Multi-directional follow-ups

In monitoring exchanges, "prior" communicative acts are defined quite clearly: reports come first, compliance statements come next, and so on. This is the *chronological priority*. However, within a structurally predetermined communicative context, as it is in the case of monitoring, chronologically prior communicative acts may react upon utterances which are not yet uttered, but which are certain to come. Take state reports: each report initiates a monitoring cycle. When the first report is filed, the monitoring body (the direct interlocutor of the state) has produced no communicative act to respond to. Still, the structure of the monitoring makes it clear that the report will be followed by a compliance statement and then by the political body's account. Therefore, reports are produced with this upcoming response in mind and can be seen as reacting upon it before the act (Figure 3). This reaction is different from the reaction to a realized communicative act. The report reacts to a projection, a hypothetical reconstruction of the compliance statement, and, somewhat paradoxically, at this stage the monitoring body is less informed on its imagined statement than the authors of the state report. However, it does not prevent a chronologically prior communicative act from reacting to a chronologically posterior communicative act.

1st state report ← *Compliance statement*

Figure 3. Following up on an anticipated utterance*

* In Figures 1–4, the forward arrow depicts a follow-up on an actual utterance, while the backward arrow depicts a follow-up on an anticipated utterance. Dashed frames indicate anticipated utterances.

In the case of the compliance statement, it follows up upon the state report, but also upon hypothesized state comments, anticipating possible reactions to critique, advice and other elements of the statement. It is also likely to take into account the forthcoming statement by the IO's political body, made up of representatives of member states and thus prone to seriously consider political implications of compliance assessment. Since the monitoring body aims at sustaining a high quality of the exchange in the long run, the anticipatory logic may extend to the distant second report (Figure 4).

1st state report → *Compliance statement* ← *State comments* ← *Final account* ← *2nd state report...*

Figure 4. Following up on actual and anticipated utterances

2.5 Follow-ups in pre-structured communication

Not only treaty monitoring, but most of other kinds of political, diplomatic and legal communication are to a great extent pre-structured. There are clear rules regulating communication within parliaments (Gruber, Bull, this volume), during debates and interviews (Hamo, Sauer, Schäffner, this volume), in negotiations and fora (Johansson, Sivenkova, this volume). Formal or informal, rigid or more flexible, these scripts make almost infallibly certain that chronologically prior utterances react, as it were, upon what follows. To account for the existence of these scripts in many types of political and diplomatic pre-structured communication, I suggest defining *follow-up in pre-structured communication as a reaction (utterance or absence of utterance) to another utterance, produced or anticipated within the given communicative exchange*. Follow-ups in pre-structured communication do not amount to any reaction to discourse or its components. The definition does not include non-discursive actions (as long as we consider silence as a discursive action; this point is further developed in this section), utterances by other actors apart from the direct interlocutors, the first (initiative) utterance in the exchange, and utterances produced by the direct interlocutors outside the exchange, including utterances on the same topic.

Interestingly, the pre-structured character of communicative exchanges can make them messier. Counterintuitive as it may sound, it is not necessarily so. Acknowledgment of the pre-determined structural component moves the focus of communication production and analysis away from the speaker and places it further in the midst of the potentially unlimited social context. "Chains" of communicative acts are but useful simplifications of the multi-voiced multi-directional communication flows, "messier, less logical, and more inconsistent practices of the moment" (Baxter and Montgomery 1996, 46). Probably, a better metaphor here is a kaleidoscope: each new utterance adds a colored element to the mix, which, illuminated by beams of context-bound interpretation, produces multiple subjective meanings.

While the multi-directional definition of follow-ups is an integral element of the reflexive framework, it is possible to arrive at it within the behaviorist framework as well. The analyst then needs to accept the structuredness of political communication and the speakers' awareness of the subsequent moves. Acting strategically, speakers try to optimize the forthcoming follow-up by adjusting their utterances ahead of time. This view is compatible with a strategic rational speaker-oriented view of communication, such as espoused by Brown and Levinson (1987).[5] It does not require moving onto the constructivist ontological platform and recognizing the immediate effect of the social, political, and ideological context on the discursive moves of the speakers. Nor does it necessarily call for opening up the "chain" of communication into its environment, where speakers respond as much to their structural roles, concerns and other elements of the relevant context as to prior communicative acts. It only makes more tangible those elements of the chain, which are not yet realized as utterances. The multi-directional definition can be attained by hardly shedding any behaviorist blood.

Anticipation is central to another important element of the expanded definition – its recognition of the fact that a follow-up can come in the form of an absence of utterance. Where an utterance is expected, silence can follow. Anticipation, particularly prominent in pre-structured communication, endows silence with a meaning: "expectation of an action will make its absence noticeable" (Bilmes 1994, 78). Within this perspective, silence is "an alternative response to a verbal stimulus" (Kurzon 1997, 22) and can be interpreted by the interlocutor in different ways (Tannen 1985; Jaworski 1993; Jaworski 1997; Ephratt 2008). Silence and omission[6] within monitoring have a fundamentally different meaning than silence and omission outside of monitoring. For example, when monitoring

5. The 'strategy' does not however need to be conscious (Brown and Levinson 1987, 85).

6. By omissions here I mean partial silences such as non-response to questions (see Kurzon 1997, 23).

procedures give states a possibility to comment on compliance statements, most states do. They can exploit this chance, for example, to negotiate a more acceptable final statement. So, when a state does not submit comments, it is a meaningful act. Since they are meaningful, silences within monitoring can be followed upon just as utterances. For instance, the monitoring body can refer to the state's failure to submit a report, comments or to answer particular questions in its subsequent compliance statement(s) and treat these omissions as elements of the state's behavior. Silence and omission are therefore integral to the parties' work on their social images and reflect variation in the directness of the discursive realization of follow-ups, as demonstrated in the following section.

3. Behaviorist framework: Strategies for enhancing social images

What makes compliance studies such a vibrant academic field and treaty monitoring so ripe with conflictual potential is the power asymmetry between states, supposed to comply, and IOs, tasked with the monitoring. Despite the continuous debate about the death or decline of the nation-state raging in international studies, states are *the* major players in international politics, the sole holders of sovereignty. The development of international law has imposed important constraints on inter-state behavior and, for several decades now, also on domestic policy-making. Still, in the absence of a world government, no unquestionably efficient procedure of holding states responsible for how they treat their own populations is in place. This means that after the challenge of making a state adhere to an international treaty regulating aspects of its behavior, the IO hosting the treaty is faced with a whole new task of regular compliance checks.

Brown and Levinson's politeness theory offers a conceptual apparatus for analyzing how participants in the monitoring deal with this antagonism: it frames the conflictuality in terms of face wants states and IOs have and studies the conscious and unconscious strategies they use to satisfy these wants (on the personification of states, see Epstein 2011).

3.1 Face theory and its application to treaty monitoring

The theory of face and facework was developed by Brown and Levinson drawing on Goffmanian and Durkheimian concepts of interaction rituals and on the folk notion of 'face', which can be 'lost' (1987, 43–44, 57, 59, 61[7]). For Goffman, face refers to the socially projected self-image, and Brown and Levinson seek to

7. In this section, page numbers refer to (Brown and Levinson 1987) unless otherwise indicated.

pinpoint "some universals in language usage" (the title of their 1987 book) in the way people cater to their wants to be acknowledged and liked ('positive face'), while remaining autonomous and unimpeded in judgments and acts ('negative face', 62).

In my analysis, I do not rely on the most-developed part of the theory: cataloguing different ways in which politeness is expressed in interaction. Rather, I am primarily interested in the claim that face wants (desires linked to the two dimensions of face) are universal and systematic – a common interest in all cultures and a recurring feature of communication.[8] Since one important aim of the theory was to shed light on the speaker's choices "in constructing an utterance intended to maintain face" (Arundale 2006, 210), it can be applied to the study of communication in multiple situations where the interlocutors' face is endangered. In the case of treaty monitoring, face theory can elucidate the discursive resources states and IOs deploy to dampen the conflictual potential in a responsive as well as anticipatory manner.[9]

As stated in the introduction, a discursive analysis of monitoring adopting the behaviorist framework and using the concept of follow-up would zoom in on the parties' facework, namely, on the discursive strategies and tactics of responding to face-threatening acts produced by their interlocutors. Managing social images and attending to face wants within treaty monitoring may be operationalized in terms of alternative discursive strategies of *cooperation* (linked to the positive face) and *independence* (linked to the negative face) (cf. Scollon, Scollon and Jones 2012, 48ff; for my detailed presentation of this framework, see Mikalayeva 2011).

The orientation towards the positive face in the interaction with the IO makes states want to show themselves cooperative, open and serious about the monitoring.[10] States can thus provide full information, signal openness and cooperative spirit, react to critique and advice, thereby attending to the concerns of the IO. On the other hand, the orientation towards negative face, inflated by the states' asymmetrical power position, can express itself in portioning the amount of information provided, paying little attention to the compliance statements of the monitoring body, and explicitly defending the state's right to interpret the treaty and its

8. In this respect, my motivation is very similar to Penman's, who uses politeness theory to establish important general communicative goals of the interactants in courtroom investigation (1990, 16–17).

9. Brown and Levinson mention the formal diplomatic protocol as the model for politeness (1987, 1).

10. Importantly, states simultaneously interact with other parties, such as citizens and domestic opposition. In these interactions, states' face wants may well differ. In domestic communication, government's positive 'face wants' may be oriented at showing rigidness and principled insistence on "national values" rather than cooperativeness: "The goal is to hit the right button with them [international partners], while not hitting the wrong button back home" (Glinert 2010, 62).

own policies as it pleases. Table 3 maps discursive options of states as intersections between their main contextual aims within the monitoring (providing information and reacting to the IO's critique) and their orientation in terms of face wants, resulting in second-order strategies and tactics.[11]

Table 3. Discursive choices of reporting states

Communicative need	Discursive strategy		
	Cooperation	**Independence**	
Providing information	Sincerity: – *Self-criticism* – *Presenting practice* – *Providing details*	Selectivity: – *Denying access* – *Omitting topics* – *Failing to respond*	Direct ↓ ↓ Indirect
Responding to critique and advice	Acceptance: – *Explicit acceptance* – *Promise of action* – *Update on the topic*	Contestation: – *Explicit rejection* – *Denial of responsibility* – *Renegotiation of the situation*	Direct ↓ ↓ Indirect

IOs and their monitoring bodies also have interests in maintaining positive and negative face. Their positive face is self-projection as professional, unbiased, modest and friendly actors, seeking approval and cooperation by providing a thorough and objective assessment, balancing criticism with well-deserved praise. For their negative face, the absence of bias is key. Legitimacy is the monitoring body's major weapon in the power play with the state. Therefore, it has to prove consistently intolerant in unquestionable cases of non-compliance, demonstrating impenetrability to pressure from states. Table 4 maps primary discursive choices of the monitoring body in terms of its contextual aims (making critique and compensating for it) and varying attention to the two dimensions of the state's face.[12]

Table 4. Discursive choices of the treaty body

Communicative need	Discursive strategy	
	Cooperation	**Independence**
Making critique	Directness	Indirectness
Compensating for critique	Praise	Justification

11. See Penman (1990) for an elaborate table representing strategies and tactics in 'face'-directed communication in courtroom interrogations.

12. The focus is on the facework of states, since, just as in the case of courtroom interrogations, it tends to be more complex than that of IOs, and facework strategies of the participants are directed primarily at the state's face, not the IO's. Indeed, the point of the monitoring exchange is to evaluate states' behavior (see Penman 1990, 34).

3.2 Treaty monitoring analyzed in terms of face wants

In the behaviorist approach to international treaty monitoring and its extension into the discursive domain with the help of face theory,[13] the parties enter the exchange with quite clearly defined wants and interests, for instance, to mitigate the conflictual potential and eventual damage to their social images, which they strategically pursue in the interaction. The departure point is the parties (speakers). The interaction is the meeting point of their desires (maintaining and enhancing face) and fears (damaging or losing face). This explanation of discursive processes sits well with the proponents of the behaviorist understanding of monitoring as a compliance-check, complicated by political and institutional configurations. Social psychology (namely, Brown and Levinson's face theory) and positivist international studies conceptualize actors as rational, strategic, endowed with externally defined general preferences and identities, and conscious and defensive of their public images. This shared understanding and vocabulary guarantees compatibility and complementarity of the behaviorist approach to international treaty monitoring and face theory and thus builds the basis for a nuanced analysis of the discursive mechanism of the monitoring exchange, its motivation and logic.

I will illustrate this type of discursive analysis and demonstrate how 'face' is mitigated in concrete instances of the monitoring exchange based on the example of discursive strategies used by states (Finland and Estonia) to react to the criticism and advice provided by a monitoring body (Advisory Committee). Such reactions are the most straightforward and clear instances of follow-ups and thus serve well as examples. Table 3 presents the repertoire of possible discursive tactics, structuring the presentation and discussion of the fragments from states' utterances.[14]

> **Example 1 (Discursive strategy of cooperation – Sub-strategy of acceptance – Tactic of explicit acceptance)**: The Government *agrees with the view of the Advisory Committee*,[15] according to which the dispute over land rights should be resolved as expeditiously as possible, in a manner that will contribute to the protection of the

13. The theory is extended here to take into account self-oriented facework strategies, hinted at but neglected in Brown and Levinson's original framework (Penman 1990, 19).

14. Responding to the AC's Opinions, authors of the state report normally indicate which parts of the Opinion they are responding to, provide quotes and thus make it easier to track a particular thread of content-related exchange. Both Reports and Opinions are pre-structured following the thematic sections and articles of the Framework Convention. The Framework Convention and all documents making part of the monitoring are available online on the website of the Council of Europe (http://www.coe.int/en/web/minorities/). To spare unnecessarily long references, I will indicate the numeric codes of the monitoring documents.

15. Here and further in the examples emphasis is mine.

culture of the Sami without interfering with the rights of the non-Sami population. Considerable efforts, which are constantly being made, are still needed in order to resolve the problems. (GVT/COM/INF/OP/I(2001)002, 7)

Example (1) shows the readiness of the state to sacrifice both its negative and positive face. By acknowledging the rightfulness of the criticism, Finland endangers its negative face. It submits itself to the interpretation and judgment of the AC and thus renounces a part of its sovereign autonomy in conducting and evaluating policy. By accepting that its behavior is deficient compared to the standard set out in the Framework Convention, Finland admits that it cannot yet meet the obligations under the treaty (positive face damaged). In terms of the realist international relations theory, this behavior is exceptional. It is equally surprising if we consider the power relationships and the formally big social distance between the interlocutors. Such overt instances of criticism acceptance or self-criticism are indeed rare in treaty monitoring (acceptance of criticism is rare in other settings as well and depends on a specific communication culture, see Sivenkova, this volume). What can help explain this discursive choice is the gain in the positive face Finland achieves by being open and cooperative. It thus deserves praise and acclaim even without making real progress in policies, at least for some time. In terms of normative compliance, this behavior is a proof of commitment to the spirit and procedures of the Framework Convention.

Example 2 (Discursive strategy of cooperation – Sub-strategy of acceptance – Tactic of explicit acceptance): The Estonian authorities *are aware* of the extent of the problem and the importance of solving it... (GVT/COM/INF/OP/II(2005)001,4)

Example (2) is similar to Example (1), but acceptance is more cautiously formulated here, with a stronger focus on the negative face: Estonia underlines that its authorities are in the know (demonstrating awareness, competence and control), so that pointing out problems by the AC does not come as a surprise. Acceptance signals that the positive face is given preference. Still, the authors of the Estonian comments also seek to preserve and accentuate the autonomy of their state and its control over the situation.

Example 3 (Discursive strategy of cooperation – Sub-strategy of acceptance – Tactic of promise of action): In the course of 2001, the Ministry of Education implements an assessment of special education, and in that connection *special attention will be paid* to the situation referred to by the Advisory Committee. (GVT/COM/INF/OP/I(2001)002, 15)

Example (3) contains a promise and can be seen as an implicit acceptance of criticism, recognition of the fault the AC had pointed to in its Opinion. While the promise endangers the state's negative face, the implicitness of the critique's acceptance shields it and the positive face from too much damage.

Example 4 (Discursive strategy of cooperation – Sub-strategy of acceptance – Tactic of providing an update on the topic): The training of teachers of schools where the language of instruction is other than Estonian and of the language training firms *has been* one of the priorities of the State Integration Programme. Special needs-assessment study with recommendations for further training *has been compiled* for Estonian language teachers in all types of schools. Various projects *have been implemented…* (GVT/COM/INF/OP/I(2002)005, 12)

Example (4) is even more implicit in that it covertly admits fault by providing updated information on the issue. Comments, in contrast to Reports, are not expected to be comprehensive and to cover all topics and areas of the Convention. If a topic appears in the Comments, often it is because of an important change in policies, practices, or in the situation of the minority population in question. Additional information, as in Example (4), often aims to inform the Committee of Ministers that some of the AC's criticisms are not warranted anymore, or that the situation is not as serious as it appeared when the Opinion was drafted. Updates can therefore be seen as implicit/indirect follow-ups on previous critique or advice by the monitoring body.

If the authors of the comments value autonomy and independent interpretation and decision-making more than cooperativeness, that is, prioritize the state's negative face, they can reject critique and advice.

Example 5 (Discursive strategy of independence – Sub-strategy of contestation – Tactic of explicit rejection): In the light of the above observations, the Government *does not find the suggestion of the Advisory Committee reasoned.*
(GVT/COM/INF/OP/I(2001)002, 20)

Example 6 (Discursive strategy of independence – Sub-strategy of contestation – Tactic of explicit rejection): In the Government's view *neither the National Board of Forestry nor any other authority has prevented* the Sami from maintaining their own culture. (GVT/COM/INF/OP/I(2001)002, 7)

Examples (5) and (6) are very direct. Here, the state does not only defend its independence and its own interpretation of policies and law. One unavoidable corollary of critique rejection is endangering the AC's face by questioning its criticism. This defensive-aggressive tactic makes a lot of sense from the point of view of realists, for whom the state's sovereignty is its most precious attribute, and the power distance between a state and an IO is important enough to permit autonomy of judgment and conduct.

Example 7 (Discursive strategy of independence – Sub-strategy of contestation – Tactic of denial of responsibility): The Government further observes that, *despite the high quality of legislation,* the practical implementation of the legislative provisions may in some cases take time, *for which there usually is a good cause.*
(GVT/COM/INF/OP/I(2001)002, 4)

Example 8 (Discursive strategy of independence – Sub-strategy of contestation – Tactic of the situation's renegotiation): However, *the purpose of remedial education is to help and support pupils with learning difficulties* so that they have equal possibilities to complete school in accordance with their capacities, at the same time with other pupils of their age. Education must be based on the strengths and individual learning and improvement needs of the pupil, supporting his or her independence and self-esteem. If the pupil has difficulties in normal education, or it is not appropriate in view of the pupil's development, the basic education is provided partly or entirely by means of remedial education. Such pupils are prepared an individual educational plan in cooperation with their custodians and teachers and other experts. As soon as there is no longer need for remedial education, the pupil is transferred back to normal education.

(GVT/COM/II(2006)004, 19)

Examples (7) and (8) are more about negotiation than refutation. In Example (7), the way in which deficiencies are recognized moves responsibility from the government to the inevitable institutional and social constraints. Governing is not an easy task, and decisions take time to implement. It can be good – hasty actions are very often not the most efficient – and, after all, time is one thing governments can legitimately claim to have no control over. Example (8) is even more interesting. It is a response by Finland to the AC's criticism of the over-enthusiastic placement of children from some minority groups (namely, Roma) in schools for pupils with learning difficulties. It does not contain outright acceptance nor rejection of the very concrete criticism by the AC. It endeavors to explain why the situation is not problematic, why it should not be addressed in terms of educational or social discrimination, but rather in terms of providing the best educational opportunities to individual pupils having problems. It works around the conflictual point very cautiously, not putting under too much stress the 'faces' of the state and of the AC. It refers to legitimate values (the best interest of the pupil), re-contextualizes the issue from the point of view of the state and thus deprives the AC of the ground from which to claim a change of policies (on the re-contextualizing function of follow-ups, see Linell cited by Fetzer and Weizman, this volume, and Johansson, this volume).

To sum up, Brown and Levinson's face theory offers a useful conceptual apparatus for analyzing how participants deal with the inherent conflictuality of the monitoring situation, driven by power asymmetry between states and IOs and the face-threatening nature of the compliance check. The theory frames conflictuality in terms of face wants and makes possible a detailed analysis of the strategies participants use to realize these wants. Its positivist and speaker-oriented assumptions can however be questioned by scholars espousing constructivist ontology.

4. Reflexive theory of monitoring: acquiring authority and building the relationship

4.1 Critique of conventional face theory and shift to a relational view of communication

The shift from conventional to relational face theory and understanding of discursive exchange in general marks the change in the focus of the analysis. The behaviorist framework highlighted the strategies of coping with the conflictual potential of monitoring and depicted interlocutors busy with wrapping their egos and social images into dampening cloths of diplomatic formulations. Reflexive framework, relying on a relational theory of communication, on the other hand, allows the monitoring exchange to have much more influence on the interlocutors' interests and identities and recognizes them as partly endogenous. The adversarial potential is still there, but its implications are quite different. The contradiction between autonomy and connectedness (or 'centripetal' and 'centrifugal' forces in Bakhtin's terminology 2006, 271–272) is a unity of oppositions for reflexivists: the identity of an autonomous actor necessarily relies on its communication with others, while communication requires "the continuing existence of the parties' unique identities" (Baxter and Montgomery 1996, 9). This intrinsically dynamic perspective sees social change as a consequence of dialectical tensions between belonging and differentiation, cooperation and independence, being approved of and left alone.

Here we are quite far from face theory as proposed by Brown and Levinson. On the one hand, they recognize some dynamism in the interaction (Brown and Levinson 1987, 285, note 9) and the fact that social factors, such as power relationship and social distance, enter into the communication exchange only through the perceptions of the interlocutors, which are context-relative (74, 79)[16]. It appears that even the face wants do not 'reside' with the interlocutors, but are "attributed by interactants to one another" (13).[17] The authors also recognize that interactions may last, so that histories of relations "are constituted, worked on, negotiated" (285–286, note 9). One (rare) example of how this works depicts a bald-on-record

16. Still, these mostly rely on 'objective' facts such as "stable social attributes" (1987, 77) and "situational sources of power" (1987, 79).

17. The nature of the relationship between language and social reality in politeness theory is a nuanced point. The authors note that they see the interaction as "the expression of social relationships" (49, 56) *and* as being "built out of strategic language use" (56). Also see page 55 for an ambiguous logical connection between two very different approaches to understanding the relationship between language use and social reality.

face-threatening act (FTA), which goes 'unpunished' and thus can alter the public definition of the relationship between the speaker and the addressee to the speaker's benefit (228–229).

Still, as Brown and Levinson's discussion of the speakers' strategies and concrete examples makes clear, they see the goals and interests ("the things desired") of the interactants as exogenous to communication (85). They point out that the interlocutors mutually *know* the social power distribution and the social distance between them, and can choose to manipulate these variables. The cited example of the 'unpunished' bald FTA and its effect are in fact a 'trick', a manipulation, which influences the public manifestation of power relationships to some extent, but is unlikely to fundamentally change it.

Another positivist dimension of politeness theory is that Brown and Levinson consider some (in fact, many) communicative acts as intrinsically, "by nature", face-threatening (60, 65). They also believe that some ways of expression of politeness are by nature better and less "costly" than others (for example, off-record demands are more polite than demands prioritizing the addressee's positive face), and that speakers know this ranking.[18] This essentialist view is incompatible with a constructivist perspective on meaning as a product of communication and interaction. To Brown and Levinson, meaning can be "to some degree negotiable", but this almost exclusively in the case of off-record strategies (69). For constructivists, it is the meanings that determine the relations between their material bearers, not the other way round (Harré et al. 2009, 7); the interlocutors themselves are "constituted and reconstituted through the various discursive practices in which they participate", and meanings are "progressively and dynamically achieved" in a "multi-faceted public process" of discourse (Davies and Harré 1990, 46).

In a nutshell, where conventional international relations theory sees a technical and political process of sovereign state policies' assessment, constructivist scholars detect communicative interaction, where meanings of compliance, sovereignty and legitimacy are co-defined by the participants. Where established facework theory sees strategic choices of individual speakers, made in a step-by-step intrinsically conflictual exchange to mitigate the danger to the 'face', relational facework theory sees a social process of mutual co-creation. The move from sovereign actor-driven communication towards communication-designed actors is a post-positivist move. The same move opens the Pandora box of context and beams the individual strategies through layers and layers of socio-political and ideological structures, systems and elements. That's how structure adds messiness.

18. So that they use appropriate strategies depending on how seriously the interlocutor's face may be damaged by what they intend to say. A miscalculation in this case may prove costly (1987, 83).

4.2 Work on the social image within the reflexive framework

In the case of the behaviorist framework, politeness theory suggested common stable interests of the participants to the monitoring process – 'face wants'. Combined with the contextual aims of the parties, centered on the provision and evaluation of information, the identification of these interests resulted in a catalogization of possible discursive choices and enabled their detailed analysis. Although the reflexive framework denies the existence of stable – and totally exogenous to communication – interests of participants to a communicative exchange, we need a conceptual basis for establishing the motivation of states and international organizations in treaty monitoring. This time, the most interesting aspect of the interaction is not how states manage the intrinsically face-threatening character of the exchange, but how IOs manage to rebalance their asymmetrical power relationship with the states to perform an objective evaluation of their conduct. This section draws on the research by reflexivist international relations scholars and seeks to establish the major components of the IOs' work on their social image, linked to different types of authority they strive to acquire.

Barnett and Finnemore offer a compelling theory of IOs' authority. They claim that the authority of IOs resides not only in the aptitude to make states behave in particular ways, but also in the ability to authoritatively indicate the right way to behave (2004, 20). Thus, IOs set up *standards* of legitimate behavior for states and define whether those standards are met. Barnett and Finnemore see compliance monitoring as more than a legal exercise. It is a major constitutive move of classifying the world: creating categories of actors ('liberal democracies', 'developing states'), new aims ('sustainable development', 'protection of human rights'), and defining shared goals ('development', 'environment protection').

This interpretive authority has four main sources (2004, 20–29). (1) States *delegate* authority to IOs at the moments of "explicit consent" (Hathaway 2008, Hurd 2011, 6), such as joining the IO or ratifying a treaty. (2) Non-biased technical and professional working procedures, the use of impersonal rules and principles of hierarchy and accountability – that is, the way in which IOs perform their functions – invests them with *rational-legal* authority. (3) The role of IOs as defenders of the dispossessed or non-powerful (refugees, children, minorities), as guards of the common interest vs. particular sovereign interests of states invests them with *moral* authority. (4) With time, employees of the IO specialize and excel in these specific tasks. At the institutional level, IOs accumulate specialized expertise, which invests them with the authority of *experts*, knowledgeable veterans matured in the battles for the cause (on expert authority, see also Hamo, this volume). These types, or sources, of authority are valid for all IOs; they are major elements in the IOs' self-presentation, self-construction, and self-negotiation, developed within the interaction and in communication with the states, but at the same time generally applicable to all cases of monitoring.

In the analysis of the communicative exchange between IOs and states, we need to distinguish two aspects of these types of authority. Firstly, – and more superficially – IOs present their work and justify their legitimacy in judging states' policies by referring to these sources of authority. Thus, in their self-presentation IOs underline the delegated authority by referring to the letter and spirit of the treaty itself and its preamble, to speeches and pronouncements of member states' representatives at important conferences and summits, to remind the states of their initial motivation and commitments. They refer to the rational-legal authority by stressing the quality of the internal procedures, the professionalism, integrity and dedication of their members, loyalty to the values of the organization and equal treatment of all states. They call to ethics, values and morality underlying the treaty and the organization itself. Finally, they stress the individual experts' and collective body's accumulated experience in dealing with the issue area covered by the treaty, claim having a comparative perspective, and capitalize on the continuity of the organization's specialized bodies and secretariats.

Table 5 provides examples of references to the four sources of IO authority in the speeches of the Council of Europe's officials on the occasion of the 5th anniversary of the Convention. For instance, the AC's President Rainer Hoffmann and his first vice-president Alan Phillips recall that the Convention was initially met with considerable pessimism (Hofmann 2004, 19; Phillips 2004, 99) and that the work of the AC first attracted "some antagonism and substantial scepticism" (Phillips 2004, 100). Becoming recognized by states as a serious interlocutor was thus among the primary tasks of the Committee; the assessment of the monitoring body's work was the prerequisite to the assessment of the states' progress in the observance of the Convention (Hofmann 2004, 23). In the same vein, the Secretary-General of the Council of Europe Walter Schwimmer noted: "we should not shy away from examining our own way of doing things, for example the effectiveness of the… supervisory mechanism" (Schwimmer 2004, 13). If the Council of Europe is successful in proving its monitoring mechanism efficient and fair, it can legitimately criticize states for failure to comply. This power does not come from the treaty itself, automatically, but has to be constructed and maintained via monitoring exchanges.

This brings us to the second – deeper – aspect of the types of IOs' authority. In fact, three of the four types of authority (except the delegated authority) are endogenous to the process of monitoring. Rational-legal, moral, and expert authority gets strengthened within a sustained interactive process, where IOs present themselves *and* behave in a certain way, that is, "form[…] and sustain[…] the social self" (Arundale 2006, 200) by action and discourse.

Rational-legal authority is enhanced by the IO developing clear and consistent monitoring procedures, maintaining a high standard of objectivity and attention to detail in its evaluation, and treating powerful and small states equally. At the level of discourse, these requirements translate into a high level of standardization in the structure, formulation, volume and timeframe of the AC's Opinions and the Committee of Ministers' Resolutions. This strong drive to uniformity demands that the same types of policies receive the same evaluation, and the same discursive choices of states receive the same follow-up from the AC. Thus, one can fruitfully study the endogenous affirmation of rational-legal authority within the monitoring mechanism by analyzing types of follow-ups the AC provides across states and issue areas.

Moral authority is enhanced by the attention to the demands of the disadvantaged, in the case of the Framework Convention – national minorities. At the level of discourse, focusing on this source of authority would logically lead to a higher level of heteroglossia, plurality of voices in the monitoring exchange, since the AC would have to consistently include in its utterances the information it receives from the representatives of minorities. One would expect to find such references especially in the follow-ups on the rejections of criticism by states, or on omissions and silences in their Reports and Comments. In this particular case, the IO would follow up simultaneously on the utterance of the direct interlocutor – the state – and on the utterances by other relevant agents (representatives of national minorities), thereby indirectly including them in the communicative exchange. The dual orientation of the AC (towards the state and the target population of the Convention) complicates the analysis, but is necessary for the IO's moral legitimacy.

Expert authority is very much the result of the interaction and communication itself. Monitoring bodies' expertise can only be built in action: by collecting and analyzing information on states' behavior, communicating with state authorities, NGOs, representatives of minorities in different regions of the country, interacting with the political bodies within the IO, discussing within the IO – including monitoring bodies of other relevant treaties within the same organization – and across organizations, and formulating well-documented and balanced accounts. For this type of authority the communicative exchange itself, its sustained character and high level of cooperativeness, are key. The IO is unable to develop expertise and expert authority if states refuse to enter in the exchange or if they prioritize uncooperative strategies: deny access to the country for field visits, fail to submit reports and comments in time or altogether, insist on a self-presentation as completely independent sovereign actors, etc. IOs are aware of the dangers of such uncooperative and low-intensity exchanges, and may try to prevent them by the means of responsive and anticipatory follow-ups on the states' utterances as well as silences.

Table 5. Four types of IO authority in the self-presentation of the Council of Europe

Authority	Topic	Examples
Delegated	– Reminding the will of the States	– the 1993 Vienna summit gave a "powerful political message" to assure the protection of national minorities (Schwimmer 2004, 11) – Council of Europe's member states are the Convention's "parents" (Hofmann 2004, 24) – the preamble of the Convention "shows clearly that the protection of national minorities is essential to stability, democratic security and peace" (Phillips 2004, 99)
Rational-legal	– Equal treatment of member states	– "any hint of undue selectivity and double standards would immediately hurt the credibility of our work" (Hofmann 2004, 20) – the Committee applies "same working methods and the same depth of objective scrutiny" to all states (ibid.)
	– Independence from political considerations	– AC is a "genuinely independent expert committee" (Hofmann 2004, 20) – it provides "a balanced and consistent interpretation of the Framework Convention" (Hofmann 2004, 19) – it has "an independent spirit… in relation to individual States" and the Committee of Ministers (Hofmann 2004, 19)
	– Pragmatism	– "our approach is measured and pragmatic" (Hofmann 2004, 22) – "we did not want to run before we had learned to walk" (ibid.)
	– Founded on law	– AC ensures that states' interpretations are "in line with general principles of international law" and "not discriminatory" (Hofmann 2004, 21) – international law needs to be "effectively implemented" (Phillips 2004, 100)
Moral	– Link to human rights	– the Convention is an "essential tool in the human rights armoury of the Council of Europe" (Schwimmer 2004, 13)
	– Need to prevent ethnic violence	– the Convention is "an effective way to fight against the return of such dark phenomena" (Hofmann 2004, 24)
	– Close cooperation with local NGOs and civil society	– NGOs act as "active godfathers" of the Convention as opposed to often passive "parents" – States (Hofmann 2004, 24) – AC established links to local Ombudsmen (Phillips 2004, 109)
Expert	– Dynamism and responsiveness	– Convention is "an instrument for developing and orchestrating change" (Schwimmer 2004, 12) – AC developed a "dynamic" and "inclusive approach" (Schwimmer 2004, 11) – the Convention "develop[s] organically", the Opinions "matur[e] over time" (Phillips 2004, 100)

In the next section I consider a case where the Framework Convention's Advisory Committee pursued this strategy of pro-active and pre-emptive follow-ups on the discursive actions of an (initially) uncooperative state, and managed to induce it into a productive exchange, and progressively strengthen its own authority and legitimacy in the process.

4.3 The case of the Framework Convention's scope of application

The puzzle mentioned by Hurd (2011) (Section 1) highlights the fact that in virtually all cases states are free to observe or not to observe rules and standards suggested by international organizations. States may interpret international norms, their meaning in the specific historic-legal context, and their application to particular cases. They can also proceed in a more straightforward and totally legal way – limit the *scope of application* of the international treaty. At ratification or later, states can specify in which policy areas, populations or territories they intend to implement the treaty. Formally, IOs have to accept and respect these limitations, but they don't always do so, as illustrated by the following case.

The Preamble of the Framework Convention refers to the "upheavals of European history [which] have shown that the protection of national minorities is essential to stability, democratic security and peace in this continent" as an inspiration for the adoption of this new treaty (page 2). Some states understood this reference narrowly, as a sign that the Convention was aimed exclusively at Central and Eastern Europe. Portugal expressed this view in its first report and declared having joined the Convention in "an act of solidarity" (ACFC/SR(2004)002, 2). Liechtenstein and San Marino mentioned the same motivation in their first reports. Although formally part of the Convention, these states did not consider themselves bound by it.

Thus, in its first report, Liechtenstein gives a brief overview of its history, geography and political system, but when it comes to the article-by-article information on the implementation of the Convention, it simply reminds having submitted a declaration while ratifying the Convention, stating that "no national minorities in the sense of the Framework Convention exist in the territory of the Principality of Liechtenstein" (ACFC/SR(1999)004, 8). Further, it notes that although Liechtenstein is "not directly concerned by the issue of national minorities", it had "expressed it solidarity" with the aims of the Convention by making voluntary financial contributions (ACFC/SR(1999)004, 9). This is where the report ends.

The Advisory Committee's follow-up on this very selective and uncooperative discursive move was nuanced. It "takes note" of the declaration and then justifies why, respecting the state's opinion, it still "considers that it is part of its duty to examine the personal scope given to the implementation of the Framework Convention" (a recurrent formula in Opinions). Because of the "rather limited…

potential for application of a number of provisions of the Framework Convention" (ACFC/INF/OP/I(2001)003, 2), the AC's only concrete recommendation to Liechtenstein is to "try to remedy any possible integration difficulties" of asylum seekers whose religion and culture are different from that of the dominant population (ACFC/INF/OP/I(2001)003, 4). The AC also expresses a belief that the Committee of Ministers is able to assist Liechtenstein in realizing the existing potential for the implementation of the Framework Convention (ACFC/INF/OP/I(2001)003, 5). It declares itself "standing ready" to be involved in the monitoring and suggests to the Committee of Ministers to invite Liechtenstein to "consider inclusion [of persons belonging to an ethnic, linguistic or religious group other than the dominant one] in the application of the Framework Convention on an article-by-article basis" within one year (ACFC/INF/OP/I(2001)003, 5).

This follow-up on an allegedly symbolic report – reflecting the refusal of the state party to enter into a serious exchange on its policies – has several noteworthy components. The fact that the AC has to refer to the authority of the Committee of Ministers is illustrative of how important state sovereignty is: firstly, the AC cannot possibly force any state to renounce its limitation on the use of the Convention, and second, it cannot give the impression that it acts without the support of the Committee of Ministers (invested with political power). It would thus be counter-productive for the AC to continue one-to-one persuasion of Liechtenstein, and it chooses a more complicated strategy of internal consolidation of opinion within the IO and channeling it through the body possessing more delegated authority than itself. Also, the AC stresses its good will and readiness to be a useful partner for the state, offering its expert services (thus referring to expert authority), and justifying its initiative by its "duty" under the Convention (moral and delegated authority).

Although it originally denied the need of the exchange itself, Liechtenstein follows up on the Opinion by publishing Comments, where it insists that the issue of asylum seekers explicitly put forward by the AC "goes beyond the scope of the Framework Convention" (Liechtenstein 2001, 2), which is, strictly speaking, true. It tactfully notes however that these remarks "are made in a spirit of constructive and ongoing dialogue with the Advisory Committee" (Liechtenstein 2001, 2). Surprisingly, the next paragraphs describe actions undertaken in Liechtenstein to address the specific needs of asylum seekers. Liechtenstein's Comments further include four paragraphs directly addressed at the Committee of Ministers. This is a peculiar fact, which stresses the complexity of the exchange and the anticipatory character of the documents making part of it (that is, Comments are a follow-up on the Opinion as well as on the anticipated Committee of Ministers' Resolution). Liechtenstein reiterates its initial declaration limiting the scope of application of the Convention so that it does not apply to Liechtenstein (Liechtenstein 2001, 3). It argues that religious minorities on its territory are mostly foreigners who cannot be "considered as minorities in the sense of the Framework Convention" (ibid.). At the same time, it recognizes that many of the foreigners live in Liechtenstein for decades.

The Committee of Ministers' Resolution should be seen as a follow-up on all the preceding utterances of this first monitoring cycle, not just on the Comments. The Resolution supports the AC, stating that there "remains potential for application of a number of provisions of the Framework Convention, albeit rather limited", but does not reiterate the AC's call to submit additional information within a year, preferring a more abstract request "to keep the Advisory Committee regularly informed" (ResCMN(2001)6). Thus, this follow-up by the IO's political body uses the preceding exchange as a fact: although unwillingly, Liechtenstein got itself into the exchange, providing the IO with a chance to build and strengthen its authority and to renegotiate their respective roles. The Resolution is clear in its (desired) anticipation of subsequent moves: the Committee of Ministers does not consider the affair closed, and expects further participation from Liechtenstein. This process of incremental construction and affirmation of authority is essentially the same mechanism that explains the creeping expansion of any bureaucracy (Barnett and Finnemore 2004, 9).

The second report by Liechtenstein still insists on the declaration, but is much longer than the first, much more detailed and provides statistics, information on state policies and measures, including on foreigners and asylum seekers. This indicates that the roles and the authority relationship between the participants are changing. The AC's follow-up – its second Opinion – is less tentative, which points in the same direction. Nonetheless, it still acknowledges the declaration made by Liechtenstein. It explicitly refers to the previous utterances of the IO (its own first Opinion and the Resolution by the Committee of Ministers) as authoritative documents, building up the momentum. The precedent is set, and the AC can capitalize on its issue expertise, matured procedural rules and ripened standard wordings developed in interaction with other states. Interestingly, the state's follow-up (Comments) on this more powerful discursive position does not mention the restrictive declaration anymore. Liechtenstein enters the exchange "for real", and its Comments go to the point of the AC's comments and recommendations.

The third report contains fewer statistics, but dutifully updates the Council of Europe on new developments and policies. It closes with a promise to "continue the dialogue with the advisory committee" and "to continue to report in this form" (ACFC/SR/III(2009)002, 6) – in the anticipation of the immediate and further removed follow-ups by the IO and by itself. The AC's follow-up on the interaction and the Report more precisely mirrors this positivity: it lauds Liechtenstein for progress and "new legal and institutional measures to strengthen protection against discrimination, racism and intolerance and to foster integration of persons with different ethnic, linguistic or religious background" (ACFC/OP/III(2009)001, 1). It also encourages the state to continue in this direction and strengthen its anti-discrimination policies, being fully supported by the Committee of Ministers in its Resolution (ResCMN(2010)9). The open and positive spirit of the exchange, which is achieved at this stage, is expressed in Liechtenstein's follow-up – its third Comments, which are the most detailed and are in fact longer than the first report. The wording of the Comments looks very cooperative; the authors thank the Advisory Committee "for the thorough and detailed analysis of the situation on the ground" and "agree[ing] in principle with its findings" (GVT/COM/III(2010)001, 2).

The refusal of the AC to accept the initial silence of Liechtenstein led – with time – to a well-functioning and highly cooperative exchange, within which the authority of the AC and the Council of Europe in general was strengthened and the relationship between it and the reporting state renegotiated. Three aspects in this process are worth highlighting.

First, the parties did not only respond to the preceding utterance of their interlocutor. Their utterances followed up on the whole prior exchange, including their own utterances. Second, the anticipatory character of the pre-structured interaction is of crucial importance. It is reflected in the discursive strategy of the AC – its orientation towards supporting Resolutions and smartly worded incitement to cooperation and requests of information from the state. It is also illustrated by the discursive behavior of Liechtenstein – its lack of anticipation at first, and its openness towards the forthcoming exchange in the third cycle. Third, silence is consequential and its meaning is negotiable. The non-tolerance of silence by the AC was at the origin of the exchange: the AC responded to the interlocutor's initial silence in an anticipatory, future-oriented way to prevent further silencing. For the IO, silence means absence or deficiency of the interaction, lack of the environment in which to develop its authority and enhance its social image. Still, partial silences may be positive. Indeed, for the sake of the existent relationship, in the third cycle Liechtenstein silences a negative aspect of the relationship – its restrictive declaration. This silence is referential (Ephratt 2008), and remains in the background, informing the participants' utterances. It can be likened to conducting a conversation with an open door – the 'door' was initially used by the Council of Europe to lure Liechtenstein in, but remains an escape way for Liechtenstein in case it feels too uncomfortable in the interaction.

As the case study makes clear, continuous interaction, intensity and regularity of the exchange within treaty monitoring are important for the success of the enterprise, because they provide the IO with sources of authority and allow to rebalance the asymmetrical departure situation. The IO's authority is strengthened within the communicative exchange, the continuity of which is upheld by multi-directed follow-ups, open into the social context of the parties.

5. Conclusion

This contribution outlined two theoretical frameworks – behaviorist and reflexive – for considering treaty monitoring as a communicative process, constituted by a series of multi-directed follow-ups and aiming at building and sustaining the interlocutors' public images. Both frameworks use a definition of follow-ups developed specifically for pre-structured communication, where the moves of the participants are set in advance and can therefore be anticipated and where absence of a move is meaningful, may be interpreted and used by the participants.

In the behaviorist framework, positivist vocabulary and logic offer common ground between international relations and discourse analysis. Treaty monitoring is understood as a conflictual situation, a technical-legal activity of evaluating states' behavior in reference to fixed international norms, complicated by political and institutional configurations. Participants – states and IOs – are strategic rational actors, and their preferences and identities are defined externally to the monitoring exchange and are rather stable. The extension of this framework into the discursive domain is performed with the help of 'face' theory, which defines general communicative aims of the speakers in terms of quite clearly defined 'wants' and interests – namely, to mitigate the conflictual potential and eventual damage to their social images in the interaction. The interaction is the meeting point of their desires (maintaining and enhancing face) and fears (damaging or losing face). These desires are strategically pursued by following up on the interlocutor's uttered and anticipated discourse and balancing between the cooperation-oriented discursive choices (linked to the speaker's positive face) and the independence-oriented choices (negative face). As an outlook for future research, I would like to highlight that cataloguing various options of follow-ups in treaty monitoring permits quantitative analysis of the parties' discourse and comparison across states, issue areas and monitoring cycles.

In the reflexive framework, the constructivist conceptual basis privileges a dialectical view of social reality and communication as mutually constraining and constituting elements. Studying treaty monitoring, reflexivist international relations scholars point out that within monitoring exchanges, structural institutional configurations between states, IOs, and "ratified bystanders" (Glinert 2010, 56) become meaningful and get transformed, either by explicit negotiation or by the sheer dynamic of the interaction. States and IOs use the written exchange to (re)construct their relationship and project a specific image (cooperative partner, independent decision-maker, consistent value-follower, rational actor, powerful entity) into the public sphere. Here, the role of the IO in negotiating a more powerful position for itself so as to be able to legitimately evaluate state policies is an issue of special interest. Main sources of IO authority (legal-rational, moral, and expert) are in fact highly endogenous to the exchange and depend on its intensity and sustained character. Development of these types of authority is advanced as a general motivation of IOs, guiding their discursive choices in the dialogue with states and shaping their follow-ups on utterances and series of utterances, realized and anticipated. The case of Liechtenstein, considered in this contribution, shows indeed that in order to be a useful concept in reflexive analysis, follow-ups need to be defined as multi-directional: using and reinterpreting (several) prior utterances as well as pre-shaping and pre-empting anticipated utterances.

Both frameworks demonstrate how silence may be a meaningful discursive act within pre-structured communication and how its inherent ambiguity (Saville-Troike 1985, 6–7; Tannen 1985, 94–97; Sobkowiak 1997, 54) may be explored and exploited by the parties. Silence indeed acquires meaning as a result of identifying what it comes to replace, "what is conventionally anticipated" in the context (Sifianou 1997, 79). Participants to treaty monitoring are aware of the meaningfulness and negotiability of silence. For example, the Advisory Committee adds a clarification to each Opinion, stating that the absence of critique on a particular point should not be interpreted as a final approval of state policies: policies and evaluation are dynamic processes. This disclaimer is necessary because critique is what is expected from the AC. Hence, when it is absent, states and "ratified bystanders" may interpret silence positively – as unconditional endorsement of the current policy line. Similarly, one would expect states to point out any incorrectness in the negative evaluation, and the abstention from refuting criticism may be interpreted as acknowledging non-compliance. Therefore, the absence of an anticipated utterance may constitute a follow-up on a prior utterance, but it can also be followed-up on in the subsequent moves of the interlocutors. In some cases, silence even may be seen as a self-directed face-threatening act, for it can damage the participant's social image. This leads me to advance this aspect of follow-ups as deserving attention in future research and to specify the definition of follow-up in pre-structured communication as follows: a reaction (utterance or absence of utterance) to another utterance, produced, anticipated *or omitted* within the given communicative exchange.

References

Alfredsson, Gudmundur, Jonas Grimheden, Bertram G. Ramcharan, and Alfred de Zayas (eds). 2001. *International Human Rights Monitoring Mechanisms*. The Hague: Martinus Nijhoff Publishers.

Alston, Philip (ed). 1995. *The United Nations and Human Rights. A Critical Appraisal*. Oxford: Clarendon Press.

Alston, Philip, and James Crawford (eds). 2000. *The Future of UN Human Rights Treaty Monitoring*. Cambridge: Cambridge UP. DOI: 10.1017/CBO9780511522284

Arundale, Robert. 2006. "Face as Relational and Interactional: A Communication Framework for Research on Face, Facework, and Politeness." *Journal of Politeness Research. Language, Behaviour, Culture* 2 (2): 193–216. DOI: 10.1515/PR.2006.011

Bakhtin, Mikhail. 2006. *The Dialogic Imagination. Four Essays by M. M. Bakhtin*. Edited by M. Holquist. Austin: University of Texas Press.

Barnett, Michael, and Martha Finnemore. 2004. *Rules for the World: International Organizations in Global Politics*. Ithaca etc: Cornell UP.

Baxter, Leslie, and Barbara Montgomery. 1996. *Relating: Dialogues and Dialectics*. New York: Guilford.

Bilmes, Jack. 1994. "Constituting Silence: Life in the World of Total Meaning." *Semiotica* 98 (1–2): 73–88.

de Boer-Buquicchio, Maud. 2008. "Opening Address at the Conference on Ten Years of Protecting National Minorities and Regional or Minority Languages, 11 March 2008." Available at http://www.coe.int/t/dghl/monitoring/minorities/6_Resources/PDF_10th_Anniv_Speech_MdeBuquicchio_en.pdf (last accessed on January 26, 2015)

Bradford, William. 2004. "International Legal Compliance: An Annotated Bibliography." *North Carolina Journal of International Law and Commercial Regulation* 30 (2): 379–428.

Brown, Penelope, and Stephen Levinson. 1987. *Politeness: Some Universals in Language Usage*. Cambridge: Cambridge University Press.

Bull, Hedley. 1977. *The Anarchical Society. A Study of Order in World Politic*. New York: Columbia University Press.

Bull, Peter. "Follow-ups in Broadcast Political Discourse: Speeches, Interviews, and Parliamentary Questions". This volume.

Davies, Bronwyn and Rom Harré. 1990. "Positioning: The Discursive Production of Selves." *Journal for the Theory of Social Behaviour* 20 (1): 43–63. DOI: 10.1111/j.1468-5914.1990.tb00174.x

Ephratt, Michal. 2008. "The Functions of Silence." *Journal of Pragmatics* 40 (11): 1909–1938. DOI: 10.1016/j.pragma.2008.03.009

Epstein, Charlotte. 2011. "Who Speaks? Discourse, the Subject and the Study of Identity in International Politics." *European Journal of International Relations* 17 (2): 327–350. DOI: 10.1177/1354066109350055

Fetzer, Anita and Elda Weizman. "Following Up across Contexts and Discourse Domains: Introduction." This volume.

Glinert, Lewis. 2010. "Apologizing to China: Elastic Apologies and the Meta-Discourse of American Diplomats." *Intercultural Pragmatics* 7 (1): 47–74. DOI: 10.1515/iprg.2010.003

Gruber, Helmut. "Intertextual References in Austrian Parliamentary Debates: Between Evaluation and Argumentation." This volume.

Hamo, Michal. *"I have Nothing to do but Agree": The Reciprocal Positioning of Journalists and Experts in Broadcast Television News Discourse.* This volume.
Harré, Rom, Fathali M. Moghaddam, Tracey Pilkerton Cairnie, Daniel Rothbart, and Steven R. Sabat. 2009. "Recent Advances in Positioning Theory". *Theory and Psychology* 19 (1): 5–31. DOI: 10.1177/0959354308101417
Hathaway, Oona. 2008. "International Delegation and State Sovereignty." *Law and Contemporary Problems* 71 (1): 115–149.
Henkin, Louis. 1994. "Human Rights and State Sovereignty." *Georgia Journal of International and Comparative Law* 25: 31-46.
Hofmann, Rainer. 2004. "The Framework Convention at the End of the First Cycle of Monitoring." In *Filling the Frame: 5 years of Monitoring the Framework Convention for the Protection of National Minorities*, 19–28. Strasbourg: Council of Europe Publishing.
Hurd, Ian. 2011. *International Organizations: Politics, Law, Practice.* Cambridge: Cambridge University Press.
Jaworski, Adam. 1993. *The Power of Silence. Social and Pragmatic Perspectives.* Newbury Park, London, New Delhi: SAGE Publications. DOI: 10.4135/9781483325460
Jaworski, Adam. 1997. "White and White: Metacommunicative and Metaphorical Silences". In *Silence. Interdisciplinary Perspectives*, ed. by Adam Jaworski, 381–401. Berlin, NY: Mouton de Gruyter.
Johansson, Marjut. "*Bravo for this Editorial! Users' Comments in Discussion Forums.*" This volume.
Liechtenstein. 2001. "Comments of the Government of Liechtenstein on the Opinion of the Advisory Committee on the Report on the Implementation of the Framework Convention for the Protection of National Minorities in Liechtenstein, 18 May 2001."
Kurzon, Dennis. 1997. *Discourse of Silence.* Amsterdam: John Benjamins. DOI: 10.1075/pbns.49
Mikalayeva, Liudmila. 2011. "Negotiating Compliance: Discursive Choices in a Formalized Setting of Diplomatic Communication." *International Journal of Communication* 21 (2): 5–28, available online at http://mikalayeva.com/onewebmedia/Negotiating_Compliance_Mikalayeva_offprint.pdf (last accessed on January 26, 2015)
Office of the United Nations Commissioner for Human Rights (OHCHR). 2005. "The United Nations Human Rights Treaty System: An Introduction to the Core Human Rights Treaties and the Treaty Bodies". Fact sheet no. 30. Available online at www2.ohchr.org/english/bodies/docs/OHCHR-FactSheet30.pdf (last accessed on January 26, 2015)
Penman, Robyn. 1990. "Facework & Politeness: Multiple Goals in Courtroom Discourse." *Journal of Language and Social Psychology* 9 (1–2): 15–38. DOI: 10.1177/0261927X9091002
Phillips, Alan. 2004. "Commentary: Economic participation of national minorities." In *Filling the Frame: 5 years of monitoring the Framework Convention for the Protection of National Minorities*, 98–110. Strasbourg: Council of Europe Publishing.
Sauer, Christoph. "Follow-Ups in Political Talk Shows and their Visual Framing." This volume.
Saville-Troike, Muriel. 1985. "The Place of Silence in an Integrated Theory of Communication". In *Perspectives of Silence*, ed. by Deborah Tannen and Muriel Saville-Troike, 3–18. Norwood: Ablex Publishing.
Schäffner, Christina. "Follow-Ups in Interpreter-Mediated Interviews and Press Conferences." This volume.
Sifianou, Maria. 1997. "Silence and Politeness". In *Silence. Interdisciplinary Perspectives*, ed. by Adam Jaworski, 63–84. Berlin, NY: Mouton de Gruyter.

Schwimmer, Walter. 2004. "Opening Speech", In *Filling the Frame: 5 years of monitoring the Framework Convention for the Protection of National Minorities*, 11–13. Strasbourg: Council of Europe Publishing.

Scollon, Ron, Suzanne Wong Scollon, and Rodney H. Jones. 2012. *Intercultural Communication: A Discourse Approach*. 3rd edition. Malden, MA, Oxford: Wiley-Blackwell.

Sivenkova, Maria. "Metacommunicative follow-ups in British, German and Russian Political Webchats." This volume.

Sobkowiak, Włodzimierz. 1997. "Silence and Markedness Theory". In *Silence. Interdisciplinary Perspectives*, ed. by Adam Jaworski, 39–61. Berlin, NY: Mouton de Gruyter.

Tannen, Deborah. 1985. "Silence: Anything But". In *Perspectives of Silence*, ed. by Deborah Tannen, and Muriel Saville-Troike, 93–111. Norwood: Ablex Publishing.

Wiener, Antje. 2004. "Contested Compliance: Interventions on the Normative Structure of World Politics." *European Journal of International Relations* 10 (2): 189–234. DOI: 10.1177/1354066104042934

Young, Oran R. 1979. *Compliance and Public Authority. A Theory with International Applications*. Baltimore: John Hopkins University Press.

Index